Congenital Disorders

Disorders

SOURCEBOOK

Fourth Edition

Health Reference Series

Fourth Edition

Congenital Disorders

SOURCEBOOK

*Basic Consumer Information about Nonhereditary
Birth Defects and Disorders Related to Prematurity,
Gestational Injuries, Prenatal and Perinatal Infections,
Maternal Health Conditions during Pregnancy, and Birth
Complications, including Cerebral Palsy, Cleft Lip and
Palate, Heart Defects, Hydrocephalus, Spina
Bifida, and More*

*Along with Facts about Risk Factors and Birth Defect
Prevention, Prenatal Care, Fetal Surgery Techniques, and
Other Treatment Options, a Glossary of Related Terms,
and a Directory of Resources for Additional
Help and Information*

OMNIGRAPHICS

615 Griswold, Ste. 901, Detroit, MI 48226

* * *

OMNIGRAPHICS
Greg Mullin, *Managing Editor*
***

Copyright © 2018 Omnigraphics

ISBN 978-0-7808-1613-8
E-ISBN 978-0-7808-1614-5

Library of Congress Cataloging-in-Publication Data

Names: Omnigraphics, Inc., issuing body.

Title: Congenital disorders sourcebook: basic consumer information about nonhereditary birth defects and disorders related to prematurity, gestational injuries, prenatal and perinatal infections, maternal health conditions during pregnancy, and birth complications, including cerebral palsy, cleft lip and palate, heart defects, hydrocephalus, spina bifida, and more; along with facts about risk factors and birth defect prevention, prenatal care, fetal surgery techniques, and other treatment options, a glossary of related terms, and a directory of resources for additional help and information.

Description: Fourth edition. | Detroit, MI: Omnigraphics, [2018] | Series: Health reference series | Includes bibliographical references and index.

Identifiers: LCCN 2017052240 (print) | LCCN 2017053489 (ebook) | ISBN 9780780816145 (eBook) | ISBN 9780780816138 (hardcover: alk. paper)

Subjects: LCSH: Abnormalities, Human--Popular works. | Developmental disabilities--Popular works.

Classification: LCC RG626 (ebook) | LCC RG626 .C597 2018 (print) | DDC 616/.043--dc23

LC record available at https://lccn.loc.gov/2017052240

Table of Contents

Part II: Prematurity and Other Birth Complications

Part III: Structural Abnormalities and Functional Impairments

Part IV: Additional Help and Information

Preface

About This Book

According to the Centers for Disease Control and Prevention (CDC), about 1 in 33 babies in the United States are born each year with a birth defect. In fact, birth defects are the leading cause of death in the first year of life. Yet the future is brightening. Recent medical advances have enabled doctors to diagnose and treat some birth defects before birth, affording affected children a much greater chance at survival. Additionally, advances in our understanding of the causes of birth defects allow prospective parents to take steps to minimize the chance that an infant will be born with these types of disorders.

Congenital Disorders Sourcebook, Fourth Edition describes the most common types of nonhereditary birth defects and disorders related to prematurity, gestational injuries, prenatal and perinatal infections, maternal health conditions during pregnancy, and birth complications, including cerebral palsy, cleft lip and palate, fetal alcohol syndrome, spina bifida, and disorders of the heart, brain, gastrointestinal tract, musculoskeletal system, urinary tract, and reproductive organs. Causes, prevention strategies, and diagnostic tests are explained, and innovative treatment strategies, including fetal surgery, are described. The book concludes with a glossary of related terms and a directory of resources for further help and information.

How to Use This Book

This book is divided into parts and chapters. Parts focus on broad areas of interest. Chapters are devoted to single topics within a part.

Part I: Prenatal Concerns and Preventing Birth Defects describes birth defects, what causes birth defects, and what can be done to prevent them. It details the most common risk factors for congenital disorders, including substance use, medications, environmental elements, and infectious diseases and other maternal health conditions with known adverse fetal effects. Disorders of the amniotic fluid and umbilical cord are also discussed. Additionally, the part offers facts about other pregnancy complications that can affect fetal health, and it describes the steps that can be taken to help ensure a healthy pregnancy.

Part II: Prematurity and Other Birth Complications provides basic information about the types of complications that can affect premature infants, including apnea of prematurity, retinopathy of prematurity, intraventricular hemorrhage (IVH) of the newborn, and jaundice. It addresses the most common health concerns with twins and other multiple births, including twin reversed arterial perfusion sequence, and unequal placental sharing. It also describes the types of infections that can be passed from mother to infant at birth, explains the screening tests that are given to newborns, and details what parents can expect in labor and delivery and in the first days after birth when a baby has a health problem.

Part III: Structural Abnormalities and Functional Impairments offers detailed information about the most common types of physical defects, including spina bifida, cerebral palsy, craniofacial and musculoskeletal defects, and defects of the brain, heart, kidney, liver, pancreas, reproductive organs, gastrointestinal tract, and urinary tract. It describes the causes and symptoms of each disorder, the diagnostic tests, and treatment techniques.

Part IV: Additional Help and Information includes a glossary of terms related to congenital disorders and a directory of resources offering additional help and support.

Bibliographic Note

This volume contains documents and excerpts from publications issued by the following government agencies: Agency for Healthcare Research and Quality (AHRQ); *Eunice Kennedy Shriver* National

Institute of Child Health and Human Development (NICHD); Centers for Disease Control and Prevention (CDC); Genetic and Rare Diseases Information Center (GARD); Genetics Home Reference (GHR); National Cancer Institute (NCI); National Eye Institute (NEI); National Institute of Diabetes and Digestive and Kidney Diseases (NIDDK); National Institute of Neurological Disorders and Stroke (NINDS); National Institute on Drug Abuse (NIDA); National Institutes of Health (NIH); National Heart, Lung, and Blood Institute (NHLBI); Office of Disease Prevention and Health Promotion (ODPHP); Office on Women's Health (OWH); U.S. Agency for International Development (USAID); U.S. Department of Health and Human Services (HHS); U.S. Environmental Protection Agency (EPA); and U.S. Food and Drug Administration (FDA).

It may also contain original material produced by Omnigraphics and reviewed by medical consultants.

About the Health Reference Series

The *Health Reference Series* is designed to provide basic medical information for patients, families, caregivers, and the general public. Each volume takes a particular topic and provides comprehensive coverage. This is especially important for people who may be dealing with a newly diagnosed disease or a chronic disorder in themselves or in a family member. People looking for preventive guidance, information about disease warning signs, medical statistics, and risk factors for health problems will also find answers to their questions in the *Health Reference Series*. The *Series*, however, is not intended to serve as a tool for diagnosing illness, in prescribing treatments, or as a substitute for the physician/patient relationship. All people concerned about medical symptoms or the possibility of disease are encouraged to seek professional care from an appropriate healthcare provider.

A Note about Spelling and Style

Health Reference Series editors use *Stedman's Medical Dictionary* as an authority for questions related to the spelling of medical terms and the *Chicago Manual of Style* for questions related to grammatical structures, punctuation, and other editorial concerns. Consistent adherence is not always possible, however, because the individual volumes within the *Series* include many documents from a wide variety of different producers, and the editor's primary goal is to present material from each source as accurately as is possible. This sometimes means that information in different chapters or sections may follow other guidelines and alternate spelling authorities. For example, occasionally a copyright holder may require that eponymous terms be shown in possessive forms (Crohn's disease vs. Crohn disease) or that British spelling norms be retained (leukaemia vs. leukemia).

Medical Review

Omnigraphics contracts with a team of qualified, senior medical professionals who serve as medical consultants for the *Health Reference Series*. As necessary, medical consultants review reprinted and originally written material for currency and accuracy. Citations including the phrase, "Reviewed (month, year)" indicate material reviewed by this team. Medical consultation services are provided to the *Health Reference Series* editors by:

Dr. Vijayalakshmi, MBBS, DGO, MD
Dr. Senthil Selvan, MBBS, DCH, MD
Dr. K. Sivanandham, MBBS, DCH, MS (Research), PhD

Our Advisory Board

We would like to thank the following board members for providing initial guidance on the development of this series:

- Dr. Lynda Baker, Associate Professor of Library and Information Science, Wayne State University, Detroit, MI

- Nancy Bulgarelli, William Beaumont Hospital Library, Royal Oak, MI

- Karen Imarisio, Bloomfield Township Public Library, Bloomfield Township, MI

- Karen Morgan, Mardigian Library, University of Michigan-Dearborn, Dearborn, MI

- Rosemary Orlando, St. Clair Shores Public Library, St. Clair Shores, MI

Health Reference Series *Update Policy*

The inaugural book in the *Health Reference Series* was the first edition of *Cancer Sourcebook* published in 1989. Since then, the *Series* has been enthusiastically received by librarians and in the medical community. In order to maintain the standard of providing high-quality health information for the layperson the editorial staff at Omnigraphics felt it was necessary to implement a policy of updating volumes when warranted.

Medical researchers have been making tremendous strides, and it is the purpose of the *Health Reference Series* to stay current with the most recent advances. Each decision to update a volume is made on an individual basis. Some of the considerations include how much new information is available and the feedback we receive from people who use the books. If there is a topic you would like to see added to the update list, or an area of medical concern you feel has not been adequately addressed, please write to:

Managing Editor
Health Reference Series
Omnigraphics
615 Griswold, Ste. 901
Detroit, MI 48226

Part One

Prenatal Concerns and Preventing Birth Defects

Chapter 1

What Are Birth Defects: An Overview

What Are Birth Defects?

Birth defects are structural or functional abnormalities present at birth that can cause physical disability, intellectual and developmental disability (IDD), and other health problems. Some may be fatal, especially if not detected and treated early. Researchers have identified thousands of different birth defects. According to the Centers for Disease Control and Prevention (CDC), birth defects are the leading cause of death for infants in the United States during the first year of life. The *Eunice Kennedy Shriver* National Institute of Child Health (NICHD) is aware that the term "birth defects" carries negative undertones and that the term does not reflect the many abilities and talents of those affected by these problems. Communities are discussing alternative terms for describing these birth problems.

What Are the Types of Birth Defects?

There are two main categories of birth defects.

This chapter includes text excerpted from "Birth Defects—Condition Information," *Eunice Kennedy Shriver* National Institute of Child Health and Human Development (NICHD), December 1, 2012. Reviewed December 2017.

Structural Birth Defects

Structural birth defects are related to a problem with body parts and structure. These can include:

- Cleft lip or cleft palate

- Heart defects, such as missing or misshaped valves

- Abnormal limbs, such as a clubfoot

- Neural tube defects, such as spina bifida, and problems related to the growth and development of the brain and spinal cord

Functional, or Developmental, Birth Defects

Functional, or developmental, birth defects are related to a problem with how a body part or body system works. These problems often lead to intellectual and developmental disability (IDD) and can include:

- **Nervous system or brain problems.** These include IDDs, behavioral disorders, speech or language difficulties, seizures, and movement trouble. Some examples of birth defects that affect the nervous system include Down syndrome, Prader-Willi syndrome, and fragile X syndrome.

- **Sensory problems.** Examples include hearing loss and visual problems, such as blindness or deafness.

- **Metabolic disorders.** These involve problems with certain chemical reactions in the body, such as conditions that limit the body's ability to rid itself of waste materials or harmful chemicals. Two common metabolic disorders are phenylketonuria and hypothyroidism.

- **Degenerative disorders.** These are conditions that might not be obvious at birth but cause one or more aspects of health to steadily get worse. Examples of degenerative disorders are muscular dystrophy and X-linked adrenoleukodystrophy, which leads to problems of the nervous system and the adrenal glands and was the subject of the movie "Lorenzo's Oil."

In some cases, birth defects are caused by a combination of factors. Some recognized patterns of birth defects affect many parts or processes in the body, leading to both structural and functional problems.

How Many People Are Affected by/at Risk for Birth Defects?

The CDC estimates that about 1 in every 33 infants born in the United States has a birth defect. Birth defects can occur during any pregnancy, but some pregnancies are at higher risk than others. The following situations place pregnant women at higher risk of having a child with a birth defect:

- **Lack of folic acid.** Women who are pregnant or who could become pregnant should take 400 micrograms of folic acid every day to prevent neural tube defects (NTDs). According to the CDC, only 2 out of every 5 women of childbearing age, however, take folic acid every day.

- **Drinking alcohol.** Drinking alcohol during pregnancy can lead to a variety of problems, including birth defects. For example, using alcohol can lead to fetal alcohol syndrome, which is characterized by IDD, physical challenges, and behavioral problems. There is no safe level of alcohol consumption during pregnancy. According to the CDC, 1 of every 10 pregnant women, and more than one-half of the women who could become pregnant, have consumed alcohol during the past month.

- **Smoking cigarettes.** Smoking cigarettes during pregnancy can lead to a variety of problems, including lung issues such as asthma. Evidence strongly suggests that certain birth defects, such as problems with the heart and intestines, are caused by smoking during pregnancy. In addition, infants of mothers who smoke during pregnancy are at higher risk for sudden infant death syndrome (SIDS).

- **Using drugs.** Using drugs during pregnancy can increase the risk of various birth defects, including IDDs and behavioral problems. For example, using cocaine during pregnancy increases the risk that the infant will be born with structural birth defects of the arms and legs, urinary system, and heart.

- **Medication use.** Certain medications are known to cause birth defects if taken during pregnancy. Thalidomide, which is currently used to treat certain cancers and other serious conditions, was once sold as a treatment for morning sickness until it was discovered that it caused severe birth defects. Infants whose mothers took thalidomide had a range of structural and functional problems, including misshapen ears and shortened limbs.

5

Although the thalidomide situation led to much stricter controls on drugs used during pregnancy, the majority of medications currently used by pregnant women have not been tested for safety or efficacy in pregnant women. Women who are pregnant or who might become pregnant should discuss all medications and supplements they take with their healthcare providers.

- **Infections.** Women who get certain infections during pregnancy are at higher risk for having a child with birth defects. Some of the more common infections that are linked to birth defects are cytomegalovirus, a common virus that spreads through body fluids and usually causes no symptoms in healthy people, and toxoplasmosis, a parasitic infection that spreads through contact with cat feces, raw meat, and contaminated food and water.

- **Obesity or uncontrolled diabetes.** A NICHD-supported research found that the risk of newborn heart defects increased with maternal obesity. Obesity is also associated with other health problems and long-term health issues. Poorly controlled blood sugar places women at higher risk of having a baby that is too large, that has breathing problems, and other poor health outcomes. These outcomes are likely regardless of whether the woman had diabetes before she got pregnant (type 1 or 2 diabetes) or whether she developed diabetes during pregnancy (gestational diabetes).

What Causes Birth Defects?

Different birth defects have different causes. A specific condition might be caused by one or more of the following problems:

- **Genetic problems.** One or more genes might have a change or mutation that results in them not working properly, such as in McCune-Albright syndrome. Similarly, a gene or part of the gene might be missing.

- **Chromosomal problems.** In some cases, a chromosome or part of a chromosome might be missing, such as in Turner syndrome, when a female is missing an X chromosome. Other birth defects result from having an extra chromosome, such as in Klinefelter syndrome (KS) and Down syndrome (DS).

- **Exposure to chemicals or other agents during pregnancy.** The infants whose mothers took thalidomide are examples of an exposure leading to birth defects. Other examples include exposure to rubella (also called German measles) and toxic chemicals, such as hydrocarbons.

How Do Healthcare Providers Diagnose Birth Defects?

Diagnosis of birth defects depends on the specific problem and parts of the body affected. For example, although their causes might not be easily detectable, structural birth defects such as clubfoot and cleft lip are visually noticeable at birth. Other birth defects are not always detectable by looking at a newborn. Newborn screening, a process that tests infant's blood for different health conditions, including many birth defects, provide one method of detecting problems before they have lifelong effects. Infants who are at high risk for certain birth defects, for example, because of their family history, can undergo additional testing at birth to detect these conditions and treat them, if needed. This type of screening has been effective in detecting some cases of Menkes disease, allowing for treatment to begin before health problems occur.

Prenatal Screening

Healthcare providers recommend that certain pregnant women, including those who are older than 35 years of age and those with a family history of certain conditions, have their fetuses tested for birth defects prenatally, while still in the womb. There are two main types of prenatal tests for birth defects.

Amniocentesis

Amniocentesis is a test that is usually performed to determine whether a fetus has a genetic disorder. In this test, a doctor takes a small amount of fluid from the womb using a long needle. The fluid, called amniotic fluid, contains cells that have genetic material that is the same as the fetus's genetic material. A laboratory grows the cells and then examines their genetic material for any problems. Some birth defects that can be detected with amniocentesis are Down syndrome and certain types of muscular dystrophy. Because amniocentesis can cause a miscarriage in about 1 out of 200 cases, it is usually only recommended for pregnancies in which the risk of genetic disorders or other problems is high.

Chorionic Villus Sampling (CVS)

This test extracts cells from inside the womb to determine whether the fetus has a genetic disorder. Using a long needle, the doctor takes cells from the chorionic villi, which are tissues in the placenta, the organ in the womb that nourishes the fetus. The genetic material in the chorionic villus cells is identical to that of the fetal cells.

Like amniocentesis, CVS can be used to test for chromosomal disorders such as Down syndrome and other genetic problems. CVS can be done earlier in pregnancy than amniocentesis, but it is also associated with a higher risk of miscarriage—about 1 in 100 cases. Healthcare providers usually only recommend CVS in women who are at high risk.

What Are the Treatments for Birth Defects?

Because the symptoms and problems caused by birth defects vary, treatments for birth defects also vary. Treatments range from medications, to therapies, to surgeries, to assistive devices. For example, in the Management of Myelomeningocele Study (MOMS), conducted through the NICHD's Maternal-Fetal Surgery Network, researchers tested a surgical procedure to correct a severe form of spina bifida while the fetus was still in the womb. Although the surgery itself carried many risks, the surgery greatly reduced health complications for the infants who received it while in utero.

Gene therapy approaches, in which a gene that is mutated or missing is replaced by a normal version of the gene, are being tested for a variety of genetic disorders. Some examples of disorders that have been treated successfully in gene therapy experiments are genetic disorders of the immune system, the muscles, and the eyes.

If someone in your family has a birth defect, discuss treatment options with that individual's healthcare provider or providers.

Chapter 2

Steps to a Healthy Pregnancy

Chapter Contents

Section 2.1

Prenatal Care

This section contains text excerpted from the following sources: Text beginning with the heading "What Is Prenatal Care?" is excerpted from "Prenatal Care," Office on Women's Health (OWH), U.S. Department of Health and Human Services (HHS), June 12, 2017; Text beginning with the heading "Pregnancy and Prenatal Care Problems" is excerpted from "Pregnancy and Prenatal Care," Centers for Disease Control and Prevention (CDC), September 15, 2017.

What Is Prenatal Care?

Prenatal care is the healthcare you get while you are pregnant. Take care of yourself and your baby by:

- Getting **early** prenatal care. If you know you're pregnant, or think you might be, call your doctor to schedule a visit.

- Getting **regular** prenatal care. Your doctor will schedule you for many checkups over the course of your pregnancy. Don't miss any—they are all important.

- Following your doctor's advice.

Why Do I Need Prenatal Care?

Prenatal care can help keep you and your baby healthy. Babies of mothers who do not get prenatal care are three times more likely to have a low birth weight and five times more likely to die than those born to mothers who do get care. Doctors can spot health problems early when they see mothers regularly. This allows doctors to treat them early. Early treatment can cure many problems and prevent others. Doctors also can talk to pregnant women about things they can do to give their unborn babies a healthy start to life.

I Am Thinking about Getting Pregnant. How Can I Take Care of Myself?

You should start taking care of yourself before you start trying to get pregnant. This is called preconception health. It means knowing how health conditions and risk factors could affect you or your unborn baby if you become pregnant. For example, some foods, habits, and medicines can harm your baby—even before he or she is conceived. Some health problems also can affect pregnancy.

Talk to your doctor before pregnancy to learn what you can do to prepare your body. Women should prepare for pregnancy before becoming sexually active. Ideally, women should give themselves at least 3 months to prepare before getting pregnant.

The five most important things you can do before becoming pregnant are:

1. Take 400 to 800 micrograms (400–800 mcg or 0.4–0.8 mg) of folic acid every day for at least 3 months before getting pregnant to lower your risk of some birth defects of the brain and spine. You can get folic acid from some foods. But it's hard to get all the folic acid you need from foods alone. Taking a vitamin with folic acid is the best and easiest way to be sure you're getting enough.

2. Stop smoking and drinking alcohol. Ask your doctor for help.

3. If you have a medical condition, be sure it is under control. Some conditions include asthma, diabetes, depression, high blood pressure, obesity, thyroid disease, or epilepsy. Be sure your vaccinations are up to date.

4. Talk to your doctor about any over-the-counter (OTC) and prescription medicines you are using. These include dietary or herbal supplements. Some medicines are not safe during pregnancy. At the same time, stopping medicines you need also can be harmful.

5. Avoid contact with toxic substances or materials at work and at home that could be harmful. Stay away from chemicals and cat or rodent feces.

I'm Pregnant. What Should I Do—or Not Do—to Take Care of Myself and My Unborn Baby?

Follow these dos and don'ts to take care of yourself and the precious life growing inside you:

11

Healthcare Dos and Don'ts

- Get early and regular prenatal care. Whether this is your first pregnancy or third, healthcare is extremely important. Your doctor will check to make sure you and the baby are healthy at each visit. If there are any problems, early action will help you and the baby.

- Take a multivitamin or prenatal vitamin with 400 to 800 micrograms (400 to 800 mcg or 0.4 to 0.8 mg) of folic acid every day. Folic acid is most important in the early stages of pregnancy, but you should continue taking folic acid throughout pregnancy.

- Ask your doctor before stopping any medicines or starting any new medicines. Some medicines are not safe during pregnancy. Keep in mind that even over-the-counter medicines and herbal products may cause side effects or other problems. But not using medicines you need could also be harmful.

- Avoid X-rays. If you must have dental work or diagnostic tests, tell your dentist or doctor that you are pregnant so that extra care can be taken.

- Get a flu shot. Pregnant women can get very sick from the flu and may need hospital care.

Food Dos and Don'ts

- Eat a variety of healthy foods. Choose fruits, vegetables, whole grains, calcium-rich foods, and foods low in saturated fat. Also, make sure to drink plenty of fluids, especially water.

- Get all the nutrients you need each day, including iron. Getting enough iron prevents you from getting anemia, which is linked to preterm birth and low birth weight. Eating a variety of healthy foods will help you get the nutrients your baby needs. But ask your doctor if you need to take a daily prenatal vitamin or iron supplement to be sure you are getting enough.

- Protect yourself and your baby from food-borne illnesses, including toxoplasmosis and listeria. Wash fruits and vegetables before eating. Don't eat uncooked or undercooked meats or fish. Always handle, clean, cook, eat, and store foods properly.

- Don't eat fish with lots of mercury, including swordfish, king mackerel, shark, and tilefish.

Lifestyle Dos and Don'ts

- Gain a healthy amount of weight. Your doctor can tell you how much weight gain you should aim for during pregnancy.

- Don't smoke, drink alcohol, or use drugs. These can cause long-term harm or death to your baby. Ask your doctor for help quitting.

- Unless your doctor tells you not to, try to get at least 2 hours and 30 minutes of moderate-intensity aerobic activity a week. It's best to spread out your workouts throughout the week. If you worked out regularly before pregnancy, you can keep up your activity level as long as your health doesn't change and you talk to your doctor about your activity level throughout your pregnancy.

- Don't take very hot baths or use hot tubs or saunas.

- Get plenty of sleep and find ways to control stress.

- Get informed. Read books, watch videos, go to a childbirth class, and talk with moms you know.

- Ask your doctor about childbirth education classes for you and your partner. Classes can help you prepare for the birth of your baby.

Environmental Dos and Don'ts

- Stay away from chemicals like insecticides, solvents (like some cleaners or paint thinners), lead, mercury, and paint (including paint fumes). Not all products have pregnancy warnings on their labels. If you're unsure if a product is safe, ask your doctor before using it. Talk to your doctor if you are worried that chemicals used in your workplace might be harmful.

- If you have a cat, ask your doctor about toxoplasmosis. This infection is caused by a parasite sometimes found in cat feces. If not treated toxoplasmosis can cause birth defects. You can lower your risk of by avoiding cat litter and wearing gloves when gardening.

- Avoid contact with rodents, including pet rodents, and with their urine, droppings, or nesting material. Rodents can carry a virus that can be harmful or even deadly to your unborn baby.

- Take steps to avoid illness, such as washing hands frequently.

- Stay away from secondhand smoke.

I Don't Want to Get Pregnant Right Now. Should I Still Take Folic Acid Every Day?

Yes! Birth defects of the brain and spine happen in the very early stages of pregnancy, often before a woman knows she is pregnant. By the time she finds out she is pregnant, it might be too late to prevent those birth defects. Also, half of all pregnancies in the United States are not planned. For these reasons, all women who are able to get pregnant need 400 to 800 mcg of folic acid every day.

How Often Should I See My Doctor during Pregnancy?

Your doctor will give you a schedule of all the doctor's visits you should have while pregnant. Most experts suggest you see your doctor:

- About once each month for weeks 4 through 28

- Twice a month for weeks 28 through 36

- Weekly for weeks 36 to birth

If you are older than 35 or your pregnancy is high risk, you'll probably see your doctor more often.

What Happens during Prenatal Visits?

During the first prenatal visit, you can expect your doctor to:

- Ask about your health history including diseases, operations, or prior pregnancies

- Ask about your family's health history

- Do a complete physical exam, including a pelvic exam and Pap test

- Take your blood and urine for lab work

- Check your blood pressure, height, and weight

- Calculate your due date

- Answer your questions

At the first visit, you should ask questions and discuss any issues related to your pregnancy. Find out all you can about how to stay healthy.

Later prenatal visits will probably be shorter. Your doctor will check on your health and make sure the baby is growing as expected. Most prenatal visits will include:

- Checking your blood pressure

- Measuring your weight gain

- Measuring your abdomen to check your baby's growth (once you begin to show)

- Checking the baby's heart rate

While you're pregnant, you also will have some routine tests. Some tests are suggested for all women, such as blood work to check for anemia, your blood type, HIV (human immunodeficiency virus), and other factors. Other tests might be offered based on your age, personal or family health history, your ethnic background, or the results of routine tests you have had.

I Am in My Late 30s and I Want to Get Pregnant. Should I Do Anything Special?

As you age, you have an increasing chance of having a baby born with a birth defect. Yet most women in their late 30s and early 40s have healthy babies. See your doctor regularly before you even start trying to get pregnant. She will be able to help you prepare your body for pregnancy.

During your pregnancy, seeing your doctor regularly is very important. Because of your age, your doctor will probably suggest some extra tests to check on your baby's health.

More and more women are waiting until they are in their 30s and 40s to have children. While many women of this age have no problems getting pregnant, fertility does decline with age. Women over 40 who don't get pregnant after six months of trying should see their doctors for a fertility evaluation.

Experts define infertility as the inability to become pregnant after trying for one year. If a woman keeps having miscarriages, it's also called infertility. If you think you or your partner may be infertile, talk to your doctor. Doctors are able to help many infertile couples go on to have healthy babies.

Where Can I Go to Get Free or Reduced-Cost Prenatal Care?

Women in every state can get help to pay for medical care during their pregnancies. This prenatal care can help you have a healthy baby. Every state in the United States has a program to help. Programs give medical care, information, advice, and other services important for a healthy pregnancy.

To find out about the program in your state:

- Call 800-311-BABY (800-311-2229). This toll-free telephone number will connect you to the Health Department in your area code.

- For information in Spanish, call 800-504-7081.

- Contact your local Health Department.

Pregnancy and Prenatal Care Problems

Each year, reports of approximately 500 women who died as a result of a pregnancy-related complication are received by the Division of Reproductive Health (DRH) at Centers for Disease Control and Prevention (CDC).

In 1999, on average there were seven infant deaths per 1000 live births. Differences in race and socioeconomic conditions can result in much higher incidences of infant mortality. The leading causes of infant death were congenital anomalies and low birthweight—two conditions that can be considerable impacted by prenatal care.

In order to have the best possible outcome for mother and child, early prenatal care is essential. Even before a woman conceives, she can be given folic acid, checked for immunity to rubella and blood type, as well as advised about smoking, drinking alcohol, and eating a healthy diet. Once a woman is pregnant, prenatal visits to a healthcare provider will include examinations to determine the health of the mother and developing fetus.

Who's at Risk?

A higher risk of death related to pregnancy has been found in women over 35 years of age, women who have borne five or more children, women who did not receive prenatal care, and Hispanic and black women. The single most important factor influencing neonatal mortality is birth weight. The rate of infant death increases significantly with decreasing birth weight for infants weighing less than 2500 grams.

Can It Be Prevented?

Some estimate that up to one half of pregnancy-related deaths could be prevented. An important element for decreasing infant mortality is to prevent low birth weight. Early prenatal care can provide necessary information to the mother and effect changes for nutrition-related and behavioral risk factors impacting the mother and baby. The following steps can be taken to prevent prenatal problems:

- Consider a preconception visit before you get pregnant.
- Start taking folic acid before conception.
- Get early prenatal care.
- Eat a well balanced diet.
- With doctor's approval, get regular exercise.
- Limit caffeine and avoid alcohol, cigarettes, and street drugs.

Section 2.2

Healthy Eating during Pregnancy

This section includes text excerpted from "Eat Healthy during Pregnancy: Quick Tips," Office of Disease Prevention and Health Promotion (ODPHP), U.S. Department of Health and Human Services (HHS), July 27, 2017.

When you are pregnant, you need more protein, iron, calcium, and folic acid. But this doesn't mean you need to eat twice as much. Making smart food choices can help you have a healthy pregnancy and a healthy baby.

Don't forget breakfast.

- Try fortified ready-to-eat or cooked breakfast cereals with fruit. Fortified cereals have added nutrients, like iron, calcium, and folic acid. Look for options with less added sugar.

- If you are feeling sick, start with a piece of whole-grain toast. Eat more food later in the morning.

Eat foods with fiber.

- Vegetables and fruits, like green peas, spinach, pears, and bananas.

- Whole grains, like brown rice, whole-wheat bread, and oatmeal.

- Beans, like black beans and kidney beans.

Choose healthy snacks.

- Low-fat or fat-free yogurt with fruit (choose options with less added sugar).

- Whole-grain crackers with fat-free or low-fat cheese.

- Carrots with hummus.

Take a prenatal vitamin with iron and folic acid every day.

Iron keeps your blood healthy. Folic acid helps prevent some birth defects. Talk with your doctor or nurse about a prenatal vitamin that's right for you.

Eat 8 to 12 ounces of seafood each week.

Fish and shellfish have nutrients that are good for your growing baby. Eat a variety of seafood 2 or 3 times a week. A 3-ounce serving is about the size of a deck of cards.

Healthy choices include:

- Salmon

- Sardines

- Shrimp

- Canned light tuna

- White (albacore) tuna—no more than 6 ounces a week

Avoid fish that are high in mercury, especially swordfish, tilefish, shark, and king mackerel. Mercury is a metal that can hurt your baby's development.

Stay away from raw fish and meat, soft cheeses, and lunch meats.

These foods may have bacteria in them that can hurt your baby. Don't eat:

- Raw (uncooked) fish, like sushi.

- Soft cheeses (like feta, Brie, and goat cheese), unless they are pasteurized.

- Raw or rare (undercooked) meats.

- Lunch meats and hot dogs, unless they are heated until steaming hot.

Limit caffeine and avoid alcohol.

- Drink decaffeinated coffee or tea.

- Drink water or seltzer instead of soda.

- Don't drink alcohol. No amount of alcohol is safe during pregnancy.

Section 2.3

Folic Acid: An Important Part of a Healthy Pregnancy

This section includes text excerpted from "Folic Acid," Office on Women's Health (OWH), U.S. Department of Health and Human Services (HHS), February 23, 2017.

Folic acid is a form of folate (a B vitamin) that everyone needs. If you can get pregnant or are pregnant, folic acid is especially important. Folic acid protects unborn babies against serious birth defects. You can get folic acid from vitamins and fortified foods, such as breads, pastas and cereals. Folate is found naturally in foods such as leafy green vegetables, oranges, and beans.

What Are Folic Acid and Folate?

Folic acid is the man-made form of folate, a B vitamin. Folate is found naturally in certain fruits, vegetables, and nuts. Folic acid is found in vitamins and fortified foods.

Folic acid and folate help the body make healthy new red blood cells. Red blood cells carry oxygen to all the parts of your body. If your body does not make enough red blood cells, you can develop anemia. Anemia happens when your blood cannot carry enough oxygen to your body, which makes you pale, tired, or weak. Also, if you do not get enough folic acid, you could develop a type of anemia called folate-deficiency anemia.

Why Do Women Need Folic Acid?

Everyone needs folic acid to be healthy. But it is especially important for women:

- **Before and during pregnancy.** Folic acid protects unborn children against serious birth defects called neural tube defects. These birth defects happen in the first few weeks of pregnancy, often before a woman knows she is pregnant. Folic acid might also help prevent other types of birth defects and early pregnancy loss (miscarriage). Since about half of all pregnancies in the United States are unplanned, experts recommend all women get enough folic acid even if you are not trying to get pregnant.

- **To keep the blood healthy by helping red blood cells form and grow.** Not getting enough folic acid can lead to a type of anemia called folate-deficiency anemia. Folate-deficiency anemia is more common in women of childbearing age than in men.

How Do I Get Folic Acid?

You can get folic acid in two ways.

1. **Through the foods you eat.** Folate is found naturally in some foods, including spinach, nuts, and beans. Folic acid is found in fortified foods (called "enriched foods"), such as breads, pastas, and cereals. Look for the term "enriched" on the ingredients list to find out whether the food has added folic acid.

2. **As a vitamin.** Most multivitamins sold in the United States contain 400 micrograms, or 100 percent of the daily value, of folic acid. Check the label to make sure.

How Much Folic Acid Do Women Need?

All women need 400 micrograms of folic acid every day. Women who can get pregnant should get 400 to 800 micrograms of folic acid from a vitamin or from food that has added folic acid, such as breakfast cereal. This is in addition to the folate you get naturally from food.

Some women may need more folic acid each day. See the chart to find out how much folic acid you need.

Table 2.1. Daily Requirement of Folic Acid for Women

If You:	Amount of Folic Acid You May Need Daily
Could get pregnant or are pregnant	400–800 micrograms. Your doctor may prescribe a prenatal vitamin with more.
Had a baby with a neural tube defect (such as spina bifida) and want to get pregnant again.	4,000 micrograms. Your doctor may prescribe this amount. Research shows taking this amount may lower the risk of having another baby with spina bifida.
Have a family member with spina bifida and could get pregnant	4,000 micrograms. Your doctor may prescribe this amount.
Have spina bifida and want to get pregnant	4,000 micrograms. Your doctor may prescribe this amount. Women with spina bifida have a higher risk of having children with the condition.
Take medicines to treat epilepsy, type 2 diabetes, rheumatoid arthritis, or lupus	Talk to your doctor or nurse. Folic acid supplements can interact with these medicines.
Are on dialysis for kidney disease	Talk to your doctor or nurse.
Have a health condition, such as inflammatory bowel disease or celiac disease, that affects how your body absorbs folic acid	Talk to your doctor or nurse.

Are Some Women at Risk for Not Getting Enough Folic Acid?

Yes, certain groups of women do not get enough folic acid each day.

- Women who can get pregnant need more folic acid (400 to 800 micrograms).

- Nearly one in three African-American women does not get enough folic acid each day.

21

- Spanish-speaking Mexican-American women often do not get enough folic acid. However, Mexican-Americans who speak English usually get enough folic acid.

Not getting enough folic acid can cause health problems, including folate-deficiency anemia, and problems during pregnancy for you and your unborn baby.

What Can Happen If I Do Not Get Enough Folic Acid during Pregnancy?

If you do not get enough folic acid before and during pregnancy, your baby is at higher risk for neural tube defects.

Neural tube defects are serious birth defects that affect the spine, spinal cord, or brain and may cause death. These include:

- **Spina bifida.** This condition happens when an unborn baby's spinal column does not fully close during development in the womb, leaving the spinal cord exposed. As a result, the nerves that control the legs and other organs do not work. Children with spina bifida often have lifelong disabilities. They may also need many surgeries.

- **Anencephaly.** This means that most or all of the brain and skull does not develop in the womb. Almost all babies with this condition die before or soon after birth.

Do I Need to Take Folic Acid Every Day Even If I'm Not Planning to Get Pregnant?

Yes. All women who can get pregnant need to take 400 to 800 micrograms of folic acid every day, even if you're not planning to get pregnant. There are several reasons why:

- Your birth control may not work or you may not use birth control correctly every time you have sex. In a survey by the Centers for Disease Control and Prevention (CDC), almost 40 percent of women with unplanned pregnancies were using birth control.

- Birth defects of the brain and spine can happen in the first few weeks of pregnancy, often before you know you are pregnant. By the time you find out you are pregnant, it might be too late to prevent the birth defects.

22

- You need to take folic acid every day because it is a water soluble B-vitamin. Water soluble means that it does not stay in the body for a long time. Your body metabolizes (uses) folic acid quickly, so your body needs folic acid each day to work properly.

What Foods Contain Folate?

Folate is found naturally in some foods. Foods that are naturally high in folate include:

- Spinach and other dark green, leafy vegetables
- Oranges and orange juice
- Nuts
- Beans
- Poultry (chicken, turkey, etc.) and meat

What Foods Contain Folic Acid?

Folic acid is added to foods that are refined or processed (not whole grain):

- Breakfast cereals (Some have 100% of the recommended daily value—or 400 micrograms—of folic acid in each serving.)
- Breads and pasta
- Flours
- Cornmeal
- White rice

Since 1998, the U.S. Food and Drug Administration (FDA) has required food manufacturers to add folic acid to processed breads, cereals, flours, corn meal, pastas, rice, and other grains. For other foods, check the nutrition facts label on the package to see if it has folic acid. The label will also tell you how much folic acid is in each serving. Sometimes, the label will say "folate" instead of folic acid.

How Can I Be Sure I Get Enough Folic Acid?

You can get enough folic acid from food alone. Many breakfast cereals have 100 percent of your recommended daily value (400 micrograms) of folic acid.

If you are at risk for not getting enough folic acid, your doctor or nurse may recommend that you take a vitamin with folic acid every day. Most U.S. multivitamins have at least 400 micrograms of folic acid. Check the label on the bottle to be sure. You can also take a pill that contains only folic acid.

If swallowing pills is hard for you, try a chewable or liquid product with folic acid.

What Should I Look for When Buying Vitamins with Folic Acid?

Look for "USP" or "NSF" on the label when choosing vitamins. These "seals of approval" mean the pills are made properly and have the amounts of vitamins it says on the label. Also, make sure the pills have not expired. If the bottle has no expiration date, do not buy it.

Ask your pharmacist for help with selecting a vitamin or folic acid-only pill. If you are pregnant and already take a daily prenatal vitamin, you probably get all the folic acid you need. Check the label to be sure.

Vitamin Label

Check the "Supplement Facts" label to be sure you are getting 400 to 800 micrograms (mcg) of folic acid

Supplement Facts		
Serving Size: 1 tablet		
Amount Per Serving		**% Daily Value**
Vitamin A	5000IU	100
Vitamin C	60mg	100
Vitamin D	400IU	100
Vitamin E	30IU	100
Thiamin	1.5mg	100
Riboflavin	1.7mg	100
Niacin	20mg	100
Vitamin B6	2mg	100
Folic Acid	400mcg	100
Vitamin B12	6mcg	100
Biotin	30mg	10
Pantothenic Acid	10mg	100
Calcium	162mg	16
Iron	18mg	100
Iodine	150mcg	100
Magnesium	100mg	25
Zinc	15mg	100
Selenium	20mcg	100
Copper	2mg	100
Manganese	3.5mg	175
Chromium	65mcg	54
Molybdenum	150mcg	200
Chloride	72mg	2
Potassium	80mg	2

Find **folic acid:** Choose a vitamin that says "400mcg" or "100%" next to folic acid

Figure 2.1. *Vitamin Label*

Can I Get Enough Folic Acid from Food Alone?

Yes, many people get enough folic acid from food alone. Some foods have high amounts of folic acid. For example, many breakfast cereals have 100 percent of the recommended daily value (400 micrograms) of folic acid in each serving. Check the label to be sure.

Some women, especially women who could get pregnant, may not get enough folic acid from food. African-American women and Mexican Americans are also at higher risk for not getting enough folic acid each day. Talk to your doctor or nurse about whether you should take a vitamin to get the 400 micrograms of folic acid you need each day.

What Is Folate-Deficiency Anemia?

Folate-deficiency anemia is a type of anemia that happens when you do not get enough folate. Folate-deficiency anemia is most common during pregnancy. Other causes of folate-deficiency anemia include alcoholism and certain medicines to treat seizures, anxiety, or arthritis.

The symptoms of folate-deficiency anemia include:

- Fatigue

- Headache

- Pale skin

- Sore mouth and tongue

If you have folate-deficiency anemia, your doctor may recommend taking folic acid vitamins and eating more foods with folate.

Can I Get Too Much Folic Acid?

Yes, you can get too much folic acid, but only from man-made products such as multivitamins and fortified foods, such as breakfast cereals. You can't get too much from foods that naturally contain folate.

You should not get more than 1,000 micrograms of folic acid a day, unless your doctor prescribes a higher amount. Too much folic acid can hide signs that you lack vitamin B12, which can cause nerve damage.

Section 2.4

Vaccinations for a Healthy Pregnancy

This section includes text excerpted from "Maternal
Vaccines: Part of a Healthy Pregnancy," Centers for Disease
Control and Prevention (CDC), August 5, 2016.

**Vaccines help protect you and your baby against serious
diseases.** You probably know that when you are pregnant, you share
everything with your baby. That means when you get vaccines, you
aren't just protecting yourself—you are giving your baby some early
protection too. Centers for Disease Control and Prevention (CDC)
recommends you get a whooping cough and flu vaccine during each
pregnancy to help protect yourself and your baby.

Vaccine Safety before, during, and after Pregnancy

Centers for Disease Control and Prevention (CDC) has guidelines
for the vaccines you need before, during, and after pregnancy. Some
vaccines, such as the measles, mumps, rubella (MMR) vaccine, should
be given a month or more **before** pregnancy. You should get the Tdap
vaccine (to help protect against whooping cough), **during** your pregnancy. Other vaccines, like the flu shot, can be given before or during
pregnancy, depending on whether or not it is flu season when you're
pregnant. It is safe for you to receive vaccines right **after** giving birth,
even while you are breastfeeding. Be sure to discuss each vaccine with
your healthcare professional before getting vaccinated.

Vaccines during Pregnancy

Whooping Cough

Whooping cough (Pertussis) can be serious for anyone, but for your
newborn, it can be life-threatening. Up to 20 babies die each year in
the United States due to whooping cough. About half of babies younger
than 1 year old who get whooping cough need treatment in the hospital. The younger the baby is when he or she gets whooping cough, the
more likely he or she will need to be treated in a hospital. It may be

26

hard for you to know if your baby has whooping cough because many babies with this disease don't cough at all. Instead, it can cause them to stop breathing and turn blue.

When you get the whooping cough vaccine during your pregnancy, your body will create protective antibodies and pass some of them to your baby before birth. These antibodies will provide your baby some short-term, early protection against whooping cough.

Flu

Flu: Changes in your immune, heart, and lung functions during pregnancy make you more likely to get seriously ill from the flu. Catching the flu also increases your chances for serious problems for your developing baby, including premature labor and delivery. Get the flu shot if you are pregnant during flu season—it's the best way to protect yourself and your baby for several months after birth from flu-related complications.

Flu seasons vary in their timing from season to season, but CDC recommends getting vaccinated by the end of October, if possible. This timing helps protect you before flu activity begins to increase.

Other Vaccines

Vaccines for Travel: If you are pregnant and planning international travel, you should talk to your doctor at least 4 to 6 weeks before your trip to discuss any special precautions or vaccines that you may need.

Hepatitis B: A baby whose mother has hepatitis B is at highest risk for becoming infected with hepatitis B during delivery. Talk to your healthcare professional about getting tested for hepatitis B and whether or not you should get vaccinated.

Additional Vaccines: Some women may need other vaccines before, during, or after they become pregnant. For example, if you have a history of chronic liver disease, your doctor may recommend the hepatitis A vaccine. If you work in a lab, or if you are traveling to a country where you may be exposed to meningococcal disease, your doctor may recommend the meningococcal vaccine.

Vaccines before and after Pregnancy

For Women Planning a Pregnancy

Even before becoming pregnant, make sure you are up to date on all your vaccines. This will help protect you and your child from serious diseases. For example, rubella is a contagious disease that can be very dangerous if you get it while you are pregnant. In fact, it can cause a miscarriage or serious birth defects. The best protection against rubella is MMR (measles-mumps-rubella) vaccine, but if you aren't up to date, you'll need it before you get pregnant. Make sure you have a **prepregnancy blood test** to see if you are immune to the disease. Most women were vaccinated as children with the MMR vaccine, but you should confirm this with your doctor. If you need to get vaccinated for rubella, you should **avoid becoming pregnant until one month after receiving the MMR vaccine** and, ideally, not until your immunity is confirmed by a blood test.

Did you know that your baby gets disease immunity (protection) from you during pregnancy? This immunity will protect your baby from some diseases during the first few months of life, but immunity decreases over time.

Your Vaccination History

It's important for you to keep an accurate record of your vaccinations. Sharing this information with your preconception and prenatal healthcare professional will help determine which vaccines you'll need during pregnancy. If you or your doctor does not have a current record of your vaccinations, you can:

- Ask your parents or other caregivers if they still have your school immunization records. Ask them which childhood illnesses you've already had because illnesses in childhood can sometimes provide immunity in adulthood.

- Contact your previous healthcare providers or other locations where you may have received vaccinations (e.g., the health department, your workplace, or local pharmacies).

Keep Protecting Your Baby after Birth

Your ob-gyn or midwife may recommend you receive some vaccines right after giving birth. Postpartum vaccination will help protect you from getting sick and you will pass some antibodies to your baby through your breastmilk. Vaccination after pregnancy is especially important if you did not receive certain vaccines before or during your pregnancy.

Your baby will also start to get his or her own vaccines to protect against serious childhood diseases.

Chapter 3

Prenatal Tests

Medical checkups and screening tests help keep you and your baby healthy during pregnancy. This is called prenatal care. It also involves education and counseling about how to handle different aspects of your pregnancy. During your visits, your doctor may discuss many issues, such as healthy eating and physical activity, screening tests you might need, and what to expect during labor and delivery.

Choosing a Prenatal Care Provider

You will see your prenatal care provider many times before you have your baby. So you want to be sure that the person you choose has a good reputation, and listens to and respects you. You will want to find out if the doctor or midwife can deliver your baby in the place you want to give birth, such as a specific hospital or birthing center. Your provider also should be willing and able to give you the information and support you need to make an informed choice about whether to breastfeed or bottlefeed.

Healthcare providers that care for women during pregnancy include:

- **Obstetricians (OB)** are medical doctors who specialize in the care of pregnant women and in delivering babies. OBs also have special training in surgery so they are also able to do a cesarean

This chapter includes text excerpted from "Pregnancy—Prenatal Care and Tests," Office on Women's Health (OWH), U.S. Department of Health and Human Services (HHS), February 1, 2017.

delivery. Women who have health problems or are at risk for pregnancy complications should see an obstetrician. Women with the highest risk pregnancies might need special care from a **maternal fetal medicine specialist.**

- **Family practice doctors** are medical doctors who provide care for the whole family through all stages of life. This includes care during pregnancy, and delivery, and following birth. Most family practice doctors cannot perform cesarean deliveries.

- A **certified nurse midwife (CNM)** and **certified professional midwife (CPM)** are trained to provide pregnancy and postpartum care. Midwives can be a good option for healthy women at low risk for problems during pregnancy, labor, or delivery. A CNM is educated in both nursing and midwifery. Most CNMs practice in hospitals and birth centers. A CPM is required to have experience delivering babies in home settings because most CPMs practice in homes and birthing centers. All midwives should have a backup plan with an obstetrician in case of a problem or emergency.

Ask your primary care doctor, friends, and family members for provider recommendations. When making your choice, think about:

- Reputation
- Personality and bedside manner
- The provider's gender and age
- Office location and hours
- Whether you always will be seen by the same provider during office checkups and delivery
- Who covers for the provider when she or he is not available
- Where you want to deliver
- How the provider handles phone consultations and after hour calls

What Is a Doula?

A doula is a professional labor coach, who gives physical and emotional support to women during labor and delivery. They offer advice on breathing, relaxation, movement, and positioning. Doulas also give emotional support and comfort to women and their partners during labor and birth. Doulas and midwives often work together during a woman's labor. A study showed that continuous doula support during labor was linked to shorter labors and much lower use of:

- Pain medicines

- Oxytocin (medicine to help labor progress)

- Cesarean delivery

Check with your health insurance company to find out if they will cover the cost of a doula. When choosing a doula, find out if she is certified by Doulas of North America (DONA) or another professional group.

Places to Deliver Your Baby

In general, women can choose to deliver at a hospital, birth center, or at home. You will need to contact your health insurance provider to find out what options are available. Also, find out if the doctor or midwife you are considering can deliver your baby in the place you want to give birth.

- **Hospitals** are a good choice for women with health problems, pregnancy complications, or those who are at risk for problems during labor and delivery. Hospitals offer the most advanced medical equipment and highly trained doctors for pregnant women and their babies. In a hospital, doctors can do a cesarean delivery if you or your baby is in danger during labor. Women can get epidurals or many other pain relief options. Also, more and more hospitals now offer onsite birth centers, which aim to offer a style of care similar to standalone birth centers.

Questions to ask when choosing a hospital:

- Is it close to your home?

- Is a doctor who can give pain relief, such as an epidural, at the hospital 24 hours a day?

- Do you like the feel of the labor and delivery rooms?

- Are private rooms available?

- How many support people can you invite into the room with you?

- Does it have a neonatal intensive care unit (NICU) in case of serious problems with the baby?

- Can the baby stay in the room with you?

- Does the hospital have the staff and setup to support successful breastfeeding?

- Does it have an onsite birth center?

- **Birth or birthing centers** give women a "homey" environment in which to labor and give birth. They try to make labor and delivery a natural and personal process by doing away with most high tech equipment and routine procedures. So, you will not automatically be hooked up to an IV. Likewise, you won't have an electronic fetal monitor around your belly the whole time. Instead, the midwife or nurse will check in on your baby from time to time with a handheld machine. Once the baby is born, all exams and care will occur in your room. Usually certified nurse midwives, not obstetricians, deliver babies at birth centers. Healthy women who are at low risk for problems during pregnancy, labor, and delivery may choose to deliver at a birth center.

  Women can not receive epidurals at a birth center, although some pain medicines may be available. If a cesarean delivery becomes necessary, women must be moved to a hospital for the procedure. After delivery, babies with problems can receive basic emergency care while being moved to a hospital.

  Many birthing centers have showers or tubs in their rooms for laboring women. They also tend to have comforts of home like large beds and rocking chairs. In general, birth centers allow more people in the delivery room than do hospitals.

  Birth centers can be inside of hospitals, a part of a hospital or completely separate facilities. If you want to deliver at a birth center, make sure it meets the standards of the Accreditation Association for Ambulatory HealthCare (AAAHC), The Joint Commission, or the American Association of Birth Centers (AABC). Accredited birth centers must have doctors who can work at a nearby hospital in case of problems with the mom or baby. Also, make sure the birth center has the staff and setup to support successful breastfeeding.

- **Homebirth** is an option for healthy pregnant women with no risk factors for complications during pregnancy, labor or delivery. It is also important women have a strong aftercare support system at home. Some certified nurse midwives and doctors will deliver babies at home. Many health insurance companies do not cover the cost of care for homebirths. So check with your plan if you'd like to deliver at home.

Home births are common in many countries in Europe. But in the United States, planned home births are not supported by the American Congress of Obstetricians and Gynecologists (ACOG). ACOG states that hospitals are the safest place to deliver a baby. In case of an emergency, says ACOG, a hospital's equipment and highly trained doctors can provide the best care for a woman and her baby.

If you are thinking about a home birth, you need to weigh the pros and cons. The main advantage is that you will be able to experience labor and delivery in the privacy and comfort of your own home. Since there will be no routine medical procedures, you will have control of your experience.

The main disadvantage of a homebirth is that in case of a problem, you and the baby will not have immediate hospital/medical care. It will have to wait until you are transferred to the hospital. Plus, women who deliver at home have no options for pain relief.

To ensure your safety and that of your baby, you must have a highly trained and experienced midwife along with a fail safe backup plan. You will need fast, reliable transportation to a hospital. If you live far away from a hospital, homebirth may not be the best choice. Your midwife must be experienced and have the necessary skills and supplies to start emergency care for you and your baby if need be. Your midwife should also have access to a doctor 24 hours a day.

Prenatal Checkups

During pregnancy, regular checkups are very important. This consistent care can help keep you and your baby healthy, spot problems if they occur, and prevent problems during delivery. Typically, routine checkups occur:

- Once each month for weeks four through 28
- Twice a month for weeks 28 through 36
- Weekly for weeks 36 to birth

Women with high risk pregnancies need to see their doctors more often.

At your first visit your doctor will perform a full physical exam, take your blood for lab tests, and calculate your due date. Your doctor might also do a breast exam, a pelvic exam, to check your uterus (womb), and a cervical exam, including a Pap test. During this first visit, your doctor will ask you lots of questions about your lifestyle, relationships, and health habits. It's important to be honest with your doctor.

After the first visit, most prenatal visits will include:

- Checking your blood pressure and weight

- Checking the baby's heart rate

- Measuring your abdomen to check your baby's growth

You also will have some routine tests throughout your pregnancy, such as tests to look for anemia, tests to measure risk of gestational diabetes, and tests to look for harmful infections.

Become a partner with your doctor to manage your care. Keep all of your appointments—every one is important! Ask questions and read to educate yourself about this exciting time.

Monitor Your Baby's Activity

After 28 weeks, keep track of your baby's movement. This will help you to notice if your baby is moving less than normal, which could be a sign that your baby is in distress and needs a doctor's care. An easy way to do this is the "count-to-10" approach. Count your baby's movements in the evening—the time of day when the fetus tends to be most active. Lie down if you have trouble feeling your baby move. Most women count 10 movements within about 20 minutes. But it is rare for a woman to count less than 10 movements within two hours at times when the baby is active. Count your baby's movements every day so you know what is normal for you. Call your doctor if you count less than 10 movements within two hours or if you notice your baby is moving less than normal. If your baby is not moving at all, call your doctor right away.

Prenatal Tests

Tests are used during pregnancy to check your and your baby's health. At your first prenatal visit, your doctor will use tests to check for a number of things, such as:

- Your blood type and rhesus (Rh) factor

- Anemia

- Infections, such as toxoplasmosis and sexually transmitted infections (STIs), including hepatitis B, syphilis, chlamydia, and human immunodeficiency virus (HIV)

- Signs that you are immune to rubella (German measles) and chickenpox.

Throughout your pregnancy, your doctor or midwife may suggest a number of other tests, too. Some tests are suggested for all women, such as screenings for gestational diabetes, Down syndrome, and HIV. Other tests might be offered based on your:

- Age

- Personal or family health history

- Ethnic background

- Results of routine tests

Some tests are screening tests. They detect risks for or signs of possible health problems in you or your baby. Based on screening test results, your doctor might suggest diagnostic tests. Diagnostic tests confirm or rule out health problems in you or your baby.

Table 3.1. Common Prenatal Tests

Test	What It Is	How It Is Done
Amniocentesis	This test can diagnosis certain birth defects, including: • Down syndrome • Cystic fibrosis • Spina bifida It is performed at 14–20 weeks. It may be suggested for couples at higher risk for genetic disorders. It also provides DNA for paternity testing.	A thin needle is used to draw out a small amount of amniotic fluid and cells from the sac surrounding the fetus. The sample is sent to a lab for testing.
Biophysical profile (BPP)	This test is used in the third trimester to monitor the overall health of the baby and to help decide if the baby should be delivered early.	BPP involves an ultrasound exam along with a nonstress test. The BPP looks at the baby's breathing, movement, muscle tone, heart rate, and the amount of amniotic fluid.

Table 3.1. Continued

Test	What It Is	How It Is Done
Chorionic villus	A test done at 10–13 weeks to diagnose certain birth defects, including: • Chromosomal disorders, including Down syndrome • Genetic disorders, such as cystic fibrosis CVS may be suggested for couples at higher risk for genetic disorders.	A needle removes a small sample of cells from the placenta to be tested.
First trimester screen	A screening test done at 11–14 weeks to detect higher risk of: • Chromosomal disorders, including Down syndrome and trisomy 18 • Other problems, such as heart defects It also can reveal multiple births. Based on test results, your doctor may suggest other tests to diagnose a disorder.	This test involves both a blood test and an ultrasound exam called nuchal translucency screening. The blood test measures the levels of certain substances in the mother's blood. The ultrasound exam measures the thickness at the back of the baby's neck. This information, combined with the mother's age, help doctors determine risk to the fetus.
Glucose challenge screening	A screening test done at 26–28 weeks to determine the mother's risk of gestational diabetes. Based on test results, your doctor may suggest a glucose tolerance test.	First, you consume a special sugary drink from your doctor. A blood sample is taken one hour later to look for high blood sugar levels.

Table 3.1. Continued

Test	What It Is	How It Is Done
Glucose tolerance test	This test is done at 26–28 weeks to diagnose gestational diabetes.	Your doctor will tell you what to eat a few days before the test. Then, you cannot eat or drink anything but sips of water for 14 hours before the test. Your blood is drawn to test your "fasting blood glucose level." Then, you will consume a sugary drink. Your blood will be tested every hour for three hours to see how well your body processes sugar.
Group B streptococcus	This test is done at 36–37 weeks to look for bacteria that can cause pneumonia or serious infection in newborn.	A swab is used to take cells from your vagina and rectum to be tested.
Maternal serum screen	A screening test done at 15–20 weeks to detect higher risk of: • Chromosomal disorders, including Down syndrome and trisomy 18 • Neural tube defects, such as spina bifida Based on test results, your doctor may suggest other tests to diagnose a disorder.	Blood is drawn to measure the levels of certain substances in the mother's blood.
Nonstress test (NST)	This test is performed after 28 weeks to monitor your baby's health. It can show signs of fetal distress, such as your baby not getting enough oxygen.	A belt is placed around the mother's belly to measure the baby's heart rate in response to its own movements.

Table 3.1. Continued

Test	What It Is	How It Is Done
Ultrasound exam	An ultrasound exam can be performed at any point during the pregnancy. Ultrasound exams are not routine. But it is not uncommon for women to have a standard ultrasound exam between 18 and 20 weeks to look for signs of problems with the baby's organs and body systems and confirm the age of the fetus and proper growth. It also might be able to tell the sex of your baby. Ultrasound exam is also used as part of the first trimester screen and biophysical profile (BPP). Based on exam results, your doctor may suggest other tests or other types of ultrasound to help detect a problem.	Ultrasound uses sound waves to create a "picture" of your baby on a monitor. With a standard ultrasound, a gel is spread on your abdomen. A special tool is moved over your abdomen, which allows your doctor and you to view the baby on a monitor.
Urine test	A urine sample can look for signs of health problems, such as: • Urinary tract infection • Diabetes • Preeclampsia If your doctor suspects a problem, the sample might be sent to a lab for more in-depth testing.	You will collect a small sample of clean, midstream urine in a sterile plastic cup. Testing strips that look for certain substances in your urine are dipped in the sample. The sample also can be looked at under a microscope.

Understanding Prenatal Tests and Test Results

If your doctor suggests certain prenatal tests, don't be afraid to ask lots of questions. Learning about the test, why your doctor is suggesting it for you, and what the test results could mean can help you cope with any worries or fears you might have. Keep in mind that screening tests do not diagnose problems. They evaluate risk. So if a screening test comes back abnormal, this doesn't mean there is a problem with your baby. More information is needed. Your doctor can explain what test results mean and possible next steps.

Avoid Keepsake Ultrasounds

You might think a keepsake ultrasound is a must have for your scrapbook. But, doctors advise against ultrasound when there is no medical need to do so. Although ultrasound is considered safe for medical purposes, exposure to ultrasound energy for a keepsake video or image may put a mother and her unborn baby at risk. Don't take that chance.

High Risk Pregnancy

Pregnancies with a greater chance of complications are called "high risk." But this doesn't mean there will be problems. The following factors may increase the risk of problems during pregnancy:

- Very young age or older than 35

- Overweight or underweight

- Problems in previous pregnancy

- Health conditions you have before you become pregnant, such as high blood pressure, diabetes, autoimmune disorders, cancer, and HIV

- Pregnancy with twins or other multiples

Health problems also may develop during a pregnancy that make it high risk, such as gestational diabetes or preeclampsia.

Women with high risk pregnancies need prenatal care more often and sometimes from a specially trained doctor. A maternal fetal medicine specialist is a medical doctor that cares for high risk pregnancies.

If your pregnancy is considered high risk, you might worry about your unborn baby's health and have trouble enjoying your pregnancy. Share your concerns with your doctor. Your doctor can explain your risks and the chances of a real problem. Also, be sure to follow your doctor's advice. For example, if your doctor tells you to take it easy, then ask your partner, family members, and friends to help you out in the months ahead. You will feel better knowing that you are doing all you can to care for your unborn baby.

Paying for Prenatal Care

Pregnancy can be stressful if you are worried about affording healthcare for you and your unborn baby. For many women, the extra expenses of prenatal care and preparing for the new baby are overwhelming. The good news is that women in every state can get help to pay for medical care during their pregnancies. Every state in the United States has a program to help. Programs give medical care, information, advice, and other services important for a healthy pregnancy.

To find out about the program in your state:

- Call 800-311-BABY (800-311-2229)—This toll-free telephone number will connect you to the Health Department in your area code.

- Call 800-504-7081 for information in Spanish.

- Call or contact your local Health Department.

You may also find help through these places:

- **Local hospital or social service agencies**—Ask to speak with a social worker on staff. She or he will be able to tell you where to go for help.

- **Community clinics**—Some areas have free clinics or clinics that provide free care to women in need.

- **Women, Infants and Children (WIC) Program**—This government program is available in every state. It provides help with food, nutritional counseling, and access to health services for women, infants, and children.

- **Places of worship**

Chapter 4

Substance Use and Pregnancy

Chapter Contents

Section 4.1

Substance Use and Risks during Pregnancy

This section includes text excerpted from "Substance Use While Pregnant and Breastfeeding," National Institute on Drug Abuse (NIDA), September 2016.

Research shows that use of tobacco, alcohol, or illicit drugs or abuse of prescription drugs by pregnant women can have severe health consequences for infants. This is because many substances pass easily through the placenta, so substances that a pregnant woman takes also, to some degree, reach the baby. Research shows that smoking tobacco or marijuana, taking prescription pain relievers, or using illegal drugs during pregnancy is associated with double or even triple the risk of stillbirth.

Risks of Stillbirth from Substance Use in Pregnancy

- Tobacco use—1.8–2.8 times greater risk of stillbirth, with the highest risk found among the heaviest smokers

- Marijuana use—2.3 times greater risk of stillbirth

- Evidence of any stimulant, marijuana, or prescription pain reliever use—2.2 times greater risk of stillbirth

- Passive exposure to tobacco—2.1 times greater risk of stillbirth

Withdrawal Symptoms

Regular drug use can produce dependence in the newborn, and the baby may go through withdrawal upon birth. Most research in this area has focused on the effects of opioid misuse (prescription pain relievers or heroin). However, more recent data has shown that use of alcohol, barbiturates, benzodiazepines, and caffeine during pregnancy may also cause the infant to show withdrawal symptoms at birth. The type and severity of an infant's withdrawal symptoms depend on the drug(s) used, how long and how often the birth mother used, how her body breaks the drug down, and whether the infant was born full term or prematurely.

Symptoms of drug withdrawal in a newborn can develop immediately or up to 14 days after birth and can include:

- blotchy skin coloring
- diarrhea
- excessive or high-pitched crying
- abnormal sucking reflex
- fever
- hyperactive reflexes
- increased muscle tone
- irritability
- poor feeding

- rapid breathing
- increased heart rate
- seizures
- sleep problems
- slow weight gain
- stuffy nose and sneezing
- sweating
- trembling
- vomiting

Effects of using some drugs could be long term and possibly fatal to the baby:

- low birth weight
- birth defects
- small head circumference
- premature birth
- sudden infant death syndrome (SIDS)

Illegal Drugs

- Marijuana
- Stimulants (Cocaine and Methamphetamine)
- 3,4-Methylenedioxymethamphetamine (MDMA) (Ecstasy, Molly)
- Heroin

Section 4.2

Alcohol Use and Pregnancy

This section includes text excerpted from "Alcohol and Pregnancy,"
Centers for Disease Control and Prevention (CDC), February 2, 2016.

Alcohol use during pregnancy can cause fetal alcohol spectrum disorders (FASDs), which are physical, behavioral, and intellectual disabilities that last a lifetime. More than 3 million U.S. women are at risk of exposing their developing baby to alcohol because they are drinking, having sex, and not using birth control to prevent pregnancy. About half of all U.S. pregnancies are unplanned and, even if planned, most women do not know they are pregnant until they are 4–6 weeks into the pregnancy. This means a woman might be drinking and exposing her developing baby to alcohol without knowing it. Alcohol screening and counseling helps people who are drinking too much to drink less. It is recommended that women who are pregnant or might be pregnant not drink alcohol at all. FASDs do not occur if a developing baby is not exposed to alcohol before birth.

Women can:

- Talk with their healthcare provider about their plans for pregnancy, their alcohol use, and ways to prevent pregnancy if they are not planning to get pregnant.

- Stop drinking alcohol if they are trying to get pregnant or could get pregnant.

- Ask their partner, family, and friends to support their choice not to drink during pregnancy or while trying to get pregnant.

- Ask their healthcare provider or another trusted person about resources for help if they cannot stop drinking on their own.

More than 3 million U.S. women are at risk of exposing their developing baby to alcohol.

Three in four women who want to get pregnant as soon as possible report drinking alcohol.

One hundred percent of fetal alcohol spectrum disorders are completely preventable.

Problem

Alcohol can harm a developing baby before a woman knows she is pregnant.

- Women who are pregnant or who might be pregnant should be aware that any level of alcohol use could harm their baby.

- All types of alcohol can be harmful, including all wine and beer.

- The baby's brain, body, and organs are developing throughout pregnancy and can be affected by alcohol at any time.

- Drinking while pregnant can also increase the risk of miscarriage, stillbirth, prematurity, and sudden infant death syndrome (SIDS).

Doctors, nurses, or other health professionals can help prevent alcohol use during pregnancy in 5 ways:

1. Provide alcohol screening and counseling to all women.

2. Recommend birth control to women who are having sex (if appropriate), not planning to get pregnant, and drinking alcohol.

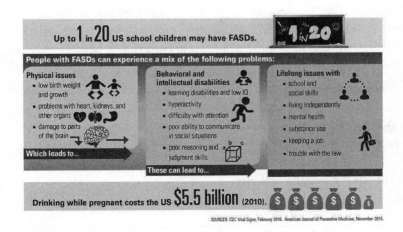

Figure 4.1. *Effects of Alcohol Use during Pregnancy*

3. Advise women who are trying to get pregnant to stop drinking alcohol.

4. Refer for additional services for women who cannot stop drinking on their own.

5. Follow up yearly or more often, as needed.

What Can Be Done

The Federal Government Is

- Requiring most health insurance plans to cover recommended alcohol screening and counseling services without cost to the patient.

- Requiring most health insurance plans to cover U.S. Food and Drug Administration (FDA)-approved methods of birth control and patient education and counseling as prescribed by a healthcare provider for women of reproductive age without cost to the patient.

- Adopting clinical guidelines to carry out alcohol screening and counseling in community health centers.

- Working with partner organizations to promote alcohol screening and counseling.

Women Can

- Talk with their healthcare provider about their plans for pregnancy, their alcohol use, and ways to prevent pregnancy if they are not planning to get pregnant.

- Stop drinking alcohol if they are trying to get pregnant or could get pregnant.

- Ask their partner, family, and friends to support their choice not to drink during pregnancy or while trying to get pregnant.

- Ask their healthcare provider or another trusted person about resources for help if they cannot stop drinking on their own.

Healthcare Providers Can

- Screen all adult patients for alcohol use at least yearly.

- Advise women not to drink at all if there is any chance they could be pregnant.

- Counsel, refer, and follow up with patients who need more help.

- Use the correct billing codes so that alcohol screening and counseling is reimbursable.

State and Local Governments Can

- Work with their Medicaid programs to make sure alcohol screening and counseling services are reimbursable.

- Encourage health insurance plans and provider organizations to support alcohol screening and counseling.

- Monitor how many adults are receiving these services in communities.

- Support proven policies and programs that work to prevent drinking too much.

Section 4.3

Tobacco Use and Pregnancy

This section includes text excerpted from "Tobacco Use and Pregnancy," Centers for Disease Control and Prevention (CDC), September 29, 2017.

How Does Smoking during Pregnancy Harm My Health and My Baby?

Most people know that smoking causes cancer, heart disease, and other major health problems. Smoking during pregnancy causes additional health problems, including premature birth (being born too early), certain birth defects, and infant death.

- Smoking makes it harder for a woman to get pregnant.

- Women who smoke during pregnancy are more likely than other women to have a miscarriage.

- Smoking can cause problems with the placenta—the source of the baby's food and oxygen during pregnancy. For example, the placenta can separate from the womb too early, causing bleeding, which is dangerous to the mother and baby.

- Smoking during pregnancy can cause a baby to be born too early or to have low birth weight—making it more likely the baby will be sick and have to stay in the hospital longer. A few babies may even die.

- Smoking during and after pregnancy is a risk factor of sudden infant death syndrome (SIDS). SIDS is an infant death for which a cause of the death cannot be found.

- Babies born to women who smoke are more likely to have certain birth defects, like a cleft lip or cleft palate.

What Are E-Cigarettes? Are They Safer than Regular Cigarettes in Pregnancy?

Electronic cigarettes (also called electronic nicotine delivery systems or e-cigarettes) come in different sizes and shapes, including "pens," "mods," (i.e., these types are modified by the user) and "tanks." Most e-cigarettes contain a battery, a heating device, and a cartridge to hold liquid. The liquid typically contains nicotine, flavorings, and other chemicals. The battery-powered device heats the liquid in the cartridge into an aerosol that the user inhales.

Although the aerosol of e-cigarettes generally has fewer harmful substances than cigarette smoke, e-cigarettes and other products containing nicotine are not safe to use during pregnancy. Nicotine is a health danger for pregnant women and developing babies and can damage a developing baby's brain and lungs. Also, some of the flavorings used in e-cigarettes may be harmful to a developing baby.

How Many Women Smoke during Pregnancy?

According to the 2011 Pregnancy Risk Assessment and Monitoring System (PRAMS) data from 24 states.

- Approximately 10 percent of women reported smoking during the last 3 months of pregnancy.

- Of women who smoked 3 months before pregnancy, 55 percent quit during pregnancy. Among women who quit smoking during pregnancy, 40 percent started smoking again within 6 months after delivery.

What Are the Benefits of Quitting?

Quitting smoking will help you feel better and provide a healthier environment for your baby.

When you stop smoking:

- Your baby will get more oxygen, even after just one day of not smoking.

- There is less risk that your baby will be born too early.

- There is a better chance that your baby will come home from the hospital with you.

- You will be less likely to develop heart disease, stroke, lung cancer, chronic lung disease, and other smoke-related diseases.

- You will be more likely to live to know your grandchildren.

- You will have more energy and breathe more easily.

- Your clothes, hair, and home will smell better.

- Your food will taste better.

- You will have more money that you can spend on other things.

- You will feel good about what you have done for yourself and your baby.

How Does Other People's Smoke (Secondhand Smoke) Harm My Health and My Child's Health?

Breathing other people's smoke make children and adults who do not smoke sick. There is no safe level of breathing others people's smoke.

- Pregnant women who breathe other people's cigarette smoke are more likely to have a baby who weighs less.

- Babies who breathe in other people's cigarette smoke are more likely to have ear infections and more frequent asthma attacks.

- Babies who breathe in other people's cigarette smoke are more likely to die from sudden infant death syndrome (SIDS). SIDS is an infant death for which a cause of the death cannot be found.

In the United States, 58 million children and adults who do not smoke are exposed to other people's smoke. Almost 25 million children and adolescents aged 3–19 years, or about 4 out of 10 children in this age group, are exposed to other people's cigarette smoke. Home and vehicles are the places where children are most exposed to cigarette smoke, and a major location of smoke exposure for adults too. Also, people can be exposed to cigarette smoke in public places, restaurants, and at work.

What Can You Do to Avoid Other People's Smoke?

There is no safe level of exposure to cigarette smoke. Breathing even a little smoke can be harmful. The only way to fully protect yourself and your loved ones from the dangers of other people's smoke is through 100 percent smoke-free environments.

You can protect yourself and your family by:

- Making your home and car smoke-free.

- Asking people not to smoke around you and your children.

- Making sure that your children's daycare center or school is smoke-free.

- Choosing restaurants and other businesses that are smoke-free. Thanking businesses for being smoke-free.

- Teaching children to stay away from other people's smoke.

- Avoiding all smoke. If you or your children have respiratory conditions, if you have heart disease, or if you are pregnant, the dangers are greater for you.

- Learn as much as you can by talking to your doctor, nurse, or healthcare provider about the dangers of other people's smoke.

Section 4.4

Marijuana and Pregnancy

This section includes text excerpted from "What You
Need to Know about Marijuana Use and Pregnancy,"
Centers for Disease Control and Prevention (CDC), April 13, 2017.

Marijuana use during pregnancy can be harmful to your baby's health. The chemicals in marijuana (in particular, tetrahydrocannabinol or THC) pass through your system to your baby and can negatively affect your baby's development. Although more research is needed to better understand how marijuana may affect you and your baby during pregnancy, the Centers for Disease Control and Prevention (CDC) recommends against using marijuana during your pregnancy.

What Are the Potential Health Effects of Using Marijuana during My Pregnancy?

- Some research shows that using marijuana while you are pregnant can cause health problems in newborns—including low birth weight and developmental problems.

- Breathing marijuana smoke can also be bad for you and your baby. Marijuana smoke has many of the same chemicals as tobacco smoke and may increase the chances for developmental problems in your baby.

Can Using Marijuana during My Pregnancy Negatively Impact My Baby after Birth?

- Research shows marijuana use during pregnancy may make it hard for your child to pay attention or to learn; these issues may only become noticeable as your child grows older.

Does Using Marijuana Affect Breastfeeding?

- Chemicals from marijuana can be passed to your baby through breast milk. THC is stored in fat and is slowly released over

51

time, meaning an infant could be exposed for a longer period of time.

- However, data on the effects of marijuana exposure to the infant through breastfeeding are limited and conflicting.

- To limit potential risk to the infant, breastfeeding mothers should reduce or avoid marijuana use.

Chapter 5

Environmental Risks and Pregnancy

Tobacco Smoke

It is well documented that maternal smoking during pregnancy is associated with poor fetal development. However, exposure to secondhand smoke during pregnancy might also result in a higher risk of poor fetal development (i.e., reduced birth weight and birth length), reduced lung function, respiratory illnesses (e.g., asthma), and cognitive deficits (e.g., impaired speech, language skills, and intelligence).

Secondhand smoke, also known as environmental tobacco smoke (ETS), contains more than 4,000 compounds, of which at least 250 have been found to be toxic to human health. Some of these chemicals can cross the placenta to the developing fetus and increase the risk of adverse birth outcomes. Children exposed to secondhand smoke after birth are more likely to suffer serious health problems such as asthma, lower respiratory tract infections, ear infections or sudden infant death syndrome (SIDS).

This chapter includes text excerpted from "Promoting Good Prenatal Health: Air Pollution and Pregnancy," U.S. Environmental Protection Agency (EPA), January 2010. Reviewed December 2017.

Carbon Monoxide

Carbon monoxide (CO) is often referred to as a silent killer. CO is a toxic gas that is difficult to detect because it is colorless, odorless, tasteless, and does not irritate the skin. Malfunctioning or improperly used fuel-burning appliances and idling automobiles in enclosed spaces are responsible for hundreds of unintentional CO-related deaths every year. Indoor sources of CO include backdrafting from woodstoves and gas water heaters, gas stoves, the improper use of generators in enclosed spaces such as homes, cigarette smoke, and unvented gas and kerosene space heaters. CO reduces the capacity of a mother's blood to carry oxygen (O^2), complicating delivery of O^2 to the developing fetus. Epidemiological and animal toxicological studies suggest that long-term exposure to ambient CO, especially during the first trimester, may increase risk for preterm birth, reduced fetal growth, and certain birth defects such as cardiac birth defects and otoacoustic deficits. The severity of CO poisoning for the fetus depends on the amount and length of exposure, as well as gestational age at the time of exposure.

In situations of suspected CO poisoning, if a pregnant woman experiences very mild symptoms, or no symptoms at all, generally it is unlikely her fetus is at significant risk. However, detecting CO poisoning in pregnant women can be more difficult because symptoms mirror conditions that normally appear in pregnancy (nausea, vomiting, and tiredness). Symptoms of high exposure to CO are serious and potentially life-threatening, and include mental confusion, lack of muscular coordination, and loss of consciousness.

Particle Pollution

Particle pollution, also known as particulate matter or PM, is the generic term for a broad class of chemically and physically diverse substances that exist as discrete particles (liquid droplets or solids) over a wide range of sizes. Particles originate from a variety of anthropogenic stationary and mobile sources as well as from natural sources. Particles may be emitted directly, or formed in the atmosphere by transformations of gaseous emissions such as sulfur oxides (SOX), nitrogen oxides (NOX), and volatile organic compounds (VOCs). The chemical and physical properties of PM vary greatly with time, region, meteorology, and source category, thus complicating the assessment of health and welfare effects. Size directly determines a particle's potential for causing health problems, with the smaller particles, those 10 micrometers in diameter or less (PM10 and PM2.5), being more dangerous. These small particles can enter the respiratory system and penetrate deep into the lungs, with possible serious health effects.

Research suggests that exposure to ambient levels of particle pollution may increase the risk for adverse cardiovascular and/or respiratory health effects. Some research has linked particle exposure to a greater risk of low birth weight (LBW) and infant mortality, especially due to respiratory causes during the postnatal period. However, outcomes are highly variable based on the size of particles, duration of exposure, and time during pregnancy when the mother is exposed. The risk of being affected by particle pollution and ground-level ozone increases with the difficulty and duration of outdoor activities, and with increased pollution levels in the area.

Ozone

Ozone is a gas composed of three oxygen atoms (O^3). "Good" ozone is a naturally formed layer in the stratosphere that helps protect life on Earth from the sun's rays. "Bad" ozone exists at ground level and can be harmful to health. Ground-level ozone is created by chemical reactions of tailpipe exhaust, gasoline vapors, industrial emissions, chemical solvents, and natural sources. Joined with particulate matter and acted on by sunlight and heat, ozone creates "smog."

Ozone can be present in indoor air as well. Ozone generators, personal air purifiers, "pure-air" generators and "super oxygen" purifiers are devices that emit ozone gas into the indoor air at levels that can irritate airways and exacerbate existing respiratory conditions. Evidence shows that at concentrations that do not exceed public health standards, ozone is ineffective at removing indoor air contaminants or biological pollutants such as mold from the air. Exposure to ozone has been linked to LBW babies. Researchers at the University of Southern California (USC) found that women who breathe air heavily polluted with ozone are at particular risk for having babies afflicted with intrauterine growth retardation (IUGR), meaning they fall below the 15th percentile of expected size. The association was even stronger for ozone exposure over the second and third trimesters. Animal studies contribute to the understanding of the role of ozone in LBW. Pregnant rats were found particularly vulnerable to lung inflammation from ozone. Researchers suspect that lung inflammation initiates a biochemical response that may harm the placenta.

Paint Fumes

When preparing the house for the new baby, be aware that exposure to paint fumes can be hazardous to the health of the mother and developing fetus. There are two general types of household paints, oil-based and water-based. Oil-based (alkyd) paint is often used on the exterior of houses because it dries very hard and withstands harsh weather for a long time. Water-based (latex) paint generally emits fewer chemical vapors, often called volatile organic compounds (VOCs), than alkyd paint, but may still contain some hazardous chemicals such as ethylene glycol ethers and biocides (e.g., mercury or formaldehyde). VOCs are emitted as a gas from various solids or liquids, including most paints, and can cause adverse health effects, especially with extended duration or frequency of exposure to fumes.

Short-term exposure to solvents from alkyd paints can be significantly higher than from latex paints. Headaches, nausea, dizziness, and fatigue are typical symptoms of paint fume inhalation and can be worse with acute, higher level exposure. Pregnant women should avoid alkyd paint, and limit the use of latex paint in order to reduce exposure to potentially harmful vapors in both home and occupational settings.

Cleaning Products

Exposure to fumes from some cleaning products during pregnancy can pose risks when used in the home and in the workplace. Common cleaning products contain a range of ingredients including solvents, strong acids and bases, and fragrances. Some of these ingredients pose health concerns, others can be bad for the environment, and some of them can release toxic fumes either individually, or if mixed together. Phthalates can be carriers for fragrance in glass cleaners, deodorizers, laundry detergents, and fabric softeners. Some phthalate compounds can be associated with potential adverse effects in male children, reduced sperm count in adult men, and increased allergic symptoms and asthma in children.

Chapter 6

X-Rays during Pregnancy: Are They Safe?

Pregnancy is a time to take good care of yourself and your unborn child. Many things are especially important during pregnancy, such as eating right, cutting out cigarettes and alcohol, and being careful about the prescription and over-the-counter (OTC) drugs you take. Diagnostic X-rays and other medical radiation procedures of the abdominal area also deserve extra attention during pregnancy.

Diagnostic X-rays can give the doctor important and even life-saving information about a person's medical condition. But like many things, diagnostic X-rays have risks as well as benefits. They should be used only when they will give the doctor information needed to treat you.

You'll probably never need an abdominal X-ray during pregnancy. But sometimes, because of a particular medical condition, your physician may feel that a diagnostic X-ray of your abdomen or lower torso is needed. If this should happen—don't be upset. The risk to you and your unborn child is very small, and the benefit of finding out about your medical condition is far greater. In fact, **the risk of *not* having a needed X-ray could be much greater than the risk from the radiation.** But even small risks should not be taken if they're unnecessary.

This chapter includes text excerpted from "Radiation-Emitting Products—X-Rays, Pregnancy and You," U.S. Food and Drug Administration (FDA), December 9, 2017.

You can reduce those risks by telling your doctor if you are, or think you might be, pregnant whenever an abdominal X-ray is prescribed. If you are pregnant, the doctor may decide that it would be best to cancel the X-ray examination, postpone it, or modify it to reduce the amount of radiation. Or, depending on your medical needs, and realizing that the risk is very small, the doctor may feel that it is best to proceed with the X-ray as planned. In any case, you should feel free to discuss the decision with your doctor.

What Kind of X-Rays Can Affect the Unborn Child?

During most X-ray examinations—like those of the arms, legs, head, teeth, or chest—your reproductive organs are not exposed to the direct X-ray beam. So these kinds of procedures, when properly done, do not involve any risk to the unborn child. However, X-rays of the mother's lower torso—abdomen, stomach, pelvis, lower back, or kidneys—may expose the unborn child to the direct X-ray beam. They are of more concern.

What Are the Possible Effects of X-Rays?

There is scientific disagreement about whether the small amounts of radiation used in diagnostic radiology can actually harm the unborn child, but it is known that the unborn child is very sensitive to the effects of things like radiation, certain drugs, excess alcohol, and infection. This is true, in part, because the cells are rapidly dividing and growing into specialized cells and tissues. If radiation or other agents were to cause changes in these cells, there could be a slightly increased chance of birth defects or certain illnesses, such as leukemia, later in life. It should be pointed out, however, that the majority of birth defects and childhood diseases occur even if the mother is not exposed to any known harmful agent during pregnancy. Scientists believe that heredity and random errors in the developmental process are responsible for most of these problems.

What If I'm X-Rayed before I Know I'm Pregnant?

Don't be alarmed. Remember that the possibility of any harm to you and your unborn child from an X-ray is very small. There are, however, rare situations in which a woman who is unaware of her pregnancy may receive a very large number of abdominal X-rays over a short period. Or she may receive radiation treatment of the lower torso. Under these circumstances, the woman should discuss the possible risks with her doctor.

How You Can Help Minimize the Risks

- Most important, tell your physician if you are pregnant or think you might be. This is important for many medical decisions, such as drug prescriptions and nuclear medicine procedures, as well as X-rays. And remember, this is true even in the very early weeks of pregnancy.

- Occasionally, a woman may mistake the symptoms of pregnancy for the symptoms of a disease. If you have any of the symptoms of pregnancy—nausea, vomiting, breast tenderness, fatigue— consider whether you might be pregnant and tell your doctor or X-ray technologist (the person doing the examination) before having an X-ray of the lower torso. A pregnancy test may be called for.

- If you are pregnant, or think you might be, do not hold a child who is being X-rayed. If you are not pregnant and you are asked to hold a child during an X-ray, be sure to ask for a lead apron to protect your reproductive organs. This is to prevent damage to your genes that could be passed on and cause harmful effects in your future descendants.

- Whenever an X-ray is requested, tell your doctor about any similar X-rays you have had recently. It may not be necessary to do another. It is a good idea to keep a record of the X-ray examinations you and your family have had taken so you can provide this kind of information accurately.

- Feel free to talk with your doctor about the need for an X-ray examination. You should understand the reason X-rays are requested in your particular case.

Chapter 7

Medications with Adverse Fetal Effects

Chapter Contents

Section 7.1

Pregnancy and Medicines: Basic Facts

This section includes text excerpted from
"Medications and Pregnancy," Centers for Disease
Control and Prevention (CDC), September 14, 2017.

If you are pregnant or thinking about becoming pregnant, talk with your doctor about any medications you are taking or thinking about taking. This includes prescription and over-the-counter (OTC) medications, as well as dietary or herbal products.

Effects of Medications during Pregnancy

The effects of taking most medications during pregnancy are little known. This is because pregnant women are often not included in studies to determine safety of new medications before they come on the market. Less than 10 percent of medications approved by the U.S. Food and Drug Administration (FDA) since 1980 have enough information to determine their risk for birth defects.

Because of studies conducted after medications come on the market, it's known that taking certain medications during pregnancy can cause serious birth defects. Examples are thalidomide (also known as Thalomid®) and isotretinoin (also known as Accutane® or Claravis®). Such medications should be avoided by all women who are or might become pregnant. For women who are taking these medications, it is important to discuss effective contraception methods with their doctor. While some medications are known to be harmful when taken during pregnancy, the safety or risk of most medications is not known. The effects depend on many factors, such as:

- How much medication is taken (sometimes called the dose).

- When during the pregnancy the medication is taken.

- Other health conditions a woman might have.

- Other medications a woman takes.

The important thing to remember is to talk to your doctor. Be sure to tell your doctor about all medications and herbal or dietary supplements you're taking or planning to take, so you can make sure you're taking only what is necessary.

Discussing Current Medications

Some pregnant women must take medications to treat health conditions. For example, if a woman has asthma, epilepsy (seizures), high blood pressure, or depression, she might need to continue to take medication to stay healthy during pregnancy. If these conditions are not treated, a pregnant woman or her unborn baby could be harmed. It is important for a woman to discuss with her doctor which medications are needed during pregnancy. She should also talk to her doctor about which medications are likely to be the safest to take during pregnancy. It is important to balance the possible risks and benefits of any medication being considered. Suddenly stopping the use of a medication may be riskier than continuing to use the medication while under a doctor's care. It is also important to know that dietary and herbal products, such as vitamins or herbs added to foods and drink, could be harmful to an unborn baby. These products can have other side effects when used during pregnancy. It's best for a woman to talk with her healthcare provider about everything she's taking or thinking about taking.

Accidental Exposure

Sometimes, women take medication before they realize that they are pregnant. When this happens, they may worry about the effects of the medication on their unborn baby. The first thing a woman who is pregnant or who is planning on becoming pregnant should do is talk with her healthcare provider. Some medications are harmful when taken during pregnancy, but others are unlikely to cause harm.

Section 7.2

Antiretroviral Drugs

This section includes text excerpted from "HIV Medicines during Pregnancy and Childbirth," AIDS*info*, U.S. Department of Health and Human Services (HHS), November 28, 2017.

Should Women with HIV Take HIV Medicines during Pregnancy?

Yes. All pregnant women with human immunodeficiency virus (HIV) should take HIV medicines during pregnancy to prevent mother-to-child transmission of HIV. HIV medicines work by preventing HIV from multiplying, which reduces the amount of HIV in the body (also called the viral load). A low viral load during pregnancy reduces the chances that any HIV will pass from mother to child during pregnancy and childbirth. Having less HIV in the body also helps keep the mother-to-be healthy.

Are HIV Medicines Safe to Use during Pregnancy?

Most HIV medicines are safe to use during pregnancy. In general, HIV medicines don't increase the risk of birth defects. When recommending HIV medicines for pregnant women with HIV, healthcare providers carefully consider the benefits and risks of specific HIV medicines.

When Should Pregnant Women with HIV Start Taking HIV Medicines?

All pregnant women with HIV should start taking HIV medicines as soon as possible during pregnancy. In general, women who are already taking HIV medicines when they become pregnant should continue taking those HIV medicines throughout their pregnancies.

What HIV Medicines Should a Pregnant Woman with HIV Take?

The choice of an HIV regimen to use during pregnancy depends on several factors, including a woman's current or past use of HIV medicines, other medical conditions she may have, and the results of drug resistance testing. In general, pregnant women with HIV can use the same HIV regimens recommended for nonpregnant adults—unless the risk of any known side effects to a pregnant woman or her baby outweighs the benefit of a regimen. Also, the regimen must be able to control a woman's HIV even with pregnancy-related changes that can affect how the body processes medicine.

In most cases, women who are already on an effective HIV regimen should continue on the same regimen throughout their pregnancies. But sometimes a woman's HIV regimen may change during pregnancy. For example, a change in HIV medicines may be needed to avoid the increased risk of a side effect during pregnancy. Sometimes, changing the dose of an HIV medicine can help offset pregnancy-related changes that make it harder for the body to absorb the medicine. But before making any changes to an HIV regimen, women should always talk to their healthcare providers.

Do Women with HIV Continue to Take HIV Medicines during Childbirth?

Yes. The risk of mother-to-child transmission of HIV is greatest during a vaginal delivery when a baby passes through the birth canal and is exposed to any HIV in the mother's blood and other fluids. During childbirth, HIV medicines that pass from mother to baby across the placenta prevent mother-to-child transmission of HIV, especially near delivery.

Women who are already taking HIV medicines when they go into labor should continue taking their HIV medicines on schedule as much as possible during childbirth.

Women with a high viral load (more than 1,000 copies/mL) or an unknown viral load near the time of delivery should receive an HIV medicine called zidovudine (brand name: Retrovir) by intravenous (IV) injection.

Zidovudine passes easily from a pregnant woman to her unborn baby across the placenta. Once in a baby's system, zidovudine protects the baby from any HIV that passes from mother to child during childbirth. For this reason, the use of zidovudine during childbirth prevents mother-to-child transmission of HIV even in women with high viral loads near the time of delivery.

Can a Cesarean Delivery Reduce the Risk of Mother-to-Child Transmission of HIV?

Yes. A scheduled cesarean delivery (sometimes called a C-section) can reduce the risk of mother-to-child transmission of HIV in women who have a high viral load (more than 1,000 copies/mL) or an unknown viral load near the time of delivery. A cesarean delivery to reduce the risk of mother-to-child transmission of HIV is scheduled for the 38th week of pregnancy, 2 weeks before a woman's expected due date.

It's unclear whether a scheduled C-section can reduce the risk of mother-to-child transmission of HIV in pregnant women with a viral load of less than 1,000 copies/mL. Of course, regardless of her viral load, a woman with HIV may have a C-section for other medical reasons.

With the help of their healthcare providers, women can decide which HIV medicines to use during childbirth and whether they should schedule a C-section to prevent mother-to-child transmission of HIV.

Do Women with HIV Continue to Take HIV Medicines after Childbirth?

Prenatal care for women with HIV includes counseling on the benefits of continuing HIV medicines after childbirth. Life-long use of HIV medicines prevents HIV from advancing to AIDS and reduces the risk of transmitting HIV. Together with their healthcare providers, women with HIV make decisions about continuing or changing their HIV medicines after childbirth.

In general, babies born to women with HIV receive zidovudine for 4 to 6 weeks after birth. (In certain situations, a baby may receive other HIV medicines in addition to zidovudine.) The HIV medicine protects the babies from infection by any HIV that may have passed from mother to child during childbirth.

Section 7.3

Selective Serotonin Reuptake Inhibitors (SSRIs)

This section includes text excerpted from "Drug Safety and Availability—FDA Drug Safety Communication: Selective Serotonin Reuptake Inhibitor (SSRI) Antidepressant Use during Pregnancy and Reports of a Rare Heart and Lung Condition in Newborn Babies," U.S. Food and Drug Administration (FDA), August 4, 2017.

The U.S. Food and Drug Administration (FDA) is updating the public on the use of selective serotonin reuptake inhibitor (SSRI) antidepressants by women during pregnancy and the potential risk of a rare heart and lung condition known as persistent pulmonary hypertension of the newborn (PPHN). The initial Public Health Advisory in July 2006 on this potential risk was based on a single published study. Since then, there have been conflicting findings from new studies evaluating this potential risk, making it unclear whether use of SSRIs during pregnancy can cause PPHN.

FDA has reviewed the additional new study results and has concluded that, given the conflicting results from different studies, it is premature to reach any conclusion about a possible link between SSRI use in pregnancy and PPHN.

PPHN occurs when a newborn baby does not adapt to breathing outside the womb. Newborns with PPHN may require intensive care support including a mechanical ventilator to increase their oxygen level. If severe, PPHN can result in multiple organ damage, including brain damage, and even death.

Information for Patients

- If you are pregnant or plan to become pregnant, talk with your healthcare professional if you are depressed or undergoing treatment for depression to determine your best treatment option during pregnancy.

- Talk to your healthcare professional about the potential benefits and risks of taking an SSRI during pregnancy.

- Do not stop taking an SSRI antidepressant without first talking to your healthcare professional. Stopping an SSRI antidepressant suddenly may cause unwanted side effects or a relapse of depression.

- Report any suspected side effects of SSRI use in pregnancy to your healthcare professional.

Section 7.4

Thalidomide

This section includes text excerpted from "Thalidomide," Centers for Disease Control and Prevention (CDC), September 15, 2017.

What's the Problem?

Taken early in pregnancy, thalidomide can cause devastating birth defects in children, most particularly shortened arms and legs, often with no elbows or knees. In spite of its tragic history of affecting more than 10,000 babies in Europe in the 1950's and 1960's when the risks were unknown, thalidomide has become available again (by prescription in the United States and over the counter in South America). In many cases, only one doseearly in pregnancy can cause harmful effects.

Who's at Risk?

Any woman who is already pregnant at the time of treatment with thalidomide or who becomes pregnant while using thalidomide could have a child with severe deformities. When the fetus is exposed to this drug during critical stages of development, limb and organ defects may result. Now that thalidomide has been approved by the U.S. Food and Drug Administration (FDA), there is the risk that it will be prescribed "off label" for other medical conditions at the discretion of physicians. Increased availability can lead to more frequent use by women of childbearing age, and, potentially, to the birth of infants with serious birth defects. Thalidomide should never be taken by women who are pregnant, planning to become pregnant, or who do not use very reliable forms of birth control.

Can It Be Prevented?

Yes. Thalidomide-affected pregnancies are completely preventable if proper precautions and guidelines are heeded. While it has been found to cause extreme malformations in unborn children, thalidomide also has a range of possible beneficial uses associated with fighting cancers, arthritis, tuberculosis, and many other diseases. Ironically, thalidomide's effectiveness at treating a wide range of illnesses may potentially make it more readily available to pregnant women, and therefore, a greater public health threat.

Section 7.5

New Research in Medications Affecting Fetal Health

This section includes text excerpted from "Treating for Two—Research," Centers for Disease Control and Prevention (CDC), March 28, 2017.

Collaborators study medication use during pregnancy to understand how specific medications might affect an unborn baby. Results of these studies give women and their healthcare providers better information on the safety or risk of using specific medications during pregnancy. This information supports their ability to make informed decisions about treatment options.

Learning the Effects of Medication during Pregnancy

The U.S. Food and Drug Administration (FDA) regulates medications to ensure their general safety and effectiveness for the U.S. population. Drug companies have to test all prescription medications to see if they are safe and effective before they can be made available to the public. Pregnant women usually are not included in these tests.

This is because of the possible risks to the unborn baby. As a result, FDA has little information about the safety of most medications during pregnancy when they first become available. But, listed below are few ways FDA works to find out more about the effects a medication might have when taken during pregnancy.

Adverse Event Reports

Drug companies are required to report problems with medicines to the FDA

Pregnancy Registries

Drug companies sometimes conduct special studies using pregnancy registries. Registries enroll pregnant women who have taken a certain medicine. Then, after these women give birth, the health of their babies is compared with the health of the babies of women who did not take the medicine. Pregnancy registries are a useful way to study the effects of a particular medication because they allow researchers to gather health information both during a pregnancy and after delivery. This allows FDA to get a clearer picture of how other health issues and life events may impact pregnancy outcomes.

Current Knowledge about Using Medication during Pregnancy

The information FDA has is limited. A study of medications approved by the U.S. Food and Drug Administration (FDA) from 1980 through 2010 found that 91 percent of the medications approved for use in adults lacked sufficient data to determine the risk of birth defects due to use of medications during pregnancy.

In addition, specific types of birth defects are rare. To determine whether or not an association between a particular medication and a specific birth defect exists, researchers need to review data from many pregnancies. This information can be hard to collect.

The good news is that Centers for Disease Control and Prevention (CDC) and other researchers are working to gather more information on medications used during pregnancy. The FDA is working hard to understand how specific medications might affect an unborn baby. Although the studies mentioned below are just one step toward determining the risk of different medications during pregnancy, they contribute to the information available to help women and their healthcare providers make treatment decisions during pregnancy.

Notable Research Findings

Over-the-counter (OTC) medications:

- Taking acetaminophen (used for pain relief) during the first trimester of pregnancy did not appear to increase the risk of major birth defects. Also, taking acetaminophen might decrease the risk of some birth defects in the baby when a pregnant woman uses it to treat a fever.

Antidepressants: Abruptly stopping the use of antidepressants can have serious consequences. Women should not change medications or stop taking medications without first talking with their doctor about the available options.

- A number of studies have identified some risks to the fetus and newborn associated with use of antidepressant medications. Selective serotonin-reuptake inhibitors (SSRIs) are a frequently prescribed group of antidepressant medications. Several studies have shown an increased risk for heart defects associated with taking SSRIs during early pregnancy. A 2007 study using data from the National Birth Defects Prevention Study (NBDPS) showed that taking SSRIs during pregnancy may increase the risk of anencephaly, craniosynostosis, or omphalocele.

- A 2010 study found that taking bupropion [Wellbutrin®] (an NDRI (norepinephrine–dopamine reuptake inhibitor) drug used to treat depression/anxiety and to quit smoking) during pregnancy might increase the risk of having a baby with certain heart defects.

- A 2013 study looked at venlafaxine use during the first trimester of pregnancy and the risk for birth defects. Researchers found that venlafaxine use during early pregnancy was not common, but that it was more common among mothers of babies born with certain birth defects, including anencephaly, some heart defects, cleft palate, and gastroschisis. This is the first study to show these links, so more research is needed to understand and confirm them.

Medications to treat chronic health conditions: Chronic health conditions are serious and without treatment may be life-threatening. Women should not change medications or stop taking medications without first talking with their healthcare provider about the available treatment options.

- **Asthma:** Pregnant women with asthma who use certain medications might have an increased risk of having a baby with a heart defect. A particular type of asthma medication, bronchodilators, might increase the risk for heart defects. Another type of medication used to treat asthma, corticosteroids, might increase the risk of having a baby born with cleft lip and/ or cleft palate. However, it is important that asthma be well controlled in pregnancy. Women should discuss the best treatment options with their healthcare provider before and during pregnancy.

- **Thyroid conditions:** Recent studies suggest that pregnant women who have a thyroid disorder might have an increased risk of having a baby with craniosynostosis, hydrocephaly (buildup of fluid on the brain), or hypospadias.

- **High blood pressure:** One study found that pregnant women who have high blood pressure (hypertension) or took certain hypertension medications appeared to have an increased risk of having a baby with certain heart defects (left or right obstructive defects or septal defects). Hypertension is a serious condition, particularly in pregnancy. Women should talk to their healthcare provider about the best medication options to manage their condition during pregnancy.

- **Autoimmune and immunodeficiency diseases:** Some recent case reports suggest that pregnant women taking mycophenolate mofetil (MMF; CellCept), which is used to help prevent transplant organ rejection or to treat lupus nephritis, have an increased risk of having a baby with birth defects. However, transplants and lupus are serious conditions, and pregnant women should not stop or start taking any type of medication that they need without first talking with a healthcare provider.

- **Epilepsy (Seizure disorders):** Epilepsy, and sometimes other conditions such as migraine headaches and mood and anxiety disorders, can be treated with antiepileptic, also called anticonvulsant, medications. Examples of these medications include valproic acid and carbamazepine. Previous studies have found that babies born to women who take certain antiepileptic medications during pregnancy have an increased risk for birth defects. Women prescribed antiepileptic medications may need to continue treatment during pregnancy. Not following a prescribed treatment plan may have worse outcomes than exposure to a particular medication. Therefore, when possible, women should discuss the best treatment options with their healthcare provider before pregnancy or as soon into the pregnancy as possible. In some cases, it may be possible to switch to a different medication that has fewer risks for causing problems during pregnancy.

- One study looked at topiramate, a medication used to treat seizures. It is also considered for treatment of sleep and eating disorders, migraines, other mental health disorders, and weight loss. Researchers found that use of topiramate during the first trimester of pregnancy was associated with an increased risk of cleft lip with or without cleft palate in infants. When making treatment decisions just before or during pregnancy, it is important that women and their healthcare providers weigh the benefits of using medications, such as topiramate, to control symptoms, along with their potential risks for birth defects.

Medications to treat infertility:

- Taking clomiphene citrate (commonly used to help women who have difficulty getting pregnant) just before or during early pregnancy might increase the risk of having a baby with certain birth defects. However, it is difficult to determine whether these findings are due to the use of the clomiphene citrate or because of some underlying health condition causing both the women's fertility and the birth defect.

- Taking progestins (used to treat infertility and an ingredient found in birth control pills) during early pregnancy might increase the risk of having a baby with hypospadias.

Medications to treat infections:

- In one study, taking penicillins, erythromycins, or cephalosporins (antibiotics used to treat infections), did not appear to increase the risk of birth defects. However, use of sulfonamide (often used in combination with trimethroprin, which is thought to increase the risk for birth defects) or nitrofurantoin was associated with several birth defects.

Medications to treat pain:

- Healthcare providers often prescribe painkillers called opioids for pain management. Unfortunately, FDA does not have enough information about the effects of prescription painkillers on a pregnant woman and her unborn baby. However, one study found that some birth defects, including spina bifida and certain heart defects, were linked with use of opioids during early pregnancy. Researchers looking at opioids in a different study also found an increased risk for spina bifida when these medications were used during pregnancy. When making treatment choices, women and their doctors should think about the benefits and risks of using opioids to manage pain.

Chapter 8

Maternal Health Conditions Affecting Pregnancy

Chapter Contents

Section 8.1

Common Maternal Health Conditions

This section includes text excerpted from "Pregnancy Complications,"
Centers for Disease Control and Prevention (CDC), June 17, 2016.

Complications of pregnancy are health problems that occur during pregnancy. They can involve the mother's health, the baby's health, or both. Some women have health problems that arise during pregnancy, and other women have health problems before they become pregnant that could lead to complications. It is very important for women to receive healthcare before and during pregnancy to decrease the risk of pregnancy complications.

Before Pregnancy

Make sure to talk to your doctor about health problems you have now or have had in the past. If you are receiving treatment for a health problem, your healthcare provider might want to change the way your health problem is managed. For example, some medicines used to treat health problems could be harmful if taken during pregnancy. At the same time, stopping medicines that you need could be more harmful than the risks posed should you become pregnant. In addition, be sure to discuss any problems you had in any previous pregnancy. If health problems are under control and you get good prenatal care, you are likely to have a normal, healthy baby.

During Pregnancy

Pregnancy symptoms and complications can range from mild and annoying discomforts to severe, sometimes life-threatening, illnesses. Sometimes it can be difficult for a woman to determine which symptoms are normal and which are not. Problems during pregnancy may include physical and mental conditions that affect the health of the mother or the baby. These problems can be caused by or can be made worse by being pregnant. Many problems are mild and do not progress; however, when they do, they may harm the mother or her baby. Keep in mind that there are ways to manage problems that come up during pregnancy. Always contact your prenatal care provider if you have any concerns during your pregnancy.

The following are some common maternal health conditions or problems a woman may experience during pregnancy:

Anemia

Anemia is having lower than the normal number of healthy red blood cells. Treating the underlying cause of the anemia will help restore the number of healthy red blood cells. Women with pregnancy related anemia may feel tired and weak. This can be helped by taking iron and folic acid supplements. Your healthcare provider will check your iron levels throughout pregnancy.

Urinary Tract Infections (UTI)

A UTI is a bacterial infection in the urinary tract. You may have a UTI if you have:

- Pain or burning when you use the bathroom.
- Fever, tiredness, or shakiness.
- An urge to use the bathroom often.
- Pressure in your lower belly.
- Urine that smells bad or looks cloudy or reddish.
- Nausea or back pain.

If you think you have a UTI, it is important to see your healthcare provider. He/she can tell if you have a UTI by testing a sample of your urine. Treatment with antibiotics to kill the infection will make it better, often in one or two days. Some women carry bacteria in their bladder without having symptoms. Your healthcare provider will likely test your urine in early pregnancy to see if this is the case and treat you with antibiotics if necessary.

Mental Health Conditions

Some women experience depression during or after pregnancy. Symptoms of depression are:

- A low or sad mood.
- Loss of interest in fun activities.

- Changes in appetite, sleep, and energy.
- Problems thinking, concentrating, and making decisions.
- Feelings of worthlessness, shame, or guilt.
- Thoughts that life is not worth living.

When many of these symptoms occur together and last for more than a week or two at a time, this is probably depression. Depression that persists during pregnancy can make it hard for a woman to care for herself and her unborn baby. Having depression before pregnancy also is a risk factor for postpartum depression. Getting treatment is important for both mother and baby. If you have a history of depression, it is important to discuss this with your healthcare provider early in pregnancy so that a plan for management can be made.

Hypertension (High Blood Pressure)

Chronic poorly-controlled high blood pressure before and during pregnancy puts a pregnant woman and her baby at risk for problems. It is associated with an increased risk for maternal complications such as preeclampsia, placental abruption (when the placenta separates from the wall of the uterus), and gestational diabetes. These women also face a higher risk for poor birth outcomes such as preterm delivery, having an infant small for his/her gestational age, and infant death. The most important thing to do is to discuss blood pressure problems with your provider before you become pregnant so that appropriate treatment and control of your blood pressure occurs before pregnancy. Getting treatment for high blood pressure is important before, during, and after pregnancy.

Gestational Diabetes Mellitus (GDM)

GDM is diagnosed during pregnancy and can lead to pregnancy complications. GDM is when the body cannot effectively process sugars and starches (carbohydrates), leading to high sugar levels in the blood stream. Most women with GDM can control their blood sugar levels by a following a healthy meal plan from their healthcare provider and getting regular physical activity. Some women also need insulin to keep blood sugar levels under control. Doing so is important because poorly controlled diabetes increases the risk of:

- Preeclampsia.
- Early delivery.

- Cesarean birth.

- Having a big baby, which can complicate delivery.

- Having a baby born with low blood sugar, breathing problems, and jaundice.

Although GDM usually resolves after pregnancy, women who had GDM have a higher risk of developing diabetes in the future.

Obesity and Weight Gain

Studies suggest that the heavier a woman is before she becomes pregnant, the greater her risk of pregnancy complications, including preeclampsia, GDM, stillbirth and cesarean delivery. Also, Centers for Disease Control and Prevention (CDC) research has shown that obesity during pregnancy is associated with increased use of healthcare and physician services, and longer hospital stays for delivery. Overweight and obese women who lose weight before pregnancy are likely to have healthier pregnancies.

Infections

During pregnancy, your baby is protected from many illnesses, like the common cold or a passing stomach bug. But some infections can be harmful to you, your baby, or both. Easy steps, such as hand washing, and avoiding certain foods, can help protect you from some infections. You won't always know if you have an infection—sometimes you won't even feel sick. If you think you might have an infection or think you are at risk, see your healthcare provider.

Hyperemesis Gravidarum

Many women have some nausea or vomiting, or "morning sickness," particularly during the first 3 months of pregnancy. The cause of nausea and vomiting during pregnancy is believed to be rapidly rising blood levels of a hormone called HCG (human chorionic gonadotropin), which is released by the placenta. However, hyperemesis gravidarum occurs when there is severe, persistent nausea and vomiting during pregnancy—more extreme than "morning sickness." This can lead to weight loss and dehydration and may require intensive treatment.

Section 8.2

Asthma

This section contains text excerpted from the following
sources: Text beginning with the heading "What's the Problem?" is
excerpted from "Asthma in Women," Centers for Disease Control
and Prevention (CDC), September 15, 2017; Text under the heading
"Findings from a Study" is excerpted from "Birth Defects—Key
Findings: Maternal Asthma Medication Use and the Risk of Selected
Birth Defects," Centers for Disease Control and Prevention (CDC),
October 22, 2014. Reviewed December 2017.

What's the Problem?

Asthma is a disease that affects people's lungs. Asthma causes
repeated episodes of wheezing, breathlessness, chest tightness, and
nighttime or early morning coughing. Asthma is a chronic lung disease.
However, asthma attacks only happen when something bothers one's
lungs. When it comes to women and asthma, the ability to breathe can
be affected by pregnancy, the menstrual cycle, and menopause. Women
who also have allergies and other asthma triggers may struggle to get
a breath of fresh air.

Who's at Risk?

Asthma affects an estimated 18.7 million adults in the United
States. Compared to male asthma patients, women with chronic
asthma also face extra challenges due to menstrual cycle, pregnancy,
and menopause. Changing estrogen levels can lead to an inflammatory response, which can bring on asthma symptoms. In addition,
asthma attacks can be very dangerous for pregnant women and their
babies, since neither of them are getting enough oxygen when an
attack happens.

Can It Be Prevented?

In most cases, the causes of asthma are unknown and there is no
absolute cure for it. However, asthma can be controlled if the patient

knows the warning signs of an attack, stays away from things that trigger an attack, and follows the advice of their doctor or other health professionals. Many doctors suggest using daily maintenance medication rather than relying only on rescue inhalers, since symptom prevention is preferable to treating symptoms once they have started.

The Bottom Line

- Asthma is a disease that affects your lungs; it is one of the most common long-term diseases of children (adults can have it, too), and causes repeated episodes of wheezing, breathlessness, chest tightness, and nighttime or early morning coughing.

- The exact cause of asthma is unknown, and asthma cannot be cured. However, if you or your child has asthma, it can be controlled by receiving ongoing medical care and education about how to manage asthma and asthma attacks, and by avoiding asthma triggers at school, work, home, outdoors, and elsewhere.

- Triggers for asthma can include mold, tobacco smoke, outdoor air pollution, dust mites, pet dander, cockroach droppings, wood smoke and infections linked to influenza, colds, and other viruses. Avoiding these triggers, along with using inhaled corticosteroids and other medicines, are the keys to preventing an asthma attack.

- Not only are women challenged with balancing known asthma triggers like pollen and mold, they also need to deal with female hormones in their bodies that are constantly changing in ways that might impact how well they can breathe.

- For women living with chronic asthma, it is important for them to avoid known asthma triggers, especially before each menstrual period is about to begin, and during pregnancy and menopause.

Findings from a Study

- Data from a study showed that using asthma medication during pregnancy:
  - Did not increase the risk for most of the birth defects studied.
  - Might increase the risk for some birth defects, such as esophageal atresia (birth defect of the esophagus or food tube),

anorectal atresia (birth defect of the anus), and omphalocele (birth defect of the abdominal wall).

- The most commonly reported asthma medications used during pregnancy were:

  - Albuterol (2%–3% of women)

  - Fluticasone (About 1% of women)

- It was difficult to determine if asthma or other health problems related to having asthma increased the risk for these birth defects, or if the increased risk was from the medication use during pregnancy.

Section 8.3

Breast Cancer Treatment and Pregnancy

This section includes text excerpted from "Breast Cancer Treatment and Pregnancy (PDQ®)–Patient Version," National Cancer Institute (NCI), July 6, 2017.

Breast cancer is a disease in which malignant (cancer) cells form in the tissues of the breast. The breast is made up of lobes and ducts. Each breast has 15 to 20 sections called lobes. Each lobe has many smaller sections called lobules. Lobules end in dozens of tiny bulbs that can make milk. The lobes, lobules, and bulbs are linked by thin tubes called ducts.

Each breast also has blood vessels and lymph vessels. The lymph vessels carry an almost colorless fluid called lymph. Lymph vessels carry lymph between lymph nodes. Lymph nodes are small bean-shaped structures that are found throughout the body. They filter substances in lymph and help fight infection and disease. Clusters of lymph nodes are found near the breast in the axilla (under the arm), above the collarbone, and in the chest.

Sometimes breast cancer occurs in women who are pregnant or have just given birth. Breast cancer occurs about once in every 3,000 pregnancies. It occurs most often between the ages of 32 and 38. Signs of breast cancer include a lump or change in the breast. These and other signs may be caused by breast cancer or by other conditions. Check with your doctor if you have any of the following:

- A lump or thickening in or near the breast or in the underarm area.

- A change in the size or shape of the breast.

- A dimple or puckering in the skin of the breast.

- A nipple turned inward into the breast.

- Fluid, other than breast milk, from the nipple, especially if it's bloody.

- Scaly, red, or swollen skin on the breast, nipple, or areola (the dark area of skin around the nipple).

- Dimples in the breast that look like the skin of an orange, called peau d'orange.

It may be difficult to detect (find) breast cancer early in pregnant or nursing women. The breasts usually get larger, tender, or lumpy in women who are pregnant, nursing, or have just given birth. This occurs because of normal hormone changes that take place during pregnancy. These changes can make small lumps difficult to detect. The breasts may also become denser. It is more difficult to detect breast cancer in women with dense breasts using mammography. Because these breast changes can delay diagnosis, breast cancer is often found at a later stage in these women.

Breast exams should be part of prenatal and postnatal care. To detect breast cancer, pregnant and nursing women should examine their breasts themselves. Women should also receive clinical breast exams during their regular prenatal and postnatal check-ups. Talk to your doctor if you notice any changes in your breasts that you do not expect or that worry you.

Tests that examine the breasts are used to detect (find) and diagnose breast cancer. The following tests and procedures may be used:

- **Physical exam and history:** An exam of the body to check general signs of health, including checking for signs of disease, such as lumps or anything else that seems unusual. A history of the patient's health habits and past illnesses and treatments will also be taken.

- **Clinical breast exam (CBE):** An exam of the breast by a doctor or other health professional. The doctor will carefully feel the breasts and under the arms for lumps or anything else that seems unusual.

- **MRI (magnetic resonance imaging):** A procedure that uses a magnet, radio waves, and a computer to make a series of detailed pictures of both breasts. This procedure is also called nuclear magnetic resonance imaging (NMRI).

- **Ultrasound exam:** A procedure in which high-energy sound waves (ultrasound) are bounced off internal tissues or organs and make echoes. The echoes form a picture of body tissues called a sonogram. The picture can be printed to look at later.

- **Mammogram:** An X-ray of the breast. A mammogram can be done with little risk to the unborn baby. Mammograms in pregnant women may appear negative even though cancer is present.

- **Blood chemistry studies:** A procedure in which a blood sample is checked to measure the amounts of certain substances released into the blood by organs and tissues in the body. An unusual (higher or lower than normal) amount of a substance can be a sign of disease.

- **Biopsy:** The removal of cells or tissues so they can be viewed under a microscope by a pathologist to check for signs of cancer. If a lump in the breast is found, a biopsy may be done.

There are four types of breast biopsies:

- **Excisional biopsy:** The removal of an entire lump of tissue.

- **Incisional biopsy:** The removal of part of a lump or a sample of tissue.

- **Core biopsy:** The removal of tissue using a wide needle.

- **Fine-needle aspiration (FNA) biopsy:** The removal of tissue or fluid, using a thin needle.

If cancer is found, tests are done to study the cancer cells. Decisions about the best treatment are based on the results of these tests and the age of the unborn baby. The tests give information about:

- How quickly the cancer may grow.

- How likely it is that the cancer will spread to other parts of the body.

- How well certain treatments might work.

- How likely the cancer is to recur (come back).

Tests may include the following:

- **Estrogen and progesterone receptor test:** A test to measure the amount of estrogen and progesterone (hormones) receptors in cancer tissue. If there are more estrogen and progesterone receptors than normal, the cancer is called estrogen and/or progesterone receptor positive. This type of breast cancer may grow more quickly. The test results show whether treatment to block estrogen and progesterone given after the baby is born may stop the cancer from growing.

- **Human epidermal growth factor type 2 receptor (HER2/neu) test:** A laboratory test to measure how many HER2/neu genes there are and how much HER2/neu protein is made in a sample of tissue. If there are more HER2/neu genes or higher levels of HER2/neu protein than normal, the cancer is called HER2/neu positive. This type of breast cancer may grow more quickly and is more likely to spread to other parts of the body. The cancer may be treated with drugs that target the HER2/neu protein, such as trastuzumab and pertuzumab, after the baby is born.

- **Multigene tests:** Tests in which samples of tissue are studied to look at the activity of many genes at the same time. These tests may help predict whether cancer will spread to other parts of the body or recur (come back).

  - **Oncotype DX:** This test helps predict whether stage I or stage II breast cancer that is estrogen receptor positive and node-negative will spread to other parts of the body. If the risk of the cancer spreading is high, chemotherapy may be given to lower the risk.

  - **MammaPrint:** This test helps predict whether stage I or stage II breast cancer that is node-negative will spread to other parts of the body. If the risk of the cancer spreading is high, chemotherapy may be given to lower the risk.

Certain factors affect prognosis (chance of recovery) and treatment options. The prognosis (chance of recovery) and treatment options depend on the following:

- The stage of the cancer (the size of the tumor and whether it is in the breast only or has spread to other parts of the body).

- The type of breast cancer.

- The age of the unborn baby.

- Whether there are signs or symptoms.

- The patient's general health.

Section 8.4

Diabetes and Pregnancy

This section includes text excerpted from "Type 1 or
Type 2 Diabetes and Pregnancy," Centers for Disease
Control and Prevention (CDC), September 29, 2017.

Blood sugar that is not well controlled in a pregnant woman with type 1 or type 2 diabetes could lead to problems for the woman and the baby:

Birth Defects

The organs of the baby form during the first two months of pregnancy, often before a woman knows that she is pregnant. Blood sugar that is not in control can affect those organs while they are being formed and cause serious birth defects in the developing baby, such as those of the brain, spine, and heart.

An Extra Large Baby

Diabetes that is not well controlled causes the baby's blood sugar to be high. The baby is "overfed" and grows extra large. Besides causing discomfort to the woman during the last few months of pregnancy, an extra large baby can lead to problems during delivery for both the mother and the baby. The mother might need a C-section to deliver the baby. The baby can be born with nerve damage due to pressure on the shoulder during delivery.

C-Section (Cesarean Section)

A C-section is a surgery to deliver the baby through the mother's belly. A woman who has diabetes that is not well controlled has a higher chance of needing a C-section to deliver the baby. When the baby is delivered by a C-section, it takes longer for the woman to recover from childbirth.

High Blood Pressure (Preeclampsia)

When a pregnant woman has high blood pressure, protein in her urine, and often swelling in fingers and toes that doesn't go away, she might have preeclampsia. It is a serious problem that needs to be watched closely and managed by her doctor. High blood pressure can cause harm to both the woman and her unborn baby. It might lead to the baby being born early and also could cause seizures or a stroke (a blood clot or a bleed in the brain that can lead to brain damage) in the woman during labor and delivery. Women with type 1 or type 2 diabetes have high blood pressure more often than women without diabetes.

Early (Preterm) Birth

Being born too early can result in problems for the baby, such as breathing problems, heart problems, bleeding into the brain, intestinal problems, and vision problems. Women with type 1 or type 2 diabetes are more likely to deliver early than women without diabetes.

Low Blood Sugar (Hypoglycemia)

People with diabetes who take insulin or other diabetes medications can develop blood sugar that is too low. Low blood sugar can be very serious, and even fatal, if not treated quickly. Seriously low blood sugar can be avoided if women watch their blood sugar closely and treat low blood sugar early.

If a woman's diabetes was not well controlled during pregnancy, her baby can very quickly develop low blood sugar after birth. The baby's blood sugar must be watched for several hours after delivery.

Miscarriage or Stillbirth

A miscarriage is a loss of the pregnancy before 20 weeks. Stillbirth means that after 20 weeks, the baby dies in the womb. Miscarriages and stillbirths can happen for many reasons. A woman who has diabetes that is not well controlled has a higher chance of having a miscarriage or stillbirth.

Tips for Women with Diabetes

If a woman with diabetes keeps her blood sugar well controlled before and during pregnancy, she can increase her chances of having a healthy baby. Controlling blood sugar also reduces the chance that a woman will develop common problems of diabetes, or that the problems will get worse during pregnancy.

Steps women can take before and during pregnancy to help prevent problems:

1. **Plan for Pregnancy**

   Before getting pregnant, see your doctor. The doctor needs to look at the effects that diabetes has had on your body already, talk with you about getting and keeping control of your blood sugar, change medications if needed, and plan for frequent follow-up. If you are overweight, the doctor might recommend that you try to lose weight before getting pregnant as part of the plan to get your blood sugar in control.

2. **See Your Doctor Early and Often**

   During pregnancy, a woman with diabetes needs to see the doctor more often than a pregnant woman without diabetes. Together, you and your doctor can work to prevent or catch problems early.

3. **Eat Healthy Foods**

   Eat healthy foods from a meal plan made for a person with diabetes. A dietitian can help you create a healthy meal plan. A dietitian can also help you learn how to control your blood sugar while you are pregnant.

4. **Exercise Regularly**

   Exercise is another way to keep blood sugar under control. It helps to balance food intake. After checking with your doctor, you can exercise regularly before, during, and after pregnancy. Get at least 30 minutes of moderate-intensity physical activity at least five days a week. This could be brisk walking, swimming, or actively playing with children.

5. **Take Pills and Insulin As Directed**

   If diabetes pills or insulin are ordered by your doctor, take it as directed in order to help keep your blood sugar under control.

6. **Control and Treat Low Blood Sugar Quickly**

   Keeping blood sugar well controlled can lead to a chance of low blood sugar at times. If you are taking diabetes pills or insulin, it's helpful to have a source of quick sugar, such as hard candy, glucose tablets or gel, on hand at all times. It's also good to teach family members and close coworkers or friends how to help in case of a severe low blood sugar reaction.

7. **Monitor Blood Sugar Often**

   Because pregnancy causes the body's need for energy to change, blood sugar levels can change very quickly. You need to check your blood sugar often, as directed by your doctor. It is important to learn how to adjust food intake, exercise, and insulin, depending on the results of your blood sugar tests.

Section 8.5

Epilepsy and Pregnancy

This section includes text excerpted from "The Epilepsies and Seizures: Hope through Research," National Institute of Neurological Disorders and Stroke (NINDS), April 2015.

What Are the Epilepsies?

The epilepsies are chronic neurological disorders in which clusters of nerve cells, or neurons, in the brain sometimes signal abnormally and cause seizures. Neurons normally generate electrical and chemical signals that act on other neurons, glands, and muscles to produce human thoughts, feelings, and actions. During a seizure, many neurons fire (signal) at the same time—as many as 500 times a second, much faster than normal. This surge of excessive electrical activity happening at the same time causes involuntary movements, sensations, emotions, and behaviors and the temporary disturbance of normal neuronal activity may cause a loss of awareness.

Epilepsy can be considered a spectrum disorder because of its different causes, different seizure types, its ability to vary in severity and impact from person to person, and its range of coexisting conditions. Some people may have convulsions (sudden onset of repetitive general contraction of muscles) and lose consciousness. Others may simply stop what they are doing, have a brief lapse of awareness, and stare into space for a short period. Some people have seizures very infrequently, while other people may experience hundreds of seizures each day. There also are many different types of epilepsy, resulting from a variety of causes. Recent adoption of the term "the epilepsies" underscores the diversity of types and causes.

In general, a person is not considered to have epilepsy until he or she has had two or more unprovoked seizures separated by at least 24 hours. In contrast, a provoked seizure is one caused by a known precipitating factor such as a high fever, nervous system infections, acute traumatic brain injury, or fluctuations in blood sugar or electrolyte levels.

Anyone can develop epilepsy. About 2.3 million adults and more than 450,000 children and adolescents in the United States currently live with epilepsy. Each year, an estimated 150,000 people are diagnosed with epilepsy. Epilepsy affects both males and females of all races, ethnic backgrounds, and ages. In the United States alone, the annual costs associated with the epilepsies are estimated to be $15.5 billion in direct medical expenses and lost or reduced earnings and productivity.

The majority of those diagnosed with epilepsy have seizures that can be controlled with drug therapies and surgery. However, as much as 30 to 40 percent of people with epilepsy continue to have seizures because available treatments do not completely control their seizures (called intractable or medication resistant epilepsy).

While many forms of epilepsy require lifelong treatment to control the seizures, for some people the seizures eventually go away. The odds of becoming seizure-free are not as good for adults or for children with severe epilepsy syndromes, but it is possible that seizures may decrease or even stop over time. This is more likely if the epilepsy starts in childhood, has been well-controlled by medication, or if the person has had surgery to remove the brain focus of the abnormal cell firing.

Many people with epilepsy lead productive lives, but some will be severely impacted by their epilepsy. Medical and research advances in the past two decades have led to a better understanding of the epilepsies and seizures. More than 20 different medications and a variety of dietary treatments and surgical techniques (including two devices) are now available and may provide good control of seizures. Devices can modulate brain activity to decrease seizure frequency. Advance neuroimaging can identify brain abnormalities that give rise to seizures which can be cured by neurosurgery. Even dietary changes can effectively treat certain types of epilepsy. Research on the underlying causes of the epilepsies, including identification of genes for some forms of epilepsy, has led to a greatly improved understanding of these disorders that may lead to more effective treatments or even to new ways of preventing epilepsy in the future.

Pregnancy and Motherhood

Women with epilepsy are often concerned about whether they can become pregnant and have a healthy child. Epilepsy itself does not interfere with the ability to become pregnant. With the right planning, supplemental vitamin use, and medication adjustments prior to pregnancy, the odds of a woman with epilepsy having a healthy pregnancy and a healthy child are similar to a woman without a chronic medical condition.

Children of parents with epilepsy have about 5 percent risk of developing the condition at some point during life, in comparison to about a 1 percent risk in a child in the general population. However, the risk of developing epilepsy increases if a parent has a clearly hereditary form of the disorder. Parents who are worried that their epilepsy may be hereditary may wish to consult a genetic counselor to determine their risk of passing on the disorder.

Other potential risks to the developing child of a woman with epilepsy or on antiseizure medication include increased risk for major congenital malformations (also known as birth defects) and adverse effects on the developing brain. The types of birth defects that have been most commonly reported with antiseizure medications include cleft lip or cleft palate, heart problems, abnormal spinal cord development (spina bifida), urogenital defects, and limb-skeletal defects. Some antiseizure medications, particularly valproate, are known to increase the risk of having a child with birth defects and/or neurodevelopmental problems, including learning disabilities, general intellectual disabilities, and autism spectrum disorder. It is important that a woman work with a team of providers that includes her neurologist and her obstetrician to learn about any special risks associated with her epilepsy and the medications she may be taking.

Although planned pregnancies are essential to ensuring a healthy pregnancy, effective birth control is also essential. Some antiseizure medications that induce the liver's metabolic capacity can interfere with the effectiveness of hormonal contraceptives (e.g., birth control pills, vaginal ring). Women who are on these enzyme-inducing antiseizure medications and using hormonal contraceptives may need to switch to a different kind of birth control that is more effective (such as different intrauterine devices, progestin implants, or long-lasting injections).

Prior to a planned pregnancy, a woman with epilepsy should meet with her healthcare team to reassess the current need for antiseizure medications and to determine a) the optimal medication to balance seizure control and avoid birth defects and b) the lowest dose for going into a planned pregnancy. Any transitions to either a new medication or dosage should be phased in prior to the pregnancy, if possible. If a woman's seizures are controlled for the 9 months prior to pregnancy, she is more likely to continue to have seizure control during pregnancy. For all women with epilepsy during pregnancy, approximately 15–25 percent will have seizure worsening, but another 15–25 percent will have seizure improvement. As a woman's body changes during pregnancy, the dose of seizure medication may need to be increased. For most medicines, monthly monitoring of blood levels of the antiseizure medicines can help to assure continued seizure control. Many of the birth defects seen with antiseizure medications occur in the first six weeks of pregnancy, often before a woman is aware she is pregnant. In addition, up to 50 percent of pregnancies in the United States are unplanned. For these reasons, the discussion about the medications should occur early between the healthcare professional and any woman with epilepsy who is in her childbearing years.

For all women thinking of becoming pregnant, using supplemental folic acid beginning prior to conception and continuing the supplement during pregnancy is an important way to lower the risk for birth defects and developmental delays. Prenatal multivitamins should also be used prior to the beginning of pregnancy. Pregnant women with epilepsy should get plenty of sleep and avoid other triggers or missed medications to avoid worsening of seizures.

Most pregnant women with epilepsy can deliver with the same choices as women without any medical complications. During the labor and delivery, it is important that the woman be allowed to take her same formulations and doses of antiseizure drugs at her usual times. If a seizure does occur during labor and delivery, intravenous short-acting medications can be given if necessary. It is unusual for the newborns of women with epilepsy to experience symptoms of withdrawal from the mother's antiseizure medication (unless she is on phenobarbital or a standing dose of benzodiazepines), but the symptoms resolve quickly and there are usually no serious or long-term effects.

The use of antiseizure medications is considered safe for women who choose to breastfeed their child. On very rare occasions, the baby may become excessively drowsy or feed poorly, and these problems should be closely monitored. However, experts believe the benefits of breastfeeding outweigh the risks except in rare circumstances. One large study showed that the children who were breastfed by mothers with epilepsy on antiseizure medications performed better on learning and developmental scales than the babies who were not breastfed. It is common for the antiseizure medication dosing to be adjusted again in the postpartum setting, especially if the dose was altered during pregnancy.

With the appropriate selection of safe antiseizure medicines during pregnancy, use of supplemental folic acid, and ideally, with prepregnancy planning, most women with epilepsy can have a healthy pregnancy with good outcomes for themselves and their developing child.

Section 8.6

Iron-Deficiency Anemia

This section includes text excerpted from "Iron-Deficiency Anemia," Office on Women's Health (OWH), U.S. Department of Health and Human Services (HHS), May 30, 2017.

Iron-deficiency anemia means that your body does not have enough iron. Your body needs iron to help carry oxygen through your blood to all parts of your body. Iron-deficiency anemia affects more women than men and is more common during pregnancy.

What Is Iron-Deficiency Anemia?

Iron-deficiency anemia is the most common type of anemia, a condition that happens when your body does not make enough healthy red blood cells or the blood cells do not work correctly. Iron-deficiency anemia happens when you don't have enough iron in your body. Your body needs iron to make hemoglobin, the part of the red blood cell that carries oxygen through your blood to all parts of your body.

Who Gets Iron-Deficiency Anemia?

Iron-deficiency anemia affects more women than men. The risk of iron-deficiency anemia is highest for women who:

- **Are pregnant.** Iron-deficiency anemia affects one in six pregnant women. You need more iron during pregnancy to support your unborn baby's development.

- **Have heavy menstrual periods.** Up to 5 percent of women of childbearing age develop iron-deficiency anemia because of heavy bleeding during their periods. Infants, small children, and teens are also at high risk for iron-deficiency anemia.

What Are the Symptoms of Iron-Deficiency Anemia?

Iron-deficiency anemia often develops slowly. In the beginning, you may not have any symptoms, or they may be mild. As it gets worse, you may notice one or more of these symptoms:

- Fatigue (very common)
- Weakness (very common)
- Dizziness
- Headaches
- Low body temperature
- Pale or yellow "sallow" skin
- Rapid or irregular heartbeat
- Shortness of breath or chest pain, especially with physical activity
- Brittle nails
- Pica (unusual cravings for ice, very cold drinks, or nonfood items like dirt or paper)

If you think you may have iron-deficiency anemia, talk to your doctor or nurse.

What Causes Iron-Deficiency Anemia?

Women can have low iron levels for several reasons:

- **Increased need for iron during pregnancy.** During pregnancy, your body needs more iron than normal to support your developing baby.

- **Iron lost through bleeding.** Bleeding can cause you to lose more blood cells and iron than your body can replace. Women may have low iron levels from bleeding caused by:

  - Digestive system problems, such as ulcers, colon polyps, or colon cancer

  - Regular, long-term use of aspirin and other over-the-counter (OTC) pain relievers

  - Donating blood too often or without enough time in between donations for your body to recover

  - Heavier or longer than normal menstrual periods

  - Uterine fibroids, which are noncancerous growths in the uterus that can cause heavy bleeding

- **Not eating enough food that contains iron.** Your body absorbs the iron in animal-based foods, such as meat, chicken, and fish, two to three times better than the iron in plant-based foods. Vegetarians or vegans, who eat little or no animal-based foods, need to choose other good sources of iron to make sure they get enough. Your body also absorbs iron from plant-based foods better when you eat them with foods that have vitamin C, such as oranges and tomatoes. But most people in the United States get enough iron from food.

- **Problems absorbing iron.** Certain health conditions, such as Crohn's disease or Celiac disease, or gastric bypass surgery for weight loss can make it harder for your body to absorb iron from food.

How Is Iron-Deficiency Anemia Diagnosed?

Talk to your doctor if you think you might have iron-deficiency anemia. Your doctor may:

- Ask you questions about your health history, including how regular or heavy your menstrual periods are. Your doctor may also ask you about any digestive system problems you may have, such as blood in your stool.

- Do a physical exam

- Talk to you about the foods you eat, the medicines you take, and your family health history

- Do blood tests. Your doctor will do a complete blood count (CBC). The CBC measures many parts of your blood. If the CBC test shows that you have anemia, your doctor will likely do another blood test to measure the iron levels in your blood and confirm that you have iron-deficiency anemia.

If you have iron-deficiency anemia, your doctor may want to do other tests to find out what is causing it.

Do I Need to Be Tested for Iron-Deficiency Anemia?

Maybe. Talk to your doctor about getting tested as part of your regular health exam if you have heavy menstrual periods or a health problem such as Crohn's disease or celiac disease.

How Is Iron-Deficiency Anemia Treated?

Treatment for iron-deficiency anemia depends on the cause:

- **Blood loss from a digestive system problem.** If you have an ulcer, your doctor may give you antibiotics or other medicine to treat the ulcer. If your bleeding is caused by a polyp or cancerous tumor, you may need surgery to remove it.

- **Blood loss from heavy menstrual periods.** Your doctor may give you hormonal birth control to help relieve heavy periods. If your heavy bleeding does not get better, your doctor may recommend surgery. Types of surgery to control heavy bleeding include endometrial ablation, which removes or destroys your uterine lining, and hysterectomy, which removes all or parts of your uterus.

- **Increased need for iron.** If you have problems absorbing iron or have lower iron levels but do not have severe anemia, your doctor may recommend:

  - Iron pills to buildup your iron levels as quickly as possible. Do not take any iron pills without first talking to your doctor or nurse.

- Eating more foods that contain iron. Good sources of iron include meat, fish, eggs, beans, peas, and fortified foods (look for cereals fortified with 100 percent of the daily value for iron).

- Eating more foods with vitamin C. Vitamin C helps your body absorb iron. Good sources of vitamin C include oranges, broccoli, and tomatoes.

If you have severe bleeding or symptoms of chest pain or shortness of breath, your doctor may recommend iron or red blood cell transfusions. Transfusions are for severe iron deficiencies only and are much less common.

What Do I Need to Know about Iron Pills?

Your doctor may recommend iron pills to help buildup your iron levels. Do not take these pills without talking to your doctor or nurse first. Taking iron pills can cause side effects, including an upset stomach, constipation, and diarrhea. If taken as a liquid, iron supplements may stain your teeth.

You can reduce side effects from iron pills by taking these steps:

- Start with half of the recommended dose. Gradually increase to the full dose.

- Take iron in divided doses. For example, if you take two pills daily, take one in the morning with breakfast and the other after dinner.

- Take iron with food (especially something with vitamin C, such as a glass of orange juice, to help your body absorb the iron).

- If one type of iron pill causes side effects, ask your doctor for another type.

- If you take iron as a liquid instead of as a pill, aim it toward the back of your mouth. This will prevent the liquid from staining your teeth. You can also brush your teeth after taking the medicine to help prevent staining.

What Can Happen If Iron-Deficiency Anemia Is Not Treated?

If left untreated, iron-deficiency anemia can cause serious health problems. Having too little oxygen in the body can damage organs.

With anemia, the heart must work harder to make up for the lack of red blood cells or hemoglobin. This extra work can harm the heart.

Iron-deficiency anemia can also cause problems during pregnancy.

How Can I Prevent Iron-Deficiency Anemia?

You can help prevent iron-deficiency anemia with the following steps:

- **Treat the cause of blood loss.** Talk to your doctor if you have heavy menstrual periods or if you have digestive system problems, such as frequent diarrhea or blood in your stool.

- **Eat foods with iron.** Good sources of iron include lean meat and chicken, dark, leafy vegetables, and beans.

- **Eat and drink foods that help your body absorb iron,** like orange juice, strawberries, broccoli, or other fruits and vegetables with vitamin C.

- **Make healthy food choices.** Most people who make healthy, balanced food choices get the iron and vitamins their bodies need from the foods they eat.

- **Avoid drinking coffee or tea with meals.** These drinks make it harder for your body to absorb iron.

- **Talk to your doctor if you take calcium pills.** Calcium can make it harder for your body to absorb iron. If you have a hard time getting enough iron, talk to your doctor about the best way to also get enough calcium.

How Much Iron Do I Need Every Day?

The table below lists how much iron you need every day. The recommended amounts are listed in milligrams (mg). See a list of good sources of iron.

Table 8.1. Iron Requirement

Age	Women	Pregnant Women	Breastfeeding Women	Vegetarian Women*
14–18 years	15 mg	27 mg	10 mg	27 mg
19–50 years	18 mg	27 mg	9 mg	32 mg
51+ years	8 mg	n/a	n/a	14 mg

Vegetarians need more iron from food than people who eat meat do. This is because the body can absorb iron from meat better than from plant-based foods.

What Foods Contain Iron?

Food sources of iron include:

- Fortified breakfast cereals (18 milligrams per serving)
- Oysters (8 milligrams per 3-ounce serving)
- Canned white beans (8 milligrams per cup)
- Dark chocolate (7 milligrams per 3-ounce serving)
- Beef liver (5 milligrams per 3-ounce serving)
- Spinach (3 milligrams per ½ cup)
- Tofu, firm (3 milligrams per ½ cup)
- Kidney beans (2 milligrams per ½ cup)
- Canned tomatoes (2 milligrams per ½ cup)
- Lean beef (2 milligrams for a 3-ounce serving)
- Baked potato (2 milligrams for a medium potato)

Do I Need More Iron during Pregnancy?

Yes. During pregnancy, your body needs more iron to support your growing baby. In fact, pregnant women need almost twice as much iron as women who are not pregnant do. Not getting enough iron during pregnancy raises your risk for premature birth or a low-birth-weight baby (less than 5½ pounds). Premature birth is the most common cause of infant death. Both premature birth and low birth weight raise your baby's risk for health and developmental problems at birth and during childhood.

If you're pregnant, talk to your doctor about these steps:

- Getting 27 milligrams of iron every day. Take a prenatal vitamin with iron every day, or talk to your doctor about taking an iron supplement (pill).
- Testing for iron-deficiency anemia.
- Testing for iron-deficiency anemia four to six weeks after childbirth.

Do I Need More Iron If I Am Breastfeeding?

No, you do not need more iron during breastfeeding. In fact, you need less iron than before you were pregnant. The amount of iron women need during breastfeeding is 10 milligrams per day for mothers age 14–18 and 9 milligrams per day for breastfeeding women older than 18.

You need less iron while breastfeeding because you likely will not lose a lot through your menstrual cycle. Many breastfeeding women do not have a period or may have only a light period. Also, if you got enough iron during pregnancy (27 milligrams a day), your breastmilk will supply enough iron for your baby.

Does Birth Control Affect My Risk for Iron-Deficiency Anemia?

It could. Hormonal birth control, such as the pill, the patch, the shot, or the hormonal intrauterine device (IUD), is often used to treat women with heavy menstrual periods. Lighter menstrual periods may reduce your risk for iron-deficiency anemia.

Also, the nonhormonal, copper IUD (Paragard) may make your menstrual flow heavier. This raises your risk for iron-deficiency anemia.

Talk to your doctor or nurse about your risk for anemia and whether hormonal birth control may help.

I Am a Vegetarian. How Can I Make Sure I Get Enough Iron?

You can help make sure you get enough iron by choosing foods that contain iron more often. Vegetarians need more iron from food than people who eat meat. This is because the body can absorb iron from meat better than from plant-based foods.

Vegetarian sources of iron include:

- Cereals and bread with added iron

- Lentils and beans

- Dark chocolate

- Dark green leafy vegetables, such as spinach and broccoli

- Tofu

- Chickpeas

- Canned tomatoes

Talk to your doctor or nurse about whether you get enough iron. Most people get enough iron from food.

Can I Get More Iron Than My Body Needs?

Yes, your body can get too much iron. Extra iron can damage the liver, heart, and pancreas. Try to get no more than 45 milligrams of iron a day, unless your doctor prescribes more. Some people get too much iron because of a condition called hemochromatosis that runs in families. You can also get too much iron from iron pills (if you also get iron from food) or from repeated blood transfusions.

Section 8.7

Obesity and Pregnancy

This section includes text excerpted from "Do Obesity and Overweight Affect Pregnancy?" *Eunice Kennedy Shriver* National Institute of Child Health and Human Development (NICHD), March 25, 2015.

Do Obesity and Overweight Affect Pregnancy?

How much a woman weighs when she gets pregnant and how much weight she gains during pregnancy can affect her health and that of her baby. Entering pregnancy with a normal body mass index (BMI) and gaining weight within the recommended levels during pregnancy are important ways to protect a mother's and a child's health.

The Institute of Medicine (IOM) recommends the following ranges of weight gain during pregnancy for American women:

- Pregnant women who are underweight (BMI of less than 18.5) should gain 28 to 40 pounds.

- Pregnant women at a normal weight (BMI of 18.5 to 24.9) should gain 25 to 35 pounds.

- Overweight pregnant women (BMI of 25 to 29.9) should gain 15 to 25 pounds.

- Obese pregnant women (BMI greater than 30) should limit weight gain to 11 to 20 pounds.

Obesity-Related Health Risks for Mothers

Women who are overweight or obese during pregnancy face several possible health risks, including high blood pressure, gestational diabetes, and an increased chance of needing a cesarean delivery.

Gestational diabetes is diabetes that begins during pregnancy. Women who have had gestational diabetes are at a higher lifetime risk for obesity and type 2 diabetes.

Obesity-Related Health Risks for Fetuses

The developing fetuses of obese women also are at increased risk for health problems. For example, researchers found a connection between maternal obesity and neural tube defects, in which the brain or spinal column does not form properly in early development. Also, research suggests that obesity increases a woman's chance of giving birth to a child with a heart defect by around 15 percent.

Gestational diabetes also can cause problems for a newborn, including dangerously low blood sugar, large body size that may cause injuries at birth, and high bilirubin levels, which can cause other health problems.

Children whose mothers had gestational diabetes also are at a higher lifetime risk for obesity and type 2 diabetes.

Preventing Obesity and Overweight in Pregnancy

In light of the rise in rates of obesity in the United States, the American Congress of Obstetricians and Gynecologists (ACOG) encourages women to seek guidance about nutrition and weight reduction from a healthcare provider if they are overweight and considering getting pregnant.

Good nutrition, staying active, and gaining the right amount of weight are important ways to promote a healthy pregnancy. The Weight-control Information Network (WIN) provides tips on maintaining a healthy pregnancy.

Section 8.8

Phenylketonuria and Pregnancy

This section includes text excerpted from "Phenylketonuria (PKU),"
Eunice Kennedy Shriver National Institute of Child
Health and Human Development (NICHD), December 5, 2012.
Reviewed December 2017.

Phenylketonuria, often called PKU, is caused by phenylalanine hydroxylase (PAH) deficiency. It is an inherited disorder that can cause intellectual and developmental disabilities (IDDs) if not treated. In PKU, the body can't process a portion of a protein called phenylalanine, which is in all foods containing protein. High levels of phenylalanine can cause brain damage. PAH deficiency produces a spectrum of disorders, including PKU, non-PKU hyperphenylalaninemia, and variant PKU. Classic PKU is caused by a complete or near-complete deficiency of PAH.

All children born in U.S. hospitals are screened routinely for PKU soon after birth, making it easier to diagnose and treat affected children early. And pregnant women may request prenatal testing to determine if their fetus is at risk for PKU.

Is Genetic Testing for Phenylketonuria (PKU) Available?

A blood sample can be used to test for the mutations that cause PKU.

Testing an Infant

A blood test that measures the phenylalanine in an infant's blood is enough to help make a PKU diagnosis. Therefore, DNA testing is not necessary. However, if a child tests positive for PKU, healthcare providers may recommend genetic testing because identifying the type of mutation involved can help guide selection of the most appropriate treatment plan.

A Deoxyribonucleic Acid (DNA) test also should be performed on a child if both parents are PKU carriers and the standard newborn blood test does not show the condition. The test will definitively indicate or rule out PKU, if the disease-causing mutations in the family have been identified.

Testing during Pregnancy

A pregnant woman can request a prenatal DNA test to learn whether or not her child will be born with PKU. To perform this test, a healthcare provider takes some cells, either through a needle inserted into the abdomen or a small tube inserted into the vagina. A genetic counselor who understands the risks and benefits of genetic testing can help explain the choices available for testing. This discussion may be particularly useful for parents who already have one child with PKU, because they have a higher-than-average chance of conceiving another child with the disorder. The disease causing mutations must have been identified before prenatal testing can be performed.

Testing Possible PKU Carriers

If a child is diagnosed with PKU, other family members may be more likely to conceive children who also will have PKU. The parents' siblings and other close blood relatives should be told that the child has PKU so that they can decide whether or not they should have DNA testing as well.

What Is Maternal PKU?

Maternal PKU is the term used when a woman who has PKU becomes pregnant. Most children born to PKU mothers do not have the disorder. But if a pregnant woman who has PKU does not strictly follow a low-phenylalanine diet, her child can develop serious problems. These include:

- Intellectual disabilities
- Having a head that is too small (microcephaly)
- Heart defects
- Low birth weight
- Behavioral problems

The newborn's problems from untreated maternal PKU are caused by the high phenylalanine levels present in the mother's blood during pregnancy—not by PKU itself. The infant does not have PKU and does not need a PKU diet. The PKU diet will not help these health problems.

Women with PKU and uncontrolled phenylalanine levels also have an increased risk of pregnancy loss.

If I Have PKU, What Steps Should I Take during Pregnancy to Protect My Infant?

If you have PKU, it is very important to follow a strict low-phenylalanine diet before becoming pregnant and throughout your pregnancy. In addition to staying on a PKU diet, also make sure to:

- Visit a PKU clinic on a regular basis

- Have your blood checked often for phenylalanine

- Ask your healthcare provider how much PKU formula to drink

Keep in mind that untreated maternal PKU can cause serious problems for a developing fetus.

A newborn's problems from untreated maternal PKU are caused by the high phenylalanine levels present in the mother's blood during pregnancy—not PKU itself. The infant does not have PKU and does not need a PKU diet. The PKU diet will not help these health problems.

Women with PKU and uncontrolled phenylalanine levels also have an increased risk of pregnancy loss.

What Determines the Severity of PKU?

A number of factors influence whether a person with PKU has mild symptoms or more severe problems.

Genetic Factors

Many different mutations of the PAH gene can cause PKU. The type of mutation greatly affects the severity of the person's symptoms.

Some mutations cause classic PKU, the most severe form of the disorder. In these cases, the enzyme that breaks down phenylalanine barely works or does not work at all. If it is not treated, classic PKU can cause severe brain damage and other serious medical problems. Some mutations allow the enzyme to work a little better than it does in classic PKU. This is sometimes called non-PKU hyperphenylalaninemia, and is also known as non-PKU HPA. Such cases come with a smaller risk of brain damage. People with very mild cases may not require treatment with a low-phenylalanine diet.

Nongenetic Factors

Genes are not the only factor that influences the severity of PKU symptoms. For example, strictly following a PKU diet greatly reduces the chances that a person will have intellectual disabilities and other problems caused by PKU. Other factors include the person's age at diagnosis and how quickly the person's blood levels of phenylalanine are brought under control.

Does a Child with PKU Need Repeated Testing?

Infants and children with PKU need frequent blood tests to measure the phenylalanine in their blood. The healthcare provider may suggest changes to the diet or formula the child receives if there is evidence of too much or too little phenylalanine. Infants with PKU will be tested about once a week for the first year of their lives. After the first year, children may be tested once or twice a month. Adults also need to be checked regularly throughout their lives. Often, blood samples can be taken at home and mailed to a laboratory.

Section 8.9

Thyroid Disease and Pregnancy

This section includes text excerpted from "Pregnancy and Thyroid Disease," National Institute of Diabetes and Digestive and Kidney Diseases (NIDDK), March 31, 2012. Reviewed December 2017.

What Is Thyroid Disease?

Thyroid disease is a disorder that affects the thyroid gland. Sometimes the body produces too much or too little thyroid hormone. Thyroid hormones regulate metabolism—the way the body uses energy—and affect nearly every organ in the body. Too much thyroid hormone is called hyperthyroidism and can cause many of the body's functions to speed up. Too little thyroid hormone is called hypothyroidism and can cause many of the body's functions to slow down.

Thyroid hormone plays a critical role during pregnancy both in the development of a healthy baby and in maintaining the health of the mother.

Women with thyroid problems can have a healthy pregnancy and protect their fetuses' health by learning about pregnancy's effect on the thyroid, keeping current on their thyroid function testing, and taking the required medications.

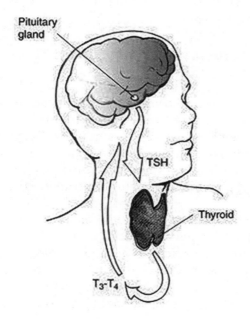

Figure 8.1. *Arthritis*

The thyroid gland's production of thyroid hormones—T3 and T4—is regulated by TSH, which is made by the pituitary gland.

What Is the Thyroid?

The thyroid is a 2-inch-long, butterfly-shaped gland weighing less than 1 ounce. Located in the front of the neck below the larynx, or voice box, it has two lobes, one on either side of the windpipe. The thyroid is one of the glands that make up the endocrine system. The glands of the endocrine system produce, store, and release hormones into the bloodstream. The hormones then travel through the body and direct the activity of the body's cells.

The thyroid gland makes two thyroid hormones, triiodothyronine (T3) and thyroxine (T4). T3 is the active hormone and is made from

T4. Thyroid hormones affect metabolism, brain development, breathing, heart and nervous system functions, body temperature, muscle strength, skin dryness, menstrual cycles, weight, and cholesterol levels.

Thyroid hormone production is regulated by thyroid-stimulating hormone (TSH), which is made by the pituitary gland in the brain. When thyroid hormone levels in the blood are low, the pituitary releases more TSH. When thyroid hormone levels are high, the pituitary responds by decreasing TSH production.

How Does Pregnancy Normally Affect Thyroid Function?

Two pregnancy-related hormones—human chorionic gonadotropin (hCG) and estrogen—cause increased thyroid hormone levels in the blood. Made by the placenta, hCG is similar to TSH and mildly stimulates the thyroid to produce more thyroid hormone. Increased estrogen produces higher levels of thyroid-binding globulin, also known as thyroxine-binding globulin, a protein that transports thyroid hormone in the blood.

These normal hormonal changes can sometimes make thyroid function tests during pregnancy difficult to interpret.

Thyroid hormone is critical to normal development of the baby's brain and nervous system. During the first trimester, the fetus depends on the mother's supply of thyroid hormone, which comes through the placenta. At around 12 weeks, the baby's thyroid begins to function on its own.

The thyroid enlarges slightly in healthy women during pregnancy, but not enough to be detected by a physical exam. A noticeably enlarged thyroid can be a sign of thyroid disease and should be evaluated. Thyroid problems can be difficult to diagnose in pregnancy due to higher levels of thyroid hormone in the blood, increased thyroid size, fatigue, and other symptoms common to both pregnancy and thyroid disorders.

Hyperthyroidism

What Causes Hyperthyroidism in Pregnancy?

Hyperthyroidism in pregnancy is usually caused by Graves disease and occurs in about one of every 500 pregnancies. Graves disease is an autoimmune disorder. Normally, the immune system protects people from infection by identifying and destroying bacteria, viruses, and other potentially harmful foreign substances. But in autoimmune diseases, the immune system attacks the body's own cells and organs.

With Graves disease, the immune system makes an antibody called thyroid-stimulating immunoglobulin (TSI), sometimes called TSH receptor antibody, which mimics TSH and causes the thyroid to make too much thyroid hormone. In some people with Graves disease, this antibody is also associated with eye problems such as irritation, bulging, and puffiness.

Although Graves disease may first appear during pregnancy, a woman with preexisting Graves disease could actually see an improvement in her symptoms in her second and third trimesters. Remission—a disappearance of signs and symptoms—of Graves disease in later pregnancy may result from the general suppression of the immune system that occurs during pregnancy. The disease usually worsens again in the first few months after delivery. Pregnant women with Graves disease should be monitored monthly.

Rarely, hyperthyroidism in pregnancy is caused by hyperemesis gravidarum—severe nausea and vomiting that can lead to weight loss and dehydration. This extreme nausea and vomiting is believed to be triggered by high levels of hCG, which can also lead to temporary hyperthyroidism that goes away during the second half of pregnancy.

How Does Hyperthyroidism Affect the Mother and Baby?

Uncontrolled hyperthyroidism during pregnancy can lead to:

- congestive heart failure
- preeclampsia—a dangerous rise in blood pressure in late pregnancy
- thyroid storm—a sudden, severe worsening of symptoms
- miscarriage
- premature birth
- low birth weight

If a woman has Graves disease or was treated for Graves disease in the past with surgery or radioactive iodine, the TSI antibodies can still be present in the blood, even when thyroid levels are normal. The TSI antibodies she produces may travel across the placenta to the baby's bloodstream and stimulate the fetal thyroid. If the mother is being treated with antithyroid medications, hyperthyroidism in the baby is less likely because these medications also cross the placenta.

Women who have had surgery or radioactive iodine treatment for Graves disease should inform their healthcare provider, so the baby can be monitored for thyroid-related problems later in the pregnancy.

Hyperthyroidism in a newborn can result in rapid heart rate, which can lead to heart failure; early closure of the soft spot in the skull; poor weight gain; irritability; and sometimes an enlarged thyroid that can press against the windpipe and interfere with breathing. Women with Graves disease and their newborns should be closely monitored by their healthcare team.

How Is Hyperthyroidism in Pregnancy Diagnosed?

Healthcare providers diagnose hyperthyroidism in pregnant women by reviewing symptoms and doing blood tests to measure TSH, T3, and T4 levels.

Some symptoms of hyperthyroidism are common features in normal pregnancies, including increased heart rate, heat intolerance, and fatigue.

Other symptoms are more closely associated with hyperthyroidism: rapid and irregular heartbeat, a slight tremor, unexplained weight loss or failure to have normal pregnancy weight gain, and the severe nausea and vomiting associated with hyperemesis gravidarum.

A blood test involves drawing blood at a healthcare provider's office or commercial facility and sending the sample to a lab for analysis. Diagnostic blood tests may include:

- **TSH test.** If a pregnant woman's symptoms suggest hyperthyroidism, her doctor will probably first perform the ultrasensitive TSH test. This test detects even tiny amounts of TSH in the blood and is the most accurate measure of thyroid activity available.

  Generally, below-normal levels of TSH indicate hyperthyroidism. However, low TSH levels may also occur in a normal pregnancy, especially in the first trimester, due to the small increase in thyroid hormones from HCG.

- **T3 and T4 test.** If TSH levels are low, another blood test is performed to measure T3 and T4. Elevated levels of free T4—the portion of thyroid hormone not attached to thyroid-binding protein—confirm the diagnosis.

  Rarely, in a woman with hyperthyroidism, free T4 levels can be normal but T3 levels are high. Because of normal pregnancy-related changes in thyroid function, test results must be interpreted with caution.

- **TSI test.** If a woman has Graves disease or has had surgery or radioactive iodine treatment for the disease, her doctor may also test her blood for the presence of TSI antibodies.

How Is Hyperthyroidism Treated during Pregnancy?

During pregnancy, mild hyperthyroidism, in which TSH is low but free T4 is normal, does not require treatment. More severe hyperthyroidism is treated with antithyroid medications, which act by interfering with thyroid hormone production.

Radioactive iodine treatment is not an option for pregnant women because it can damage the fetal thyroid gland. Rarely, surgery to remove all or part of the thyroid gland is considered for women who cannot tolerate antithyroid medications.

Antithyroid medications cross the placenta in small amounts and can decrease fetal thyroid hormone production, so the lowest possible dose should be used to avoid hypothyroidism in the baby.

Antithyroid medications can cause side effects in some people, including:

- allergic reactions such as rashes and itching
- a decrease in the number of white blood cells in the body, which can lower a person's resistance to infection
- liver failure, in rare cases

Stop your antithyroid medication and call your healthcare provider right away if you develop any of the following signs and symptoms while taking antithyroid medications:

- fatigue
- weakness
- vague abdominal pain
- loss of appetite
- a skin rash or itching
- easy bruising
- yellowing of the skin or whites of the eyes, called jaundice
- persistent sore throat
- fever

In the United States, healthcare providers prescribe the antithyroid medication methimazole (Tapazole, Northyx) for most types of hyperthyroidism.

Experts agree that women in their first trimester of pregnancy should probably not take methimazole due to the rare occurrence of damage to the fetus. Another antithryroid medication, propylthiouracil (PTU), is available for women in this stage of pregnancy or for women who are allergic to or intolerant of methimazole and have no other treatment options.

Healthcare providers may prescribe PTU for the first trimester of pregnancy and switch to methimazole for the second and third trimesters.

Some women are able to stop antithyroid medication therapy in the last 4 to 8 weeks of pregnancy due to the remission of hyperthyroidism that occurs during pregnancy. However, these women should continue to be monitored for recurrence of thyroid problems following delivery.

Studies have shown that mothers taking antithyroid medications may safely breastfeed. However, they should take only moderate doses, less than 10–20 milligrams daily, of the antithyroid medication methimazole. Doses should be divided and taken after feedings, and the infants should be monitored for side effects.

Women requiring higher doses of the antithyroid medication to control hyperthyroidism should not breastfeed.

Hypothyroidism

What Causes Hypothyroidism in Pregnancy?

Hypothyroidism in pregnancy is usually caused by Hashimoto disease and occurs in three to five out of every 1,000 pregnancies. Hashimoto disease is a form of chronic inflammation of the thyroid gland.

Like Graves disease, Hashimoto disease is an autoimmune disorder. In Hashimoto disease, the immune system attacks the thyroid, causing inflammation and interfering with its ability to produce thyroid hormones.

Hypothyroidism in pregnancy can also result from existing hypothyroidism that is inadequately treated or from prior destruction or removal of the thyroid as a treatment for hyperthyroidism.

How Does Hypothyroidism Affect the Mother and Baby?

Some of the same problems caused by hyperthyroidism can occur with hypothyroidism. Uncontrolled hypothyroidism during pregnancy can lead to:

- preeclampsia
- anemia—too few red blood cells in the body, which prevents the body from getting enough oxygen
- miscarriage
- low birth weight
- stillbirth
- congestive heart failure, rarely

Because thyroid hormones are crucial to fetal brain and nervous system development, uncontrolled hypothyroidism—especially during the first trimester—can affect the baby's growth and brain development.

How Is Hypothyroidism in Pregnancy Diagnosed?

Like hyperthyroidism, hypothyroidism is diagnosed through a careful review of symptoms and measurement of TSH and T4 levels.

Symptoms of hypothyroidism in pregnancy include extreme fatigue, cold intolerance, muscle cramps, constipation, and problems with memory or concentration. High levels of TSH and low levels of free T4 generally indicate hypothyroidism. Because of normal pregnancy-related changes in thyroid function, test results must be interpreted with caution.

The TSH test can also identify subclinical hypothyroidism—a mild form of hypothyroidism that has no apparent symptoms. Subclinical hypothyroidism occurs in 2–3 percent of pregnancies Test results will show high levels of TSH and normal free T4.

Experts differ in their opinions as to whether asymptomatic pregnant women should be routinely screened for hypothyroidism. But if subclinical hypothyroidism is discovered during pregnancy, treatment is recommended to help ensure a healthy pregnancy.

How Is Hypothyroidism Treated during Pregnancy?

Hypothyroidism is treated with synthetic thyroid hormone called thyroxine—a medication which is identical to the T4 made by the thyroid. Women with preexisting hypothyroidism will need to increase their prepregnancy dose of thyroxine to maintain normal thyroid function. Thyroid function should be checked every 6 to 8 weeks during pregnancy. Synthetic thyroxine is safe and necessary for the well-being of the fetus if the mother has hypothyroidism.

Eating, Diet, and Nutrition

During pregnancy, the body requires higher amounts of some nutrients to support the health of the mother and growing baby. Experts recommend pregnant women maintain a balanced diet and take a prenatal multivitamin and mineral supplement containing iodine to receive most nutrients necessary for thyroid health.

Dietary Supplements

Because the thyroid uses iodine to make thyroid hormone, iodine is an important mineral for a mother during pregnancy. During pregnancy, the baby gets iodine from the mother's diet. Women need more iodine when they are pregnant—about 250 micrograms a day. In the United States, about 7 percent of pregnant women may not get enough iodine in their diet or through prenatal vitamins. Choosing iodized salt—salt supplemented with iodine—over plain salt and prenatal vitamins containing iodine will ensure this need is met.

However, people with autoimmune thyroid disease may be sensitive to harmful side effects from iodine. Taking iodine drops or eating foods containing large amounts of iodine—such as seaweed, dulse, or kelp—may cause or worsen hyperthyroidism and hypothyroidism.

To help ensure coordinated and safe care, people should discuss their use of dietary supplements with their healthcare provider.

Chapter 9

Infectious Diseases with Adverse Fetal Effects

Chapter Contents

Section 9.1

Prevent Infections during Pregnancy

This section includes text excerpted from "Prevent
Infections during Pregnancy," Centers for Disease Control and
Prevention (CDC), June 5, 2017.

If you're pregnant or planning a pregnancy, there are simple steps
you can take to protect your fetus or newborn from infections that
cause serious health problems.

Cytomegalovirus (CMV)

A pregnant woman infected with Cytomegalovirus (CMV) can pass
the virus to her baby during pregnancy. Most babies born with CMV
infection will be fine and will not have symptoms or develop health
problems. However, some babies will have permanent problems, such
as hearing or vision loss or intellectual disabilities, at birth, or develop
problems later on.

CMV is passed from infected people to others through body fluids,
such as saliva, urine, blood, vaginal secretions, and semen. Infants
and young children are more likely to shed CMV in their saliva
and urine than older children and adults. For pregnant women,
the two most common ways they are exposed to CMV is through
contact with saliva and urine of children with CMV infection and
sexual activity.

Regular hand washing, particularly after changing diapers, is a
commonly recommended step to decrease the spread of infections and
may reduce exposures to CMV.

Group B Strep

If you are pregnant—or know anyone who is—you need to know
about group B strep. About 1 in 4 women in the United States carry
the bacteria that cause group B strep infection. Babies can get very
sick and even die if their mothers pass group B strep bacteria to them
during childbirth. If you are pregnant, talk to your doctor or midwife

about getting tested for group B strep. If you test positive you will get an antibiotic during labor to prevent the bacteria from spreading to your baby. It's important to get tested for group B strep during each pregnancy.

Remember:

- Talk with your doctor or midwife about getting a group B strep test when you are 35 through 37 weeks pregnant.

- If the test shows that you carry the bacteria, talk with your doctor or midwife about a plan for your labor. Be sure to tell them if you are allergic to penicillin or other antibiotics.

- If you go into labor or your water breaks before you are tested for group B strep, remind the labor and delivery staff that you have not had a group B strep test.

Listeriosis

Listeriosis is a rare but serious infection caused by eating food contaminated with bacteria called *Listeria*. Listeriosis mostly affects pregnant women, newborns, older adults, and people with weakened immune systems. Pregnant women are 10 times more likely than other people to get listeriosis. About 1 in 6 cases of listeriosis are associated with pregnancy.

Pregnant women typically experience only fever and other flu like symptoms, such as fatigue and muscle aches. However, infections during pregnancy can lead to miscarriage, stillbirth, premature delivery, or life-threatening infection of the newborn.

In general, you can protect yourself from listeriosis by following these guidelines:

- Avoid eating cheese made from raw (unpasteurized) milk.

  - Soft cheeses made with pasteurized milk, including commercial cottage cheese, cream cheese, and mozzarella, are generally regarded as safe. However, some soft cheeses made with pasteurized milk, including Hispanic style soft cheeses, have become contaminated with *Listeria* during processing. This could occur again.

- Avoid raw (unpasteurized) milk.

- Do not eat raw or lightly cooked sprouts of any kind (including alfalfa, clover, radish, and mung bean sprouts).

117

- Eat cut melon right away or refrigerate it at 40°F or colder and for no more than 7 days. Throw away cut melons left at room temperature for more than 4 hours.

- Avoid eating hot dogs, lunch meats, cold cuts, other deli meats (such as bologna), or fermented or dry sausages unless they are heated to an internal temperature of 165°F or until steaming hot just before serving. Don't let juice from hot dog and lunch meat packages get on other foods, utensils, and food preparation surfaces. Wash hands after handling hot dogs, lunch meats, and deli meats.

- Do not eat refrigerated pâté or meat spreads from a deli or meat counter or from the refrigerated section of a store. Foods that do not need refrigeration, like canned or shelf-stable pâté and meat spreads, are safe to eat. Refrigerate these foods after opening.

- Do not eat refrigerated smoked seafood unless it is in a cooked dish, such as a casserole, or unless it is canned or shelf-stable.

If you are pregnant and Hispanic, your risk of getting listeriosis is even greater. Pregnant Hispanic women are about 24 times more likely than other people to get listeriosis. Be aware that some Hispanic style cheeses, such as queso fresco, that were made from pasteurized milk but were contaminated when the cheese was being made, have also caused *Listeria* infections. Hispanic style soft cheeses include queso fresco, queso blanco, queso blando, queso Cotija, queso panela, queso ranchero, cuajada en terrón, and others. Learn about additional ways to reduce your risk for listeriosis.

If you are pregnant and have a fever and other symptoms of possible listeriosis, such as fatigue and muscle aches, within two months after eating a possibly contaminated food, you should seek medical care and tell the doctor about eating possibly contaminated food. If you are infected, your healthcare provider can give you antibiotics that can protect your fetus or newborn. If you ate food possibly contaminated with *Listeria* and do not feel sick, most experts believe you do not need tests or treatment, even if you are in a group that is more likely to get listeriosis.

Zika

Zika virus can be passed from a pregnant woman to her developing baby during pregnancy or around the time of birth. Zika virus infection during pregnancy is a cause of microcephaly and has been linked to other pregnancy problems and serious birth defects, including miscarriage, stillbirth, eye defects, hearing loss, and impaired growth. Zika is primarily spread through the bite of an infected Aedes aegypti or Aedes albopictus mosquito. However, Zika can also be spread during sex by a person infected with Zika to his or her sex partners.

The Centers for Disease Control and Prevention (CDC) has issued a travel notice (Level 2 Practice Enhanced Precautions) for people traveling to places where Zika virus is spreading. Specific areas where Zika is spreading are often difficult to determine and are likely to change over time.

Pregnant Women

- Should not travel to areas with Zika.

- Who must travel to one of these areas should talk to their doctor or healthcare provider first and strictly follow steps to prevent mosquito bites during the trip.

- Should talk with their doctor and consider postponing nonessential travel to countries in CDC's special travel considerations.

- Who have a sex partner who lives in or has traveled to an area with Zika should protect themselves by using condoms correctly, from start to finish, every time they have sex, or they should not have sex during the pregnancy. This includes vaginal, anal, oral sex, and the sharing of sex toys.

Women Trying to Become Pregnant

- Should consider avoiding nonessential travel to areas with Zika.

- Who must travel to one of these areas should consult with their healthcare provider first before traveling to areas with Zika, and they and their partners should strictly follow steps to prevent mosquito bites during the trip.

- Who have a sex partner who lives in or has traveled to an area with Zika should protect themselves from getting Zika during sex.

Partners of Pregnant Women Who Live in or Have Traveled to an Area with Zika

- Should take steps to prevent mosquito bites.

- Should use a condom correctly, from start to finish, every time they have sex, or not have sex during the pregnancy. This includes vaginal, anal, and oral sex and the sharing of sex toys. Condoms include male or female condoms. Not having sex is the only way to be sure that Zika will not spread through sex.

- Should talk to a healthcare provider about how to prevent sexual transmission of Zika during pregnancy and reduce the risk of birth defects related to Zika.

Section 9.2

Chickenpox

This section includes text excerpted from "Chickenpox (Varicella)," Centers for Disease Control and Prevention (CDC), July 1, 2016.

People at High Risk for Complications

Pregnant Women

Pregnant women who get varicella are at risk for serious complications; they are at increased risk for developing pneumonia, and in some cases, may die as a result of varicella. Some studies have suggested that both the frequency and severity of VZV pneumonia are higher when varicella is acquired during the 3rd trimester although other studies have not supported this observation.

If a pregnant woman gets varicella in her 1st or early 2nd trimester, her baby has a small risk (0.4–2.0 percent) of being born with congenital varicella syndrome (CVS). The baby may have scarring on the skin; abnormalities in limbs, brain, and eyes; and low birth weight. If a woman develops varicella rash from 5 days before to 2 days after delivery, the newborn will be at risk for neonatal varicella. Historically, the mortality rate for neonatal varicella was reported to be about 30 percent but the availability of VZV immune globulin and intensive supportive care have reduced the mortality to about 7 percent.

Immunocompromised Persons

Immunocompromised persons who get varicella are at risk of developing visceral dissemination (VZV infection of internal organs) leading to pneumonia, hepatitis, encephalitis, and disseminated intravascular coagulopathy. They can have an atypical varicella rash with more lesions, and they can be sick longer than immunocompetent persons who get varicella. New lesions may continue to develop for more than 7 days, may appear on the palms and soles, and may be hemorrhagic.

People with HIV or Acquired Immune Deficiency Syndrome (AIDS)

Most adults, including those who are HIV positive have already had varicella disease and are VZV seropositive. As a result, varicella is relatively uncommon among HIV infected adults.

Section 9.3

Cytomegalovirus (CMV) and Pregnancy

This section includes text excerpted from "Cytomegalovirus (CMV) and Congenital CMV Infection," Centers for Disease Control and Prevention (CDC), June 17, 2016.

About one out of every 200 infants are born with congenital cytomegalovirus (CMV) infection. However, only about one in five infants with congenital CMV infection will have long-term health problems.

Transmission

A pregnant woman can pass CMV to her fetus following primary infection, reinfection with a different CMV strain, or reactivation of a previous infection during pregnancy. The risk of transmission is greatest in the third trimester whereas risk of complications to the infant is greatest if infection occurs during the first trimester. Risk of transmission for primary infection is 30–40 percent in the first and second trimesters, and 40–70 percent in the third trimester.

Signs and Symptoms

Most infants with congenital CMV infection never have health problems. About 10 percent of infants with congenital CMV infection will have health problems that are apparent at birth, which include:

- Premature birth,
- Liver, lung and spleen problems,
- Low birth weight,
- Microcephaly, and
- Seizures.

About 40–60 percent of infants born with signs of congenital CMV infection at birth will have long-term health problems, such as:

- Hearing loss.
- Vision loss.
- Intellectual disability,
- Microcephaly,
- Lack of coordination,
- Weakness or problems using muscles, and
- Seizures.

Some infants without signs of congenital CMV infection at birth may later have hearing loss, but do not appear to have other long-term health problems. Hearing loss may be present at birth or may develop later in infants who passed their newborn hearing test. About 10–20 percent of infants with congenital CMV infection who have no signs at birth will have, or later develop, hearing loss.

Diagnosing Congenital CMV Infection

Congenital CMV infection is diagnosed by detection of CMV in the urine, saliva, blood, or other tissues within two to three weeks after birth. Only tests that detect CMV live virus (through viral culture) or CMV deoxyribonucleic acid (DNA) (through polymerase chain reaction (PCR)) can be used to diagnose congenital CMV infection. Congenital CMV infection cannot be diagnosed using samples collected more than two to three weeks after birth because testing after this time cannot distinguish between congenital infection and an infection acquired during and after delivery.

Serological tests are not recommended for diagnosing congenital CMV infection. Maternal immunoglobulin G (IgG) antibodies pass through the placenta during pregnancy; thus, CMV IgG testing of infants may reflect maternal antibody status, and does not necessarily indicate infection in the infant. Maternal IgM antibodies do not cross the placenta and, thus, CMV IgM in the newborn would indicate congenital infection, but is only present in 25–40 percent of newborns with congenital infection.

Treatment and Management

- Antiviral medications, such as ganciclovir or valganciclovir, may improve hearing and developmental outcomes in infants with symptoms of congenital CMV disease. Ganciclovir can have serious side effects, and has only been studied in infants with symptomatic congenital CMV disease. There is limited data on the effectiveness of ganciclovir or valganciclovir to treat infants with isolated hearing loss.

- Any infant diagnosed with congenital CMV infection should have his or her hearing and vision tested regularly. Most infants with congenital CMV grow up healthy. However, if the child has delayed onset of hearing or vision problems, early detection may improve outcomes.

Section 9.4

Listeriosis and Pregnancy

This section includes text excerpted from "Listeria (Listeriosis)," Centers for Disease Control and Prevention (CDC), December 12, 2016.

What Is Listeriosis?

Listeriosis is a serious infection caused by the germ *Listeria monocytogenes*. People usually become ill with listeriosis after eating contaminated food. The disease primarily affects pregnant women, newborns, older adults, and people with weakened immune systems. It's rare for people in other groups to get sick with *Listeria* infection.

Listeriosis is usually a mild illness for pregnant women, but it causes severe disease in the fetus or newborn baby. Some people with *Listeria* infections, most commonly adults 65 years and older and people with weakened immune systems, develop severe infections of the bloodstream (causing sepsis) or brain (causing meningitis or encephalitis). *Listeria* infections can sometimes affect other parts of the body, including bones, joints, and sites in the chest and abdomen.

What Are the Symptoms of Listeriosis?

Listeriosis can cause a variety of symptoms, depending on the person and the part of the body affected. *Listeria* can cause fever and diarrhea similar to other foodborne germs, but this type of *Listeria* infection is rarely diagnosed. Symptoms in people with invasive listeriosis, meaning the bacteria has spread beyond the gut, depend on whether the person is pregnant.

- **Pregnant women:** Pregnant women typically experience only fever and other flu like symptoms, such as fatigue and muscle aches. However, infections during pregnancy can lead to miscarriage, stillbirth, premature delivery, or life-threatening infection of the newborn.

- **People other than pregnant women:** Symptoms can include headache, stiff neck, confusion, loss of balance, and convulsions in addition to fever and muscle aches.

People with invasive listeriosis usually report symptoms starting 1 to 4 weeks after eating food contaminated with *Listeria*; some people have reported symptoms starting as late as 70 days after exposure or as early as the same day of exposure.

How Is Listeriosis Diagnosed and Treated?

Listeriosis is usually diagnosed when a bacterial culture (a type of laboratory test) grows *Listeria monocytogenes* from a body tissue or fluid, such as blood, spinal fluid, or the placenta. Listeriosis is treated with antibiotics.

How Do People Get Infected with Listeria?

Listeriosis is usually caused by eating food contaminated with *Listeria monocytogenes*. If infection occurs during pregnancy, *Listeria* bacteria can spread to the baby through the placenta.

What Should I Do If I Ate a Food That May Have Been Contaminated with Listeria?

You should seek medical care and tell the doctor about eating possibly contaminated food if you have a fever and other symptoms of possible listeriosis, such as fatigue and muscle aches, within two months after eating possibly contaminated food. This is especially important if you are pregnant. Talk with your medical provider if you have questions about what to do after eating possibly contaminated food.

Is Listeriosis a Serious Disease?

Most people with invasive listeriosis require hospital care, and about one in five people with the infection die. When listeriosis occurs during pregnancy, it can cause miscarriage, stillbirth, or newborn death. Listeriosis during pregnancy results in fetal loss in about 20 percent and newborn death in about 3 percent of cases.

How Many People Get Listeriosis Every Year?

Every year, about 1,600 people get listeriosis in the United States.

Section 9.5

Lymphocytic Choriomeningitis Virus

This section includes text excerpted from "Lymphocytic Choriomeningitis (LCM)," Centers for Disease Control and Prevention (CDC), May 6, 2014. Reviewed December 2017.

Lymphocytic choriomeningitis, or LCM, is a rodent-borne viral infectious disease caused by lymphocytic choriomeningitis virus (LCMV), a member of the family *Arenaviridae*, that was initially isolated in 1933. The primary host of LCMV is the common house mouse, *Mus musculus*. Infection in house mouse populations may vary by geographic location, though it is estimated that 5 percent of house mice throughout the United States carry LCMV and are able to transmit virus for the duration of their lives without showing any sign of illness. Other types of rodents, such as hamsters, are not the natural reservoirs but can become infected with LCMV from wild mice at the breeder, in the pet store, or home environment. Humans are more likely to contract LCMV from house mice, but infections from pet rodents have also been reported.

LCMV infections have been reported in Europe, the Americas, Australia, and Japan, and may occur wherever infected rodent hosts of the virus are found. The disease has historically been underreported, often making it difficult to determine incidence rates or estimates of prevalence by geographic region. Several serologic studies conducted in urban areas have shown that the prevalence of LCMV antibodies in human populations range from 2 percent to 5 percent.

Additionally, pregnancy-related infection has been associated with congenital hydrocephalus, chorioretinitis, and mental retardation.

Transmission

LCMV infections can occur after exposure to fresh urine, droppings, saliva, or nesting materials from infected rodents. Transmission may also occur when these materials are directly introduced into broken skin, the nose, the eyes, or the mouth, or presumably, via the bite of an infected rodent. Person-to-person transmission has not been reported, with the exception of vertical transmission from infected mother to fetus, and rarely, through organ transplantation.

Signs and Symptoms

LCMV is most commonly recognized as causing neurological disease, as its name implies, though infection without symptoms or mild febrile illnesses are more common clinical manifestations. For infected persons who do become ill, onset of symptoms usually occurs 8–13 days after exposure to the virus as part of a biphasic febrile illness. This initial phase, which may last as long as a week, typically begins with any or all of the following symptoms: fever, malaise, lack of appetite, muscle aches, headache, nausea, and vomiting. Other symptoms appearing less frequently include sore throat, cough, joint pain, chest pain, testicular pain, and parotid (salivary gland) pain.

Following a few days of recovery, a second phase of illness may occur. Symptoms may consist of meningitis (fever, headache, stiff neck, etc.), encephalitis (drowsiness, confusion, sensory disturbances, and/or motor abnormalities, such as paralysis), or meningoencephalitis (inflammation of both the brain and meninges). LCMV has also been known to cause acute hydrocephalus (increased fluid on the brain), which often requires surgical shunting to relieve increased intracranial pressure. In rare instances, infection results in myelitis (inflammation of the spinal cord) and presents with symptoms such as muscle weakness, paralysis, or changes in body sensation. An association between LCMV infection and myocarditis (inflammation of the heart muscles) has been suggested.

Previous observations show that most patients who develop aseptic meningitis or encephalitis due to LCMV survive. No chronic infection has been described in humans, and after the acute phase of illness, the virus is cleared from the body. However, as in all infections of the central nervous system, particularly encephalitis, temporary or permanent neurological damage is possible. Nerve deafness and arthritis have been reported.

Women who become infected with LCMV during pregnancy may pass the infection on to the fetus. Infections occurring during the first trimester may result in fetal death and pregnancy termination, while in the second and third trimesters, birth defects can develop. Infants infected *In utero* can have many serious and permanent birth defects, including vision problems, mental retardation, and hydrocephaly (water on the brain). Pregnant women may recall a flu-like illness during pregnancy, or may not recall any illness. LCM is usually not fatal. In general, mortality is less than 1 percent.

Risk of Exposure

Individuals of all ages who come into contact with urine, feces, saliva, or blood of wild mice are potentially at risk for infection. Owners of pet mice or hamsters may be at risk for infection if these animals originate from colonies that were contaminated with LCMV, or if their animals are infected from other wild mice. Human fetuses are at risk of acquiring infection vertically from an infected mother. Laboratory workers who work with the virus or handle infected animals are also at risk. However, this risk can be minimized by utilizing animals from sources that regularly test for the virus, wearing proper protective laboratory gear, and following appropriate safety precautions.

Diagnosis

During the first phase of the disease, the most common laboratory abnormalities are a low white blood cell count (leukopenia) and a low platelet count (thrombocytopenia). Liver enzymes in the serum may also be mildly elevated. After the onset of neurological disease during the second phase, an increase in protein levels, an increase in the number of white blood cells or a decrease in the glucose levels in the cerebrospinal fluid (CSF) is usually found. Laboratory diagnosis is usually made by detecting IgM and IgG antibodies in the CSF and serum. Virus can be detected by PCR or virus isolation in the CSF at during the acute stage of illness.

Treatment

Aseptic meningitis, encephalitis, or meningoencephalitis requires hospitalization and supportive treatment based on severity. Anti-inflammatory drugs, such as corticosteroids, may be considered under specific circumstances. Although studies have shown that ribavirin, a drug used to treat several other viral diseases, is effective against LCMV in vitro, there is no established evidence to support its routine use for treatment of LCM in humans.

Prevention

LCMV infection can be prevented by avoiding contact with wild mice and taking precautions when handling pet rodents (i.e., mice, hamsters, or guinea pigs).

Rarely, pet rodents may become infected with LCMV from wild rodents. Breeders, pet stores, and pet owners should take measures to prevent infestations of wild rodents. Pet rodents should not come into contact with wild rodents. If you have a pet rodent, wash your hands with soap and water (or waterless alcohol-based hand rubs when soap is not available and hands are not visibly soiled) after handling rodents or their cages and bedding.

If you have a rodent infestation in and around your home, take the following precautions to reduce the risk of LCMV infection:

- Seal up rodent entry holes or gaps with steel wool, lath metal, or caulk.

- Trap rats and mice by using an appropriate snap trap.
- Clean up rodent food sources and nesting sites and take precautions when cleaning rodent-infected areas:
  - Use cross-ventilation when entering a previously unventilated enclosed room or dwelling prior to cleanup.
  - Put on rubber, latex, vinyl or nitrile gloves.
  - Do not stir up dust by vacuuming, sweeping, or any other means.
  - Thoroughly wet contaminated areas with a bleach solution or household disinfectant.
  - Hypochlorite (bleach) solution: Mix 1 and 1/2 cups of household bleach in 1 gallon of water.
  - Once everything is wet, take up contaminated materials with damp towel and then mop or sponge the area with bleach solution or household disinfectant.
  - Spray dead rodents with disinfectant and then double-bag along with all cleaning materials and throw bag out in an appropriate waste disposal system.
  - Remove the gloves and thoroughly wash your hands with soap and water (or waterless alcohol-based hand rubs when soap is not available and hands are not visibly soiled).

The geographic distributions of the rodent hosts are widespread both domestically and abroad. However, infrequent recognition and diagnosis, and historic underreporting of LCM, have limited scientists' ability to estimate incidence rates and prevalence of disease among humans. Understanding the epidemiology of LCM and LCMV infections will help to further delineate risk factors for infection and develop effective preventive strategies. Increasing physician awareness will improve disease recognition and reporting, which may lead to better characterization of the natural history and the underlying immuno-pathological mechanisms of disease, and stimulate future therapeutic research and development.

Section 9.6

Rubella (German Measles) and Pregnancy

This section includes text excerpted from "Rubella (German Measles, Three Day Measles)—Pregnancy and Rubella," Centers for Disease Control and Prevention (CDC), September 15, 2017.

Rubella is very dangerous for a pregnant woman and her developing baby. Anyone who is not vaccinated against rubella is at risk of getting the disease. Although rubella was declared eliminated from the United States in 2004, cases can occur when unvaccinated people are exposed to infected people, mostly through international travel. Women should make sure they are protected from rubella before they get pregnant. Infection with rubella virus causes the most severe damage when the mother is infected early in pregnancy, especially in the first 12 weeks (first trimester). During 2005–2015, eight babies with CRS have been reported in the United States.

Congenital Rubella Syndrome (CRS)

Congenital rubella syndrome (CRS) is a condition that occurs in a developing baby in the womb whose mother is infected with the rubella virus. Pregnant women who contract rubella are at risk for miscarriage or stillbirth, and their developing babies are at risk for severe birth defects with devastating, lifelong consequences. CRS can affect almost everything in the developing baby's body. The most common birth defects from CRS can include:

- Deafness
- Cataracts
- Heart defects
- Intellectual disabilities
- Liver and spleen damage
- Low birth weight
- Skin rash at birth

Less common complications from CRS can include:

- Glaucoma

- Brain damage

- Thyroid and other hormone problems

- Inflammation of the lungs

Although specific symptoms can be treated, there is no cure for CRS. Since there is no cure, it is important for women to get vaccinated before they get pregnant.

Vaccine Recommendations

Women who are planning to become pregnant should check with their doctor to make sure they are vaccinated before they get pregnant. Because measles, mumps, and rubella (MMR) vaccine is an attenuated (weakened) live virus vaccine, pregnant women who are not vaccinated should wait to get MMR vaccine until after they have given birth. Adult women of childbearing age should avoid getting pregnant for at least four weeks after receiving MMR vaccine. Pregnant women should NOT get MMR vaccine. If you get rubella or are exposed to rubella while you're pregnant, contact your doctor immediately.

Section 9.7

Sexually Transmitted Diseases (STDs) and Pregnancy

This section includes text excerpted from "Sexually Transmitted Diseases (STDs)," Centers for Disease Control and Prevention (CDC), February 11, 2016.

Vaccine Recommendations for Sexually Transmitted Diseases (STDs)

Sexually transmitted diseases (STDs) can complicate pregnancy and may have serious consequences for both a woman and her developing baby. A healthcare provider caring for pregnant women plays a key role in safeguarding the health of both a mother and her unborn child. A critical component of appropriate prenatal care is ensuring that pregnant women are tested for STDs. Pregnant women should be tested for STDs starting early in their pregnancy and repeated close to delivery, as needed.

Table 9.1. CDC's Screening Recommendations for Pregnant Women

Disease	CDC Recommendation
Chlamydia	**First prenatal visit:** Screen all pregnant women <25 years of age and older pregnant women at increased risk for infection. **Third trimester:** Rescreen if <25 years of age or at continued high risk. **Risk Factors:** • New or multiple sex partners • Sex partner with concurrent partners • Sex partner who has a sexually-transmitted disease (STD) NOTE: Pregnant women found to have chlamydial infection should have a test-of-cure three to four weeks after treatment and then be retested within three months.
Gonorrhea	**First prenatal visit:** Screen all pregnant women <25 years of age and older pregnant women at increased risk for gonorrhea at first prenatal visit. **Third trimester:** Rescreen for women at continued high risk. **Risk Factors:** • Living in a high-morbidity area • Previous or coexisting STI • New or multiple sex partners • Inconsistent condom use among persons not in mutually monogamous relationships • Exchanging sex for money or drugs
Syphilis	**First prenatal visit:** Screen all pregnant women. **Early third trimester:** Rescreen women who are • At high risk for syphilis, • Who live in areas with high numbers of syphilis cases, and/or • Who were not previously tested, or had a positive test in the first trimester.

Table 9.1. Continued

Disease	CDC Recommendation
Hepatitis B (HBV)	**First prenatal visit:** Screen all pregnant women. **Third trimester:** Test those who were not screened prenatally, those who engage in behaviors that put them at high risk for infection, and those with signs or symptoms of hepatitis at the time of admission to the hospital for delivery. **Risk Factors:** • Having had more than one sex partner in the previous six months • Evaluation or treatment for an STD • Recent or current injection-drug use • An HBsAg-positive sex partner
Hepatitis C (HCV)	**First prenatal visit:** Screen all pregnant women at increased risk. **Risk Factors:** • Past or current injection-drug use • Having received a blood transfusion before July 1992 • Receipt of unregulated tattoo • Long-term dialysis • Known exposure to HCV

Bacterial Vaginosis

Bacterial vaginosis (BV), a common cause of vaginal discharge in women of childbearing age, is a polymicrobial clinical syndrome resulting from a change in the vaginal community of bacteria. Although BV is often not considered an STD, it has been linked to sexual activity. Women may have no symptoms or may complain of a foul smelling, fishy, vaginal discharge. BV during pregnancy has been associated with serious pregnancy complications, including premature rupture of the membranes surrounding the baby in the uterus, preterm labor, premature birth, chorioamnionitis, as well as endometritis. While there is no evidence to support screening for BV in pregnant women at high risk for preterm delivery, symptomatic women should be evaluated and treated. There are no known direct effects of BV on the newborn.

Chlamydia

Bacterial vaginosis (BV), a common cause of vaginal discharge in women of childbearing age, is a polymicrobial clinical syndrome resulting from a change in the vaginal community of bacteria. Although BV is often not considered an STD, it has been linked to sexual activity. Women may have no symptoms or may complain of a foul smelling, fishy, vaginal discharge. BV during pregnancy has been associated with serious pregnancy complications, including premature rupture of the membranes surrounding the baby in the uterus, preterm labor, premature birth, chorioamnionitis, as well as endometritis. While there is no evidence to support screening for BV in pregnant women at high risk for preterm delivery, symptomatic women should be evaluated and treated. There are no known direct effects of BV on the newborn.

Gonorrhea

Gonorrhea is a common STD in the United States. Untreated gonococcal infection in pregnancy has been linked to miscarriages, premature birth and low birth weight, premature rupture of membranes, and chorioamnionitis. Gonorrhea can also infect an infant during delivery as the infant passes through the birth canal. If untreated, infants can develop eye infections. Because gonorrhea can cause problems in both the mother and her baby, it is important for providers to accurately identify the infection, treat it with effective antibiotics, and closely follow up to make sure that the infection has been cured.

Hepatitis B

Hepatitis B is a liver infection caused by the hepatitis B virus (HBV). A mother can transmit the infection to her baby during pregnancy. While the risk of an infected mother passing HBV to her baby varies, depending on when she becomes infected, the greatest risk happens when mothers become infected close to the time of delivery. Infected newborns also have a high risk (up to 90%) of becoming chronic HBV carriers themselves. Infants who have a lifelong infection with HBV are at an increased risk for developing chronic liver disease or liver cancer later in life. Approximately 25 percent of infants who develop chronic HBV infection will eventually die from chronic liver disease. By screening your pregnant patients for the infection and providing treatment to at risk infants shortly after birth, you can help prevent mother to child transmission of HBV.

Hepatitis C

Hepatitis C is a liver infection caused by the hepatitis C virus (HCV), and can be passed from an infected mother to her child during pregnancy. In general, an infected mother will transmit the infection to her baby 10 percent of the time, but the chances are higher in certain subgroups, such as women who are also infected with human immunodeficiency virus (HIV). In some studies, infants born to HCV infected women have been shown to have an increased risk for being small for gestational age, premature, and having a low birth weight. Newborn infants with HCV infection usually do not have symptoms, and a majority will clear the infection without any medical help.

Herpes Simplex Virus

Herpes simplex virus (HSV) has two distinct virus types that can infect the human genital tract, HSV1 and HSV2. Infections of the newborn can be of either type, but most are caused by HSV2. Generally, the symptoms of genital herpes are similar in pregnant and in nonpregnant women; however, the major concern regarding HSV infection relates to complications linked to infection of the newborn. Although transmission may occur during pregnancy and after delivery, the risk of transmission to the neonate from an infected mother is high among women who acquire genital herpes near the time of delivery and low among women with recurrent herpes or who acquire the infection during the first half of pregnancy. HSV infection can have very serious effects on newborns, especially if the mother's first outbreak occurred during the third trimester. Cesarean section is recommended for all women in labor with active genital herpes lesions or early symptoms, such as vulvar pain and itching.

Human Immunodeficiency Virus

Human immunodeficiency virus (HIV) is the virus that causes acquired immune deficiency syndrome, or AIDS. HIV destroys specific blood cells that are crucial to helping the body fight diseases. According to the Centers for Disease Control and Prevention's (CDC) 2015 HIV surveillance data, women make up 24 percent of all adults and adolescents living with diagnosed HIV infection in the United States. The most common ways that HIV passes from mother to child are during pregnancy, labor, and delivery, or through breastfeeding. However, when HIV is diagnosed before or during pregnancy and appropriate steps are taken, the risk of mother to child transmission can be lowered to less than 2 percent. A mother who knows early in her pregnancy that she is HIV positive has more time to consult with her healthcare provider and decide on effective ways to protect her health and that of her unborn baby.

135

Human Papillomavirus

Human papillomaviruses (HPV) are viruses that most commonly involve the lower genital tract, including the cervix, vagina, and external genitalia. Genital warts frequently increase in number and size during pregnancy. Genital warts often appear as small cauliflower like clusters which may burn or itch. If a woman has genital warts during pregnancy, you may select to delay treatment until after delivery. When large or spread out, genital warts can complicate a vaginal delivery. In cases where there are large genital warts that are blocking the birth canal, a cesarean section may be recommended. Infection of the mother may be linked to the development of laryngeal papillomatosis in the newborn—a rare, noncancerous growth in the larynx.

Syphilis

Syphilis is primarily a sexually transmitted disease, but it may be transmitted to a baby by an infected mother during pregnancy. Transmission of syphilis to a developing baby can lead to a serious multisystem infection, known as congenital syphilis (CS). There has been a sharp increase in the number of congenital syphilis cases in the United States. Syphilis has been linked to premature births, stillbirths, and, in some cases, death shortly after birth. Untreated infants that survive tend to develop problems in multiple organs, including the brain, eyes, ears, heart, skin, teeth, and bones.

Trichomoniasis

Vaginal infection due to the sexually transmitted parasite *Trichomonas vaginalis* is very common. Although most people report no symptoms, others complain of itching, irritation, unusual odor, discharge, and pain during urination or sex. If you have a pregnant patient with symptoms of trichomoniasis, she should be evaluated for *Trichomonas vaginalis* and treated appropriately. Infection in pregnancy has been linked to premature rupture of membranes, preterm birth, and low birth weight infants. Rarely, the female newborn can acquire the infection when passing through the birth canal during delivery and have vaginal discharge after birth.

Screening and prompt treatment are recommended at least annually for all HIV infected women, based on the high prevalence of *Trichomonas vaginalis* infection, the increased risk of pelvic inflammatory disease (PID) associated with this infection, and the ability of treatment to reduce genital tract viral load and vaginal HIV shedding.

This includes HIV infected women who are pregnant, as *T. vaginalis* infection is a risk factor for vertical transmission of HIV. For other pregnant women, screening may be considered at the discretion of the treating clinician, as the benefit of routine screening for pregnant women has not been established. Screening might be considered for persons receiving care in high prevalence settings (e.g., STD clinics or correctional facilities) and for asymptomatic persons at high risk for infection. Decisions about screening might be informed by local epidemiology of *T. vaginalis* infection. However, data are lacking on whether screening and treatment for asymptomatic trichomoniasis in high prevalence settings or persons at high risk can reduce any adverse health events and health disparities or reduce community burden of infection.

STD Treatment during Pregnancy

STDs, such as chlamydia, gonorrhea, syphilis, and trichomoniasis can all be treated and cured with antibiotics that are safe to take during pregnancy. Viral STDs, including genital herpes, hepatitis B, and HIV cannot be cured. However, in some cases these infections can be treated with antiviral medications or other preventive measures to reduce the risk of passing the infection to the baby.

STD Prevention during Pregnancy

The most reliable way to avoid transmission of STDs is to abstain from oral, vaginal, and anal sex or to be in a long-term, mutually monogamous relationship with a partner known to be uninfected. For patients who are being treated for an STD other than HIV (or whose partners are undergoing treatment), counseling that encourages abstinence from sexual intercourse until completion of the entire course of medication is crucial. Latex male condoms, when used consistently and correctly, can reduce the risk of transmitting or acquiring STDs and HIV.

Section 9.8

Toxoplasmosis and Pregnancy

This section includes text excerpted from "Parasites-Toxoplasmosis
(Toxoplasma infection)—Pregnant Women," Centers for Disease
Control and Prevention (CDC), August 25, 2017.

When Should I Be Concerned about Toxoplasmosis?

Generally if you have been infected with *Toxoplasma* before becoming pregnant your unborn child is protected by your immunity. Some experts suggest waiting for 6 months after a recent infection to become pregnant.

How Do I Know If I Have Been Infected with Toxoplasma?

Your healthcare provider may suggest a blood test to check for antibodies to *Toxoplasma* if you are pregnant.

How Can Toxoplasma Affect My Unborn Child?

If you are newly infected with *Toxoplasma* while you are pregnant, or just before pregnancy, then you can pass the infection on to your baby. You may not have any symptoms from the infection. Most infected infants do not have symptoms at birth but can develop serious symptoms later in life, such as blindness or mental disability. Occasionally infected newborns have serious eye or brain damage at birth.

How Is Toxoplasmosis Spread?

Cats play an important role in the spread of toxoplasmosis. They become infected by eating infected rodents, birds, or other small animals. The parasite is then passed in the cat's feces. Kittens and cats can shed millions of parasites in their feces for as long as 3 weeks after infection. Mature cats are less likely to shed *Toxoplasma*. Cats and kittens prefer litter boxes, garden soils, and sandboxes for elimination, and you may be exposed unintentionally by touching your mouth after changing a litter box, or while gardening without gloves. Fruits and vegetables may have contact with contaminated soil or water also, and you can be infected by eating fruits and vegetables if they are not cooked, washed, or peeled.

Do I Have to Give up My Cat If I'm Pregnant or Planning on Becoming Pregnant?

No. You should follow these helpful tips to reduce your risk of environmental exposure to *Toxoplasma*.

- Avoid changing cat litter if possible. If no one else can perform the task, wear disposable gloves and wash your hands with soap and water afterwards.

- Ensure that the cat litter box is changed daily. The *Toxoplasma* parasite does not become infectious until 1 to 5 days after it is shed in a cat's feces.

- Feed your cat commercial dry or canned food, not raw or undercooked meats.

- Keep cats indoors.

- Avoid stray cats, especially kittens. Do not get a new cat while you are pregnant.

- Keep outdoor sandboxes covered.

- Wear gloves when gardening and during contact with soil or sand because it might be contaminated with cat feces that contain *Toxoplasma*. Wash hands with soap and water after gardening or contact with soil or sand.

Is Treatment Available?

If you are infected during pregnancy, medication is available. You and your baby should be closely monitored during your pregnancy and after your baby is born.

What Are the Best Ways to Protect Myself or My Unborn Child against Toxoplasmosis?

Cat owners and women who are exposed to cats should follow the tips above regarding reducing expose to *Toxoplasma*.

You should also:

Cook food to safe temperatures. A food thermometer should be used to measure the internal temperature of cooked meat. Do not sample meat until it is cooked. The United States Department of Agriculture (USDA) recommends the following for meat preparation.

For Whole Cuts of Meat (Excluding Poultry)

Cook to at least 145°F (63°C) as measured with a food thermometer placed in the thickest part of the meat, then allow the meat to rest* for three minutes before carving or consuming.

For Ground Meat (Excluding Poultry)

Cook to at least 160°F (71°C); ground meats do not require a rest* time.

For All Poultry (Whole Cuts and Ground)

Cook to at least 165°F (74°C), and for whole poultry allow the meat to rest* for three minutes before carving or consuming.

*According to USDA, "A 'rest time' is the amount of time the product remains at the final temperature, after it has been removed from a grill, oven, or other heat source. During the three minutes after meat is removed from the heat source, its temperature remains constant or continues to rise, which destroys pathogens."

- Freeze meat for several days at sub zero (0°F) temperatures before cooking to greatly reduce chance of infection.

- Peel or wash fruits and vegetables thoroughly before eating.

- Wash cutting boards, dishes, counters, utensils, and hands with hot soapy water after contact with raw meat, poultry, seafood, or unwashed fruits, or vegetables.

- Avoid drinking untreated water.

Should a Woman Breastfeed Her Infant If She Had Contracted a Toxoplasma Infection during Her Pregnancy?

Yes. Among healthy women, the possibility of breast milk transmission of *Toxoplasma* infection is not likely. While *Toxoplasma* infection has been associated with infants who consumed unpasteurized goat's milk, there are no studies documenting breast milk transmission of *Toxoplasma gondii* in humans. In the event that a nursing woman experiences cracked and bleeding nipples or breast inflammation within several weeks immediately following an acute *Toxoplasma* infection (when the organism is still circulating in her bloodstream), it is theoretically possible that she could transmit *Toxoplasma gondii* to the infant through her breast milk. Immune suppressed women could have circulating *Toxoplasma* for even longer periods of time. However, the likelihood of human milk transmission is very small.

Section 9.9

Zika and Pregnancy

This section includes text excerpted from "Zika Virus—Pregnancy," Centers for Disease Control and Prevention (CDC), November 6, 2017.

What We Know

Zika primarily spreads through infected mosquitoes. You can also get Zika through sex without a condom with someone infected by Zika, even if that person does not show symptoms of Zika. There is no vaccine to prevent or medicine to treat Zika. Zika virus can be passed from a pregnant woman to her fetus. Infection during pregnancy can cause a birth defect called microcephaly and other severe fetal brain defects.

What We Do Not Know

- How likely it is that Zika infection will affect your pregnancy.
- If your baby will have birth defects if you are infected while pregnant.
- The full range of health effects that Zika virus infection during pregnancy might lead to.

Pregnant Women

How to Protect Yourself

- Pregnant women should not travel to areas with risk of Zika (i.e., with documented or likely Zika virus transmission).

- Pregnant women should consider postponing travel to yellow cautionary areas in the United States.

What to Do If You Live in or Travel to an Area with Risk of Zika

If you live in or must travel to one of these areas, talk to your doctor or other healthcare provider first and strictly follow steps to prevent mosquito bites and practice safe sex.

During Travel or While Living in an Area with Risk of Zika

- Take steps to prevent mosquito bites.

- Take steps to prevent getting Zika through sex by using condoms from start to finish every time you have sex (oral, vaginal, or anal) or by not having sex during your entire pregnancy.

After Travel

- Talk to a doctor or other healthcare provider after travel to an area with risk of Zika.

- If you develop a fever with a rash, headache, joint pain, red eyes, or muscle pain talk to your doctor immediately and tell him or her about your travel.

- Take steps to prevent mosquito bites for 3 weeks after returning.

- Take steps to prevent passing Zika through sex by using condoms from start to finish every time you have sex (oral, vaginal, or anal) or by not having sex.

Women and Their Partners Trying to Become Pregnant

How to Protect Yourself

- Check the Centers for Disease Control and Prevention (CDC's) travel website (www.cdc.gov/zika/geo/index.html) for areas with risk of Zika.

- Talk to your doctor or other healthcare provider before traveling to areas with risk of Zika and take steps to plan for travel.
- Take steps to prevent mosquito bites and prevent sexual transmission.

Consider Waiting to Get Pregnant If You Travel to or Live in an Area with Risk of Zika

If You Are Traveling to an Area with Risk of Zika

Talk with your healthcare provider about your pregnancy plans and possible Zika risk before travel.

Table 9.2. Time Constraints and Risks of Zika

Traveling Partner	How Long to Wait
If only the male partner travels to an area with risk of Zika	The couple should consider using condoms or not having sex for at least 6 months • After the male partner returns, even if he doesn't have symptoms, or • From the start of the male partner's symptoms or the date he was diagnosed with Zika
If only the female partner travels to an area with risk of Zika	The couple should consider using condoms or not having sex for at least 2 months • After the female partner returns, even if she doesn't have symptoms, or • From the start of the female partner's symptoms or the date she was diagnosed with Zika
If both partners travel to an area with risk of Zika	The couple should consider using condoms or not having sex for at least 6 months • After returning from an area with risk of Zika, even if they don't have symptoms, or • From the start of the male partner's symptoms or the date he was diagnosed with Zika

If You Have Ongoing Exposure

- Take steps to prevent mosquito bites.
- Because of your ongoing exposure to Zika, talk with your healthcare provider about your plans for pregnancy, your risk of Zika virus infection, the possible health effects of Zika virus infection on a baby, and ways to protect yourself from Zika.
- If you or your partner develop symptoms of Zika or test positive for Zika, you should follow the suggested timeframes above before trying to conceive.

Talk with Your Doctor or Other Healthcare Provider

- Decisions about pregnancy planning are personal and complex, and circumstances will vary for women and their partners. Women and their partners should discuss pregnancy planning with a trusted doctor or healthcare provider. As part of preconception counseling, women and their partners who are thinking about pregnancy should talk with their doctor or healthcare provider about

- Their reproductive life plans, including pregnancy intentions and timing of pregnancy

- Their potential exposures to Zika during pregnancy

- Their partner's potential Zika exposures

Preventing Unintended Pregnancy during the Zika Virus Outbreak

Zika virus infection during pregnancy can cause microcephaly and other severe brain defects. Zika virus has also been linked to a number of other poor pregnancy outcomes. Avoiding or delaying pregnancy during a Zika virus outbreak is a way to reduce the number of pregnancies affected by Zika virus.

How to Prevent Unintended Pregnancy

If you decide that now is not the right time to have a baby, talk to your doctor or other healthcare provider about ways to prevent pregnancy. If you are sexually active, the best way to prevent unintended pregnancy is to use an effective form of birth control correctly and consistently every time you have sex. It is important to find a type of birth control that is safe, effective, and works for you.

Types of Reversible Birth Control

There are many different types of birth control; some have hormones and some don't. Also, some methods are permanent while others are reversible.

Among reversible birth control methods, IUDs (intrauterine devices) and contraceptive implants are the most effective at preventing pregnancy. Because they do not require you to do anything once they are in place, they are as effective as permanent methods (e.g., vasectomy, tubal sterilization) and can last up to 3–10 years, depending on the method used. However they can be removed at any time if you decide you want to become pregnant. Because these methods can last for long periods of time, they are known as long-acting reversible contraception (LARC).

While IUDs and contraceptive implants don't require you to do anything after they are in place, other methods require more effort—like with birth control pills you have to remember to take a pill every day, and with condoms you have to use them the right way every time you have sex. Because these methods require more effort for most women they are less effective than IUDs and implants at preventing pregnancy.

Highly Effective Reversible Birth Control Methods

IUDs and implants are highly effective methods—Fewer than 1 in 100 women can expect to get pregnant during the first year of use. These methods include:

- **Copper T intrauterine device (IUD)**—This IUD is a small device that is shaped in the form of a "T." Your doctor places it inside your uterus to prevent pregnancy. It can stay in your uterus up to 10 years.

- **Hormonal IUD**—This is a small T-shaped device, just like the Copper T IUD. It also needs to be placed inside your uterus by a doctor. It releases a small amount of hormone (progestin) each day to keep you from getting pregnant. It can stay in your uterus up to 3–5 years depending on which type you choose.

- **Implant**—The implant is a thin rod that is inserted under the skin of your upper arm. It is so small that most people cannot see it after it has been inserted. The rod contains a hormone (progestin) that is released into your body. The implant can work up to 3 years.

Moderately Effective Birth Control Methods

These methods are moderately effective—approximately 6 to 12 per 100 women can expect to get pregnant during the first year of use. These methods include:

- **Injection or "shot"**—If you choose this method you will get a shot of a hormone (progestin) in the buttocks or arm every 3 months from your doctor.

- **Birth control pills**—also called, "combined oral contraceptives," these pills are prescribed by a doctor and contain the hormones estrogen and progestin. A pill must be taken at the same time each day. If you are older than 35 years and smoke, have a history of blood clots or breast cancer, your doctor may advise you not to take the pill.

- **Progestin only pill**—also called, "the mini pill" Unlike the combined pill, the progestin only pill only contains one hormone, progestin. It is also prescribed by a doctor. It is very important that you take it the same time each day. This method, and other progestin only birth control methods (e.g., hormonal IUDs, implants, or shots), may be a good option for you if you cannot take estrogen.

- **Patch**—The patch looks like a square bandage and is worn on the lower abdomen, buttocks, or upper body (but not on the breasts). This method is prescribed by a doctor. It releases the hormones progestin and estrogen. You put on a new patch once a week for three weeks. During the fourth week, you do not wear a patch, so you can have your period. Women who weigh more than 198 pounds may be more likely than women who weigh less to become pregnant when using the patch.

- **Vaginal contraceptive ring**—The ring releases the hormones progestin and estrogen. This method is prescribed by a doctor. You place the ring inside your vagina for three weeks, take it out for the week you have your period, and then put in a new ring.

- **Diaphragm or cervical cap**—These methods are placed inside your vagina to cover the cervix to block sperm. The diaphragm is shaped like a shallow cup. The cervical cap is a thimble shaped cup. Before sex, you insert them with a spermicide to block or kill sperm. Visit your doctor for a proper fitting because diaphragms and cervical caps come in different sizes.

Least Effective Birth Control Methods

These methods are least effective—12 or more per 100 women can expect to get pregnant during the first year of use. These methods include:

- **Male condom**—A male condom is worn by a man and keeps sperm from getting into a woman's body. Latex condoms, the most common type, help prevent pregnancy and sexually

transmitted diseases (STDs), including human immunodeficiency virus (HIV), and Zika, as do the newer synthetic condoms.
"Natural" or "lambskin" condoms also help prevent pregnancy,
but may not protect against Zika or STDs, including HIV. About
18 pregnancies per 100 women who use this method will get
pregnant during the first year of use. Condoms are the only
birth control that reduces your risk of pregnancy, Zika, and
STDs. Condoms must be used correctly and consistently every
time you have sex.

- **Female condom**—The female condom is worn by a woman and
  helps keep sperm from getting into her body. It is packaged with
  a lubricant and is available at drug stores. It can be inserted up
  to 8 hours before sex. Female condoms may help prevent STDs.
  About 12 pregnancies occur per 100 women who use female
  condoms.

- **Spermicides**—These products work by killing sperm and come
  in several forms—foam, gel, cream, film, suppository, or tablet.
  Place them in your vagina no more than 1 hour before intercourse, and leave them in place at least 6–8 hours after you have
  sex. You can use a spermicide in addition to a male condom, diaphragm, or cervical cap. They can be purchased at drug stores.
  On average, 28 pregnancies occur per 100 women who use spermicides as their primary method of birth control.

- **Natural family planning or fertility awareness**—Understanding your monthly fertility pattern can help you plan to get
  pregnant or avoid getting pregnant. Your fertility pattern is the
  number of days in the month when you are fertile (able to get
  pregnant), days when you are infertile, and days when fertility
  is unlikely, but possible. If you have a regular menstrual cycle,
  you have about 9 or more fertile days each month. If you are
  practicing this method of birth control, you do not have sex on
  the days you are fertile, or you use a barrier method of birth
  control like a male or female condom on those days. Pregnancy
  rates can vary, on average, 24 pregnancies occur per 100 women
  who use natural family planning or fertility awareness as their
  primary method of birth control.

Permanent Methods of Birth Control

Less than 1 in 100 women who use permanent birth control methods
will get pregnant each year. These methods include:

- **Female sterilization**—tubal ligation or "tying tubes" A woman can have her fallopian tubes tied (or closed) so that sperm and eggs cannot meet for fertilization. The procedure can be done in a hospital or in an outpatient surgical center. You can go home the same day of the surgery and resume your normal activities within a few days. This method is effective immediately.

- **Transcervical sterilization**—A thin tube is used to thread a tiny device into each fallopian tube. It irritates the fallopian tubes and causes scar tissue to grow and permanently plug the tubes. It can take about 3 months for the scar tissue to grow, so you should use another form of birth control during this time. Return to your doctor for a test to see if scar tissue has fully blocked your fallopian tubes.

- **Male sterilization**—vasectomy. This operation is done to keep a man's sperm from going to his penis, so his ejaculate does not contain sperm in it that can fertilize an egg. The procedure is done at an outpatient surgical center. The man can go home the same day. Recovery time is less than 1 week. After the operation, a man visits his doctor for tests to count his sperm and to make sure the sperm count has dropped to zero; this takes about 12 weeks. Another form of birth control should be used until the man's sperm count has dropped to zero.

Emergency Contraception

Emergency contraception is NOT a regular method of birth control. Emergency contraception can be used if you did not use birth control during sex or if your birth control method failed (e.g., your condom broke or slipped off).

Chapter 10

Amniotic Fluid Disorders

Chapter Contents

Section 10.1

Oligohydramnios

Oligohydramnios is a pregnancy condition characterized by deficient amniotic fluid (AF), commonly called "waters," within the sac (the amnion) that holds the fetus. Generated from the maternal plasma about 12 days postconception, the amniotic fluid is mostly water along with small amounts of electrolytes, nutrients, hormones, and antibodies. At about 20 weeks of gestation, fetal urine adds to the amniotic fluid and subsequently becomes a substantial component of it. Besides providing protection to the fetus from mechanical shocks and assisting in thermoregulation, the fluid also plays an important role in fetal development involving musculoskeletal, digestive, and respiratory organs.

Causes of Oligohydramnios

- Idiopathic

- Premature rupture of the amniotic sac prior to labor

- Intrauterine growth restriction; discordant fetal growth not in line with expected gestational growth

- Pregnancy extending beyond 42 weeks

- Fetal birth anomalies, especially renal and urinary tract defects, leading to low urine output

- Twin-to-twin transfusion syndrome, a condition affecting monochorionic twins (fetuses sharing a placenta) and characterized by intrauterine blood transfusion from a "donor" twin to a "recipient" twin

- Fetal demise

- Uteroplacental insufficiency arising from preeclampsia (gestational hypertension and proteinuria), chronic hypertension, abruptio placentae (placental detachment), a thrombotic disorder, or other maternal disorders

- Medications, including ACE (angiotensin-converting enzyme) inhibitors used as antihypertensives, and NSAIDs (nonsteroidal anti-inflammatory drugs)

Complications of Oligohydramnios

Oligohydramnios can complicate pregnancies by increasing the risks of adverse outcomes for the fetus. Mild forms of AF insufficiency may be common, requiring little intervention. Severe and persistent cases, however, can result in preterm premature rupture of the amnion and also cause abnormal fetal development and limb contractures. Pulmonary hypoplasia, a condition characterized by poor lung development in utero, is a substantial cause of neonatal mortality and is considered one of the most serious consequences of oligohydramnios. Low amniotic fluid volumes can greatly compromise fetal breathing movements and lead to poorly developed bronchopulmonary segments, alveoli, and air sacs that aid in gaseous exchange.

Reduced AF volumes can also lead to umbilical cord compression, a condition that obstructs blood supply to the fetus and reduces uptake of nutrients and oxygen from the placenta. Cord compression can lead to perinatal asphyxia, a serious complication caused by oxygen deprivation leading to brain damage and, in severe cases, fetal death.

Diagnosing Oligohydramnios

Oligohydamnios does not cause any obvious symptoms, other than reduced fetal movements and a smaller than expected uterine size as evidenced by a smaller "bump." Most cases of oligohydramnios show up incidentally during a routine scan or during surveillance for other conditions. A physical examination showing discrepancies in fundal height (uterine size) measurements and fetal growth as evidenced by palpation may indicate the need for further investigation to establish low fluid volumes.

Optimum volumes of fluid are considered markers for fetal well-being. While amniotic fluid volumes vary significantly throughout pregnancy, the fifth percentile for a particular gestational age is usually used as cutoff value for establishing a diagnosis of oligohydramnios. Amniotic fluid volumes can be quantified using the indirect method usually involving dye-dilution techniques via amniocentesis.

Dye-dilution techniques provide actual AF volumes on par with values obtained through direct measurement at the time of a cesarean section; but they are less frequently used because the procedures are lengthy and invasive. The most commonly used diagnostic procedure is the ultrasound, which estimates vertical pockets of amniotic fluid. Magnetic resonance imaging (MRI), although impractical for frequent screenings, may sometimes be used to assess AF volumes.

Treatment

Management of oligohydramnios depends on the cause, severity, implications on fetal health, and gestational age. While low amniotic fluid levels in the first two trimesters may be managed with simple treatments that involve maintaining adequate maternal hydration through increased intake of fluids, or an intravenous injection, successful management of more serious forms of inadequate fluid levels may require constant monitoring to assess the AF levels and provide timely interventions.

Amnioinfusion

This method aims to restore normal AF volume to prevent fetal complications, particularly after the mid trimester when pulmonary development can be compromised by reduced AF volumes. Amnioinfusion can be achieved by two methods: transabdominal and trancervical. In the first, a needle is introduced into the amnion via the uterine wall under ultrasonographic guidance, and a solution of saline (or another suitable isotonic solution) is delivered until normal fluid levels are restored. Oligohydramnios during labor is typically treated with transcervical amnioninfusion to prevent decelerating fetal heart rate and fetal distress. This method involves delivering saline, or another appropriate infusion, into the amniotic sac via a catheter placed in the cervix.

References

1. Dulay, Antonette T, MD. "Oligohydramnios," MSD Manuals, October 2017.

2. "Low Amniotic Fluid Levels: Oligohydramnios," American Pregnancy Association, May 26, 2017.

3. "Amniotic Fluid Problems/Hydramnios/Oligohydramnios," Stanford Children's Health, n.d.

4. "Unequal Placental Sharing," UCSF Fetal Treatment Center, n.d.

5. "Unequal Placental Sharing," UCSF Benioff Children's Hospital, n.d.

Section 10.2

Polyhydramnios

"Polyhydramnios," © 2017 Omnigraphics.
Reviewed December 2017.

Polyhydramnios is excessive accumulation of amniotic fluid in the amniotic sac—the membranes within which the fetus develops—otherwise known as the "bag of waters." The fluid plays an important role in cushioning the fetus from mechanical shock and helps in the development of fetal organs. Thought to affect fewer than 2 percent of pregnancies, polyhydramnios can be either: chronic (a gradual buildup of fluid over several weeks) or acute (characterized by rapid increase of fluid volume within a short duration).

Etiology

While most mild cases of polyhydramnios are idiopathic—with only one-fifth of them caused by an underlying disease or condition—the majority of moderate-to-severe cases are associated with potential etiologies, which may include:

- Fetal anemia caused by deficiency of red blood cells

  - Fetal malformations, including abnormal development of cardiovascular, musculoskeletal, and central nervous systems; gastrointestinal obstruction; and renal defects

  - Twin-to-twin transfusion syndrome, a condition affecting monochorionic twins (fetuses sharing a placenta) and characterized by intrauterine blood transfusion from a "donor" twin to a "recipient" twin

- Chromosomal abnormalities such as Down syndrome and Edwards syndrome

- Maternal viral infections such as those caused by rubella or cytomegalovirus

- Maternal diabetes mellitus, pre-existing or gestational

- Maternal and fetal blood incompatibility

Signs and Symptoms of Polyhydramnios

Moderate-to-severe cases of polyhydramnios may manifest as a larger or heavier "bump," maternal dyspnea (shortness of breath), excessive weight gain, and edema in lower extremities. Polyhydramnios also tends to worsen other pregnancy-associated symptoms such as indigestion, constipation, and varicose veins.

Complications

Polyhydramnios is associated with an increased risk of perinatal mortality and other obstetric complications, which arise from over-expansion of the uterus. Potential risks of excessive amniotic fluid levels include:

- **Preterm labor:** Labor contractions occurring before 37 weeks' gestation.

- **Premature rupture of membranes:** Breaking of the amnion before the onset of labor.

- **Placental abruption (also known as abruptio placentae):** Detachment of placenta from the uterine wall.

- **Umbilical cord prolapse:** The descent of cord into the birth canal ahead of the fetus causing cord compression and oxygen deprivation for the fetus.

- **Postpartum hemorrhage:** Caused by increased distension of the uterus.

- **Fetal malposition:** Abnormally presented fetus (e.g., breech).

- **Fetal macrosomia:** Significantly larger than average birth weight (more than 4000 g).

Diagnostic Tests

The principal criterion used to establish polyhydramnios is the amniotic fluid index (AFI), which is typically assessed by a comprehensive ultrasonographic evaluation. The uterus is divided into four quadrants and the deepest amniotic pocket of each quadrant is measured to evaluate AFI. In addition to ultrasound evaluations, other maternal and fetal diagnostic tests may be required to screen for gestational diabetes, maternal infections, fetal anemia, and clinically suspected chromosomal abnormalities, conditions that are considered potential causes for polyhydramnios.

Treatment Options to Reduce Amniotic Fluid Volume

The prognosis of polyhydramnios depends largely on its etiology and severity. While mild, idiopathic cases of polyhydramnios usually require little or no intervention, moderate-to-severe cases are treated by either pharmacological intervention or amnioreduction.

Nonsteroidal anti-inflammatory drugs (NSAIDs), although known to reduce amniotic fluid volumes, are not widely used in clinical practice, owing to complications in fetal development and adverse side effects for the mother.

Amnioreduction involves draining the gestational sac to balance amniotic fluid levels, and is usually performed via amniocentesis, an invasive process in which a needle is inserted into the amniotic sac via the uterus. The procedure is performed under ultrasound guidance and sterile conditions, and labor-suppressant medication is administered to the patient to prevent uterine contractions and preterm labor, inherent risks of amnioreduction.

Prognosis for Polyhydramnios

The prognosis for polyhydramnios depends largely on the etiology, gestation age, and severity of the condition. While mild cases of fluid buildup may have little effect on pregnancy outcomes, severe cases with coexisting conditions like small-for-gestational-age fetuses are usually associated with poor pregnancy outcomes.

Furthermore, polyhydramnios may also be a marker for developmental disorders; regular monitoring and follow-up diagnostic tests may be required to assess fetal growth and developmental anomalies.

References

1. "Polyhydramnios," Mayo Clinic, November 18, 2017.

2. "Polyhydramnios," MedlinePlus, April 15, 2015.

3. "Polyhydramnios (Too Much Amniotic Fluid)," NHS, April 4, 2017.

4. "Polyhydramnios: High Amniotic Fluid during Pregnancy," American Pregnancy Association, June 25, 2017.

Chapter 11

Umbilical Cord Abnormalities

A narrow tube-like structure, the umbilical cord, serves as the primary connection between the mother and baby. It connects the developing baby to the placenta. The cord is also called the baby's "supply line" as it delivers oxygen and nutrients to the baby, carries blood back and forth between the baby and the placenta, and removes the baby's waste products.

After a woman conceives, the umbilical cord starts to develop after 5 weeks of conception. It gradually becomes longer, until 28 weeks of pregnancy, reaching 22–24 inches in length. The cord comprises three blood vessels: two arteries and one vein. The waste is removed from the baby to the placenta by the arteries (waste is transferred to the mother's blood and is disposed of by her kidneys). The vein transports oxygen and nutrients from the placenta (connected to mother's blood supply) to the developing baby. Wharton's jelly, a gelatin-like tissue protects these blood vessels. The cord is literally the baby's lifeline, and it cannot survive the gestational period without the umbilical cord. However, there are several cord abnormalities that can occur that are medical emergencies and need immediate medical attention.

There are numerous cord abnormalities from false knots that do not have adverse effects on the baby or mom to vasa previa, which often

"Umbilical Cord Abnormalities," © 2017 Omnigraphics. Reviewed December 2017.

leads to fetal death. Problems of the cord can occur during pregnancy or during labor and delivery. In a few cases, they are found before delivery through an ultrasound; but they are usually found only during delivery when there is direct examination of the cord. Some common umbilical cord abnormalities are discussed below.

Umbilical Cord Prolapse

The prolapse happens when the umbilical cord slips through the cervix into the vagina before the baby descends into the birth canal. Normally, the baby comes out first through the birth canal trailing the umbilical cord behind it. The prolapse can cause the cord to be wrapped around the baby's body or get trapped in the birth canal that leads to further complications. The baby's oxygen supply may decrease as the pressure on the cord reduces or cuts off blood flow from the placenta to the baby. Around 1 in 300 births experience cord prolapse. Some common reasons for the prolapse include:

- Breech delivery (foot-first) position
- Preterm labor
- Excessive amount of amniotic fluid
- The umbilical cord is unusually long
- Healthcare provider ruptures the membranes to speed up labor

The cord prolapse is a medical emergency and needs immediate medical attention; the doctor can confirm the prolapse by doing a pelvic examination. After the membranes (bag of waters) have ruptured, if the healthcare provider detects heart rate abnormalities in the baby, umbilical cord prolapse may be a possibility. Pressure on the cord must be lifted immediately, and the mother should be made ready for prompt cesarean delivery in the case of emergency.

Single Umbilical Artery

In this particular cord abnormality, the umbilical cord has only two blood vessels instead of three. There is only one artery and one vein; mostly the left artery is absent. About 1 percent of cords in singletons and 5 percent of cords in multiple pregnancies (twins, triplets, and more) have this abnormality, the cause of which is unknown. Central nervous system problems, urinary tract defects, and heart and chromosomal abnormalities are some of the risks in single umbilical artery for infants. An ultrasound helps to identify the abnormality, and healthcare providers may suggest certain prenatal tests to rule out birth defects; tests can include a detailed ultrasound and echocardiography (fetal heart evaluation through special ultrasound).

Vasa Previa

The terms "vasa" and "previa" mean "vessels" and "before," respectively, in Latin. Vasa previa occurs when blood vessels from the cord or placenta crosses the cervix below the baby's positioning. The blood vessels may tear when the membrane ruptures or the cervix dilates as they are unprotected by the Wharton's jelly in the cord or tissue in the placenta. Even if they do not tear, the pressure on the blood vessels may make the baby suffer due to lack of oxygen.

This condition occurs in 1 of 2,500 births; it can be diagnosed during pregnancy by doing an ultrasound. Fetal deaths can be prevented by performing a cesarean section at about 35 weeks of gestation. However, most of the affected babies are stillborn when vasa previa is diagnosed at delivery.

Painless vaginal bleeding can occur in pregnant woman with vasa previa; hence, when the bleeding happens, a healthcare provider needs to be consulted to avoid future complications. The risk for vasa previa can be increased if a pregnant woman:

- is expecting multiple pregnancies (twin, triplet, or more)

- has a velamentous insertion (instead of insertion of umbilical cord in the center of the placenta, the cord is inserted into the fetal membranes)

- has placenta previa (low-lying placenta)

Umbilical Cord Knots

Umbilical cord knots happen during pregnancy or delivery. Knot formation during pregnancy can happen while the baby moves around in the amniotic fluid. If the umbilical cord is long, knots can occur. If the knot remains loose the baby is unaffected; however, if the knots tighten then the baby's oxygen supply can get cut off leading to heart rate abnormalities. It can also result in miscarriage and stillbirth. Knots can form during the delivery when the baby with a nuchal loop (umbilical cord wrapped around the baby's neck) is pulled through the loop.

Umbilical Cord Cyst

An abnormal growth on the umbilical cord is known as the umbilical cord cyst. There are true and false cysts.

- True cysts are remaining cells from fetal development.
- False cysts are filled with fluid.

Research suggests that both types of cysts can lead to birth defects—they include kidney defects, abdominal defects, and chromosomal abnormalities. The healthcare provider may conduct tests to rule out birth defects after an ultrasound confirms umbilical cord cysts. They are usually detected and treated during the first trimester.

Nuchal Cord

The nuchal cord is the umbilical cord wrapped around the baby's neck. Also known as nuchal loops, they rarely cause any problems. Almost 25 percent of the babies are born with a nuchal loop, and they are generally healthy. An ultrasound may show some heart rate abnormalities during labor and delivery for babies with a nuchal cord because of the pressure on the cord. However, the pressure is not serious to cause fetal death or other major complications. Even if the nuchal cord is wrapped around other parts of the baby's body, it causes no harm. Rarely a cesarean delivery is required for babies with a nuchal loop.

Cord Stricture

Cord stricture is a sharp narrowing of the umbilical cord, which is a common cause of fetal death during second trimester before birth. The cause of this condition is unknown. An early detection in cord stricture is difficult; hence the risk of fetal death is increased. However, even if the baby survives, a few medical conditions such as septal defects, cleft lip, and trisomy 18 can occur.

References

1. "Complications and Loss—Umbilical Cord Abnormalities," March of Dimes, February 2008.

2. Beall, Marie Helen; Isaacs, Christine. "Umbilical Cord Complications," September 9, 2015.

3. Jick, Bryan. "Umbilical Cord Abnormalities," Pregnancy Corner, June 2017.

4. "Umbilical Cord Problems," Birth Injury Guide, n.d.

Chapter 12

Other Pregnancy Complications

Chapter Contents

Section 12.1

Amniotic Band Syndrome

This section includes text excerpted from "Amniotic Band
Syndrome," Genetic and Rare Diseases Information
Center (GARD), National Center for Advancing
Translational Sciences (NCATS), March 21, 2017.

Amniotic band syndrome refers to a condition in which bands
develop from the inner lining of the amnion. The amnion is the sac
that surrounds the baby in the womb. As the baby develops in the
womb, the bands may attach to and affect the development of different
areas of the body. This may result in constriction of the affected area or
even amputation. The signs and symptoms vary greatly depending on
the area(s) of the body involved and may include: shortened or absent
digits (fingers and/or toes) or limbs (arms and/or legs), an opening in
the abdomen through which various abdominal organs can protrude
(abdominal wall defects), protrusion of a portion of the brain and its
surrounding membranes through a skull defect (encephalocele), and
cleft lip and/or palate. In most instances, the cause of amniotic bands
remains unknown. Researchers have suggested two main theories to
explain the development: the extrinsic theory and the intrinsic theory.
The extrinsic theory states that amniotic band syndrome occurs due to
factors found outside of the developing baby (externally); the intrinsic
theory states that amniotic band syndrome occurs due to factors found
within the baby (internally). Treatment differs depending on the severity of the condition and the areas of the body affected and may include
surgery, physical therapy, and occupational therapy.

Symptoms

The symptoms of amniotic band syndrome depend on the severity
and location of the constrictions. The mildest constrictions affect only
the superficial skin and may not require treatment. Deeper constrictions may block lymphatic vessels, impair blood flow, and require
immediate surgical care. When the bands affect the limbs, the lower
part of the limbs are most often involved, especially the middle, long,

and index fingers of the hand. When the feet are involved, the bands most commonly affect the big toe.

Pressure from the bands may result in additional abnormalities, such as underdevelopment of a limb, bone abnormalities, amputations, leg-length discrepancy, and club feet. Constriction bands across the head and face may lead to facial clefts. Severe clefts affecting vital organs are often life-threatening.

The Human Phenotype Ontology (HPO) provides the following list of features that have been reported in people with this condition. Much of the information in the HPO comes from Orphanet, a European rare disease database. If available, the list includes a rough estimate of how common a feature is (its frequency). Frequencies are based on a specific study and may not be representative of all studies.

Cause

Amniotic bands are caused by damage to a part of the placenta called the amnion. Damage to the amnion may produce fiber-like bands that can trap parts of the developing baby.

Diagnosis

The earliest reported detection of an amniotic band is at 12 weeks gestation, by vaginal ultrasound. On ultrasound the bands appear as thin, mobile lines, which may be seen attached to or around the baby. However these bands may be difficult to detect by ultrasound, and are more often diagnosed by the results of the fusion, such as missing or deformed limbs.

Treatment

Mild cases may not require treatment, however all bands need monitoring as growth occurs to watch for progressive constriction and swelling. Other constrictions may require surgical management; surgical options will vary depending on the abnormality. People with amniotic band syndrome who have amputations may benefit from the use of prosthetics.

Prognosis

Because the prognosis of people with amniotic band syndrome can vary from patient to patient, the best person to provide your family with information regarding your child's prognosis, is the healthcare providers involved in their care. In general, the outlook for infants with a single band involving the superficial skin of the wrist and/or hand is good. While the family and child will need to adjust to the cosmetic difference, the functional use of the hand is normal. Deeper bands can be associated with complications (i.e., blockage of lymph and blood vessels) that can worsen over time and may require surgery. Some people with amniotic band syndrome are born with acrosyndactyly, a fusion of the fingers that may limit the hand function and cause stiffness of the joints. In many cases a good ability to hold and grasp may be obtained with reconstructive procedures.

Section 12.2

Preeclampsia and Eclampsia

This section includes text excerpted from "Preeclampsia and Eclampsia," *Eunice Kennedy Shriver* National Institute of Child Health and Human Development (NICHD), August 26, 2017.

Preeclampsia and eclampsia are pregnancy-related high blood pressure disorders. In preeclampsia, the mother's high blood pressure reduces the blood supply to the fetus, which may get less oxygen and fewer nutrients. Eclampsia is when pregnant women with preeclampsia develop seizures or coma.

About Preeclampsia and Eclampsia

Preeclampsia and eclampsia are part of the spectrum of high blood pressure, or hypertensive, disorders that can occur during pregnancy. At the mild end of the spectrum is gestational hypertension, which occurs when a woman who previously had normal blood pressure develops high blood pressure when she is more than 20 weeks pregnant and her blood pressure returns to normal within 12 weeks after delivery. This problem usually occurs without other symptoms. In many cases, gestational hypertension does not harm the mother or fetus. Severe gestational hypertension, however, may be associated with preterm birth and infants who are small for their age at birth. And about 15 percent to 25 percent of women with gestational hypertension go on to develop preeclampsia.

Preeclampsia is similar to gestational hypertension, because it also describes high blood pressure at or after 20 weeks of pregnancy in a woman whose blood pressure was normal before pregnancy. But preeclampsia can also include blood pressure at or greater than 140/90 mmHg, increased swelling, and protein in the urine. The condition can be serious and is a leading cause of preterm birth (before 37 weeks of pregnancy). If it is severe enough to affect brain function, causing seizures or coma, it is called eclampsia.

One of the serious complications of hypertensive disorders in pregnancy is haemolysis, elevated liver enzymes, low platelet count (HELLP) syndrome, a situation in which a pregnant woman with pre-eclampsia or eclampsia suffers damage to the liver and blood cells. The letters in the name HELLP stand for the following problems:

- H – Hemolysis, in which oxygen carrying red blood cells break down

- EL – Elevated Liver enzymes, showing damage to the liver

- LP – Low Platelet count, meaning that the cells responsible for stopping bleeding are low.

What Causes Preeclampsia and Eclampsia?

The causes of preeclampsia and eclampsia are not known. These disorders previously were believed to be caused by a toxin, called "toxemia," in the blood, but healthcare providers now know that is not true. Nevertheless, preeclampsia is sometimes still referred to as "toxemia."

To learn more about preeclampsia and eclampsia, scientists are investigating many factors that could contribute to the development and progression of these diseases, including:

- Placental abnormalities, such as insufficient blood flow

- Genetic factors

- Environmental exposures

- Nutritional factors

- Maternal immunology and autoimmune disorders

- Cardiovascular and inflammatory changes

- Hormonal imbalances

What Are the Risks of Preeclampsia and Eclampsia to the Mother?

Risks during Pregnancy

Preeclampsia during pregnancy is mild in 75 percent of cases. However, a woman can progress from mild to severe preeclampsia or to full eclampsia very quickly—even in a matter of days. Both preeclampsia and eclampsia can cause serious health problems for the mother and infant.

Women with preeclampsia are at increased risk for damage to the kidneys, liver, brain, and other organ and blood systems. Preeclampsia may also affect the placenta. The condition could lead to a separation of the placenta from the uterus (referred to as placental abruption), preterm birth, and pregnancy loss or stillbirth. In some cases, preeclampsia can lead to organ failure or stroke.

In severe cases, preeclampsia can develop into eclampsia, which includes seizures. Seizures in eclampsia may cause a woman to lose consciousness and twitch uncontrollably. If the fetus is not delivered, these conditions can cause the death of the mother and/or the fetus.

Expecting mothers rarely die from preeclampsia in the developed world, but it is still a major cause of illness and death globally. According to the World Health Organization (WHO), preeclampsia and eclampsia cause 14 percent of maternal deaths each year, or about 50,000–75,000 women worldwide.

Risks after Pregnancy

In "uncomplicated preeclampsia," the mother's high blood pressure and other symptoms usually go back to normal within 6 weeks of the infant's birth. However, studies have shown that women who had preeclampsia are four times more likely to later develop hypertension (high blood pressure) and are twice as likely to later develop ischemic heart disease (reduced blood supply to the heart muscle, which can cause heart attacks), a blood clot in a vein, and stroke as are women who did not have preeclampsia.

Less commonly, mothers who had preeclampsia could experience permanent damage to their organs, such as their kidneys and liver. They could also experience fluid in the lungs. In the days following birth, women with preeclampsia remain at increased risk for developing eclampsia and seizures.

What Are the Risks of Preeclampsia and Eclampsia to the Fetus?

Preeclampsia may be related to problems with the placenta early in the pregnancy. Such problems pose risks to the fetus, including:

- Lack of oxygen and nutrients, which can impair fetal growth

- Preterm birth

- Stillbirth if placental abruption (separation of the placenta from the uterine wall) leads to heavy bleeding in the mother

- Death: According to the Preeclampsia Foundation each year, about 10,500 infants in the United States and about half a million worldwide die due to preeclampsia.

- Stillbirths are more likely to occur when the mother has a more severe form of preeclampsia, including HELLP syndrome.

Infants whose mothers had preeclampsia are also at increased risk for later problems, even if they were born at full term (39 weeks of pregnancy). Infants born preterm due to preeclampsia face a higher risk of some long-term health issues, mostly related to being born early, including learning disorders, cerebral palsy, epilepsy, deafness, and blindness. Infants born preterm may also have to be hospitalized for a long time after birth and may be smaller than infants born full term. Infants who experienced poor growth in the uterus may later be at higher risk of diabetes, congestive heart failure, and high blood pressure.

How Many Women Are Affected by or at Risk of Preeclampsia?

The exact number of women who develop preeclampsia is not known. Some estimates suggest that preeclampsia affects 2 percent to 8 percent of all pregnancies globally and about 3.4 percent in the United States.

The condition is estimated to account for 10 percent to 15 percent of maternal deaths worldwide. Disorders related to high blood pressure are the second leading cause of stillbirths and early neonatal deaths in developing nations.

In addition, HELLP syndrome occurs in about 10 percent to 20 percent of all women with severe preeclampsia or eclampsia.

Risk Factors for Preeclampsia

Although preeclampsia occurs primarily in first pregnancies, a woman who had preeclampsia in a previous pregnancy is seven times more likely to develop preeclampsia in a later pregnancy.

Other factors that can increase a woman's risk include:

- Chronic high blood pressure or kidney disease before pregnancy
- High blood pressure or preeclampsia in an earlier pregnancy
- Obesity. Overweight or obese women are also more likely to have preeclampsia in more than one pregnancy.
- Age. Women older than 40 are at higher risk.
- Multiple gestation (being pregnant with more than one fetus)
- African American ethnicity. Also, among women who have had preeclampsia before, nonwhite women are more likely than white women to develop preeclampsia again in a later pregnancy.
- Family history of preeclampsia. According to the World Health Organization (WHO), among women who have had preeclampsia, about 20 percent to 40 percent of their daughters and 11 percent to 37 percent of their sisters also will get the disorder.

Preeclampsia is also more common among women who have histories of certain health conditions, such as migraines, diabetes, rheumatoid arthritis, lupus, scleroderma, urinary tract infections, gum disease, polycystic ovary syndrome, multiple sclerosis, gestational diabetes, and sickle cell disease.

Preeclampsia is also more common in pregnancies resulting from egg donation, donor insemination, or *in vitro* fertilization.

The U.S. Preventative Services Task Force (USPSTF) recommends that women who are at high risk for preeclampsia take low dose aspirin starting after 12 weeks of pregnancy to prevent preeclampsia. Women who are pregnant or who are thinking about getting pregnant should talk with their healthcare provider about preeclampsia risk and ways to reduce the risk.

What Are the Symptoms of Preeclampsia, Eclampsia, and HELLP Syndrome?

Preeclampsia

Possible symptoms of preeclampsia include:

- High blood pressure

- Too much protein in the urine

- Swelling in a woman's face and hands (a woman's feet might swell too, but swollen feet are common during pregnancy and may not signal a problem)

- Systemic problems, such as headache, blurred vision, and right upper quadrant abdominal pain

Eclampsia

The following symptoms are cause for immediate concern:

- Seizures

- Severe headache

- Vision problems, such as temporary blindness

- Abdominal pain, especially in the upper right area of the belly

- Nausea and vomiting

- Smaller urine output or not urinating very often

HELLP Syndrome

HELLP syndrome can lead to serious complications, including liver failure and death.

A pregnant woman with HELLP syndrome might bleed or bruise easily and/or experience abdominal pain, nausea or vomiting, headache, or extreme fatigue. Although most women who develop HELLP syndrome already have high blood pressure and preeclampsia, sometimes the syndrome is the first sign. In addition, HELLP syndrome can occur without a woman having either high blood pressure or protein in her urine.

How Do Healthcare Providers Diagnose Preeclampsia, Eclampsia, and HELLP Syndrome?

A healthcare provider will check a pregnant woman's blood pressure and urine during each prenatal visit. If the blood pressure reading is considered high (140/90 or higher), especially after the 20th week of pregnancy, the healthcare provider will likely perform blood tests and more extensive lab tests to look for extra protein in the urine (called proteinuria) as well as other symptoms.

The American College of Obstetricians and Gynecologists (ACOG) provides the following criteria for a diagnosis of gestational hypertension, preeclampsia, eclampsia, and HELLP syndrome.

Gestational hypertension is diagnosed if a pregnant woman has high blood pressure but no protein in the urine. Gestational hypertension occurs when women whose blood pressure levels were normal before pregnancy develop high blood pressure after 20 weeks of pregnancy. Gestational hypertension can progress into preeclampsia.

Mild preeclampsia is diagnosed when a pregnant woman has:

- Systolic blood pressure (top number) of 140 mmHg or higher or diastolic blood pressure (bottom number) of 90 mmHg or higher

  - Urine with 0.3 or more grams of protein in a 24-hour specimen (a collection of every drop of urine within 24 hours) or a protein to creatinine ratio greater than 0.3

  or

  - Blood tests that show kidney or liver dysfunction

  - Fluid in the lungs and difficulty breathing

  - Visual impairments

Severe preeclampsia occurs when a pregnant woman has any of the following:

- Systolic blood pressure of 160 mmHg or higher or diastolic blood pressure of 110 mmHg or higher on two occasions at least 4 hours apart while the patient is on bed rest

- Urine with 5 or more grams of protein in a 24 hour specimen or 3 or more grams of protein on 2 random urine samples collected at least 4 hours apart

- Test results suggesting kidney or liver damage—for example, blood tests that reveal low numbers of platelets or high liver enzymes

- Severe, unexplained stomach pain that does not respond to medication

- Symptoms that include visual disturbances, difficulty breathing, or fluid buildup

Eclampsia occurs when women with preeclampsia develop seizures. The seizures can happen before or during labor or after the baby is delivered.

HELLP syndrome is diagnosed when laboratory tests show hemolysis (burst red blood cells release hemoglobin into the blood plasma), elevated liver enzymes, and low platelets. There also may or may not be extra protein in the urine.

Some women may also be diagnosed with **superimposed preeclampsia**—a situation in which the woman develops preeclampsia on top of high blood pressure that was present before she got pregnant. Healthcare providers look for an increase in blood pressure and either protein in the urine, fluid buildup, or both for a diagnosis of superimposed preeclampsia.

In addition to tests that might diagnose preeclampsia or similar problems, healthcare providers may do other tests to assess the health of the mother and fetus, including:

- Blood tests to see how well the mother's liver and kidneys are working

- Blood tests to check blood platelet levels to see how well the mother's blood is clotting

- Blood tests to count the total number of red blood cells in the mother's blood

- A maternal weight check

- An ultrasound to assess the fetus's size

- A check of the fetus's heart rate

- A physical exam to look for swelling in the mother's face, hands, or legs as well as abdominal tenderness or an enlarged liver

What Are the Treatments for Preeclampsia, Eclampsia, and HELLP Syndrome?

The only cure for preeclampsia and eclampsia is delivering the fetus.

Treatment decisions for preeclampsia, eclampsia, and HELLP syndrome need to take into account how severe the condition is, the potential for maternal complications, how far along the pregnancy is, and the potential risks to the fetus. Ideally, the healthcare provider will minimize risks to the mother while giving the fetus as much time as possible to mature before delivery.

The U.S. Preventative Services Task Force recommends that women at high risk for preeclampsia take low dose aspirin starting after 12 weeks of pregnancy to prevent the condition from occurring.

Preeclampsia Treatment

If the pregnancy is at 37 weeks or later, the healthcare provider will usually want to deliver the fetus to treat preeclampsia and avoid further complications.

If the pregnancy is at less than 37 weeks, however, the woman and her healthcare provider may consider treatment options that give the fetus more time to develop, depending on how severe the condition is. A healthcare provider may consider the following options:

- If the preeclampsia is mild, it may be possible to wait to deliver. To help prevent further complications, the healthcare provider may ask the woman to go on bed rest to try to lower blood pressure and increase the blood flow to the placenta.

- Close monitoring of the woman and her fetus will be needed. Tests for the mother might include blood and urine tests to see if the preeclampsia is progressing, such as tests to assess platelet counts, liver enzymes, kidney function, and urinary protein levels. Tests for the fetus might include ultrasound, heart rate monitoring, assessment of fetal growth, and amniotic fluid assessment.

- Anticonvulsive medication, such as magnesium sulfate, might be used to prevent a seizure.

- In some cases, such as with severe preeclampsia, the woman will be admitted to the hospital so she can be monitored closely and continuously. Treatment in the hospital might include intravenous medication to control blood pressure and prevent seizures or other complications as well as steroid injections to help speed up the development of the fetus's lungs.

When a woman has severe preeclampsia and is at 34 weeks of pregnancy or later, the American College of Obstetricians and Gynecologists recommends delivery as soon as medically possible. If the pregnancy is at less than 34 weeks, healthcare providers will probably prescribe corticosteroids to help speed up the maturation of the fetal lungs before attempting delivery.

Preterm delivery may be necessary, even if that means likely complications for the infant, because of the risk of severe maternal complications.

The symptoms of preeclampsia usually go away within 6 weeks of delivery.

Eclampsia Treatment

Eclampsia—the onset of seizures in a woman with preeclampsia—is considered a medical emergency. Immediate treatment, usually in a hospital, is needed to stop the mother's seizures, treat blood pressure levels that are too high, and deliver the fetus.

Magnesium sulfate (a type of mineral) may be given to treat active seizures and prevent future seizures. Antihypertensive medications may be given to lower the blood pressure.

HELLP Syndrome Treatment

HELLP syndrome, a severe complication of preeclampsia and eclampsia, can lead to serious complications for the mother, including liver failure and death, as well as the fetus. The healthcare provider may consider the following treatments after a diagnosis of HELLP syndrome:

- Delivery of the fetus

- Hospitalization to provide intravenous medication to control blood pressure and prevent seizures or other complications as well as steroid injections to help speed up the development of the fetus's lungs.

Section 12.3

Rh Incompatibility

This section includes text excerpted from "Rh Incompatibility,"
National Heart, Lung, and Blood Institute (NHLBI),
January 1, 2011. Reviewed December 2017.

What Is Rh Incompatibility?

Rh incompatibility is a condition that occurs during pregnancy if a woman has Rh-negative blood and her baby has Rh-positive blood.

"Rh-negative" and "Rh-positive" refer to whether your blood has Rh factor. Rh factor is a protein on red blood cells. If you have Rh factor, you're Rh-positive. If you don't have it, you're Rh-negative. Rh factor is inherited (passed from parents to children through the genes). Most people are Rh-positive.

Whether you have Rh factor doesn't affect your general health. However, it can cause problems during pregnancy.

Other Names for Rh Incompatibility

- Rh disease

- Rh induced hemolytic disease of the newborn

Who Is at Risk for Rh Incompatibility?

An Rh negative woman who conceives a child with an Rh-positive man is at risk for Rh incompatibility.

Rh factor is inherited (passed from parents to children through the genes). If you're Rh-negative and the father of your baby is Rh-positive, the baby has a 50 percent or more chance of having Rh-positive blood.

Simple blood tests can show whether you and the father of your baby are Rh-positive or Rh-negative.

If you're Rh-negative, your risk of problems from Rh incompatibility is higher if you were exposed to Rh-positive blood before the pregnancy. This may have happened during:

- An earlier pregnancy (usually during delivery). You also may have been exposed to Rh-positive blood if you had bleeding or abdominal trauma (for example, from a car accident) during the pregnancy.

- An ectopic pregnancy, a miscarriage, or an induced abortion. (An ectopic pregnancy is a pregnancy that starts outside of the uterus, or womb.)

- A mismatched blood transfusion or blood and marrow stem cell transplant.

- An injection or puncture with a needle or other object containing Rh-positive blood.

Certain tests also can expose you to Rh-positive blood. Examples include amniocentesis and chorionic villus sampling (CVS).

Amniocentesis is a test that you may have during pregnancy. Your doctor uses a needle to remove a small amount of fluid from the sac around your baby. The fluid is then tested for various reasons.

CVS also may be done during pregnancy. For this test, your doctor threads a thin tube through the vagina and cervix to the placenta. He or she removes a tissue sample from the placenta using gentle suction. The tissue sample is tested for various reasons.

Unless you were treated with the medicine that prevents Rh antibodies (Rh immune globulin) after each of these events, you're at risk for Rh incompatibility during current and future pregnancies.

What Are the Signs and Symptoms of Rh Incompatibility?

Rh incompatibility doesn't cause signs or symptoms in a pregnant woman. In a baby, the condition can lead to hemolytic anemia. Hemolytic anemia is a condition in which red blood cells are destroyed faster than the body can replace them.

Red blood cells contain hemoglobin, an iron rich protein that carries oxygen to the body. Without enough red blood cells and hemoglobin, the baby won't get enough oxygen.

Hemolytic anemia can cause mild to severe signs and symptoms in a newborn, such as jaundice and a buildup of fluid.

Jaundice is a yellowish color of the skin and whites of the eyes. When red blood cells die, they release hemoglobin into the blood. The hemoglobin is broken down into a compound called bilirubin. This compound gives the skin and eyes a yellowish color. High levels of bilirubin can lead to brain damage in the baby.

The buildup of fluid is a result of heart failure. Without enough hemoglobin carrying red blood cells, the baby's heart has to work harder to move oxygen rich blood through the body. This stress can lead to heart failure.

Heart failure can cause fluid to buildup in many parts of the body. When this occurs in a fetus or newborn, the condition is called hydrops fetalis.

Severe hemolytic anemia can be fatal to a newborn at the time of birth or shortly after.

How Is Rh Incompatibility Diagnosed?

Rh incompatibility is diagnosed with blood tests. To find out whether a baby is developing hemolytic anemia and how serious it is, doctors may use more advanced tests, such as ultrasound.

Specialists Involved

An obstetrician will screen for Rh incompatibility. This is a doctor who specializes in treating pregnant women. The obstetrician also will monitor the pregnancy and the baby for problems related to hemolytic anemia. He or she also will oversee treatment to prevent problems with future pregnancies.

A pediatrician or hematologist treats newborns who have hemolytic anemia and related problems. A pediatrician is a doctor who specializes in treating children. A hematologist is a doctor who specializes in treating people who have blood diseases and disorders.

Diagnostic Tests

If you're pregnant, your doctor will order a simple blood test at your first prenatal visit to learn whether you're Rh-positive or Rh-negative.

If you're Rh-negative, you also may have another blood test called an antibody screen. This test shows whether you have Rh antibodies in your blood. If you do, it means that you were exposed to Rh-positive blood before and you're at risk for Rh incompatibility.

If you're Rh-negative and you don't have Rh antibodies, your baby's father also will be tested to find out his Rh type. If he's Rh-negative too, the baby has no chance of having Rh-positive blood. Thus, there's no risk of Rh incompatibility.

However, if the baby's father is Rh-positive, the baby has a 50 percent or more chance of having Rh-positive blood. As a result, you're at high risk of developing Rh incompatibility.

If your baby's father is Rh-positive, or if it's not possible to find out his Rh status, your doctor may do a test called amniocentesis.

For this test, your doctor inserts a hollow needle through your abdominal wall into your uterus. He or she removes a small amount of fluid from the sac around the baby. The fluid is tested to learn whether the baby is Rh-positive. (Rarely, an amniocentesis can expose you to Rh-positive blood).

Your doctor also may use this test to measure bilirubin levels in your baby. Bilirubin builds up as a result of red blood cells dying too quickly. The higher the level of bilirubin is, the greater the chance that the baby has hemolytic anemia.

If Rh incompatibility is known or suspected, you'll be tested for Rh antibodies one or more times during your pregnancy. This test often is done at least once at your sixth or seventh month of pregnancy.

The results from this test also can suggest how severe the baby's hemolytic anemia has become. Higher levels of antibodies suggest more severe hemolytic anemia.

To check your baby for hemolytic anemia, your doctor also may use a test called Doppler ultrasound. He or she will use this test to measure how fast blood is flowing through an artery in the baby's head.

Doppler ultrasound uses sound waves to measure how fast blood is moving. The faster the blood flow is, the greater the risk of hemolytic anemia. This is because the anemia will cause the baby's heart to pump more blood.

How Is Rh Incompatibility Treated?

Rh incompatibility is treated with a medicine called Rh immune globulin (IG). Treatment for a baby who has hemolytic anemia will vary based on the severity of the condition.

Goals of Treatment

The goals of treating Rh incompatibility are to ensure that your baby is healthy and to lower your risk for the condition in future pregnancies.

Treatment for Rh Incompatibility

If Rh incompatibility is diagnosed during your pregnancy, you'll receive Rh immune globulin in your seventh month of pregnancy and again within 72 hours of delivery.

You also may receive Rh immune globulin if the risk of blood transfer between you and the baby is high (for example, if you've had a miscarriage, ectopic pregnancy, or bleeding during pregnancy).

Rh immune globulin contains Rh antibodies that attach to the Rh-positive blood cells in your blood. When this happens, your body doesn't react to the baby's Rh-positive cells as a foreign substance. As a result, your body doesn't make Rh antibodies. Rh immune globulin must be given at the correct times to work properly.

Once you have formed Rh antibodies, the medicine will no longer help. That's why a woman who has Rh-negative blood must be treated with the medicine with each pregnancy or any other event that allows her blood to mix with Rh-positive blood.

Rh immune globulin is injected into the muscle of your arm or buttock. Side effects may include soreness at the injection site and a slight fever. The medicine also may be injected into a vein.

Treatment for Hemolytic Anemia

Several options are available for treating hemolytic anemia in a baby. In mild cases, no treatment may be needed. If treatment is needed, the baby may be given a medicine called erythropoietin and iron supplements. These treatments can prompt the body to make red blood cells.

If the hemolytic anemia is severe, the baby may get a blood transfusion through the umbilical cord. If the hemolytic anemia is severe and the baby is almost full term, your doctor may induce labor early. This allows the baby's doctor to begin treatment right away.

A newborn who has severe anemia may be treated with a blood exchange transfusion. The procedure involves slowly removing the newborn's blood and replacing it with fresh blood or plasma from a donor.

Newborns also may be treated with special lights to reduce the amount of bilirubin in their blood. These babies may have jaundice (a yellowish color of the skin and whites of the eyes). High levels of bilirubin cause jaundice.

Reducing the blood's bilirubin level is important because high levels of this compound can cause brain damage. High levels of bilirubin often are seen in babies who have hemolytic anemia. This is because the compound forms when red blood cells break down.

How Can Rh Incompatibility Be Prevented?

Rh incompatibility can be prevented with Rh immune globulin, as long as the medicine is given at the correct times. Once you have formed Rh antibodies, the medicine will no longer help.

Thus, a woman who has Rh-negative blood must be treated with Rh immune globulin during and after each pregnancy or after any other event that allows her blood to mix with Rh-positive blood.

Early prenatal care also can help prevent some of the problems linked to Rh incompatibility. For example, your doctor can find out early whether you're at risk for the condition.

If you're at risk, your doctor can closely monitor your pregnancy. He or she will watch for signs of hemolytic anemia in your baby and provided treatment as needed.

Living with Rh Incompatibility

If you have Rh-negative blood, injections of Rh immune globulin can reduce your risk of Rh incompatibility in future pregnancies. It's important to get this medicine every time you give birth to an Rh-positive baby or come in contact with Rh-positive blood.

If you're Rh-negative, your risk of problems from Rh incompatibility is higher if you were exposed to Rh-positive blood before your current pregnancy. This may have happened during:

- An earlier pregnancy (usually during delivery). You also may have been exposed to Rh-positive blood if you had bleeding or abdominal trauma (for example, from a car accident) during the pregnancy.

- An ectopic pregnancy, a miscarriage, or an induced abortion. (An ectopic pregnancy is a pregnancy that starts outside of the uterus, or womb.)

- A mismatched blood transfusion or blood and marrow stem cell transplant.

- An injection or puncture with a needle or other object containing Rh-positive blood.

You also can be exposed to Rh-positive blood during certain tests, such as amniocentesis and chorionic villus sampling.

Unless you were treated with Rh immune globulin after each of these events, you're at risk for Rh incompatibility during current and future pregnancies.

Let your doctor know about your risk early in your pregnancy. This allows him or her to carefully monitor your pregnancy and promptly treat any problems that arise.

Part Two

Prematurity and Other Birth Complications

Chapter 13

Preterm Labor and Birth

Preterm birth is when a baby is born too early, before 37 weeks of pregnancy have been completed. In 2016, preterm birth affected about 1 of every 10 infants born in the United States. Preterm birth rates decreased from 2007–2014, and Centers for Disease Control and Prevention (CDC) research shows that this decline is due, in part, to declines in the number of births to teens and young mothers. However, the preterm birth rate rose for the second straight year in 2016. Additionally, racial and ethnic differences in preterm birth rates remain. For example, in 2016, the rate of preterm birth among African-American women (14%) was about 50 percent higher than the rate of preterm birth among white women (9%).

A developing baby goes through important growth throughout pregnancy; including in the final months and weeks. For example, the brain, lungs, and liver need the final weeks of pregnancy to fully develop.

Babies born too early (especially before 32 weeks) have higher rates of death and disability. In 2015, preterm birth and low birth weight accounted for about 17 percent of infant deaths. Babies who survive may have:

This chapter contains text excerpted from the following sources: Text in this chapter begins with excerpts from "Maternal and Infant Health—Preterm Birth," Centers for Disease Control and Prevention (CDC), November 27, 2017; Text beginning with the heading "What Is Preterm Labor and Birth?" is excerpted from "Preterm Labor and Birth—Condition Information," *Eunice Kennedy Shriver* National Institute of Child Health and Human Development (NICHD), March 16, 2014. Reviewed December 2017.

- Breathing problems

- Feeding difficulties

- Cerebral palsy

- Developmental delay

- Vision problems

- Hearing problems

Preterm births may also take an emotional toll and be a financial burden for families.

What Is Preterm Labor and Birth?

In general, a normal human pregnancy is about 40 weeks long (9.2 months). Healthcare providers now define "full-term" birth as birth that occurs between 39 weeks and 40 weeks and 6 days of pregnancy. Infants born during this time are considered full-term infants.

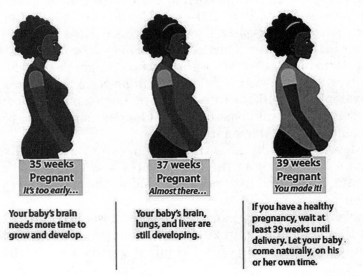

Figure 13.1. *Your Baby Grows throughout Your Entire Pregnancy*

(Source: "Maternal and Infant Health—Preterm Birth," Centers for Disease Control and Prevention (CDC).)

Infants born in the 37th and 38th weeks of pregnancy—previously called term but now referred to as "early term"—face more health risks than do those born at 39 or 40 weeks.

Deliveries before 37 weeks of pregnancy are considered "preterm" or premature:

- Labor that begins before 37 weeks of pregnancy is preterm or premature labor.

- A birth that occurs before 37 weeks of pregnancy is a preterm or premature birth.

- An infant born before 37 weeks in the womb is a preterm or premature infant. (These infants are commonly called "preemies" as a reference to being born prematurely.)

"Late preterm" refers to 34 weeks through 36 weeks of pregnancy. Infants born during this time are considered late-preterm infants, but they face many of the same health challenges as preterm infants. More than 70 percent of preterm infants are born during the late-preterm time frame.

Preterm birth is the most common cause of infant death and is the leading cause of long-term disability in children. Many organs, including the brain, lungs, and liver, are still developing in the final weeks of pregnancy. The earlier the delivery, the higher the risk of serious disability or death.

Infants born prematurely are at risk for cerebral palsy (a group of nervous system disorders that affect control of movement and posture and limit activity), developmental delays, and vision and hearing problems.

Late-preterm infants typically have better health outcomes than those born earlier, but they are still three times more likely to die in the first year of life than are full-term infants. Preterm births can also take a heavy emotional and economic toll on families.

What Are the Symptoms of Preterm Labor?

Preterm labor is any labor that occurs from 20 weeks through 36 weeks of pregnancy. Here are the symptoms:

- Contractions (tightening of stomach muscles, or birth pains) every 10 minutes or more often

- Change in vaginal discharge (leaking fluid or bleeding from the vagina)

- Feeling of pressure in the pelvis (hip) area

- Low, dull backache

- Cramps that feel like menstrual cramps

- Abdominal cramps with or without diarrhea

It is normal for pregnant women to have some uterine contractions throughout the day. It is not normal to have frequent uterine contractions, such as six or more in one hour. Frequent uterine contractions, or tightenings, may cause the cervix to begin to open. If a woman thinks that she might be having preterm labor, she should call her doctor or go to the hospital to be evaluated.

How Many People Are Affected by Preterm Labor and Birth?

According to the Centers for Disease Control and Prevention (CDC), preterm birth affected about 1 of every 10 infants born in the United States.

Going into preterm labor does not always mean that a pregnant woman will deliver the baby prematurely. Up to one-half of women who experience preterm labor eventually deliver at 37 weeks of pregnancy or later.

In some cases, intervention from a healthcare provider is needed to stop preterm labor. In other cases, the labor may stop on its own. A woman who thinks she is experiencing preterm labor should contact a healthcare provider immediately.

How Many Women Are at Risk for Preterm Labor and Delivery?

Any pregnant woman could experience preterm labor and delivery. But there are some factors that increase a woman's risk of going into labor or giving birth prematurely.

What Causes Preterm Labor and Birth?

The causes of preterm labor and premature birth are numerous, complex, and only partly understood. Medical, psychosocial, and biological factors may all play a role in preterm labor and birth.

There are three main situations in which preterm labor and premature birth may occur:

- **Spontaneous preterm labor and birth.** This term refers to unintentional, unplanned delivery before the 37th week of pregnancy. This type of preterm birth can result from a number of causes, such as infection or inflammation, although the cause of spontaneous preterm labor and delivery is usually not known. A history of delivering preterm is one of the strongest predictors for subsequent preterm births.

- **Medically indicated preterm birth.** If a serious medical condition—such as preeclampsia—exists, the healthcare provider might recommend a preterm delivery. In these cases, healthcare providers often take steps to keep the baby in the womb as long as possible to allow for additional growth and development, while also monitoring the mother and fetus for health issues. Providers also use additional interventions, such as steroids, to help improve outcomes for the baby.

- **Nonmedically indicated (elective) preterm delivery.** Some late-preterm births result from inducing labor or having a cesarean delivery even though there is not a medical reason to do so, even though this practice is not recommended. Research indicates that even babies born at 37 or 38 weeks of pregnancy are at higher risk for poor health outcomes than are babies born at 39 weeks of pregnancy or later. Therefore, unless there are medical problems, healthcare providers should wait until at least 39 weeks of pregnancy to induce labor or perform a cesarean delivery to prevent possible health problems.

What Are the Risk Factors for Preterm Labor and Birth?

There are several risk factors for preterm labor and premature birth, including ones that researchers have not yet identified. Some of these risk factors are "modifiable," meaning they can be changed to help reduce the risk. Other factors cannot be changed.

Healthcare providers consider the following factors to put women at high risk for preterm labor or birth:

- Women who have delivered preterm before, or who have experienced preterm labor before, are considered to be at high risk for preterm labor and birth.

- Being pregnant with twins, triplets, or more (called "multiple gestations") or the use of assisted reproductive technology is associated with a higher risk of preterm labor and birth. One study showed that more than 50 percent of twin births occurred preterm, compared with only 10 percent of births of single infants.

- Women with certain abnormalities of the reproductive organs are at greater risk for preterm labor and birth than are women who do not have these abnormalities. For instance, women who have a short cervix (the lower part of the uterus) or whose cervix shortens in the second trimester (fourth through sixth months) of pregnancy instead of the third trimester are at high risk for preterm delivery.

Certain medical conditions, including some that occur only during pregnancy, also place a woman at higher risk for preterm labor and delivery. Some of these conditions include:

- Urinary tract infections.

- Sexually transmitted infections.

- Certain vaginal infections, such as bacterial vaginosis and trichomoniasis.

- High blood pressure.

- Bleeding from the vagina.

- Certain developmental abnormalities in the fetus.

- Pregnancy resulting from *in vitro* fertilization.

- Being underweight or obese before pregnancy.

- Short time period between pregnancies (less than 6 months between a birth and the beginning of the next pregnancy).

- Placenta previa, a condition in which the placenta grows in the lowest part of the uterus and covers all or part of the opening to the cervix.

- Being at risk for rupture of the uterus (when the wall of the uterus rips open). Rupture of the uterus is more likely if you have had a prior cesarean delivery or have had a uterine fibroid removed.

- Diabetes (high blood sugar) and gestational diabetes (which occurs only during pregnancy).

- Blood clotting problems.

Other factors that may increase risk for preterm labor and premature birth include:

- **Ethnicity.** Preterm labor and birth occur more often among certain racial and ethnic groups. Infants of African American

188

mothers are 50 percent more likely to be born preterm than are infants of white mothers

- **Age of the mother.**
  - Women younger than age 18 are more likely to have a preterm delivery.
  - Women older than age 35 are also at risk of having preterm infants because they are more likely to have other conditions (such as high blood pressure and diabetes) that can cause complications requiring preterm delivery.
- **Certain lifestyle and environmental factors**, including:
  - Late or no healthcare during pregnancy
  - Smoking
  - Drinking alcohol
  - Using illegal drugs
  - Domestic violence, including physical, sexual, or emotional abuse
  - Lack of social support
  - Stress
  - Long working hours with long periods of standing
  - Exposure to certain environmental pollutants

Is It Possible to Predict Which Women Are More Likely to Have Preterm Labor and Birth?

There is no definitive way to predict preterm labor or premature birth. Many research studies are focusing on this important issue. By identifying which women are at increased risk, healthcare providers may be able to provide early interventions, treatments, and close monitoring of these pregnancies to prevent preterm delivery or to improve health outcomes. However, in some situations, healthcare providers know that a preterm delivery is very likely. Some of these situations are described below.

Shortened Cervix

As a preparation for birth, the cervix (the lower part of the uterus) naturally shortens late in pregnancy. However, in some women, the cervix shortens prematurely, around the fourth or fifth month of pregnancy, increasing the risk for preterm delivery.

In some cases, a healthcare provider may recommend measuring a pregnant woman's cervical length, especially if she previously had preterm labor or a preterm birth. Ultrasound scans may be used to measure cervical length and identify women with a shortened cervix.

"Incompetent"

The cervix normally remains closed during pregnancy. In some cases, the cervix starts to open early, before a fetus is ready to be born. Healthcare providers may refer to a cervix that begins to open as an "incompetent" cervix. The process of cervical opening is painless and unnoticeable, without labor contractions or cramping. Approximately 5 to 10 out of 1,000 pregnant women are diagnosed as having an incompetent cervix.

To try to prevent preterm birth, a doctor may place a stitch around the cervix to keep it closed. This procedure is called cervical cerclage. *Eunice Kennedy Shriver* National Institute of Child Health and Human Development (NICHD)-supported research has found that, in women with a prior preterm birth who have a short cervix, cerclage may improve the likelihood of a full-term delivery.

How Do Healthcare Providers Diagnose Preterm Labor?

If a woman is concerned that she could be showing signs of preterm labor, she should call her healthcare provider or go to the hospital to be evaluated. In particular, a woman should call if she has more than six contractions in an hour or if fluid or blood is leaking from the vagina.

Physical Exam

If a woman is experiencing signs of labor, the healthcare provider may perform a pelvic exam to see if:

- The membranes have ruptured

- The cervix is beginning to get thinner (efface)

- The cervix is beginning to open (dilate)

- Any of these situations could mean the woman is in preterm labor.

- Providers may also do an ultrasound exam and use a monitor to electronically record contractions and the fetal heart rate.

Fetal Fibronectin (fFN) Test

This test is used to detect whether the protein fetal fibronectin is being produced. fFN is like a biological "glue" between the uterine lining and the membrane that surrounds the fetus.

Normally fFN is detectable in the pregnant woman's secretions from the vagina and cervix early in the pregnancy (up to 22 weeks, or about 5 months) and again toward the end of the pregnancy (1–3 weeks before labor begins). It is usually not present between 24 and 34 weeks of pregnancy (5½–8½ months). If fFN is detected during this time, it may be a sign that the woman may be at risk of preterm labor and birth.

In most cases, the fFN test is performed on women who are showing signs of preterm labor. Testing for fFN can predict with about 50 percent accuracy which pregnant women showing signs of preterm labor are likely to have a preterm delivery. It is typically used for its negative predictive value, meaning that if it is negative, it is unlikely that a woman will deliver within the next 7 days.

What Treatments Are Used to Prevent Preterm Labor and Birth?

Treatment options for preventing preterm labor or birth are somewhat limited, in part because the cause of preterm labor or birth is often unknown. But there are a few options, described below.

- **Hormone treatment.** The only preventive drug therapy is progesterone, a hormone produced by the body during pregnancy, which is given to women at risk of preterm birth, such as those with a prior preterm birth. The NICHD's Maternal-Fetal Medicine Units Network (MFMU) found that progesterone given to women at risk of preterm birth due to a prior preterm birth reduces chances of a subsequent preterm birth by one-third. This preventive therapy is given beginning at 16 weeks of gestation and continues to 37 weeks of gestation. The treatment works among all ethnic groups and can improve outcomes for infants.

- **Cerclage.** A surgical procedure called cervical cerclage is sometimes used to try to prevent early labor in women who have an incompetent (weak) cervix and have experienced early pregnancy loss accompanied by a painless opening (dilation) of the cervix (the bottom part of the uterus). In the cerclage procedure, a doctor stitches the cervix closed. The stitch is then removed closer to the woman's due date.

- **Bed rest.** Contrary to expectations, confining the mother to bed rest does not help to prevent preterm birth. In fact, bed rest can make preterm birth even more likely among some women.

Women should discuss all of their treatment options—including the risks and benefits—with their healthcare providers. If possible, these discussions should occur during regular prenatal care visits, before there is any urgency, to allow for a complete discussion of all the issues.

Chapter 14

Complications of Prematurity

Chapter Contents

Section 14.1

Apnea of Prematurity

This section includes text excerpted from "Use of Methylxanthine
Therapies for the Treatment and Prevention of Apnea of
Prematurity," U.S. Department of Health and Human Services
(HHS), April 2014. Reviewed December 2017.

Apnea of prematurity (AOP) is a common complication of preterm
birth, which affects more than 80 percent of neonates with a birth
weight less than 1,000 grams. Methylxanthine therapies, including
caffeine and theophylline, are a mainstay in the treatment and prevention of AOP.

Apnea in preterm neonates occurs as a result of immature respiratory control. Episodes of AOP and its associated hypoxemia and bra-
dycardia are characterized by a pause in breathing for greater than 15
seconds, accompanied with an oxygen saturation (SpO2) less than 80
percent for more than 4 seconds, and a heart rate less than 67 percent
from baseline for more than 4 seconds in neonates less than 37 weeks'
gestation. The incidence of apneic episodes corresponds inversely to
the gestational age and birth weight of the neonate. Neonates born at
30–31 weeks' gestation experience AOP at a higher incidence rate than
neonates born at 32–33 or 34–35 weeks' gestation (54 percent versus
15 percent versus 7 percent). Additionally, there is an 84 percent incidence rate of apnea occurring in neonates weighing less than 1 kilo-
gram at birth, regardless of gestational age. Thus, preterm neonates
are at an increased risk of apnea than term neonates due to their low
gestational age and low birth weight.

Although AOP is a time-limited developmental disorder that
resolves with maturation, pharmaceutical interventions are frequently used to reduce the frequency of apneic events, decreasing
hypoxemic and bradycardic events. Methylxanthine therapies, such
as caffeine citrate and theophylline, are the primary pharmaceutical agents used in the treatment and prevention of AOP. Methylxanthines act as central nervous system stimulants and have been
proven to increase respiratory drive, lower the threshold of sensitivity to hypercapnia, and increase the contractility of the diaphragm.

Methylxanthines are frequently prescribed to prevent apneic episodes around the periextubation period and to facilitate weaning off of mechanical ventilation.

Methylxanthine therapies act as nonspecific adenosine receptor antagonists. Caffeine and theophylline are both substrates for cytochrome P450 (CYP) 1A2, which accounts for more than 95 percent of the primary metabolism of caffeine. Caffeine primarily undergoes hepatic N-demethylation to paraxanthine, theobromine, and theophylline. Theophylline (1,3-dimethylxanthine) is closely related to caffeine; however, it undergoes N-demethylation to give rise to 1-methylxanthine, which is also a product of CYP1A2-mediated metabolism of caffeine via the intermediate metabolite paraxanthine. In neonates, this typical metabolic pathway may be disrupted by retrograde conversion of theophylline to caffeine, which occurs via methylation. The standard dosing regimen of caffeine citrate includes an intravenous loading dose of 20 milligrams/kilograms followed by a maintenance dose of 5 milligrams/kilograms/day. The standard theophylline regimen involves an oral loading dose of 5–6 milligrams/kilograms, followed by a maintenance dose of 1–3 milligrams/kilograms/12 hours. Although caffeine and theophylline feature similar molecular structures, caffeine and theophylline display slight variations in their clinical efficacy when used in the treatment and prevention of AOP.

Section 14.2

Bronchopulmonary Dysplasia (BPD)

This section includes text excerpted from "What Is Bronchopulmonary Dysplasia?" National Heart, Lung, and Blood Institute (NHLBI), January 12, 2012. Reviewed December 2017.

What Is Bronchopulmonary Dysplasia (BPD)?

Bronchopulmonary dysplasia, or BPD, is a serious lung condition that affects infants. BPD mostly affects premature infants who need oxygen therapy (oxygen given through nasal prongs, a mask, or a breathing tube).

Most infants who develop BPD are born more than 10 weeks before their due dates, weigh less than 2 pounds (about 1,000 grams) at birth, and have breathing problems. Infections that occur before or shortly after birth also can contribute to BPD.

Some infants who have BPD may need long-term breathing support from nasal continuous positive airway pressure (NCPAP) machines or ventilators.

What Causes BPD?

BPD develops as a result of an infant's lungs becoming irritated or inflamed. The lungs of premature infants are fragile and often aren't fully developed. They can easily be irritated or injured within hours or days of birth. Many factors can damage premature infants' lungs.

Ventilation

Newborns who have breathing problems or can't breathe on their own may need ventilator support. Ventilators are machines that use pressure to blow air into the airways and lungs.

Although ventilator support can help premature infants survive, the machine's pressure might irritate and harm the babies' lungs. For this reason, doctors only recommend ventilator support when necessary.

High Levels of Oxygen

Newborns who have breathing problems might need oxygen therapy (oxygen given through nasal prongs, a mask, or a breathing tube). This treatment helps the infants' organs get enough oxygen to work well.

However, high levels of oxygen can inflame the lining of the lungs and injure the airways. Also, high levels of oxygen can slow lung development in premature infants.

Infections

Infections can inflame the lungs. As a result, the airways narrow, which makes it harder for premature infants to breathe. Lung infections also increase the babies need for extra oxygen and breathing support.

Heredity

Studies show that heredity may play a role in causing BPD. More studies are needed to confirm this finding.

Who Is at Risk for BPD?

The more premature an infant is and the lower his or her birth weight, the greater the risk of BPD.

Most infants who develop BPD are born more than 10 weeks before their due dates, weigh less than 2 pounds (about 1,000 grams) at birth, and have breathing problems. Infections that occur before or shortly after birth also can contribute to BPD.

The number of babies who have BPD is higher now than in the past. This is because of advances in care that help more premature infants survive.

Many babies who develop BPD are born with serious respiratory distress syndrome (RDS). However, some babies who have mild RDS or don't have RDS also develop BPD. These babies often have very low birth weights and one or more other conditions, such as patent ductus arteriosus (PDA) and sepsis.

PDA is a heart problem that occurs soon after birth in some babies. Sepsis is a serious bacterial infection in the bloodstream.

What Are the Signs and Symptoms of BPD?

Many babies who develop BPD are born with serious RDS. The signs and symptoms of RDS at birth are:

- Rapid, shallow breathing

- Sharp pulling in of the chest below and between the ribs with each breath

- Grunting sounds

- Flaring of the nostrils

Babies who have RDS are treated with surfactant replacement therapy. They also may need oxygen therapy (oxygen given through nasal prongs, a mask, or a breathing tube).

Shortly after birth, some babies who have RDS also are treated with nasal continuous positive airway pressure (NCPAP) or ventilators (machines that support breathing).

Often, the symptoms of RDS start to improve slowly after about a week. However, some babies get worse and need more oxygen or breathing support from NCPAP or a ventilator.

A first sign of BPD is when premature infants—usually those born more than 10 weeks early—still need oxygen therapy by the time they reach their original due dates. These babies are diagnosed with BPD.

197

Infants who have severe BPD may have trouble feeding, which can lead to delayed growth. These babies also may develop:

- **Pulmonary hypertension (PH).** PH is increased pressure in the pulmonary arteries. These arteries carry blood from the heart to the lungs to pick up oxygen.

- **Cor pulmonale.** Cor pulmonale is failure of the right side of the heart. Ongoing high blood pressure in the pulmonary arteries and the lower right chamber of the heart causes this condition.

How Is BPD Diagnosed?

Infants who are born early—usually more than 10 weeks before their due dates—and still need oxygen therapy by the time they reach their original due dates are diagnosed with BPD.

BPD can be mild, moderate, or severe. The diagnosis depends on how much extra oxygen a baby needs at the time of his or her original due date. It also depends on how long the baby needs oxygen therapy.

To help confirm a diagnosis of BPD, doctors may recommend tests, such as:

- **Chest X-ray.** A chest X-ray takes pictures of the structures inside the chest, such as the heart and lungs. In severe cases of BPD, this test may show large areas of air and signs of inflammation or infection in the lungs. A chest X-ray also can detect problems (such as a collapsed lung) and show whether the lungs aren't developing normally.

- **Blood tests.** Blood tests are used to see whether an infant has enough oxygen in his or her blood. Blood tests also can help determine whether an infection is causing an infant's breathing problems.

- **Echocardiography.** This test uses sound waves to create a moving picture of the heart. Echocardiography is used to rule out heart defects or pulmonary hypertension as the cause of an infant's breathing problems.

How Is BPD Treated?

Preventive Measures

If your doctor thinks you're going to give birth too early, he or she may give you injections of a corticosteroid medicine. The medicine can speed up surfactant production in your baby. Surfactant is a liquid that coats the inside of the lungs. It helps keep the lungs open so your infant can breathe in air once he or she is born.

Corticosteroids also can help your baby's lungs, brain, and kidneys develop more quickly while he or she is in the womb. Premature babies who have very low birth weights also might be given corticosteroids within the first few days of birth. Doctors sometimes prescribe inhaled nitric oxide shortly after birth for babies who have very low birth weights. This treatment can help improve the babies' lung function. These preventive measures may help reduce infants' risk of RDS, which can lead to BPD.

Section 14.3

Intraventricular Hemorrhage (IVH) of the Newborn

This section includes text excerpted from "Pathogenesis and Prevention of Intraventricular Hemorrhage," U.S. Department of Health and Human Services (HHS), March 2014. Reviewed December 2017.

Intraventricular hemorrhage (IVH) is a major neurological complication of prematurity. Pathogenesis of intraventricular hemorrhage is attributed to built-in fragility of germinal matrix vasculature and to the fluctuation in the cerebral blood flow. This fluctuation results from a wide range of respiratory and hemodynamic instability associated with the preterm infants. Prenatal glucocorticoid exposure remains the most effective means of preventing IVH. Therapies targeted to enhance the stability of the germinal matrix vasculature and minimize fluctuation in the cerebral blood flow might lead to more effective strategies in preventing IVH.

In the United States, about 12,000 premature infants develop intraventricular hemorrhage (IVH) every year. The incidence of moderate-to-severe IVH has remained almost stationary during the last two decades. IVH is a major problem in premature infants, as a large number of them develop neurologic sequelae. Approximately 50–75 percent of preterm survivors with IVH develop cerebral palsy, mental retardation, and/or hydrocephalus. Approximately, a quarter of nondisabled survivors develop psychiatric disorders and problems with executive function. According to the U.S. Census Bureau and the *Eunice Kennedy Shriver* National Institute of Child Health and Human Development (NICHD) Neonatal Research Network, over 3600 new cases of mental retardation each year are children who were born premature and suffered IVH. Hence, IVH and its resultant neurologic and psychiatric sequelae continue to be a major public health concern worldwide.

IVH usually starts in the periventricular germinal matrix. The subependymal germinal matrix is highly vascular and is selectively vulnerable to hemorrhage. After 24 gestational weeks (gw), thickness of the germinal matrix decreases, and it almost disappears by 36–37 gw. When hemorrhage in the germinal matrix is large, the underlying ependyma breaks and germinal matrix hemorrhage progresses to IVH, as blood fills the lateral cerebral ventricle.

Prenatal Pharmacological Treatments to Prevent IVH

Glucocorticoids (GCs)

In the United States, the preterm birth rate is about 12.5 percent and approximately 75 percent women in premature labor with gestational age of less than 34 weeks are treated with either betamethasone or dexamethasone. A number of studies have confirmed that prenatal Glucocorticoids (GC) reduces both severity and incidence of IVH. Prenatal GC stops angiogenesis in the germinal matrix microvasculature and thus trims the undeveloped and fragile vasculature, which are vulnerable to hemorrhage. Thus, GC exposure stabilizes the blood-brain barrier (BBB) of the germinal matrix. Moreover, it reduces the incidence and severity of respiratory distress syndrome, which might minimize fluctuation in the cerebral blood flow (CBF). Postnatal betamethasone (0.1 mg/kg) also reduces cerebral flow velocity possibly by exerting a vasoconstrictor effect on cerebral vessels in preterm infants. Similarly, prenatal betamethasone has been shown to reduce cerebral blood flow by increasing cerebrovascular resistance in fetal sheep model.

The optimal effects of prenatal GC have been observed after a complete course of 2 doses of betamethasone or 4 doses of dexamethasone when administered within a week of delivery of the premature newborn. However, benefits have also been noted with incomplete courses of GCs. Comparison of the two GCs—betamethasone and dexamethasone—has not conclusively shown superiority of one over the other and clinicians should choose whatever is available. Betamethasone exposed infants exhibit less severe respiratory distress syndrome, but more IVH, compared to prenatal dexamethasone treated infants. There has been concern that prenatal dexamethasone might increase the incidence of periventricular leukomalacia. However, a subsequent study on a larger population clearly showed that there is no difference in the incidence of cystic PVL between dexamethasone and betamethasone exposed infants. Importantly, prenatal betamethasone is associated with a reduced risk for neonatal death compared with dexamethasone. Together, there is no recommendation for the use of one GC over the other, despite multiple clinical trials undertaken. Another key issue related to the use of prenatal steroid is single versus repeated course. Unfortunately, there is no agreement among the experts on the advantage of single versus multiple course of GCs. There are concerns that multiple course of prenatal GC might have adverse effects on brain and other organ systems.

Phenobarbital and Magnesium Sulfate

As etiopathogenesis of IVH was more mysterious in 80s than now, a number of agents without a concrete rationale were tried to prevent IVH. Phenobarbital and vitamin K are important to mention here, as these medications attracted the attention of investigators. Initial studies showed some protective effect of phenobarbital, however, subsequent clinical trials failed to confirm the protective effect of phenobarbital in preventing IVH. Maternal treatment of vitamin K or magnesium sulfate to prevent IVH did not demonstrate any benefit either.

Postnatal Pharmacological Treatment to Prevent IVH

Indomethacin

Indomethacin, commonly used in premature neonates to close patent ductus arteriosus, has been shown to prevent IVH in several clinical trials. Indomethacin, a nonselective cyclo-oxygenase (COX) inhibitor, weakens cerebral vascular hyperemic responses induced by hypoxia, hypercapnia, hypertension, and asphyxia. It reduces changes in the BBB permeability after cerebral ischemia and promotes maturation of basement membrane. The maturation of basal lamina upon indomethacin treatment can be attributed to COX2 inhibition, which suppresses angiogenesis and matures the germinal matrix vasculature.

In a number of clinical trials, indomethacin treatment has shown short-term benefit of reducing the incidence of IVH. Secondary analyses of a multicenter study based on gender have shown that indomethacin treatment reduces the rate of IVH in male infants, but not in female infants. However, another study on a larger population of preterm infants showed just a weak differential effect of indomethacin by sex. Since indomethacin reduces the occurrence of IVH, it was anticipated that this treatment would improve the neurodevelopment outcome of the infants. However, indomethacin treatment failed to reduce the rate of cerebral palsy, deafness and blindness on long-term follow-up. A meta-analyses of 19 clinical trials also did not show any improvement in the long-term outcome of indomethacin treated infants. Together, indomethacin prophylaxis has immediate benefits of reduction in symptomatic patent ductus arteriosus, and severe IVH; however, this does not impact long-term neurodevelopmental outcomes. Hence, indomethacin is not recommended for routine prophylaxis against IVH. However, indomethacin is still being used in some neonatal units depending on clinical circumstances and personal preferences.

Ibuprofen is another nonselective COX inhibitor that has shown promise in closing patent ductus arteriosus. This compound does not reduce CBF, in contrast to indomethacin. More importantly, ibuprofen does not prevent IVH in premature infants.

Section 14.4

Jaundice and Kernicterus

This section includes text excerpted from "Facts about Jaundice and Kernicterus," Centers for Disease Control and Prevention (CDC), November 7, 2016.

Jaundice is the yellow color seen in the skin of many newborns. Jaundice happens when a chemical called bilirubin builds up in the baby's blood. During pregnancy, the mother's liver removes bilirubin for the baby, but after birth the baby's liver must remove the bilirubin. In some babies, the liver might not be developed enough to efficiently get rid of bilirubin. When too much bilirubin builds up in a new baby's body, the skin and whites of the eyes might look yellow. This yellow coloring is called jaundice.

When severe jaundice goes untreated for too long, it can cause a condition called kernicterus. Kernicterus is a type of brain damage that can result from high levels of bilirubin in a baby's blood. It can cause athetoid cerebral palsy and hearing loss. Kernicterus also causes problems with vision and teeth and sometimes can cause intellectual disabilities. Early detection and management of jaundice can prevent kernicterus.

Signs and Symptoms

Jaundice usually appears first on the face and then moves to the chest, belly, arms, and legs as bilirubin levels get higher. The whites of the eyes can also look yellow. Jaundice can be harder to see in babies with darker skin color. The baby's doctor or nurse can test how much bilirubin is in the baby's blood.

See your baby's doctor the same day if your baby:

- Is very yellow or orange (skin color changes start from the head and spread to the toes).

- Is hard to wake up or will not sleep at all.

- Is not breastfeeding or sucking from a bottle well.

- Is very fussy.

- Does not have enough wet or dirty diapers.

Get emergency medical help if your baby:

- Is crying inconsolably or with a high pitch.

- Is arched like a bow (the head or neck and heels are bent backward and the body forward).

- Has a stiff, limp, or floppy body.

- Has strange eye movements.

Diagnosis

Before leaving the hospital with your newborn, you can ask the doctor or nurse about a jaundice bilirubin test.

A doctor or nurse may check the baby's bilirubin using a light meter that is placed on the baby's head. This results in a transcutaneous bilirubin (TcB) level. If it is high, a blood test will likely be ordered.

The best way to accurately measure bilirubin is with a small blood sample from the baby's heel. This results in a total serum bilirubin (TSB) level. If the level is high, based upon the baby's age in hours and other risk factors, treatment will likely follow. Repeat blood samples will also likely be taken to ensure that the TSB decreases with the prescribed treatment.

Bilirubin levels are usually the highest when the baby is 3–5 days old. At a minimum, babies should be checked for jaundice every 8–12 hours in the first 48 hours of life and again before 5 days of age.

Treatment

When being treated for high bilirubin levels, the baby will be undressed and put under special lights. The lights will not hurt the baby. This can be done in the hospital or even at home. The baby's milk intake may also need to be increased. In some cases, if the baby has very high bilirubin levels, the doctor will do a blood exchange transfusion. Jaundice is generally treated before brain damage is a concern. Putting the baby in sunlight is not recommended as a safe way of treating jaundice.

Risk Factors

About 60 percent of all babies have jaundice. Some babies are more likely to have severe jaundice and higher bilirubin levels than others. Babies with any of the following risk factors need close monitoring and early jaundice management:

Preterm Babies

Babies born before 37 weeks, or 8.5 months, of pregnancy might have jaundice because their liver is not fully developed. The young liver might not be able to get rid of so much bilirubin.

Babies with Darker Skin Color

Jaundice may be missed or not recognized in a baby with darker skin color. Checking the gums and inner lips may detect jaundice. If there is any doubt, a bilirubin test should be done.

East Asian or Mediterranean Descent

A baby born to an East Asian or Mediterranean family is at a higher risk of becoming jaundiced. Also, some families inherit conditions (such as G6PD deficiency), and their babies are more likely to get jaundice.

Feeding Difficulties

A baby who is not eating, wetting, or stooling well in the first few days of life is more likely to get jaundice.

Sibling with Jaundice

A baby with a sister or brother that had jaundice is more likely to develop jaundice.

Bruising

A baby with bruises at birth is more likely to get jaundice. A bruise forms when blood leaks out of a blood vessel and causes the skin to look black and blue. The healing of large bruises can cause high levels of bilirubin and your baby might get jaundice.

Blood Type

Women with an O blood type or Rh negative blood factor might have babies with higher bilirubin levels. A mother with Rh incompatibility should be given Rhogam.

If You're Concerned

If you think your baby has jaundice you should call and visit your baby's doctor right away. Ask your baby's doctor or nurse about a jaundice bilirubin test. If your baby does have jaundice, it is important to take jaundice seriously and stick to the follow-up plan for appointments and recommended care. Make sure your baby is getting enough to eat. The process of removing waste also removes bilirubin in your baby's blood. If you are breastfeeding, you should nurse the baby at least 8–12 times a day for the first few days. This will help you make enough milk for the baby and will help keep the baby's bilirubin level down. If you are having trouble breastfeeding, ask your doctor, nurse, or a lactation coach for help.

Section 14.5

Necrotizing Enterocolitis

This section includes text excerpted from "Necrotizing Enterocolitis
(NEC)—Condition Information," *Eunice Kennedy Shriver* National
Institute of Child Health and Human Development (NICHD),
December 4, 2012. Reviewed December 2017.

What Is Necrotizing Enterocolitis (NEC)?

Necrotizing enterocolitis, or NEC, is a common disease of the intestinal tract in which the tissue lining the intestine becomes inflamed,
dies, and can slough off. The condition typically affects infants who
are born preterm or who are already sick, and it usually occurs before
the newborn leaves the hospital. NEC usually begins within the first
2–3 weeks after birth in preterm infants who otherwise appear to be
getting healthier.

What Are the Symptoms of NEC?

In NEC, some of the tissue lining an infant's intestine becomes
diseased and can die. The bacteria in the infant's intestine can then
penetrate the dead or decaying intestinal tissue, infect the wall of the
intestine, and enter the bloodstream, causing systemic or bloodstream
infection. The surviving tissue becomes swollen and inflamed; as a
result, the infant is unable to digest food or otherwise move food through
the digestive tract. The symptoms of NEC can develop over a period of
days or appear suddenly. Commonly reported symptoms include:

- Poor tolerance of feeding (not being able to digest food)

- Bloating or swelling of the stomach (abdominal distention)

- Stomach discoloration, usually bluish or reddish

- Pain when someone touches the abdomen

- Blood in the stools or a change in their volume or frequency

- Diarrhea, with change in the color and consistency of the stool,
  often containing frank (visible) blood

- Decreased activity (lethargy)

- Vomiting greenish-yellow liquid

- Inability to maintain normal temperature

- Episodes of low heart rate or apnea, a temporary stop in breathing

- In advanced cases, the blood pressure may drop and the pulse may become weak. Infants may develop fluid in the abdominal cavity or infection of the tissue lining the stomach (a condition called peritonitis), or they could go into shock. The affected area of the intestine may develop a hole or perforation in the wall requiring emergency surgery. Pressure from the abdomen can cause a severe difficulty in breathing. In this case, the infant may need support from a breathing machine, or respirator.

How Many Infants Are Affected by or at Risk of NEC?

According to a review of evidence, all newborn infants born preterm (before 37 weeks of pregnancy) or born with a low birth weight (less than 2,500 grams, or about 5.5 pounds) are at increased risk for NEC. The smaller the infant or the more premature the delivery, the greater the risk.

The *Eunice Kennedy Shriver* National Institute of Child Health and Human Development (NICHD) estimates that NEC affects about 9,000 of the 480,000 infants born preterm each year in the United States.

The population most at risk for NEC is increasing because with technological advances in care the number of very low birth weight infants who survive continues to grow. The percentage of very low birth weight infants who develop NEC remains steady, however, at about 7 percent.

NEC continues to be one of the leading causes of illness and death among preterm infants. Fifteen to forty percent of infants with NEC die from the disease.

Although NEC mostly occurs in preterm infants, it occasionally occurs in infants born at term. One study found that about 9 percent of all NEC cases that occurred in one children's hospital over 30 years were in full-term infants. Full-term infants with NEC often have another serious illness or risk factor, such as congenital heart disease or restricted growth in the womb. NEC may also have a different disease process in full-term versus preterm infants.

How Do Healthcare Providers Diagnose NEC?

The development of symptoms such as the inability to tolerate feeding, bloody stools, or distention of the abdomen could indicate NEC. The condition is usually confirmed by an abdominal X-ray. If the X-ray reveals a "bubbly" appearance in the wall of the intestine or air outside the infant's intestine (in the peritoneal cavity) the diagnosis is confirmed. Other X-ray signs include air in a vein of the liver called the portal vein, swollen intestines, or a lack of gas in the abdomen.

Other useful tests include looking for blood in the infant's stool. If necessary, the healthcare provider can use a chemical that reveals blood not visible to the eye.

In addition, healthcare providers may test the infant's blood to check for infection, which could suggest NEC. They may also use a blood test for lactic acid, which can indicate whether the body is getting enough oxygen or an infection that increases the metabolic rate and production of lactic acid.

Blood and stool tests, combined with the abdominal X-ray, can help the healthcare provider determine the seriousness of the infant's condition.

What Are the Common Treatments for NEC?

The treatment for NEC varies with the severity of the disease. Three stages (Bell stages) have been defined for NEC.

- **Stage 1, suspected NEC**, includes symptoms such as bloody stools, diminished activity (lethargy), slow heart rate, an unstable temperature, mild abdominal bloating, and vomiting.

- **Stage 2, definite NEC**, includes all the symptoms of stage 1 as well as slightly reduced blood platelet levels, a slight excess of lactic acid, no bowel sounds, pain when the abdomen is touched, reduced or no intestinal movement, and the growth of gas-filled spaces in the walls of the intestine.

- **Stage 3, advanced NEC**, includes the symptoms of stages 1 and 2 plus periods of not breathing, low blood pressure, a lowered number of certain white blood cells, blood clot formation, a stop in urination, inflammation of tissue in the abdomen, increased pain when the abdomen is touched, redness in the abdomen, a buildup of fluid and gas in the abdominal cavity, and excess acid.

The treatment for stage 1 patients includes vigorous supportive care, resting the intestine by feeding through an intravenous tube instead of the mouth, and continued diagnostic and monitoring tests to ensure that the disease is not progressing. Treatments for stage 2 patients include continuation of stage 1 treatments and the use of antibiotics. Emergency surgery is sometimes performed for stage 3 patients.

Other treatments offered at all stages of NEC include:

- Inserting a tube through the nasal passages or mouth into the infant's stomach to remove air and fluid

- Taking blood samples to look for bacteria and giving antibiotic treatment through an intravenous tube

- Measuring and monitoring the infant's belly for swelling. If it becomes so swollen that it interferes with breathing, the infant may be given oxygen or put on a ventilator.

Many infants respond to treatment within 72 hours, and physicians may decide to put these infants back on regular feeding. (Generally, infants are not fed for up to 2 weeks or longer with confirmed NEC.) However, if the condition worsens or a hole develops in the intestine or bowel, surgery may be needed.

What Causes NEC?

The cause of NEC is not well known. In premature infants, the cause may be related to the immaturity of the child's digestive system. NEC involves infection and inflammation in the child's gut, which may stem from the growth of dangerous bacteria or the growth of bacteria in parts of the intestine where they do not usually live.

Other possible causes of NEC that are related to having an immature gut include:

- Inability to digest food and pass it through, allowing a buildup of toxic substances

- Inadequate blood circulation to the gut

- Inability of the infant's digestive system to keep out dangerous bacteria

- Inadequate ability of the immature intestine to provide an adequate structural barrier to bacteria. This barrier usually matures in the unborn infant starting about week 26 (11–12 weeks before a full-term birth).

- The inability of the immature gut to secrete its normal biochemical defenses

Because premature infants may lack any or all of these abilities, they may be more vulnerable to the types of inflammation that lead to NEC.

Full-term infants who get NEC almost always do so because they are already sick or, in some cases, have a low body weight for their gestational age. They might have congenital heart disease or have had vascular bypass surgery, for example, possibly affecting the blood supply to the intestines.

Full-term infants are usually diagnosed with NEC earlier than are premature infants (day 5 versus day 13 on average), possibly because they start feeding earlier. The condition is equally life threatening in premature and full-term infants.

A NICHD-supported study found that a common type of medication, sometimes given to infants for acid reflux and called "H2-blockers," was associated with a slight increase in the risk of NEC in preterm infants.

Section 14.6

Respiratory Distress Syndrome (RDS)

This section includes text excerpted from "What Is Respiratory Distress Syndrome?" National Heart, Lung, and Blood Institute (NHLBI), January 24, 2012. Reviewed December 2017.

What Is Respiratory Distress Syndrome (RDS)?

Respiratory distress syndrome (RDS) is a breathing disorder that affects newborns. RDS rarely occurs in full-term infants. The disorder is more common in premature infants born about 6 weeks or more before their due dates.

RDS is more common in premature infants because their lungs aren't able to make enough surfactant. Surfactant is a liquid that coats the inside of the lungs. It helps keep them open so that infants can breathe in air once they're born.

Without enough surfactant, the lungs collapse and the infant has to work hard to breathe. He or she might not be able to breathe in enough oxygen to support the body's organs. The lack of oxygen can damage the baby's brain and other organs if proper treatment isn't given. Most babies who develop RDS show signs of breathing problems and a lack of oxygen at birth or within the first few hours that follow.

What Causes RDS?

The main cause of RDS is a lack of surfactant in the lungs. Surfactant is a liquid that coats the inside of the lungs.

A fetus's lungs start making surfactant during the third trimester of pregnancy (weeks 26 through labor and delivery). The substance coats the insides of the air sacs in the lungs. This helps keep the lungs open so breathing can occur after birth. Without enough surfactant, the lungs will likely collapse when the infant exhales (breathes out). The infant then has to work harder to breathe. He or she might not be able to get enough oxygen to support the body's organs. Some full-term infants develop RDS because they have faulty genes that affect how their bodies make surfactant.

Who Is at Risk for RDS?

Certain factors may increase the risk that your infant will have RDS. These factors include:

- Premature delivery. The earlier your baby is born, the greater his or her risk for RDS. Most cases of RDS occur in babies born before 28 weeks of pregnancy.

- Stress during your baby's delivery, especially if you lose a lot of blood.

- Infection.

- Your having diabetes.

Your baby also is at greater risk for RDS if you require an emergency cesarean delivery (C-section) before your baby is full term. You may need an emergency C-section because of a condition, such as a detached placenta, that puts you or your infant at risk.

Planned C-sections that occur before a baby's lungs have fully matured also can increase the risk of RDS. Your doctor can do tests before delivery that show whether it's likely that your baby's lungs are fully developed. These tests assess the age of the fetus or lung maturity.

211

What Are the Signs and Symptoms of RDS?

Signs and symptoms of RDS usually occur at birth or within the first few hours that follow. They include:

- Rapid, shallow breathing
- Sharp pulling in of the chest below and between the ribs with each breath
- Grunting sounds
- Flaring of the nostrils

The infant also may have pauses in breathing that last for a few seconds. This condition is called apnea.

RDS Complications

Depending on the severity of an infant's RDS, he or she may develop other medical problems.

Lung Complications

Lung complications may include a collapsed lung (atelectasis), leakage of air from the lung into the chest cavity (pneumothorax), and bleeding in the lung (hemorrhage).

Some of the life-saving treatments used for RDS may cause bronchopulmonary dysplasia, another breathing disorder.

Blood and Blood Vessel Complications

Infants who have RDS may develop sepsis, an infection of the bloodstream. This infection can be life threatening.

Lack of oxygen may prevent a fetal blood vessel called the ductus arteriosus from closing after birth as it should. This condition is called patent ductus arteriosus, or PDA.

The ductus arteriosus connects a lung artery to a heart artery. If it remains open, it can strain the heart and increase blood pressure in the lung arteries.

Other Complications

Complications of RDS also may include blindness and other eye problems and a bowel disease called necrotizing enterocolitis. Infants who have severe RDS can develop kidney failure.

Some infants who have RDS develop bleeding in the brain. This bleeding can delay mental development. It also can cause mental retardation or cerebral palsy.

How Is RDS Diagnosed?

RDS is common in premature infants. Thus, doctors usually recognize and begin treating the disorder as soon as babies are born.

Doctors also do several tests to rule out other conditions that could be causing an infant's breathing problems. The tests also can confirm that the doctors have diagnosed the condition correctly.

The tests include:

- **Chest X-ray.** A chest X-ray creates a of the structures inside the chest, such as the heart and lungs. This test can show whether your infant has signs of RDS. A chest X-ray also can detect problems, such as a collapsed lung, that may require urgent treatment.

- **Blood tests.** Blood tests are used to see whether an infant has enough oxygen in his or her blood. Blood tests also can help find out whether an infection is causing the infant's breathing problems.

- **Echocardiography (echo).** This test uses sound waves to create a moving picture of the heart. Echo is used to rule out heart defects as the cause of an infant's breathing problems.

How Is RDS Treated?

Treatment for RDS usually begins as soon as an infant is born, sometimes in the delivery room.

Most infants who show signs of RDS are quickly moved to a neonatal intensive care unit (NICU). There they receive around-the-clock treatment from healthcare professionals who specialize in treating premature infants.

The most important treatments for RDS are:

- Surfactant replacement therapy.

- Breathing support from a ventilator or nasal continuous positive airway pressure (NCPAP) machine. These machines help premature infants breathe better.

- Oxygen therapy.

Surfactant Replacement Therapy

Surfactant is a liquid that coats the inside of the lungs. It helps keep them open so that an infant can breathe in air once he or she is born.

Babies who have RDS are given surfactant until their lungs are able to start making the substance on their own. Surfactant usually is given through a breathing tube. The tube allows the surfactant to go directly into the baby's lungs.

Once the surfactant is given, the breathing tube is connected to a ventilator, or the baby may get breathing support from NCPAP.

Surfactant often is given right after birth in the delivery room to try to prevent or treat RDS. It also may be given several times in the days that follow, until the baby is able to breathe better.

Some women are given medicines called corticosteroids during pregnancy. These medicines can speed up surfactant production and lung development in a fetus. Even if you had these medicines, your infant may still need surfactant replacement therapy after birth.

Breathing Support

Infants who have RDS often need breathing support until their lungs start making enough surfactant. The ventilator was connected to a breathing tube that ran through the infant's mouth or nose into the windpipe.

Nowadays, more and more infants are receiving breathing support from NCPAP. NCPAP gently pushes air into the baby's lungs through prongs placed in the infant's nostrils.

Oxygen Therapy

Infants who have breathing problems may get oxygen therapy. Oxygen is given through a ventilator or NCPAP machine, or through a tube in the nose. This treatment ensures that the infant's organs get enough oxygen to work well.

Other Treatments

Other treatments for RDS include medicines, supportive therapy, and treatment for PDA. PDA is a condition that affects some premature infants.

Medicines

Doctors often give antibiotics to infants who have RDS to control infections (if the doctors suspect that an infant has an infection).

Supportive Therapy

Treatment in the NICU helps limit stress on babies and meet their basic needs of warmth, nutrition, and protection. Such treatment may include:

- Using a radiant warmer or incubator to keep infants warm and reduce the risk of infection.

- Ongoing monitoring of blood pressure, heart rate, breathing, and temperature through sensors taped to the babies' bodies.

- Using sensors on fingers or toes to check the amount of oxygen in the infant's blood.

- Giving fluids and nutrients through needles or tubes inserted into the infants' veins. This helps prevent malnutrition and promotes growth. Nutrition is critical to the growth and development of the lungs. Later, babies may be given breast milk or infant formula through feeding tubes that are passed through their noses or mouths and into their throats.

- Checking fluid intake to make sure that fluid doesn't buildup in the babies' lungs.

Treatment for PDA

PDA is a possible complication of RDS. In this condition, a fetal blood vessel called the ductus arteriosus doesn't close after birth as it should.

The ductus arteriosus connects a lung artery to a heart artery. If it remains open, it can strain the heart and increase blood pressure in the lung arteries.

How Can RDS Be Prevented?

Taking steps to ensure a healthy pregnancy might prevent your infant from being born before his or her lungs have fully developed. These steps include:

- Seeing your doctor regularly during your pregnancy

- Following a healthy diet

- Avoiding tobacco smoke, alcohol, and illegal drugs

- Managing any medical conditions you have

- Preventing infections

If you're having a planned cesarean delivery (C-section), your doctor can do tests before delivery to show whether it's likely that your baby's lungs are fully developed. These tests assess the age of the fetus or lung maturity.

Your doctor may give you injections of a corticosteroid medicine if he or she thinks you may give birth too early. This medicine can speed up surfactant production and development of the lungs, brain, and kidneys in your baby.

Treatment with corticosteroids can reduce your baby's risk of RDS. If the baby does develop RDS, it will probably be fairly mild.

Corticosteroid treatment also can reduce the chances that your baby will have bleeding in the brain.

Living with RDS

Caring for a premature infant can be challenging. You may experience:

- Emotional distress, including feelings of guilt, anger, and depression.

- Anxiety about your baby's future.

- A feeling of a lack of control over the situation.

- Financial stress.

- Problems relating to your baby while he or she is in the neonatal intensive care unit (NICU).

- Fatigue (tiredness).

- Frustration that you can't breastfeed your infant right away. (You can pump and store your breast milk for later use.)

Take Steps to Manage Your Situation

You can take steps to help yourself during this difficult time. For example, take care of your health so that you have enough energy to deal with the situation.

Learn as much as you can about what goes on in the NICU. You can help your baby during his or her stay there and begin to bond with the baby before he or she comes home.

Learn as much as you can about your infant's condition and what's involved in daily care. This will allow you to ask questions and feel more confident about your ability to care for your baby at home.

Seek out support from family, friends, and hospital staff. Ask the case manager or social worker at the hospital about what you'll need after your baby leaves the hospital. The doctors and nurses can assist with questions about your infant's care. Also, you may want to ask whether your community has a support group for parents of premature infants.

Parents are encouraged to visit their baby in the NICU as much as possible. Spend time talking to your baby and holding and touching him or her (when allowed).

Ongoing Care for Your Infant

Your baby may need special care after leaving the NICU, including:

- Special hearing and eye exams
- Speech or physical therapy
- Specialty care for other medical problems caused by premature birth

Talk to your child's doctor about ongoing care for your infant and any other medical concerns you have.

Section 14.7

Retinopathy of Prematurity (ROP)

This section includes text excerpted from "Facts about Retinopathy of Prematurity (ROP)," National Eye Institute (NEI), June 2014. Reviewed December 2017.

What Is Retinopathy of Prematurity (ROP)?

Retinopathy of prematurity (ROP) is a potentially blinding eye disorder that primarily affects premature infants weighing about 2¾ pounds (1250 grams) or less that are born before 31 weeks of gestation (A full-term pregnancy has a gestation of 38–42 weeks). The smaller a baby is at birth, the more likely that baby is to develop

ROP. This disorder—which usually develops in both eyes—is one of the most common causes of visual loss in childhood and can lead to lifelong vision impairment and blindness. ROP was first diagnosed in 1942.

How Many Infants Have ROP?

With advances in neonatal care, smaller and more premature infants are being saved. These infants are at a much higher risk for ROP. Not all babies who are premature develop ROP. There are approximately 3.9 million infants born in the United States each year; of those, about 28,000 weigh 2¾ pounds or less. About 14,000–16,000 of these infants are affected by some degree of ROP. The disease improves and leaves no permanent damage in milder cases of ROP. About 90 percent of all infants with ROP are in the milder category and do not need treatment. However, infants with more severe disease can develop impaired vision or even blindness. About 1,100–1,500 infants annually develop ROP that is severe enough to require medical treatment. About 400–600 infants each year in the United States become legally blind from ROP.

Are There Different Stages of ROP?

Yes. ROP is classified in five stages, ranging from mild (stage I) to severe (stage V):

- **Stage I**—Mildly abnormal blood vessel growth. Many children who develop stage I improve with no treatment and eventually develop normal vision. The disease resolves on its own without further progression.

- **Stage II**—Moderately abnormal blood vessel growth. Many children who develop stage II improve with no treatment and eventually develop normal vision. The disease resolves on its own without further progression.

- **Stage III**—Severely abnormal blood vessel growth. The abnormal blood vessels grow toward the center of the eye instead of following their normal growth pattern along the surface of the retina. Some infants who develop stage III improve with no treatment and eventually develop normal vision. However, when infants have a certain degree of Stage III and "plus disease" develops, treatment is considered. "Plus disease" means that the blood vessels of the retina have become enlarged and twisted, indicating a worsening of the disease. Treatment at this point has a good chance of preventing retinal detachment.

- **Stage IV**—Partially detached retina. Traction from the scar produced by bleeding, abnormal vessels pulls the retina away from the wall of the eye.

- **Stage V**—Completely detached retina and the end stage of the disease. If the eye is left alone at this stage, the baby can have severe visual impairment and even blindness.

Most babies who develop ROP have stages I or II. However, in a small number of babies, ROP worsens, sometimes very rapidly. Untreated ROP threatens to destroy vision.

Can ROP Cause Other Complications?

Yes. Infants with ROP are considered to be at higher risk for developing certain eye problems later in life, such as retinal detachment, myopia (nearsightedness), strabismus (crossed eyes), amblyopia (lazy eye), and glaucoma. In many cases, these eye problems can be treated or controlled.

What Causes ROP?

ROP occurs when abnormal blood vessels grow and spread throughout the retina, the tissue that lines the back of the eye. These abnormal blood vessels are fragile and can leak, scarring the retina and pulling it out of position. This causes a retinal detachment. Retinal detachment is the main cause of visual impairment and blindness in ROP.

Several complex factors may be responsible for the development of ROP. The eye starts to develop at about 16 weeks of pregnancy, when the blood vessels of the retina begin to form at the optic nerve in the back of the eye. The blood vessels grow gradually toward the edges of the developing retina, supplying oxygen and nutrients. During the last 12 weeks of a pregnancy, the eye develops rapidly. When a baby is born full-term, the retinal blood vessel growth is mostly complete (The retina usually finishes growing a few weeks to a month after birth). But if a baby is born prematurely, before these blood vessels have reached the edges of the retina, normal vessel growth may stop. The edges of the retina, the periphery may not get enough oxygen and nutrients.

Scientists believe that the periphery of the retina then sends out signals to other areas of the retina for nourishment. As a result, new abnormal vessels begin to grow. These new blood vessels are fragile and weak and can bleed, leading to retinal scarring. When these scars shrink, they pull on the retina, causing it to detach from the back of the eye.

Are There Other Risk Factors for ROP?

In addition to birth weight and how early a baby is born, other factors contributing to the risk of ROP include anemia, blood transfusions, respiratory distress, breathing difficulties, and the overall health of the infant

An ROP epidemic occurred in the 1940s and early 1950s when hospital nurseries began using excessively high levels of oxygen in incubators to save the lives of premature infants. During this time, ROP was the leading cause of blindness in children in the United States. In 1954, scientists funded by the National Institutes of Health determined that the relatively high levels of oxygen routinely given to premature infants at that time were an important risk factor, and that reducing the level of oxygen given to premature babies reduced the incidence of ROP. With newer technology and methods to monitor the oxygen levels of infants, oxygen use as a risk factor has diminished in importance.

Although it had been suggested as a factor in the development of ROP, researchers supported by the National Eye Institute (NEI) determined that lighting levels in hospital nurseries has no effect on the development of ROP.

How Is ROP Treated?

The most effective proven treatments for ROP are laser therapy or cryotherapy. Laser therapy "burns away" the periphery of the retina, which has no normal blood vessels. With cryotherapy, physicians use an instrument that generates freezing temperatures to briefly touch spots on the surface of the eye that overlie the periphery of the retina. Both laser treatment and cryotherapy destroy the peripheral areas of the retina, slowing or reversing the abnormal growth of blood vessels. Unfortunately, the treatments also destroy some side vision.

Both laser treatments and cryotherapy are performed only on infants with advanced ROP, particularly stage III with "plus disease."

Both treatments are considered invasive surgeries on the eye, and doctors don't know the long-term side effects of each.

In the later stages of ROP, other treatment options include:

- **Scleral buckle.** This involves placing a silicone band around the eye and tightening it. This keeps the vitreous gel from pulling on the scar tissue and allows the retina to flatten back down onto the wall of the eye. Infants who have had a sclera buckle need to have the band removed months or years later, since the eye continues to grow; otherwise they will become nearsighted. Sclera buckles are usually performed on infants with stage IV or V.

- **Vitrectomy.** Vitrectomy involves removing the vitreous and replacing it with a saline solution. After the vitreous has been removed, the scar tissue on the retina can be peeled back or cut away, allowing the retina to relax and lay back down against the eye wall. Vitrectomy is performed only at stage V.

What Happens If Treatment Does Not Work?

While ROP treatment decreases the chances for vision loss, it does not always prevent it. Not all babies respond to ROP treatment, and the disease may get worse. If treatment for ROP does not work, a retinal detachment may develop. Often, only part of the retina detaches (stage IV). When this happens, no further treatments may be needed, since a partial detachment may remain the same or go away without treatment. However, in some instances, physicians may recommend treatment to try to prevent further advancement of the retinal detachment (stage V). If the center of the retina or the entire retina detaches, central vision is threatened, and surgery may be recommended to reattach the retina.

Section 14.8

Transient Tachypnea of the Newborn

This section includes text excerpted from "Diuretics for Transient Tachypnoea of the Newborn," *Eunice Kennedy Shriver* National Institute of Child Health and Human Development (NICHD), September 18, 2015.

Transient tachypnoea of the newborn (TTN) was first described by Avery 1966. It is generally considered a benign condition that occurs in about 1 percent of newborns. In infants born at term, TTN leads to rapid respiration (>60 bpm), grunting and retraction at, or shortly after, birth. Investigations for infection will be negative and the oxygen requirement usually does not rise above 40percent. Chest X-ray shows streaky interstitial or pleural fluid, prominent interlobar fissures, perihilar vascular markings and sometimes hyperinflation. The symptoms often resolve by 48 hours, occasionally lasting as long as five days. The condition is more common in term infants born by elective cesarean section. It may be difficult to distinguish between congenital pneumonia and TTN and many infants receive antibiotics until blood cultures are known to be negative. TTN is regarded as being synonymous with wet lung, benign unexplained respiratory distress in the newborn, neonatal tachypnoea and type 2 RDS. The underlying pathology of TTN is not well understood. The most commonly proposed mechanism is a delay in the resorption of foetal lung fluid after birth. Lung liquid that has been rendered high in protein by either mild asphyxia or amniotic fluid aspiration may contribute to the problem. In addition, elective cesarean section deprives the foetus of the effect of endogenous catecholamines on resorption of lung liquid.

The reported prevalence of TTN varies, with some studies attributing up to 40 percent of neonatal respiratory distress to TTN; and an overall incidence of around 11 per 1000 births. With a tendency to delivery by elective cesarean section for an increasing number of obstetric and foetal indications, the number of infants admitted to neonatal units with TTN is likely to rise.

There are no specific biochemical or haematological markers and the diagnosis is essentially clinical with typical radiological features on chest X-ray. The natural history is of gradual improvement of respiratory signs as foetal lung fluid is reabsorbed. Treatment is supportive with oxygen to maintain acceptable saturations and occasionally continuous positive airway pressure (CPAP) and even endotracheal ventilation to obtain adequate oxygenation and carbon dioxide clearance. TTN usually settles within 24 hours but may persist for several days and in its more severe forms may be associated with secondary surfactant-deficient lung disease; and in extreme cases, persistent pulmonary hypertension.

Description of the Intervention

Diuretics have been shown to affect fluid dynamics in the lung by both diuretic and nondiuretic actions. The diuretic response following intravenous furosemide is more rapid than oral furosemide and injection of furosemide is considered safer in infants with respiratory distress.

How the Intervention Might Work

In theory, diuresis should increase the plasma oncotic pressure and draw water from the lungs into the pulmonary vascular bed. This has been shown not to be the case in an adult canine model. It seems more likely that nondiuretic effects are predominant, with several authors showing improved pulmonary dynamics without demonstrable diuresis. Given the effects of furosemide on the fluid-overloaded lung, it is reasonable to hypothesise that it might alter the clinical course of TTN.

Chapter 15

Pregnancy Concerns with Twins and Other Multiple Births

Chapter Contents

Section 15.1

Twins, Triplets, and Other Multiples

This section includes text excerpted from "Twins, Triplets, and Other Multiples," Office on Women's Health (OWH), U.S. Department of Health and Human Services (HHS), February 1, 2017.

Information about Multiples

More women are having babies after age 30. Women in their 30s are more likely than younger women to conceive more than one baby naturally. Another reason is that more women are using fertility treatments to help them conceive.

How Twins Are Formed

Twins form in one of two ways:

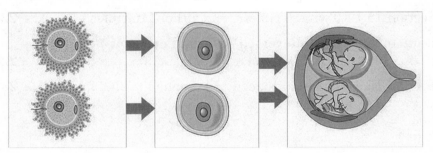

Figure 15.1. *Identical Twins Illustration*

Identical twins occur when a single fertilized egg splits into two. Identical twins look almost exactly alike and share the exact same genes. Most identical twins happen by chance.

Fraternal twins occur when two, separate eggs are fertilized by two, separate sperm. Fraternal twins do not share the exact same genes—they are no more alike than they are to their siblings from different pregnancies. Fraternal twins tend to run in some families. Multiple births can be fraternal, identical, or a combination. Multiples associated with fertility treatments are mainly fraternal.

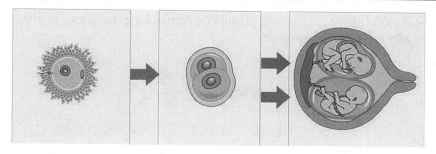

Figure 15.2. *Fraternal Twins Illustration*

Pregnancy with Multiples

Years ago, most twins came as a surprise. Now, thanks to advances in prenatal care, most women learn about a multiple pregnancy early. You might suspect you are pregnant with multiples if you have more severe body changes, including:

- Rapid weight gain in the first trimester
- Intense nausea and vomiting
- Extreme breast tenderness

Your doctor can confirm whether you are carrying more than one baby through ultrasound. If you are pregnant with twins or other multiples, you will need to see your doctor more often than women who are carrying only one baby because your risk of complications is greater. Women carrying more than one baby are at higher risk of:

- Preterm birth
- Low birth weight
- Preeclampsia
- Gestational diabetes
- Cesarean birth

More frequent prenatal visits help your doctor to monitor your and your babies' health. Your doctor will also tell you how much weight to gain, if you need to take extra vitamins, and how much activity is safe. With close monitoring, your babies will have the best chance of being born near term and at a healthy weight.

After delivery and once your babies come home, you may feel over-whelmed and exhausted. Ask for help from your partner, family, and friends. Volunteer help and support groups for parents of multiples also can ease the transition.

Section 15.2

Twin Reversed Arterial Perfusion (TRAP) Sequence

"Twin Reversed Arterial Perfusion (TRAP) Sequence," © 2017 Omnigraphics. Reviewed December 2017.

Twin reversed arterial perfusion (TRAP) sequence is a rare and random phenomenon found in monochorionic pregnancies (fetuses sharing a common placenta). Seen to occur in 1 out of 100 monochorionic pregnancies, TRAP sequence usually has a poor prognosis and typically presents with an acardiac fetus characterized by severely maldeveloped internal organs and external structures, and an absent heart (hence the name acardiac). The other twin, called the "pump fetus," shows a normal growth pattern but has a cardiac system that pumps blood for both the fetuses (hence the name "pump twin"). The pump fetus feeds the acardiac fetus through interconnected blood vessels, called anastomoses, present in the shared placenta. While the exact pathogenesis of TRAP remains unclear, studies indicate that vascular disruptions caused by anastomoses during early embryonic development may contribute to atrophy of heart and other organs in the acardiac twin. Studies have also indicated that certain genetic anomalies may be linked to the failure of primary embryonic heart development, one of the leading consequences of TRAP sequence. The acardiac twin is nonviable with a near 100-percent mortality rate. The pump fetus, on the other hand, has a better survival rate—more than 50 percent—with regular monitoring and appropriate management.

Complications of TRAP

Cardiac failure in the pump twin is one of the major risks associated with TRAP sequence. The risk varies proportionally with the size of the acardiac twin; the larger the acardiac twin, the higher the blood volume that is required to be pumped by the pump twin and, consequently, the greater the risk of cardiac failure in the pump twin. TRAP sequence is also complicated with polyhyramnios, or excessive amniotic fluid buildup in the gestational sac, a condition typically associated with adverse perinatal outcomes in the form of premature rupture of fetal membranes and preterm delivery.

Prenatal Diagnosis of TRAP Sequence

Diagnosis is usually done based on findings during a routine ultrasound scan, which shows the presence of a single placenta (monochorionicity). This is usually backed up by additional tests to confirm the diagnosis; these include amniocentesis and fetal echocardiograms to investigate abnormal heart function of the pump twin. Advances in color Doppler ultrasound have made it possible to evaluate the reversed arterial flow in the acardiac fetus as early as 11 weeks of gestation. Doppler tests also help to rule out single twin demise characterized by lack of blood flow as opposed to the presence of appreciable blood flow to the acardiac fetus in a TRAP sequence. Early diagnosis of TRAP sequence is important to provide timely intervention for improving the prognosis of the pump fetus, or for termination of pregnancy in cases wherein outlook for the pump fetus is poor and the mortality risk is high.

Treatment

Managing monochorionic twin pregnancies in which one fetus is compromised and the other is normal poses therapeutic challenges. While early delivery may compromise the healthy fetus, delayed management may also increase the risks of fetal demise and adverse neurological outcomes in the pump twin. The goal of intervention, therefore, is to maintain the viability of the pump fetus and prevent adverse perinatal outcomes.

Selective reduction of the nonviable acardiac fetus is one of the most common methods adopted to salvage the pump twin. This is usually considered when a diagnosis of cardiac insufficiency with polyhydramnios indicates imminent heart failure and preterm birth of the viable pump fetus. Congestive heart failure is often accompanied by hydrops fetalis, a serious condition characterized by abnormal fluid accumulation in two or more fetal compartments (the membranes surrounding the heart, lungs, or abdomen). These conditions are known to significantly increase fetal and neonatal mortality risk of the pump twin.

Selective termination of the acardiac fetus is based on arresting the vascular communication between the fetuses and is carried out via one of the following procedures:

Bipolar coagulation: Recommended for smaller gestational age pregnancies, this procedure obliterates blood flow to the acardiac fetus by sealing off its umbilical cord near the placenta. A set of hollow needles, called trocars, is inserted into the gestational sac via the abdomen. A forceps is introduced through the trocar to grasp the cord that is then obliterated by coagulation using laser or electric current.

Radiofrequency ablation (RFA): Under ultrasound guidance, a needle is inserted into the cord insertion site of the acardiac twin and blood flow is arrested by the application of high-frequency alternating currents to coagulate the cord. This is the most commonly used minimally invasive procedure and is associated with fewer risks compared to certain other methods that target the umbilical cord.

Mode of Delivery for TRAP Sequence

Following selective reduction of acardiac fetus, a healthy pump fetus can be managed in much the same way as a normal singleton fetus; however, the chances of preterm labor increases with TRAP sequence fetal interventions. Also, an uncomplicated TRAP pregnancy in which the acardiac fetus is relatively small is easily managed with fairly good outcomes for the pump twin. Under the circumstances, the patient may be able to have a vaginal delivery, unless an obstetric indication requires a cesarean section.

However, if preterm birth is indicated in a TRAP sequence that is associated with complications to the pump twin, then delivery may be induced or a cesarean section may be required to facilitate early delivery. After birth, the pump twin may need to be placed in a neonatal intensive care unit (NICU) to screen for congenital anomalies and receive specialized care.

References

1. "Labor and Delivery," *Eunice Kennedy Shriver* National Institute of Child Health and Human Development (NICHD), n.d.

2. Simpson, Lynn L., "TRAP Syndrome," Clinical Advisor, n.d.

3. "Twin Reversed Arterial Perfusion," Johns Hopkins University, n.d.

Section 15.3

Unequal Placental Sharing

"Unequal Placental Sharing," © 2017 Omnigraphics.
Reviewed December 2017.

Unequal placental sharing, although relatively uncommon, is one of the complications seen in fetuses sharing a common placenta, otherwise known as a monochorionic twin pregnancy. The placenta, a fetomaternal tissue that protects and nourishes the fetus, starts developing before the zygote (fertilized egg) is implanted on the uterine wall and continues to grow throughout pregnancy. Regarded as the life-support system for the growing embryo, the placenta provides a pathway for gaseous exchange and nutrient intake via maternal blood circulation, helps eliminate metabolic waste, and secretes hormones to sustain pregnancy. In monochorionic twin pregnancies, the placenta (originally designed for a single fetus) is unequally apportioned; it favors one of the fetuses, with more than 60 percent of the maternal blood supply, which can lead to serious complications, including discordant fetal growth and developmental abnormalities in the other fetus.

Risks and Complications of Unequal Placental Sharing

Selective Intrauterine Growth Restriction (SIUGR)

One of the most common outcomes of unequal placental sharing is selective intrauterine growth restriction (SIUGR), which typically affects only one of the fetuses. Seen in more than 15 percent of monochorionic twin pregnancies, SIUGR can lead to significant perinatal morbidity and mortality if left unmanaged. In addition to poor growth, there is increased risk of cardiovascular abnormalities and neurodevelopmental impairment.

SIUGR and Twin-to-Twin Transfusion Syndrome (TTTs)

The umbilical cord of each fetus embeds in the placenta and creates anastomoses—shared vascular connections linking their respective blood vessels, the existence of which can determine the well-being of one or both fetuses. Virtually all monochorionic fetuses have interconnected blood vessels within the common placenta, but whether it complicates the pregnancy depends largely on the type and number of blood vessels shared. Placental anastomoses can link the artery of one fetus to the artery of the other fetus (AA anastomoses); the vein of one fetus to the vein of the other fetus (VV anastomoses); or the artery of one fetus to the vein of the other fetus (AV anastomoses). While the blood flow in AA and VV anastomoses are bidirectional and may be equally distributed between the circulations of the fetuses, the same is not true for AV anastomoses. The higher arterial pressure creates a unidirectional shunt leading to a net transfusion of blood from one fetus to the other. This condition, called twin-to-twin transfusion syndrome, is one of the serious complications of unequal placental sharing. Untreated, TTTS can lead to lower blood/amniotic fluid volumes and restricted growth in the "donor" twin and a disproportionately higher blood volume and increased risk of cardiac failure in the "recipient" twin.

Diagnosis of SIUGR

After monochorionic twin pregnancy has been confirmed, an ultrasound scan is the first step in establishing SIUGR. The in utero diagnosis with an ultrasound typically uses three parameters to confirm SIUGR.

- The estimated fetal weight of one of the twins falls short of the 10th percentile of the expected gestational weight.

- Ruling out twin-to-twin transfusion syndrome (TTTS): Interconnecting blood vessels that allow disproportionate blood flow from one twin (donor) to the other (recipient).

- Absent or reversed flow in the fetal umbilical artery of the growth-restricted twin.

Prenatal Management and Treatment of SIUGR

Early diagnosis, close surveillance, and fetal intervention are keys to successful management of SIUGR. A maternal fetal specialist monitors the pregnancy with weekly ultrasound scans. Fetal echocardiography, a noninvasive high-resolution ultrasound, is often used to evaluate cardiovascular function of the fetus. Doppler studies may also be used to assess blood flow to vital organs and the umbilicus. It is particularly important to monitor the growth-restricted fetus for intrauterine fetal demise to prevent an adverse outcome for the normally growing fetus. Clinical decisions are usually based on type and severity of SIUGR, parental wishes, and gestational age.

Common management protocol includes:

Selective Cord Occlusion

A minimally invasive procedure, this involves arresting blood flow to the growth-restricted fetus; in doing so, it minimizes the risk of preterm labor or growth abnormality in the normal fetus. This ultrasound-guided procedure may involve cord ligation using electric current, laser occlusion, or radiofrequency ablation to perform selective termination of the smaller fetus. This intervention is usually recommended when the growth-restricted fetus is deemed unlikely to survive. In severe cases of unequal placental sharing, the intrauterine demise of the growth-restricted fetus may cause blood flow from the appropriately growing fetus to the demised, leading to a drastic drop of blood pressure and possible concomitant death of the other twin or long-term adverse neurological outcomes in the surviving twin.

Fetoscopic Laser Photocoagulation

A small laparoscope—called fetoscope—is introduced into the uterus, and the blood vessels that cause unequal sharing of the placenta are ablated (sealed) using a laser. The procedure is typically performed when TTTS coexists with SIUGR, causing blood flow imbalances in the fetuses. However, laser ablation is not a first-line treatment for SIUGR, and depends largely on the number and size of interconnected blood vessels between the twins.

Preterm Delivery

If SIUGR is discovered later in the pregnancy, or if it continues to progress after the pregnancy reaches its 24th–26th week, delivery of the babies via cesarean birth is considered to avoid endangering the lives of one or both twins.

Postnatal Management of SIUGR

SIUGR babies delivered prematurely will face problems typically associated with preterm births, including anemia, jaundice, or respiratory problems. Intrauterine growth restriction in the compromised twin, however, may be associated with several long-term complications that vary in severity depending on the extent of SIUGR and the gestational period. Growth-restricted babies delivered between 24 and 32 weeks have special needs and may need to be placed in a neonatal intensive care unit (NICU). Besides breathing and feeding problems, they may require screening by neonatologists to rule out neurological sequelae of SIUGR, which may be present even when birth is not premature.

References

1. "Unequal Placental Sharing," Mount Sinai Hospital, n.d.

2. "Perinatal Outcome of Monochorionic Twins with Selective IUGR Compared with Uncomplicated Monochorionic Twins," Twin Research and Human Genetics, October 2011.

3. "Uneven Growth of Twins May Begin Shortly after Conception," King's College London, November 12, 2015.

4. "Selective Intrauterine Growth Restriction," The Johns Hopkins University, n.d.

Chapter 16

Labor and Delivery Concerns in Complicated Pregnancies

What Is Induction of Labor?

Labor induction is the use of medications or other methods to cause, or induce, labor. This practice is used to make contractions start.

When Would a Provider Induce Labor?

Induction is usually limited to situations when there is a problem with the pregnancy, or when a baby is overdue. Several weeks before labor begins, the cervix begins to soften (called "ripening"), thin out, and open to prepare for delivery. If the cervix is not ready, especially if labor has not started 2 weeks or more after your due date, your healthcare provider may recommend labor induction. A healthcare provider may also recommend labor induction if there is a health risk to mother or fetus.

Healthcare providers use a scoring system, called the Bishop score, to determine how ready the cervix is for labor. The scoring system ranges from 0–13. A score of less than 6 means the cervix may need a procedure to prepare it for labor.

This chapter includes text excerpted from "Labor and Delivery: Topic Information," *Eunice Kennedy Shriver* National Institute of Child Health and Human Development (NICHD), December 18, 2014. Reviewed December 2017.

Preparing the Cervix for Labor

If the cervix is not ready for labor, a healthcare provider may suggest one of the following to ripen the cervix:

- **Stripping the membranes.** Your healthcare provider can disconnect the thin tissue of the amniotic sac containing the fetus from the wall of the uterus. Stripping the membranes causes the body to release prostaglandins, which soften the cervix and cause contractions.

- **Giving prostaglandins.** This drug may be inserted into the vagina or given by mouth. The body naturally makes these chemicals to ripen the cervix.

- **Inserting a catheter.** A small tube with an inflatable balloon on the end can be placed in the cervix to widen it.

How Is Labor Induced?

Once the cervix is ripe, a healthcare provider may recommend one of the following techniques to start contractions or make them stronger:

- **Amniotomy.** A healthcare provider uses a tool to make a small hole in the amniotic sac, causing it to rupture (or the water to break) and contractions to start.

- **Giving oxytocin (also called Pitocin).** Oxytocin is a hormone the body naturally makes that causes contractions. It is given to start labor or to speed up labor that has already begun.

Can Induction Be Requested?

In most cases, induction is limited to situations when there is a problem with the pregnancy, or when a baby is overdue. But sometimes labor induction is requested for reasons other than a problem with the pregnancy.

- A woman might want labor induction for several reasons, including:

- Physical discomfort at the end of pregnancy

- Concern with getting to the hospital in time

- Ensuring her own healthcare provider or midwife can be at the delivery

- Ensuring her spouse or partner can be at the delivery
- Scheduling issues with work or child care

It is best not to induce labor before 39 weeks of pregnancy (full term) unless there is a medical reason. Preterm infants (born before 37 weeks) and early term infants (born in the 37th and 38th weeks of pregnancy) are at increased risk of illness and even death.

Cesarean Section (C-Section)

A C-section, short for cesarean section, is also called cesarean birth. Cesarean birth is the delivery of a baby through surgical cuts in a woman's abdomen and uterus. The uterus is then closed with stitches that later dissolve. Stitches or staples also close the skin on the belly.

When Is Cesarean Delivery Needed?

Cesarean delivery may be necessary in the following circumstances:

- **A pregnancy with two or more fetuses (multiple pregnancy).** A cesarean delivery may be needed if labor has started too early (preterm labor), if the fetuses are not in good positions in the uterus for natural delivery, or if there are other problems.

- **Labor is not progressing.** Contractions may not open the cervix enough for the baby to move into the vagina.

- **The infant's health is in danger.** The umbilical cord, which connects the fetus to the uterus, may become pinched, or the fetus may have an abnormal heart rate. In these cases, a C-section allows the baby to be delivered quickly to address and resolve the baby's health problems.

- **Problems with the placenta.** Sometimes the placenta is not formed or working correctly, is in the wrong place in the uterus, or is implanted too deeply or firmly in the uterine wall. This can cause problems, such as depriving the fetus of needed oxygen and nutrients or vaginal bleeding.

- **The baby is too large.** Women with gestational diabetes, especially if their blood sugar levels are not well controlled, are at increased risk for having large infants. And larger infants are at risk for complications during delivery. These include shoulder dystocia, when the infant's head is delivered through the vagina but the shoulders are stuck.

- **The baby is breech, or in a breech presentation,** meaning the baby is coming out feet first instead of head first.

- **The mother has an infection, such as HIV or herpes,** that could be passed to the baby during vaginal birth. Cesarean delivery could help prevent transmission of the virus to the infant.

- **The mother has a medical condition.** A C-section enables the healthcare provider to better manage the mother's health issues.

Women who have a cesarean delivery may be given pain medication with an epidural block, a spinal block, or general anesthesia. An epidural block numbs the lower part of the body through an injection in the spine. A spinal block also numbs the lower part of the body but through an injection directly into the spinal fluid. Women who receive general anesthesia, often used for emergency cesarean deliveries, will not be awake during the surgery.

What Are the Risks of a C-Section?

Cesarean birth is a type of surgery, meaning it has risks and possible complications for both mother and infant.

Possible risks from a C-section (which are also associated with vaginal birth) include:

- Infection

- Blood loss

- Blood clots in the legs, pelvic organs, or lungs

- Injury to surrounding structures, such as the bowel or bladder

- Reaction to medication or anesthesia used

A woman who has a C-section also may have to stay in the hospital longer. The more C-sections a woman has, the greater her risk for certain medical problems and problems with future pregnancies, such as uterine rupture and problems with the placenta.

Can a C-Section Be Requested?

Some women may want to have a cesarean birth even if vaginal delivery is an option. Women should discuss this option in detail with their healthcare provider before making a final decision about a C-section. As is true for vaginal births, unless there is a medical necessity, delivery should not occur before 39 weeks of pregnancy (called full term).

Common Complications during Labor and Delivery

Labor and delivery are different for everyone. Complications sometimes happen. Possible complications include (but are not limited to):

- **Labor that does not progress.** Sometimes the cervix does not dilate in a timely manner to ready the body for delivery. If labor is not progressing, a healthcare provider may give the woman medications to speed up labor, or the woman may need a cesarean delivery.

- **Abnormal heart rate of the baby.** Many times an abnormal heart rate during labor does not mean there is a problem. A healthcare provider will likely ask the woman to switch positions to help the infant get more blood flow. In certain instances or if test results show there is a problem, delivery might have to happen right away. When this happens, the woman is more likely to need a cesarean delivery, or the healthcare provider will need to do an episiotomy (a surgical cut between the vagina and anus) to widen the vaginal opening for delivery.

- **Perinatal asphyxia.** This condition occurs when the baby does not get enough oxygen in the uterus, during labor and delivery, or just after birth.

- **Shoulder dystocia.** In this situation, the infant's head has come out of the vagina but one of the shoulders becomes stuck.

- **Excessive bleeding.** If delivery results in tears to the uterus or if the uterus does not contract to deliver the placenta, heavy bleeding can result. Worldwide, such bleeding is a leading cause of maternal death. The *Eunice Kennedy Shriver* National Institute of Child Health and Human Development (NICHD) has supported studies to investigate the use of misoprostol to reduce bleeding, especially in resource-poor settings.

Chapter 17

Screening Tests for Newborns

Chapter Contents

Section 17.1

Newborn Screening Tests:
What You Need to Know

This section includes text excerpted from documents published by two public domain sources. Text under headings marked 1 is excerpted from "Newborn Screening Is Important for Your Baby," Centers for Disease Control and Prevention (CDC), September 15, 2014. Reviewed December 2017; Text under headings marked 2 are excerpted from "Newborn Screening—How Are Newborn Screening Tests Done?" *Eunice Kennedy Shriver* National Institute of Child Health and Human Development (NICHD), July 4, 2012. Reviewed December 2017.

Newborn Screening Is Important[1]

The nursery is decorated, the car seat is ready, and you can't wait to bring your new baby home. But before your newborn comes home, he or she will need some important screening done at the hospital. This screening is called newborn screening and includes a blood test, hearing screening, and, in many hospitals, screening for critical congenital heart defects (CCHD). Newborn screening is important because even if your baby looks healthy, some medical conditions can't be seen just by looking. If your baby was not born in a hospital or was not screened before leaving the hospital, take him or her to the doctor's office or hospital to be screened as soon as possible.

What Is the Purpose of Newborn Screening?[2]

The intent of newborn screening is to detect potentially fatal or disabling conditions in newborns. Identifying infants with these conditions early on provides a window of opportunity for treatment, often before the infant displays any signs or symptoms of a disease or condition. Such early detection and treatment can have a profound impact on the severity of the condition in the child. The consequences of many of the screened for conditions, if left undiagnosed and untreated, can be dire, often causing irreversible neurological damage; intellectual, developmental, and physical disabilities; and even death.

What Disorders Are Newborns Screened for in the United States?[2]

The Discretionary Advisory Committee on Heritable Disorders in Newborns and Children (DACHDNC) recommends that every newborn screening program in the United States include a uniform screening panel of 31 primary and 26 secondary conditions. This panel is called the Recommended Uniform Screening Panel (RUSP).

In addition to making recommendations on newborn screening to the Secretary, U.S. Department of Health and Human Services (HHS), DACHDNC reviews evidence for the inclusion of new conditions in the screening panel and advises the Secretary on the most appropriate application of universal newborn screening tests, technologies, policies, guidelines, and standards.

What Are Some Examples of the Benefits of Newborn Screening?[2]

Many conditions included today in newborn screening no longer cause serious impairment or illness if treated properly after their early identification and diagnosis—but they once did. The three examples that follow are conditions that cause very serious developmental and intellectual disabilities, or death, if they are not detected and treated early enough to prevent damage from the beginning. With the ability to test for these conditions soon after birth and to start treatment as soon as they are detected, babies who not very long ago might have died in infancy or early childhood, or needed specialized care, can grow to healthy adulthood.

Severe Combined Immune Deficiency (SCID)

One of the newest additions to the newborn screening panel is an inherited condition that makes a child's body unable to fight off infections, called Severe Combined Immune Deficiency (SCID) policy. This condition is also known as "bubble boy syndrome (BBS)." In infants born with this condition, certain portions of the immune system do not work properly. If untreated, children with SCID rarely live past the age of two years. However, when SCID is identified and treated early, children can live longer, healthier lives.

SCID is rare, with best estimates that between 40 and 100 infants are diagnosed each year in the United States. Because SCID is a new-comer to the newborn screening panel and not all states yet screen for it, infants with the condition might be dying of infections without being diagnosed.

Infants should be evaluated for SCID and other types of immune system problems if they have:

- A high number of infections

- Infections that do not improve with antibiotic treatment for 2 or more months

- Diarrhea

- Poor weight gain or growth (called "failure to thrive")

- Fungal infections in the mouth (called "thrush") that will not go away

An infant with any of these warning signs should be tested for SCID right away.

Phenylketonuria (PKU)

Phenylketonuria (PKU) is a metabolic disorder that is detected by newborn screening. In PKU, the body cannot digest or process one of the building blocks of proteins, an amino acid called phenylalanine, or Phe. Phe is found naturally in many foods, especially high protein foods.

PKU was the first condition for which a screening test was developed and the first condition for which widespread newborn testing was implemented in the 1960s. If PKU is left untreated, the Phe builds up in the infant's body and brain. By 3–6 months of age, infants with untreated PKU begin to show symptoms of intellectual and developmental disabilities (IDDs). These disabilities can become severe if Phe remains at high levels.

Fortunately, PKU is treatable. The treatment consists of a diet containing little or no Phe and higher levels of other amino acids. If children with the condition are placed on this diet at birth, they grow normally and usually show no symptoms or health problems. Before newborn screening programs could detect PKU in the first few hours after birth, PKU was one of the leading causes of intellectual disability (IDD) in the United States. Today, as a result of newborn screening programs that allow for almost immediate treatment of the condition, PKU has been virtually eliminated as a cause of IDD in this country.

Galactosemia

Another metabolic disorder included in newborn screening is galactosemia, which means being unable to use galactose. Galactose is one of two simple sugars that make up lactose, the sugar in milk. People with galactosemia cannot use any milk or milk products.

If infants with galactosemia consume milk or milk products (human or animal) they will develop damage to their liver, brain, kidneys, and eyes from substances that build up in their systems. Untreated infants with galactosemia can die of a serious blood infection or of liver failure. Some survive but have IDD and other damage to the brain and nervous system. A milder form of galactosemia still needs treatment. Children who are not treated may develop early cataracts, an unsteady gait, and delays in learning, talking, and growth.

The treatment for galactosemia is not to consume any milk or milk products and to avoid other foods that contain this sugar. If this disease is diagnosed very early and the infant is placed on a rigorous galactose free diet, she or he may live a relatively normal life, although mild IDD may still develop. If not placed on a galactose free diet immediately, an infant will develop symptoms in the first few days of life.

Before it could be detected either before birth or through a newborn screening program, galactosemia was a frequent cause of IDD or early death. At present, this inherited disease occurs in about 1 in every 50,000 babies born in the United States.

How Many Infants Are Screened in the United States?[2]

All 50 states; Washington, DC; and the Commonwealth of Puerto Rico have newborn screening programs, and nearly every child born in the United States or Puerto Rico is screened shortly after birth.

• All states require newborn screening for at least 26 health conditions. Each state's public health department decides both the number and types of conditions on its testing panel. Most states allow parents to opt out for religious or other reasons.

• More than 4 million infants are born each year in the United States, and most of them are screened.

• Most states report participation of 99.9 percent or higher. For example:

- Maryland reported that during the last several years, fewer than five families opted out of newborn screening each year, although there have been approximately 75,000 births annually.

- In Wyoming, there were 6,800 infants born in 2007, but only two families opted out of screening.

Disorders Identified

- Centers for Disease Control and Prevention (CDC) data show that about 12,500 newborns per year are diagnosed with one of the 29 core conditions that are detected through newborn screening. This means that almost 1 out of every 300 newborns screened is eventually diagnosed.

- Early diagnosis and treatment in many cases can significantly improve the chances of healthy development and positive outcomes.

How Are Newborn Screening Tests Done?[2]

Newborn screening typically consists of a blood test and a hearing test. First, hospital staff fill out a newborn screening card with the infant's vital information—name, sex, weight, date and time of birth—and the date and time of the blood collection. Part of the card consists of special absorbent paper used to collect the blood sample.

Heel Stick Blood Test

After warming and careful sterilizing of the infant's heel, blood is taken through a "heel stick." The absorbent portion of the screening card is then placed in contact with the blood drop. This procedure is repeated with a series of new drops of blood until all the printed circles on the card contain a blood sample. These blood samples are used to conduct the screening tests, which are done in carefully controlled high volume clinical laboratories.

Hearing Test

Hospital staff typically use one of two methods for the hearing test. Both are quick (5–10 minutes) and safe.

- **Otoacoustic emissions (OAE).** This test determines if certain parts of the infant's ear respond to sound. A miniature earphone and microphone are placed in the ear, and sounds are played. If the infant has normal hearing, the microphone picks up an echo reflected back into the ear canal. Failure to detect an echo means there may be a loss of hearing.

- **Auditory brain stem response (ABR).** This test evaluates the auditory brain stem—the part of the auditory nerve that carries sound from the ear to the brain—and the brain's response to sound. Miniature earphones are placed in the ear, and sounds are played. Electrodes (small, sticky electric conductors) are placed on the infant's head to detect the brain's response to the sounds. If the infant's brain does not respond consistently to the sounds, there may be a hearing problem.

Pulse Oximetry

In some cases, hospital staff will perform pulse oximetry to measure how much oxygen is in the infant's blood. Pulse oximetry is usually performed after the infant is 24 hours old. Hospital staff place a sensor on the infant's skin for a couple of minutes, and the sensor measures the level of oxygen in the blood through the skin.

Low blood oxygen can indicate that a newborn has heart problems. Pulse oximetry can help identify infants with a condition called critical congenital heart disease (CCHD). Annually, CCHD accounts for 24 percent of all infant deaths that are due to birth defects. This type of screening can identify infants who need to be seen by a heart specialist and receive lifesaving care.

Other Blood Tests

Some states require a second blood test that repeats the initial set of screenings.

- The first screening is performed 24–48 hours after the infant is born, ideally before the infant leaves the hospital. For some conditions, the screening is not valid if the blood is taken before a newborn is 24 hours old.

- The second screening is performed when the infant is 10 days–2 weeks old to ensure that the child's doctor has the most accurate results possible.

How Are My Newborn's Screening Results Used?[2]

After a newborn is screened, parents may not hear anything at all about the results. In fact, most parents do not. This usually means that the child's tests did not detect any of the conditions screened for—or, as the child's healthcare provider might say, the results were "negative" or "in range." Parents with concerns should feel free to contact their physician and ask about the results. Most states notify parents only when the results are out of range for a particular condition.

Out of Range Results

If the screening detects one or more conditions, the result is "positive" or more accurately, "out of range." Your child's healthcare provider or someone from the state health department will notify you, usually within 2–3 weeks.

A positive result does not mean your child definitely has the condition detected. Sometimes, the tests produce a "false positive," meaning that even though the test result was positive, your infant does not actually have the disease.

If the test result is positive, it is very important that your infant receives additional testing right away. Your child's healthcare provider will perform a diagnostic test to determine whether your baby actually has the condition. Screening tests and diagnostic tests are not the same tests. If your baby is diagnosed with a condition, his or her healthcare provider and other providers will recommend a course of treatment.

Baby's First Test (www.babysfirsttest.org/newborn-screening/states) provides a list of the conditions screened for in the newborn screening panel for most states. This list includes symptoms of each condition and the test(s) used to diagnose a condition or confirm a positive screening result.

The Importance of Following Through

Newborn screening is used to test for serious medical conditions. If not treated, some of these conditions can cause lifelong health problems; others can cause early death. If your child's healthcare provider or the state health department calls you about your infant's newborn screening test, it is important to follow up quickly. Call them back and follow their instructions to get care for your baby.

Newborn screening makes early diagnosis possible so that treatment can begin immediately—before serious problems can occur or become permanent. This approach helps to ensure the best possible outcomes for your baby.

Treatment[1]

Sometimes, all that is needed is a change in your baby's diet. For example, babies with PKU cannot process phenylalanine well. Phenylalanine is found in many protein rich foods and some sweeteners and can build up in the body of a baby with PKU, resulting in brain damage. This can be prevented if a baby with PKU is put on a special diet early.

For other conditions, your baby might need to take medicine. Babies with hypothyroidism do not make enough thyroid hormone and without treatment can have slowed growth and brain damage. Taking thyroid hormone medication shortly after birth can prevent these problems.

Although treatments for some conditions are more complicated, it is still helpful to know about the condition early. A baby with sickle cell disease (SCD) is at risk for harmful infections. Identifying these babies right away means that they can receive a daily dose of penicillin, an antibiotic medicine, to help avoid infections and prevent serious problems.

Many hospitals have started screening for critical congenital heart defects. Some babies born with a heart defect can appear healthy at first and go home with their families before their heart defect is detected. These babies risk having serious complications within the first days of life and often require emergency care. Newborn screening can identify some of these babies so they can be seen by heart specialists and receive care and treatment that can prevent disability and death early in life.

Section 17.2

Apgar Score

"Apgar Score," © 2017 Omnigraphics. Reviewed December 2017.

The Apgar test is the first test given to infants after their birth. It is given at the first minute and, again, at the fifth minute. Developed in 1952 by Virginia Apgar, an anesthesiologist, the test is designed to evaluate the physical condition of an infant right after birth and suggest if emergency care or medical attention is necessary. The first-minute test score determines how well the child has endured the birthing process, and the fifth-minute test score determines how well the infant adapts to life outside the womb.

The Apgar test uses five factors to evaluate the baby's condition. Apgar scores range from 0–2 for each condition, with 2 being the best score and 0 indicating a need for immediate medical care. A doctor, midwife, or nurse would do the tests and combine the five factors for the final score between 0 and 10 — 10 being the highest score possible, indicating the baby is very healthy. The factors taken into consideration for Apgar scoring are as follows:

- Skin color (appearance)

- Heart rate (pulse)

- Reflexes (grimace response)

- Muscle tone (activity)

- Breathing effort (respiration)

What Do the Apgar Scores Mean?

Each of the five factors is scored with a 0, 1, or 2 based on observations. The following are the interpretations for the score:

Skin Color (Appearance)

- If the skin is bluish-gray or pale on the entire body, the test score is 0.

- If the hands and feet are bluish and the rest of the body is in normal color (pink), the test score is 1.

- If the entire body is in normal color (pink), the test score is 2.

Heart Rate (Pulse)

- The most important assessment, the heartbeat is evaluated by a stethoscope.

- The test score is 0 if there is no heartbeat.

- The test score is 1 if the heart rate is less than 100 beats per minute.

- The test score is 2 if the heart rate is greater than 100 beats per minute.

Reflexes (Grimace response)

- Grimace response refers to response toward stimulation, such as a mild pinch:

- The test score is 0 if there is no response to airways being suctioned.

- The test score is 1 if there is a grimace during suction.

- The test score is 2 if there a grimace, cough, sneeze, or vigorous cry.

Muscle Tone Activity

- **The test score is 0 if there is no movement and the muscles are loose and floppy.**

- The test score is 1 if there is some bending of arms and legs.

- The test score is 2 if there is active movement.

Breathing Effort (Respiration)

- The test score is 0 if no breathing takes place.

- The test score is 1 if there is slow or irregular respiration takes place.

- The test score is 2 if there is a strong cry.

An infant who has a test score of 8 or above is considered a healthy baby. However, a score below 8 may require medical attention such as helping him or her breathe through suction. It does not mean the baby is unhealthy nor has major health issues. Some infants are born with a medical condition that needs to be treated; others may just need time to get accustomed to the new environment outside the womb.

If the scores of the test given at the first minute are low or do not look good, another test is given at the fifth minute and the scores are recalculated. The doctors and nurses will continue to monitor the baby and give the needed medical care and treatment. Very rarely, a test is given in the 10th minute of birth. Most of the infants score low in the first minute and eventually the scores are higher at the fifth-minute test.

The test does not predict a child's long-term health, intellectual status, behavior, or personality. Only few infants score a perfect 10. A slightly lower Apgar score is common for some newborns that were born after a complicated labor, cesarean delivery, or high-risk pregnancy. If the healthcare provider has concerns about the baby's Apgar score, he or she will let the parent know about the baby's present health condition, cause of the problem, and the treatment administrated. As time progresses, most babies do well with necessary medical attention.

References

1. Hirsch, Larissa. "What Is the Apgar Score?" Kidshealth, July 2014.

2. "Apgar Score," U.S. National Library of Medicine (NLM), November 6, 2017.

3. "Your Child's First Test: The APGAR," American Pregnancy Association, August 2015.

4. "The Apgar Score," BabyCenter, n.d.

Section 17.3

Newborn Hearing Screening

This section includes text excerpted from "Hearing, Ear Infections,
and Deafness—Your Baby's Hearing Screening," National
Institute on Deafness and Other Communication Disorders
(NIDCD), June 19, 2017.

Most children hear and listen to sounds at birth. They learn to talk
by imitating the sounds they hear around them and the voices of their
parents and caregivers. But that's not true for all children. In fact,
about two or three out of every 1,000 children in the United States are
born with detectable hearing loss in one or both ears. More lose hearing
later during childhood. Children who have hearing loss may not learn
speech and language as well as children who can hear. For this reason,
it's important to detect deafness or hearing loss as early as possible.

Because of the need for prompt identification of and intervention
for childhood hearing loss, universal newborn hearing screening programs currently operate in all U.S. states and most U.S. territories.
With help from the federal government, every state has established
an Early Hearing Detection and Intervention (EHDI) program. As a
result, more than 96 percent of babies have their hearing screened
within 1 month of birth.

Why Is It Important to Have My Baby's Hearing Screened Early?

The most important time for a child to learn language is in the first
3 years of life, when the brain is developing and maturing. In fact,
children begin learning speech and language in the first 6 months of
life. Research suggests that children with hearing loss who get help
early develop better language skills than those who don't.

When Will My Baby's Hearing Be Screened?

Your baby's hearing should be screened before he or she leaves
the hospital or birthing center. If your baby's hearing was not tested

within the first month of life, or if you haven't been told the results of the hearing screening, ask your child's doctor. Quick action will be important if the screening shows a possible problem.

How Will My Baby's Hearing Be Screened?

Two different tests are used to screen for hearing loss in babies. Your baby can rest or sleep during both tests.

- **Otoacoustic emissions (OAE)** test whether some parts of the ear respond to sound. During this test, a soft earphone is inserted into your baby's ear canal. It plays sounds and measures an "echo" response that occurs in ears with normal hearing. If there is no echo, your baby might have hearing loss.

- **The auditory brainstem response (ABR)** tests how the auditory nerve and brainstem (which carry sound from the ear to the brain) respond to sound. During this test, your baby wears small earphones and has electrodes painlessly placed on his or her head. The electrodes adhere and come off like stickers, and should not cause discomfort.

What Should I Do If My Baby's Hearing Screening Reveals a Possible Problem?

If the results show that your baby may have hearing loss, make an appointment with a pediatric audiologist—a hearing expert who specializes in the assessment and management of children with hearing loss. This follow-up exam should be done by the time your baby is 3 months old. The audiologist will conduct tests to determine whether your baby has a hearing problem and, if so, the type and severity of that problem.

If you need help finding a pediatric audiologist, ask your pediatrician or the hospital staff who conducted your baby's screening. They may even be able to help you schedule an appointment. You can also try the directories provided by the American Academy of Audiology (ADA) or the American Speech–Language–Hearing Association (ASHA). If the follow-up examination confirms that your baby has hearing loss, he or she should begin receiving intervention services before the age of 6 months.

The pediatric audiologist may recommend that your baby visit a physician specializing in ear, nose, and throat disorders (an otolaryngologist), who can determine possible causes of hearing loss and recommend intervention options. If your child has siblings, the audiologist or otolaryngologist may also recommend that their hearing be tested.

The Follow-up Exam Revealed That My Baby's Hearing Is Fine. Does That Mean We Don't Need to Check His or Her Hearing Again?

Hearing loss can occur at any time of life. Some inherited forms of hearing loss don't appear until a child is older. In addition, illness, ear infection, head injury, certain medications, and loud noise are all potential causes of hearing loss in children. Use Your Baby's Hearing and Communicative Development Checklist to monitor and track your child's communication milestones through age 5. If you have concerns, talk to your pediatrician right away.

Table 17.1. Your Baby's Hearing and Communicative Development Checklist

Birth–3 Months		
Reacts to loud sounds	YES	NO
Calms down or smiles when spoken to	YES	NO
Recognizes your voice and calms down if crying	YES	NO
When feeding, starts or stops sucking in response to sound	YES	NO
Coos and makes pleasure sounds	YES	NO
Has a special way of crying for different needs	YES	NO
Smiles when he or she sees you	YES	NO
4–6 Months		
Follows sounds with his or her eyes	YES	NO
Responds to changes in the tone of your voice	YES	NO
Notices toys that make sounds	YES	NO
Pays attention to music	YES	NO
Babbles in a speech-like way and uses many different sounds, including sounds that begin with p, b, and m	YES	NO
Laughs	YES	NO

Table 17.1. Continued

Birth–3 Months		
Babbles when excited or unhappy	YES	NO
Makes gurgling sounds when alone or playing with you	YES	NO
7 Months–1 Year		
Enjoys playing peek-a-boo and pat-a-cake	YES	NO
Turns and looks in the direction of sounds	YES	NO
Listens when spoken to	YES	NO
Understands words for common items such as "cup," "shoe," or "juice"	YES	NO
Responds to requests ("Come here")	YES	NO
Babbles using long and short groups of sounds ("tata, upup, bibibi")	YES	NO
Babbles to get and keep attention	YES	NO
Communicates using gestures such as waving or holding up arms	YES	NO
Imitates different speech sounds	YES	NO
Has one or two words ("Hi," "dog," "Dada," or "Mama") by first birthday	YES	NO
1–2 Years		
Knows a few parts of the body and can point to them when asked	YES	NO
Follows simple commands ("Roll the ball") and understands simple questions ("Where's your shoe?")	YES	NO
Enjoys simple stories, songs, and rhymes	YES	NO
Points to pictures, when named, in books	YES	NO
Acquires new words on a regular basis	YES	NO
Uses some one- or two-word questions ("Where kitty?" or "Go bye-bye?")	YES	NO
Puts two words together ("More cookie")	YES	NO
Uses many different consonant sounds at the beginning of words	YES	NO
2–3 Years		
Has a word for almost everything	YES	NO

Table 17.1. Continued

2–3 Years		
Uses two- or three-word phrases to talk about and ask for things	YES	NO
Uses k, g, f, t, d, and n sounds	YES	NO
Speaks in a way that is understood by family members and friends	YES	NO
Names objects to ask for them or to direct attention to them	YES	NO
3–4 Years		
Hears you when you call from another room	YES	NO
Hears the television or radio at the same sound level as other	YES	NO
family members	YES	NO
Answers simple "Who?" "What?" "Where?" and "Why?" questions	YES	NO
Talks about activities at daycare, preschool, or friends' homes	YES	NO
Uses sentences with four or more words	YES	NO
Speaks easily without having to repeat syllables or words	YES	NO
4–5 Years		
Pays attention to a short story and answers simple questions about it	YES	NO
Hears and understands most of what is said at home and in school	YES	NO
Uses sentences that give many details	YES	NO
Tells stories that stay on topic	YES	NO
Communicates easily with other children and adults	YES	NO
Says most sounds correctly except for a few (l, s, r, v, z, ch, sh, and th)	YES	NO
Uses rhyming words	YES	NO
Names some letters and numbers	YES	NO
Uses adult grammar	YES	NO

How Can I Help My Child Succeed If He or She Has Hearing Loss?

When interventions begin early, children with hearing loss can develop language skills that help them communicate freely and learn actively. The federal Individuals with Disabilities Education Act (IDEA) ensures that all children with disabilities have access to the services they need to get a good education. Your community may also offer additional services to help support your child.

Talk to and communicate with your child often. Other ways to support your child include:

- Keep all doctor's appointments.

- Learn sign language or other strategies to support better communication.

- Join a support group.

What Types of Intervention Services Are Available?

Your baby's healthcare team will help you find services and methods to overcome communication barriers. You may also be referred to a speech language pathologist or a teacher who is experienced in working with children with hearing loss.

Depending on your baby's hearing loss and communication needs, some of these devices and tools may help to maximize his or her communication skills.

- **Hearing aids.** Worn in or behind the ear, hearing aids help make sounds louder. Hearing aids can be used for different degrees of hearing loss in babies as young as 1 month. A pediatric audiologist who is experienced in treating infants and children can help you choose the best hearing aid and make sure that it fits securely and is properly adjusted.

- **Cochlear implants.** If your child won't benefit from a hearing aid, your doctor may suggest a cochlear implant. This electronic device can provide a sense of sound to people who are profoundly deaf or hard of hearing. The device converts sounds into electrical signals and carries them past the nonworking part of the inner ear to the brain. Cochlear implants can be surgically placed in children as young as 12 months, or sometimes earlier. With training, children with cochlear implants can learn to recognize sounds and understand speech. Studies have also shown that eligible children who receive a cochlear implant before 18 months of age can develop language skills at a rate comparable to children with normal hearing, and many succeed in mainstream classrooms. Some doctors now recommend the use of two cochlear implants, one for each ear. An otolaryngologist who specializes in cochlear implants can help you decide if a cochlear implant is appropriate for your child.

- **Assistive devices.** As your child grows, other devices may be useful. Some devices help children hear better in a classroom. Others amplify one on one conversations or make talking on the phone or watching television (TV) and videos easier.

What Other Language and Communication Options Might Be Available for My Child?

Children who are deaf or hard of hearing can learn to communicate in several ways, including American Sign Language (ASL). Find out as much as you can about the communication choices, and ask your healthcare team to refer you to experts if you want to know more. Because language development begins early, regardless of the communication mode you choose, you should engage with your child and begin intervention as soon as possible.

Here are the main options to help children with hearing loss express themselves and interact with others:

- **Auditory oral and auditory verbal options** combine natural hearing ability and hearing devices, such as hearing aids and cochlear implants, with other strategies to help children develop speech and English language skills. Auditory oral options use visual cues such as lipreading and sign language, while auditory verbal options work to strengthen listening skills.

- **Signed English** is a system that uses signs to represent words or phrases in English. Signed English is designed to enhance the use of both spoken and written English.

- **American Sign Language (ASL)** is a language used by some children who are deaf and their families and communities. ASL consists of hand signs, body movements, and facial expressions. ASL has its own grammar, which is different from English. It has no written form.

- **Combined options** use portions of the various methods listed above. For example, some deaf children who use auditory oral

259

options also learn sign language. Children who use ASL also learn to read and write in English. Combined options can expose children who are deaf or hard of hearing to many ways to communicate with others.

Will My Child Be Successful in School?

Like all children, children who are deaf or hard of hearing can develop strong academic, social, and emotional skills and succeed in school. Find out how your school system helps children with hearing loss. With your input, your child's school will develop an Individualized Education Program (IEP) for your child, and you should ask if an educational audiologist is available to be part of the academic team. Explore programs outside of school that may help you and your child, and talk with other parents who have already dealt with these issues. The Individuals with Disabilities Education Act ensures that children with hearing loss receive free, appropriate, early intervention services from birth through the school years.

Baby's Hearing Screening Timeline for Parents

By 1 Month Old

- Make sure that your baby's hearing is screened either before you leave the hospital or immediately afterward. After the screening, find out the results. If your newborn was not screened in the hospital, schedule a screening to occur by the time your baby is 1 month old.

By 3 Months Old

- If your baby does not pass the hearing screening, immediately schedule a follow-up appointment with a pediatric audiologist. Ask your doctor or hospital for a list of pediatric audiologists or use the directories provided by the American Academy of Audiology (AAA) and the American Speech–Language–Hearing Association (ASHA).

- If you must cancel the follow-up appointment, reschedule it! Make sure you take your baby to a follow-up examination by age 3 months.

By 6 Months Old

- If the follow-up exam shows that your baby has hearing loss, start your baby in some form of intervention by the time he or she is 6 months old. Intervention can include hearing devices, such as hearing aids or cochlear implants; communication methods, including oral approaches (such as lipreading) or manual approaches (such as American Sign Language); or a combination of options, including assistive devices.

Ongoing

• Remain active and involved in your child's progress.

• If you move, make sure that your child's doctors and specialists have your new address.

• Even if your child passed the follow-up exam, continue to monitor his or her communication development. If you have concerns, speak with your child's doctor. If your child has risk factors for childhood hearing loss, speak with an audiologist about how often his or her hearing should be monitored.

Section 17.4

Pulse Oximetry Screening for Critical Congenital Heart Defects

This section includes text excerpted from "Pulse Oximetry Screening for Critical Congenital Heart Defects," Centers for Disease Control and Prevention (CDC), August 29, 2014. Reviewed December 2017.

What Are Critical Congenital Heart Defects?

The seven defects classified as critical congenital heart defects (CCHDs) are hypoplastic left heart syndrome (HLHS), pulmonary atresia (PA) (with intact septum), Tetralogy of Fallot (TOF), total anomalous pulmonary venous return (TAPVR), transposition of the great arteries (TGA), tricuspid atresia (TA), and truncus arteriosus (TA). Babies with one these CCHDs are at significant risk for death or disability if their heart defect is not diagnosed and treated soon after birth. These seven CCHDs among some babies potentially can be detected using pulse oximetry screening, which is a test to determine the amount of oxygen in the blood and pulse rate. Certain hospitals routinely screen all newborns using pulse oximetry screening. However, pulse oximetry screening is not currently included in newborn screening in most states.

Other heart defects can be just as severe as these seven CCHDs and also require treatment soon after birth. However, pulse oximetry screening may not detect these heart defects as consistently as the seven disorders listed as CCHDs.

Why Is Screening for Critical Congenital Heart Defects Important?

Some babies born with a heart defect can appear healthy at first and can be sent home with their families before their heart defect is detected. It has been estimated that at least 300 infants with an unrecognized CCHD are discharged each year from newborn nurseries in the United States. These babies are at risk for having serious problems within the first few days or weeks of life and often require emergency care.

Pulse oximetry newborn screening can identify some infants with a CCHD before they show any signs. Once identified, babies with a CCHD can be seen by cardiologists (heart doctors) and can receive specialized care and treatment that could prevent death or disability early in life. Treatment can include medications and surgery.

How Are Babies Screened?

Pulse oximetry is a simple bedside test to determine the amount of oxygen in a baby's blood and the baby's pulse rate. Low levels of oxygen in the blood can be a sign of a CCHD. The test is done using a machine called a pulse oximeter, with sensors placed on the baby's skin. The test is painless and takes only a few minutes. Pulse oximetry screening does not replace a complete history and physical examination, which sometimes can detect a CCHD before oxygen levels in the blood become low. Pulse oximetry screening, therefore, should be used along with the physical examination.

When Are Babies Screened?

Screening is done when a baby is 24–48 hours of age. If the baby is to be discharged from the hospital before he or she is 24 hours of age, screening should be done as late as possible before discharge. Pulse oximetry screening is not currently included in newborn screening in most states.

What Are Pulse Oximetry Screening Results?

If the results are "negative" (in range result), it means that the baby's test results did not show signs of a CCHD. This type of screening test does not detect all CCHDs, so it is possible to still have a critical or other heart defect with a negative screening result. If the results are "positive" ("fail" or out of range result), it means that the baby's test results showed low levels of oxygen in the blood. This can be a sign of a CCHD. This does not always mean that the baby has a CCHD. It just means that more testing is needed.

The baby's doctor might recommend that the infant get screened again or have more specific tests, like an echocardiogram (an ultrasound picture of the heart), to diagnose a CCHD. Babies who are found to have a CCHD also might be evaluated by a clinical geneticist. This could help identify genetic syndromes associated with these heart defects and inform families about future risks.

Chapter 18

Perinatal Infections

Chapter Contents

Section 18.1

Group B Streptococcal Infection

This section includes text excerpted from "Group B Strep Home—
Group B Strep Infection in Newborns," Centers for Disease Control
and Prevention (CDC), May 23, 2016.

Group B *Streptococcus* (group B strep) is a type of bacteria that
causes illness in people of all ages. Also known as GBS, group B strep
disease can be especially severe in newborns, most commonly causing
sepsis (infection of the blood), pneumonia (infection in the lungs), and
sometimes meningitis (infection of the fluid and lining around the
brain and spinal cord).

Types of Infection

Among babies, there are two main types of group B strep disease:

- Early-onset—occurs during the first week of life

- Late-onset—occurs from the first week through three months of
life

Early-onset disease used to be the most common type of disease in
babies. Nowadays, because of effective early-onset disease prevention,
early and late-onset disease occur at similar low rates.

For early-onset disease, group B strep most commonly causes sepsis
(infection of the blood), pneumonia (infection in the lungs), and sometimes meningitis (infection of the fluid and lining around the brain).
Similar illnesses are associated with late-onset group B strep disease.
Meningitis is more common with late-onset group B strep disease than
with early-onset group B strep disease.

How It Spreads

In cases of early-onset disease (occurs in babies younger than 1
week old), group B strep bacteria are most often passed from mother
to baby during labor and birth. Antibiotics given to the mother during

labor can be very effective at preventing the spread of group B strep bacteria to the baby.

Late-onset disease (occurs in babies 1 week through 3 months old) is sometimes due to passing of the bacteria from mother to newborn, but the bacteria may come from another source. For a baby whose mother does not test positive for group B strep bacteria, the source of infection for late-onset disease can be hard to figure out and is often unknown.

Risk Factors

Some pregnant women are at an increased risk of having a baby who develops early-onset group B strep disease. Some risk factors include:

- Testing positive for group B strep bacteria late in the current pregnancy (35–37 weeks pregnant)
- Detecting group B strep bacteria in urine (pee) during the current pregnancy
- Delivering early (before 37 weeks of pregnancy)
- Developing a fever during labor
- Having a long time between water breaking and delivering (18 hours or more)
- Having a previous baby who developed early-onset disease

The risk factors for late-onset group B strep disease are not as well understood as those for early-onset disease. Late-onset disease is more common among babies who are born prematurely (before 37 weeks of pregnancy). Babies whose mothers tested positive for group B strep bacteria also are at increased risk of late-onset disease.

Symptoms

The symptoms of group B strep disease can seem like other health problems in newborns and babies. Most newborns with early-onset disease (occurs in babies younger than 1 week old) have symptoms on the day of birth. Babies who develop late-onset disease may appear healthy at birth and develop symptoms of group B strep disease after the first week through the first three months of life.

Some symptoms include:

- Fever

- Difficulty feeding
- Irritability or lethargy (limpness or hard to wake up the baby)
- Difficulty breathing
- Blue-ish color to skin

Complications

For both early- and late-onset group B strep disease, and particularly for babies who had meningitis (infection of the fluid and lining around the brain and spinal cord), there may be long-term problems such as deafness and developmental disabilities. Care for sick babies has improved a lot in the United States. However, 2–3 out of every 50 babies (4–6 percent) who develop group B strep disease will die.

On average, about 1,000 babies in the United States get early-onset group B strep disease each year, with rates higher among prematurely born babies (born before 37 weeks) and blacks. Group B strep bacteria may also cause some miscarriages, stillbirths, and preterm deliveries. However, there are many different factors that lead to stillbirth, preterm delivery, or miscarriage and, most of the time, the cause is not known.

Diagnosis

Group B strep disease is diagnosed by taking samples of a baby's sterile body fluids, such as blood or spinal fluid. These samples are cultured (bacteria grown in the laboratory) to see if group B strep bacteria are present, which can take a few days.

If a mother who tested positive for group B strep bacteria received antibiotics during labor, doctors will check on the baby once he or she is born. The baby likely won't need extra antibiotics or other medicine after birth, unless the doctor says they are needed.

For both early-onset (occurs in babies younger than 1 week old) and late-onset (occurs in babies 1 week through 3 months old) disease, if a group B strep infection is suspected, doctors will take a sample of the baby's blood and spinal fluids or take a chest X-ray to confirm the diagnosis.

Treatment

Group B strep disease in newborns and older babies is treated with antibiotics (medicine used to kill bacteria in the body), such as penicillin or ampicillin, given through intravenous (IV). For babies with severe illness, other procedures, in addition to antibiotics, may be needed.

Section 18.2

Hepatitis B

This section includes text excerpted from "Viral Hepatitis— Hepatitis B FAQs for the Public," Centers for Disease Control and Prevention (CDC), May 23, 2016.

What Is Hepatitis B?

Hepatitis B is a contagious liver disease that ranges in severity from a mild illness lasting a few weeks to a serious, lifelong illness. It results from infection with the Hepatitis B virus. Hepatitis B can be either "acute" or "chronic."

How Is Hepatitis B Spread?

Hepatitis B is spread when blood, semen, or other body fluid infected with the Hepatitis B virus enters the body of a person who is not infected. People can become infected with the virus during activities such as:

- Birth (spread from an infected mother to her baby during birth)
- Sex with an infected partner
- Sharing needles, syringes, or other drug-injection equipment
- Sharing items such as razors or toothbrushes with an infected person
- Direct contact with the blood or open sores of an infected person
- Exposure to blood from needle sticks or other sharp instruments

How Serious Is Chronic Hepatitis B?

Chronic Hepatitis B is a serious disease that can result in long-term health problems, including liver damage, liver failure, liver cancer, or even death. Approximately 1,800 people die every year from Hepatitis B-related liver disease.

Can Hepatitis B Be Prevented?

Yes. The best way to prevent Hepatitis B is by getting the Hepatitis B vaccine. The Hepatitis B vaccine is safe and effective and is usually given as 3–4 shots over a 6-month period.

What Is Hepatitis B Immune Globulin (HBIG)?

Hepatitis B immune globulin is a substance made from human blood samples that contains antibodies against the Hepatitis B virus. It is given as a shot and can provide short-term protection (approximately 3 months) against Hepatitis B.

Are Pregnant Women Tested for Hepatitis B?

Yes. When a pregnant woman comes in for prenatal care, she will be given a series of routine blood tests, including one that checks for the presence of Hepatitis B virus infection. This test is important because women infected with this virus can pass Hepatitis B to their babies during birth. But this can be prevented by giving the infant Hepatitis B immune globulin (HBIG) and the first Hepatitis B vaccine at birth, and then completing the series.

What If a Pregnant Woman Has Hepatitis B?

If a pregnant woman has Hepatitis B, she can pass the infection to her baby during birth. But this can be prevented through a series of vaccinations and HBIG for her baby beginning at birth. Without vaccination, babies born to women with Hepatitis B virus infection can develop chronic infection, which can lead to serious health problems.

How Does a Baby Get Hepatitis B?

A baby can get Hepatitis B from an infected mother during childbirth.

Can a Baby Be Protected from Getting Hepatitis B from His or Her Mother during Birth?

Yes, almost all cases of Hepatitis B can be prevented if a baby born to an infected woman receives the necessary shots at the recommended times The infant should receive a shot called HBIG and the first dose of Hepatitis B vaccine within 12 hours of birth. Two or 3 additional shots of vaccine are needed over the next 1–6 months to help prevent Hepatitis B. The timing and total number of shots will be influenced by several factors, including the type of vaccine and the baby's age and birth weight. In addition, experts recommend that the baby get an antibody test 1–2 months after completion of the vaccine series at age 9–12 months to make sure he or she is protected from the disease. To best protect your baby, follow the advice of his or her doctor.

What Happens If a Baby Gets Hepatitis B?

Most newborns who become infected with Hepatitis B virus do not have symptoms, but they have a 90 percent chance of developing chronic Hepatitis B. This can eventually lead to serious health problems, including liver damage, liver cancer, and even death.

Do Babies Need the Hepatitis B Vaccine Even If a Pregnant Woman Does Not Have Hepatitis B?

Yes. The Hepatitis B vaccine is recommended for all infants. Centers for Disease Control and Prevention (CDC) recommends that the infant get the first shot before leaving the hospital.

Why Is the Hepatitis B Vaccine Recommended for All Babies?

Hepatitis B vaccine is recommended for all babies so that they will be protected from a serious but preventable disease. Babies and young children are at much greater risk for developing a chronic infection if infected, but the vaccine can prevent this.

Section 18.3

Human Immunodeficiency Virus (HIV)

This section includes text excerpted from "Pregnancy and HIV,"
Office on Women's Health (OWH), U.S. Department of Health and
Human Services (HHS), March 16, 2016.

A diagnosis of human immunodeficiency virus (HIV) does not mean you can't have children. But you can pass HIV to your baby during the pregnancy, while in labor, while giving birth, or by breastfeeding. The good news is that there are many ways to lower the risk of passing HIV to your unborn baby to almost zero.

What Can I Do before Getting Pregnant to Lower My Risk of Passing HIV to My Baby?

If you plan to become pregnant, talk to your doctor right away. Your doctor can talk with you about how HIV can affect your health during pregnancy and your unborn baby's health. Your doctor can work with you to prepare for a healthy pregnancy before you start trying to become pregnant.

Everyone living with HIV should take HIV medicines to stay healthy. If you are thinking about becoming pregnant and are not taking HIV treatment, it is important that you begin, because this will lower your chances of passing the virus to your baby when you become pregnant.

There are ways for you to get pregnant that will limit your partner's risk of HIV infection. You can ask your doctor about ways to get pregnant and still protect your partner.

I Do Not Have HIV, but My Partner Does. Can I Get Pregnant without Getting HIV?

Women have a higher risk of HIV infection during vaginal sex than men. If you do not have HIV but your male partner does, the risk of getting HIV while trying to get pregnant can be reduced but not totally eliminated.

Talk to your doctor about HIV medicine you can take (called pre-exposure prophylaxis or PrEP) to help protect you and your baby from HIV.

You may also want to consider donor sperm or assisted reproductive technology (ART), such as semen washing or in vitro fertilization, to get pregnant. These options can be expensive and may not be covered by your health insurance.

I'm Pregnant. Will My Baby Have HIV?

If you just found out you are pregnant, see your doctor right away. Find out what you can do to take care of yourself and to give your baby a healthy start to life.

With your doctor's help, you can decide on the best treatment for you and your baby before, during, and after the pregnancy. You should also take these steps before and during your pregnancy to help you and your baby stay healthy.

Just because you have HIV doesn't mean your child will get HIV. In the United States, before effective treatment was available, about 25 percent of pregnant mothers with HIV passed the virus to their babies. But now, if you take HIV treatment and have an undetectable viral load, your risk of passing HIV to your baby is less than 1 percent.

What Can I Do to Lower My Risk of Passing HIV to My Baby?

Thanks to more HIV testing and new medicines, the number of children infected with HIV during pregnancy, labor and childbirth, and breastfeeding has decreased by 90 percent since the mid-1990s.

The steps below can lower the risk of giving HIV to your baby:

Step 1: Tell your doctor you want to get pregnant. Your doctor can help you decide if you need to change your treatments to lower your viral load, to help you get pregnant without passing HIV to your partner, and to prevent you from passing the virus to your baby. He or she will also help you get as healthy as possible before you get pregnant to improve your chances of a healthy pregnancy and baby. Don't stop using condoms for sexually transmitted infections (STI) prevention and another method of birth control for pregnancy prevention until your doctor says you are healthy enough to start trying.

Step 2: Get prenatal care. Prenatal care is the care you receive from your doctor while you are pregnant. You need to work closely with your doctor throughout your pregnancy to monitor your treatment, your health, and your baby's health.

Step 3: Start HIV treatment. You can start treatment before pregnancy to lower the risk of passing HIV to your baby. If you are already on treatment, do not stop, but do see your doctor right away. Some HIV drugs should not be used while you're pregnant. For other drugs, you may need a different dosage.

Step 4: Manage side effects. Side effects from HIV medicines can be especially challenging during pregnancy, but it is still important that you take your medicine as directed by your doctor. Talk to your doctor about any side effects you have and about ways to manage them.

Step 5: Do not breastfeed. You can pass the virus to your baby through your breastmilk even if you are taking medicine. The best way to avoid passing HIV to your baby is to feed your infant formula instead of breastfeeding.

Step 6: Make sure your baby is tested for HIV right after birth. You should choose a doctor or clinic experienced in caring for babies exposed to HIV. They will tell you what follow-up tests your baby will need and when. Talk to your doctor about whether your baby may benefit from starting treatment right away.

Step 7: Ask your pediatric HIV specialist if your baby might benefit from anti-HIV medicines before you know if your baby is HIV-positive or HIV-negative. Research has shown that giving combination HIV drugs to newborns is better at preventing HIV than taking AZT (azidothymidine, an antiretroviral medicine) alone.

Can I Take HIV Medicine during Pregnancy?

HIV-infected pregnant women should take HIV medicines. These medicines can lower the risk of passing HIV to a baby and improve the mother's health.

If you haven't used any HIV drugs before pregnancy and are in your first trimester, your doctor will help you decide if you should start treatment. Here are some things to consider:

- Nausea and vomiting may make it hard to take the HIV medicine early during pregnancy.

- It is possible the medicine may affect your baby. Your doctor will prescribe medicine that is safe to use during pregnancy.

- HIV is more commonly passed to a baby late in pregnancy or during delivery. HIV can be passed early in pregnancy if your viral load is detectable.

- Studies show treatment works best at preventing HIV in a baby if it is started before pregnancy or as early as possible during pregnancy.

If you are taking HIV drugs and find out you're pregnant in the first trimester, talk to your doctor about sticking with your current treatment plan. Some things you can talk about with your doctor include:

- Whether to continue or stop HIV treatment in the first trimester. Stopping HIV medicine could cause your viral load to go up. If your viral load goes up, the risk of infection also goes up. Your disease also could get worse and cause problems for your baby. So this is a serious decision to make with your doctor.

- What effects your HIV medicines may have on the baby.

- Whether you are at risk for drug resistance. This means the HIV medicine you take no longer works against HIV. Never stop taking your HIV medicine without first talking to your doctor.

Can I Get Help Paying for Care during Pregnancy?

If you are pregnant, Medicaid may pay for your prenatal care. If you are pregnant and living with HIV, Medicaid might pay for counseling, medicine to lower the risk of passing HIV to your baby, and treatment for HIV. Each state makes its own rules regarding Medicaid. Contact your local or county medical assistance, welfare, or social services office to learn more. If you are unable to find that number, search your state's department of health.

If you don't think you qualify for assistance, check again. Sometimes states change their Medicaid rules. You may also access care through the Ryan White Human Immunodeficiency Virus/Acquired Immune Deficiency Syndrome (HIV/AIDS) Program.

Chapter 19

What to Expect When Your Baby Is in the Neonatal Intensive Care Unit (NICU)

The birth of a baby brings much joy and is a wonderful experience. However, there can be many complications in the birthing process. Once the baby is out of the mother's womb, he or she has to make several adjustments to get adapted to the physical environment, independent of the mother's circulation and placenta for physiologic functions. The infant's body systems undergo major changes and should be able to do the following functions effectively:

- The lungs must be able to inhale and exhale air.

- The cardiac and pulmonary circulation should function effectively.

- The digestive system has to digest food and excrete waste.

- The kidneys have to work effectively by balancing fluids and chemicals and excreting unwanted fluids and electrolytes.

- The liver and the immunologic system have to function independently.

If the above functions do not happen in the baby's body or if a baby is born prematurely, the baby could be placed in the neonatal intensive care unit (NICU).

What Is the Neonatal Intensive Care Unit (NICU)?

The neonatal intensive care unit is a special area of the hospital where newborns are admitted if they show signs of health issues during the first few days of life. Babies who are born prematurely or encounter problems during delivery may also be moved to the NICU to be kept under special care. The NICU is also called an intensive care nursery, a newborn intensive care, or special care nursery. If infants need special treatment, they are usually admitted within 24 hours of birth. The severity of the condition will determine the stay in the NICU.

The NICU can be an overwhelming place for parents, with equipment, small babies in incubators, hospital staff, and other parents. A baby in the NICU gets medical care from many providers who specialize in neonatal care:

- **Neonatologist:** A doctor who has taken special training to treat newborns that need intensive care.

- **Pediatric residents, neonatology fellows**: Doctors who pursue training in neonatology at different levels.

- **Registered nurse:** The nurse who has the training to give medical care.

- **Neonatal nurse practitioner:** A nurse with additional training in neonatology care.

- **Respiratory therapist:** A therapist who helps with the infant's breathing.

- **Speech-language pathologist:** A specialist who helps babies with feeding and swallowing problems.

- **A nutritionist:** A person who helps with the baby's diet.

- **Cardiologist:** A doctor who specializes in diagnosing and treating diseases or conditions of the heart and blood vessels.

- **Neurologist:** A doctor who treats disorders that affect the brain, spinal cord, and nerves.

- **Pharmacists:** A trained medical professional in charge of the infant's medications.

- **Occupational therapist:** A medical professional who helps with the baby's movement issues.

- **A chaplain:** A person who provides counsel, support, and comfort to parents.

- **A social worker:** A person who helps parents to get the services they need and lends support by connecting the families to the therapists.

The infant's providers may keep changing—it depends on the length of the baby's hospital stay and the baby's condition. In some NICUs, the nurses may change every day; in others, a particular nurse would be assigned to an infant. Sometimes, doctors might also be changed. Parents need to talk to the healthcare providers about the baby's condition and the tests and treatments that he or she is undergoing. If parents are unable to go into the NICU because of their own condition, then talking to a provider on the healthcare team will give them a better understanding of the baby's condition.

Questions to Ask the Healthcare Providers in the NICU

Constant conversation with healthcare providers gives parents a better understanding of the baby's condition while in the NICU. Nurses see the baby every day and can give the parents updates about the baby's condition, and explain the diagnosis and treatment plan. However, if the parents have questions and other issues, they could discuss it with the attending neonatologist, neonatal nurse practitioner, neonatal fellow, or another member of the NICU healthcare team. Certain questions parents might want to ask the neonatologist or nurses include:

- How long does the baby have to stay in the NICU?
- What are the health issues?
- Who is involved with taking care of the baby?
- What medicines does the baby have to take?
- What are the types of tests that would be done on the baby?
- What can the baby's diet contain?
- When can the baby be nursed or bottle-fed by the parent, and how?
- Can the baby be touched?

- Will someone help the mother to nurse the baby?

- Will parents be allowed inside the NICU?

- Is there help from someone who can run the parents through the process?

Nurses can give detailed information about the baby's condition and when the parents can visit the baby in the NICU. For more help coping with the situation, a social worker can be contacted. For example, if you need to stay over in the hospital or a nearby place, the social worker will help you find accommodations, cots, or recliners.

What to Expect in the NICU?

The NICU experience can be intimidating for parents because the unit is often busy with lots of activity, people, and beeping monitors. However, to make the babies as comfortable as possible, the unit is made dim and quiet. Each baby gets care tailored to his or her specific needs.

Since not all the organs may be fully developed for the baby, some health issues may occur during the infant's stay in the NICU. Some of them may include:

- In a premature baby, a breathing problem—respiratory distress syndrome (RDS)—may happen, and he or she may require respiratory support. The baby's ability to breathe on its own happens with time, as the lungs develop and get stronger.

- Bleeding in the brain, heart murmur, low blood count, anemia, infections, or intestinal problems.

After settling down in the NICU, infants might be on a feeding schedule based on their developmental progress. Some babies are born too early or maybe too sick to eat on their own; hence, a feeding tube is attached to their stomach through the mouth.

An infant might be on medicines as directed by the healthcare provider to help the breathing process, blood pressure, or heart rate. To ensure the baby's progress, the doctors may want to do more tests, such as blood and urine tests, X-rays, and ultrasounds. For complicated cases, the doctors may place a line into an artery or vein to take blood for the test, so that the baby would not be disturbed as often. NICU staff will ensure the baby is given the best care possible. One of the best things a parent can do is not to be afraid to ask questions or seek help when their child is in the NICU.

NICU Equipment

The NICU equipment listed below help with the baby's treatment, depending on his or her condition and diagnosis:

- **Feeding tubes:** Often, babies in the NICU do not get enough calories; hence, breast milk or formula milk is given through the feeding tube. The tube is placed in the stomach of the baby through the mouth. The tubes are not painful because they are taped to one place to not move or cause friction.

- **IV (intravenous) catheter and lines:** Most babies in the NICU have IV catheters for fluids and medication. They are given on the hands, arms, legs, feet, or scalp. IV catheters are thin, flexible tubes placed inside the vein with the help of a small needle. The needle is removed after the insertion of the tube into the vein. Instead of giving the baby injection several times, IV catheters help in giving medication through several drops at a time.

- **Arterial lines:** These are placed in the artery, not in the vein, and help in monitoring blood pressure and oxygen levels.

- **Infant warmers:** These are beds with radiant heaters over them; babies can be touched by parents in the warmers.

- **Isolettes:** These small beds enclosed in clear, hard plastic help babies maintain the correct body temperature. Isolettes have holes that allow doctors and nurses to examine and parents to touch the baby.

- **Monitors:** Babies are connected to monitors so that the health-care team can be aware of all the vital signs. A single monitor is secured to chest leads, which are painless stickers connected to wires that can count the baby's heart rate and breathing rate. A pulse oximetry machine helps display the baby's blood oxygen levels on the screen. Even the temperature is displayed on the monitor with the help of a temperature robe, a coated wire attached to the baby's skin with a patch.

- **Phototherapy:** A therapy mostly done for infants with jaundice for a few days. Phototherapy helps get rid of bilirubin, which causes jaundice. The infant is made to lie on a special blanket and has lights attached to their isolettes or beds. The eyes are protected from the light by using eye pads.

- **Ventilators:** Ventilators are used to help the baby breathe. Babies are connected to the ventilator through an endotracheal tube (a plastic tube inserted in the windpipe through the nose or mouth). Infants who have a longer stay at the NICU may undergo a tracheostomy (a plastic tube is placed into the trachea).

How Can the Parent Take Care of the Baby in the NICU?

Parental bonding plays a major role in the well-being of the baby in the NICU. Parents are allowed to visit and spend time with their baby in the NICU. Other visitors may be restricted.

Research suggests that kangaroo care, a skin-to-skin contact between a baby and a parent, speeds recovery of the baby. This is how it works:

- The mother needs to place the baby near her chest underneath her shirt so that the baby rests on the mother's skin.

- The shirt can be loosely closed over the baby to keep him or her warm.

Parents need to hold, touch, and talk to their baby as much as possible; this can improve the outcome of treatment and future health. Depending on the child's condition, parents are allowed to hold the baby, even if he or she is connected to medical equipment. The healthcare provider may suggest a minimal touch when babies could become stressed; however, parents can still spend time with the baby, talk, and sing to them.

The best way to help babies in the NICU is for parents to be there and observe their behaviors, such as:

- When a baby needs rest.

- When a baby bonds with the parent.

- What time of the day the baby is most alert.

- What types of interaction the baby likes (stroking, singing, etc.)

- How well the baby responds to the parents before getting tired.

References

1. Greenspan, Jay S. "When Your Baby Is in the NICU?" October 2014.

2. "Your Baby's NICU Stay," March of Dimes, April 2017.

3. "Parenting in the Neonatal Intensive Care Unit (NICU) Parenting in the NICU," Phoenix Children's Hospital, n.d.

Part Three

Structural Abnormalities and Functional Impairments

Chapter 20

Arteriovenous Malformations

What Are Arteriovenous Malformations?

Arteriovenous malformations (AVMs) are abnormal, snarled tangles of blood vessels that cause multiple irregular connections between the arteries and veins. These malformations most often occur in the spinal cord and in any part of the brain or on its surface, but can develop elsewhere in the body. Normally, arteries carry oxygen-rich blood away from the heart to the body's cells, organs, and tissues; veins return blood with less oxygen to the lungs and heart. But in an AVM, the absence of capillaries—a network of small blood vessels that connect arteries to veins and deliver oxygen to cells—creates a shortcut for blood to pass directly from arteries to veins and bypass tissue, which can lead to tissue damage and the death of nerve cells and other cells. Over time, some AVMs get progressively larger as the amount of blood flow increases.

In some cases, a weakened blood vessel may burst, spilling blood into the brain (hemorrhage) that can cause stroke and brain damage. Other neurological problems include headache, weakness, seizures, pain, and problems with speech, vision, or movement. In most cases, people with neurological AVMs experience few, if any, significant symptoms. It is unclear why AVMs form. Most often AVMs are congenital,

This chapter includes text excerpted from "Arteriovenous Malformations and Other Vascular Lesions of the Central Nervous System Fact Sheet," National Institute of Neurological Disorders and Stroke (NINDS), September 2015.

but they can appear sporadically. In some cases the AVM may be inherited, but it is more likely that other inherited conditions increase the risk of having an AVM. The malformations tend to be discovered only incidentally, usually during treatment for an unrelated disorder or at autopsy. It is estimated that brain AVMs occur in less than one percent of the general population; each year about one percent of those with AVMs will die as a direct result of the AVM. Treatment options depend on the type of AVM, its location, noticeable symptoms, and the general health condition of the individual.

What Are the Symptoms?

Symptoms can vary greatly in severity; in some people the severity of symptoms becomes debilitating or even life-threatening. Seizures and headaches that may be severe are the most generalized symptoms of AVMs, but no particular type of seizure or headache pattern has been identified. Seizures can be focal (meaning they involve a small part of the brain) or generalized (widespread), involving convulsions, a loss of control over movement, or a change in a person's level of consciousness. Headaches can vary greatly in frequency, duration, and intensity, sometimes becoming as severe as migraines. Pain may be on either one side of the head or on both sides. Sometimes a headache consistently affecting one side of the head may be closely linked to the site of an AVM. Most often, the location of the pain is not specific to the malformation and may encompass most of the head.

AVMs also can cause a wide range of more specific neurological symptoms that vary from person to person, depending primarily upon the location of the AVM. Such symptoms may include:

- muscle weakness or paralysis in one part of the body

- a loss of coordination (ataxia) that can lead to such problems as gait disturbances

- difficulties carrying out tasks that require planning (apraxia)

- back pain or weakness in the lower extremities caused by a spinal AVM

- dizziness

- visual problems such as a loss of part of the visual field, inability to control eye movement, or swelling of a part of the optic nerve

- difficulty speaking or understanding language (aphasia)

- abnormal sensations such as numbness, tingling, or spontaneous pain
- memory deficits
- confusion, hallucinations, or dementia

AVMs may also cause subtle learning or behavioral disorders in some people during their childhood or adolescence, long before more obvious symptoms become evident. Symptoms caused by AVMs can appear at any age. Because the abnormalities tend to result from a slow buildup of neurological damage over time, they are most often noticed when people are in their twenties or older. If AVMs do not become symptomatic by the time people reach their late forties or early fifties, they tend to remain stable and are less likely to produce symptoms. Some pregnant women may experience a sudden onset or worsening of symptoms due to accompanying cardiovascular changes, especially increases in blood volume and blood pressure.

Although most neurological AVMs have very few, if any, significant symptoms, one particularly severe type of AVM causes symptoms to appear at, or very soon after, birth. Called a vein of Galen defect after the major blood vessel involved, this lesion is located deep inside the brain. It is frequently associated with hydrocephalus (an accumulation of fluid within certain spaces in the brain, often with visible enlargement of the head), swollen veins visible on the scalp, seizures, failure to thrive, and congestive heart failure. Children born with this condition who survive past infancy often remain developmentally impaired.

How Do AVMs Damage the Brain and Spinal Cord?

AVMs damage the brain or spinal cord through three basic mechanisms: by reducing the amount of oxygen reaching neurological tissues; by causing bleeding (hemorrhage) into surrounding tissues; and by compressing or displacing parts of the brain or spinal cord.

- AVMs affect oxygen delivery to the brain or spinal cord by altering normal patterns of blood flow using the arteries, veins, and capillaries. In AVMs arteries pump blood directly into veins through a passageway called afistula. Since the network of capillaries is bypassed, the rate of blood flow is uncontrolled and too rapid to allow oxygen to be dispersed to surrounding tissues. As a result, the cells that make up these tissues become oxygen-depleted and begin to deteriorate, sometimes dying off completely.

- This abnormally rapid rate of blood flow frequently causes blood pressure inside the vessels located in the central portion of an AVM directly adjacent to the fistula—an area doctors refer to as the nidus—to rise to dangerously high levels. The arteries feeding blood into the AVM often become swollen and distorted; the veins that drain blood away from it often become abnormally constricted (a condition called stenosis). Also, the walls of the involved arteries and veins are often abnormally thin and weak. Aneurysms—balloon-like bulges in blood vessel walls that are susceptible to rupture—may develop in association with approximately half of all neurological AVMs due to this structural weakness.

- Bleeding into the brain, called intracranial hemorrhage, can result from the combination of high internal pressure and vessel wall weakness. Such hemorrhages are often microscopic in size (called microbleeds), causing limited damage and few significant symptoms. (Generally, microbleeds do not have short-term consequences on brain function, but microbleeds over time can lead to an increased risk of dementia and cognitive disruption.) Even many nonsymptomatic AVMs show evidence of past bleeding. But massive hemorrhages can occur if the physical stresses caused by extremely high blood pressure, rapid blood flow rates, and vessel wall weakness are great enough. If a large enough volume of blood escapes from a ruptured AVM into the surrounding brain, the result can be a catastrophic stroke. AVMs account for approximately two percent of all hemorrhagic strokes that occur each year.

- Even in the absence of bleeding or significant oxygen depletion, large AVMs can damage the brain or spinal cord simply by their presence. They can range in size from a fraction of an inch to more than 2.5 inches in diameter, depending on the number and size of the blood vessels making up the lesion. The larger the lesion, the greater the amount of pressure it exerts on surrounding brain or spinal cord structures. The largest lesions may compress several inches of the spinal cord or distort the shape of an entire hemisphere of the brain. Such massive AVMs can constrict the flow of cerebrospinal fluid—a clear liquid that normally nourishes and protects the brain and spinal cord—by distorting or closing the passageways and open chambers (ventricles) inside the brain that allow this fluid to circulate freely. As cerebrospinal fluid accumulates, hydrocephalus results. This fluid buildup further increases the amount of pressure on fragile neurological structures, adding to the damage caused by the AVM itself.

Where Do Neurological AVMs Tend to Form?

AVMs can form virtually anywhere in the brain or spinal cord—wherever arteries and veins exist. Some are formed from blood vessels located in the dura mater or in the pia mater, the outermost and innermost, respectively, of the three membranes surrounding the brain and spinal cord. (The third membrane, called the arachnoid, lacks blood vessels). AVMs of the dura mater affect the function of the spinal cord by transmitting excess pressure to the venous system of the spinal cord. AVMs of the spinal cord affect the function of the spinal cord by hemorrhage, by reducing blood flow to the spinal cord, or by causing excess venous pressure. Spinal AVMs frequently cause attacks of sudden, severe back pain, often concentrated at the roots of nerve fibers where they exit the vertebrae, with pain that is similar to that caused by a slipped disk. These lesions also can cause sensory disturbances, muscle weakness, or paralysis in the parts of the body served by the spinal cord or the damaged nerve fibers. A spinal cord AVM can lead to degeneration of the nerve fibers within the spinal cord below the level of the lesion, causing widespread paralysis in parts of the body controlled by those nerve fibers.

AVMs on the surface of the cerebral hemispheres—the uppermost portions of the brain—exert pressure on the cerebral cortex, the brain's "gray matter." Depending on their location, these AVMs may damage portions of the cerebral cortex involved with thinking, speaking, understanding language, hearing, taste, touch, or initiating and controlling voluntary movements. AVMs located on the frontal lobe close to the optic nerve or on the occipital lobe (the rear portion of the cerebrum where images are processed) may cause a variety of visual disturbances.

AVMs also can form from blood vessels located deep inside the interior of the cerebrum (the main portion of the brain). These AVMs may compromise the functions of three vital structures:

1. the thalamus, which transmits nerve signals between the spinal cord and upper regions of the brain,

2. the basal ganglia surrounding the thalamus, which coordinate complex movements and plays a role in learning and memory, and

291

3. the hippocampus, which plays a major role in memory.

AVMs can affect other parts of the brain besides the cerebrum. The hindbrain is formed from two major structures:

1. the cerebellum, which is nestled under the rear portion of the cerebrum and

2. the brain stem, which serves as the bridge linking the upper portions of the brain with the spinal cord.

These structures control finely coordinated movements, maintain balance, and regulate some functions of internal organs, including those of the heart and lungs. AVM damage to these parts of the hindbrain can result in dizziness, giddiness, vomiting, a loss of the ability to coordinate complex movements such as walking, or uncontrollable muscle tremors.

What Are the Health Consequences of AVMs?

The greatest potential danger posed by AVMs is hemorrhage. Most episodes of bleeding remain undetected at the time they occur because they are not severe enough to cause significant neurological damage. But massive, even fatal, bleeding episodes do occur. Whenever an AVM is detected, the individual should be carefully and consistently monitored for any signs of instability that may indicate an increased risk of hemorrhage.

A few physical characteristics appear to indicate a greater-than-usual likelihood of clinically significant hemorrhage:

*   Smaller AVMs have a greater likelihood of bleeding than do larger ones.

*   Impaired drainage by unusually narrow or deeply situated veins increases the chances of hemorrhage.

*   Pregnancy appears to increase the likelihood of clinically significant hemorrhage, mainly because of increases in blood pressure and blood volume.

*   AVMs that have hemorrhaged once are about nine times more likely to bleed again during the first year after the initial hemorrhage than are lesions that have never bled.

The damaging effects of a hemorrhage are related to lesion location. Bleeding from AVMs located deep inside the interior tissues, or parenchyma, of the brain typically causes more severe neurological damage than does hemorrhage by lesions that have formed in the dural or pial membranes or on the surface of the brain or spinal cord. (Deeply located bleeding is usually referred to as an intracerebral or parenchymal hemorrhage; bleeding within the membranes or on the surface of the brain is known as subdural or subarachnoid hemorrhage.) Therefore, location is an important factor to consider when weighing the relative risks surgery to treat AVMs.

What Other Types of Vascular Lesions Affect the Central Nervous System?

Besides AVMs, three other main types of vascular lesion can arise in the brain or spinal cord:

1. Cavernous malformations,

2. Capillary telangiectases, and

3. Venous malformations.

These lesions may form virtually anywhere within the central nervous system, but unlike AVMs, they are not caused by high-velocity blood flow from arteries into veins. Instead of a combination of arteries and veins, these low-flowing lesions involve only one type of blood vessel. These lesions are less unstable than AVMs and do not pose the same relatively high risk of significant hemorrhage. In general, low-flow lesions tend to cause fewer troubling neurological symptoms and require less aggressive treatment than do AVMs.

Cavernous malformations are formed from groups of tightly packed, abnormally thin-walled, small blood vessels that displace normal neurological tissue in the brain or spinal cord. The vessels are filled with slow-moving or stagnant blood that is usually clotted or in a state of decomposition. Like AVMs, cavernous malformations can range in size from a few fractions of an inch to several inches in diameter, depending on the number of blood vessels involved. Some people develop multiple lesions. Although cavernous malformations usually do not hemorrhage as severely as AVMs do, they sometimes leak blood into surrounding tissues because the walls of the involved blood vessels are extremely fragile. Although they are often not as symptomatic as AVMs, cavernous malformations can cause seizures in some people. After AVMs, cavernous malformations are the type of vascular lesion most likely to require treatment.

Capillary telangiectases are groups of abnormally swollen capillaries and usually measure less than an inch in diameter. Telangiectases are usually benign and rarely cause extensive damage to surrounding brain or spinal cord tissues. Any isolated hemorrhages that occur are microscopic in size. However, in some inherited disorders in which people develop large numbers of these lesions, telangiectases can contribute to the development headaches or seizures.

Venous malformations consist of abnormally enlarged veins. The structural defect usually does not interfere with the function of the blood vessels, and venous malformations rarely hemorrhage. As with telangiectases, most venous malformations do not produce symptoms, remain undetected, and follow a benign course.

What Causes Vascular Lesions?

The cause of vascular anomalies of the central nervous system (CNS) is not yet well understood. Scientists believe the anomalies most often result from mistakes that occur during embryonic or fetal development. These mistakes may be linked to genetic mutations in some cases. A few types of vascular malformations are known to be hereditary and thus are known to have a genetic basis. Some evidence also suggests that at least some of these lesions are acquired later in life as a result of injury to the CNS.

During fetal development, new blood vessels continuously form and then disappear as the human body changes and grows. These changes in the body's vascular map continue after birth and are controlled by angiogenic factors, chemicals produced by the body that stimulate new blood vessel formation and growth. Researchers have identified changes in the chemical structures of various angiogenic factors in some people who have AVMs or other vascular abnormalities of the central nervous system. However, it is not yet clear how these chemical changes actually cause changes in blood vessel structure.

By studying patterns of occurrence in families, researchers have established that one type of cavernous malformation involving multiple lesion formation is caused by a genetic mutation in chromosome 7. This genetic mutation appears in many ethnic groups, but it is especially frequent in a large population of Hispanic Americans living in the Southwest; these individuals share a common ancestor in whom the genetic change occurred. Some other types of vascular defects of the central nervous system are part of larger medical syndromes known to be hereditary. They include hereditary hemorrhagic telangiectasia, Sturge-Weber syndrome, and Klippel-Trenaunay syndrome.

How Are AVMs and Other Vascular Lesions Detected?

One of the more distinctive signs clinicians use to diagnose an AVM is an auditory phenomenon called a bruit—a rhythmic, whooshing sound caused by excessively rapid blood flow through the arteries and veins of an AVM. The sound is similar to that made by a torrent of water rushing through a narrow pipe. A bruit can sometimes become a symptom when it is especially severe. When audible to individuals, the bruit may compromise hearing, disturb sleep, or cause significant psychological distress.

An array of imaging technologies can be used to uncover the presence of AVMs. Cerebral angiography, also called cerebral arteriography, provides the most accurate pictures of blood vessel structure in brain AVMs. A special water-soluble dye, called a contrast agent, is injected into an artery and highlights the structure of blood vessels so that it can be seen on X-rays. CT scans (computed axial tomography) use X-rays to create an image of the head, brain, or spinal cord and are especially useful in revealing the presence of hemorrhage. MRI (magnetic resonance imaging) uses magnetic fields and radio waves to create detailed images that can show subtle changes in neurological tissues. Magnetic resonance angiography (MRA) can record the pattern and velocity of blood flow through vascular lesions as well as the flow of cerebrospinal fluid throughout the brain and spinal cord. Transcranial doppler (TCD) ultrasound can diagnose medium-size to large AVMS and also detect the presence and extent of hemorrhage. It evaluates blood flow through the brain by directing high-frequency sound waves through the skull at particular arteries. The resulting sound wave signals that bounce back from blood cells are interpreted by a computer to make an image of the velocity of blood flow.

How Are AVMs and Other Vascular Lesions Treated?

There are several options for treating AVMs. Although medication can often lessen general symptoms such as headache, back pain, and seizures caused by AVMs and other vascular lesions, the definitive treatment for AVMs is either surgery or focused radiation therapy. Venous malformations and capillary telangiectases rarely require surgery. Cavernous malformations are usually well defined enough for surgical removal, but surgery on these lesions is less common than for AVMs because they do not pose the same risk of hemorrhage.

Because so many variables are involved in treating AVMs, doctors must assess the danger posed to individuals largely on a case-by-case basis. A hemorrhage from an untreated AVM can cause serious neurological deficits or death, leading many clinicians to recommend surgical intervention whenever the physical characteristics of an AVM appear to indicate a greater-than-usual likelihood of significant bleeding and subsequent neurological damage. However, surgery on any part of the central nervous system carries some risk of serious complications or death. There is no easy formula that can allow physicians and individuals to reach a decision on the best course of therapy.

An AVM grading system developed in the mid-1980s can help healthcare professionals estimate the risk of surgery based on the size of the AVM, location in the brain and surrounding tissue involvement, and any leakage.

Three surgical options are used to treat AVMs; conventional surgery, endovascular embolization, and radiosurgery. The choice of treatment depends largely on the size and location of an AVM. Endovascular embolization and radiosurgery are less invasive than conventional surgery and offer safer treatment options for some AVMs located deep inside the brain.

- **Conventional surgery** involves entering the brain or spinal cord and removing the central portion of the AVM, including the fistula, while causing as little damage as possible to surrounding neurological structures. This surgery is most appropriate when an AVM is located in a superficial portion of the brain or spinal cord and is relatively small in size. AVMs located deep inside the brain generally cannot be approached through conventional surgical techniques because there is too great a possibility that functionally important brain tissue will be damaged or destroyed.

- In **endovascular embolization** the surgeon guides a catheter through the arterial network until the tip reaches the site of the AVM. The surgeon then injects a substance (such as fast-drying glue-like substances, fibered titanium coils, and tiny balloons) that will travel through blood vessels and create an artificial blood clot in the center of an AVM. Since embolization usually does not permanently obliterate the AVM, it is usually used as an adjunct to surgery or to radiosurgery to reduce the blood flow through the AVM and make the surgery safer.

- **Radiosurgery** is an even less invasive therapeutic approach often used to treat small AVMs that haven't ruptured. A beam of highly focused radiation is aimed directly on the AVM and damages the walls of the blood vessels making up the lesion. Over the course of the next several months, the irradiated vessels gradually degenerate and eventually close, leading to the resolution of the AVM.

Embolization frequently proves incomplete or temporary, although new embolization materials have led to improved results. Radiosurgery often has incomplete results as well, particularly when an AVM is large, and it poses the additional risk of radiation damage to surrounding normal tissues. Even when successful, complete closure of an AVM takes place over the course of many months following radiosurgery. During that period, the risk of hemorrhage is still present. However, both techniques can treat deeply situated AVMs that had previously been inaccessible. And in many individuals, staged embolization followed by conventional surgical removal or by radiosurgery is now performed, resulting in further reductions in death and complication rates.

Chapter 21

Birthmarks and Giant Congenital Melanocytic Nevus

Birthmarks are abnormalities of the skin that are present when a baby is born. There are two types of birthmarks. Vascular birthmarks are made up of blood vessels that have not formed correctly. They are usually red. Two types of vascular birthmarks are hemangiomas and port-wine stains. Pigmented birthmarks are made of a cluster of pigment cells which cause color in skin. They can be many different colors, from tan to brown, gray to black, or even blue. Moles can be birthmarks.

No one knows what causes many types of birthmarks, but some run in families. Your baby's doctor will look at the birthmark to see if it needs any treatment or if it should be watched. Pigmented birthmarks aren't usually treated, except for moles. Treatment for vascular birthmarks includes laser surgery. Most birthmarks are not serious,

This chapter contains text excerpted from the following sources: Text in this chapter begins with excerpts from "Birthmarks," MedlinePlus, National Institutes of Health (NIH), April 18, 2016; Text beginning with the heading "What Is an Infantile Hemangioma (IH)?" is excerpted from "Treating Infantile Hemangiomas in Children," Agency for Healthcare Research and Quality (AHRQ), June 21, 2016; Text under the heading "What Is Giant Congenital Melanocytic Nevus" is excerpted from "Giant Congenital Melanocytic Nevus," Genetics Home Reference (GHR), National Institutes of Health (NIH), December 12, 2017.

and some go away on their own. Some stay the same or get worse as you get older. Usually birthmarks are only a concern for your appearance. But certain types can increase your risk of skin cancer. If your birthmark bleeds, hurts, itches, or becomes infected, call your healthcare provider.

What Is an Infantile Hemangioma (IH)?

An infantile hemangioma (IH) is a birthmark that happens when a group of blood vessels and other cells do not grow normally. The mark starts as a small bump or colored patch on the skin and may grow quickly. Its color depends on how deep in the skin the IH is. Often, you cannot see the IH at birth. The mark starts to appear in the first few weeks of life.

- An IH on the outer layer of skin is usually bright red and raised. This type of IH used to be called a "strawberry hemangioma" or "strawberry mark."

- An IH that grows under the skin may make the skin look blue or may have no color. Tiny red blood vessels may also show up on the skin.

- Sometimes an IH is both on the outer layer of skin and under the skin.

An IH can form anywhere on the body, but it often forms on the head or neck. An IH can range in size. It may stay as small as the tip of a crayon. Or, it may grow as big as a baseball or larger. The IH may grow very quickly in the first few months of life and may continue to grow until around 1 year of age or older. Once the IH reaches its largest size, it usually starts to shrink and fade. It often takes several years for the IH to shrink and fade. The IH may not go away completely, or it may leave a scar.

How Common Is an IH?

- Out of every 100 babies, about 4–5 babies have an IH.

- IHs are more common in white babies.

- Girls have an IH more often than boys.

- Premature babies (those born before 37 weeks of pregnancy) have a higher risk of having an IH.

What Problems Can an IH Cause, and When Should an IH Be Treated?

Most IHs go away on their own over several years with no problems. But, an IH may cause problems in some cases.

- An IH may leave a scar or extra skin in some children.

- If your child's IH is in a visible place, such as on the face, talk with your child's healthcare professional about whether you should consider treatment.

- Sometimes, an IH can blister (ulcerate) or become infected.

- An infected IH may hurt and could leave a worse scar.

- Signs of an infected IH may include pain, redness, crustiness, discharge, or a bad smell coming from the IH. Call your child's healthcare professional if your child has any of these symptoms.

- An IH near the eyes, nose, or mouth could cause problems with seeing, breathing, or eating. These problems are rare but may be permanent if the IH is not treated early.

- For these more severe IHs, your child's healthcare professional may send your child to a specialist.

If your child's IH does not start to shrink and go away on its own, talk with your child's healthcare professional about whether treatment may be needed.

How Is an IH Treated?

Most IHs do not need treatment and will go away on their own. Your child's healthcare professional may check the IH over time to make sure it is shrinking and is not causing any problems. If the IH needs treatment, your child's healthcare professional will probably first suggest a medicine. Laser treatments can be used to treat IHs but are not used as often. In some cases, surgery to remove the IH may be needed. Usually, healthcare professionals only suggest surgery if the IH is likely to cause serious problems (such as problems with seeing, breathing, or eating) and if medicines did not work to treat the IH.

Medicines

Table 21.1 gives information about medicines to treat IH. Which medicine your child's healthcare professional recommends depends on

301

many things, such as your child's age and the size and location of your child's IH. Treatment with medicines taken by mouth or gel drops put on the IH usually lasts about 9–15 months.

Table 21.1. Medicines for Treating Infantile Hemangiomas

Medicine	Name (Brand)	How It Is Taken	More Information
Beta Blockers	Propranolol (Hemangeol™)	Taken by mouth daily	• Beta blockers are used to treat many conditions, such as high blood pressure, irregular heartbeat, and migraine headaches. • Propranolol (Hemangeol™) is the first medicine to be approved by the U.S. Food and Drug Administration (FDA) for IHs. • Timolol (Timoptic-XE®) was made to treat glaucoma (an eye condition). Some healthcare professionals now use it to treat some types of IHs.* • Atenolol (Tenormin®) and Nadolol (Corgard®) were made to treat high blood pressure. Some healthcare professionals may also use these medicines to treat IHs.*
	Timolol (Timoptic-XE®)	Gel drops put on the IH daily	
	Atenolol (Tenormin®)	Taken by mouth daily	
	Nadolol (Corgard®)		
Steroids	Methylprednisolone (Medrol®)	Taken by mouth daily	Steroids are used to treat many conditions, such as arthritis, asthma, and skin conditions. Healthcare professionals have also used steroids to treat IHs.*
	Prednisolone (Flo-Pred®, Prelone®)		
	Triamcinolone (Kenalog®)	Shot given monthly**	

* The U.S. Food and Drug Administration (FDA) approves medicines to treat certain conditions. A healthcare professional may choose to prescribe a medicine for a condition other than what the FDA has approved it for. This is called "off-label" use, and healthcare professionals often prescribe medicines this way.

** The number of shots needed to treat an IH depends on the specific type of IH your child has. Talk with your child's healthcare professional about how many shots your child may need.

What Is Giant Congenital Melanocytic Nevus?

Giant congenital melanocytic nevus is a skin condition characterized by an abnormally dark, noncancerous skin patch (nevus) that is composed of pigment-producing cells called melanocytes. It is present from birth (congenital) or is noticeable soon after birth. The nevus may be small in infants, but it will usually grow at the same rate the body grows and will eventually be at least 40 cm (15.75 inches) across. The nevus can appear anywhere on the body, but it is more often found on the trunk or limbs. The color ranges from tan to black and can become darker or lighter over time. The surface of a nevus can be flat, rough, raised, thickened, or bumpy; the surface can vary in different regions of the nevus, and it can change over time. The skin of the nevus is often dry and prone to irritation and itching (dermatitis). Excessive hair growth (hypertrichosis) can occur within the nevus. There is often less fat tissue under the skin of the nevus; the skin may appear thinner there than over other areas of the body.

People with giant congenital melanocytic nevus may have more than one nevus (plural: nevi). The other nevi are often smaller than the giant nevus. Affected individuals may have one or two additional nevi or multiple small nevi that are scattered over the skin; these are known as satellite or disseminated nevi.

Affected individuals may feel anxiety or emotional stress due to the impact the nevus may have on their appearance and their health. Children with giant congenital melanocytic nevus can develop emotional or behavior problems.

Some people with giant congenital melanocytic nevus develop a condition called neurocutaneous melanosis, which is the presence of pigment-producing skin cells (melanocytes) in the tissue that covers the brain and spinal cord. These melanocytes may be spread out or grouped together in clusters. Their growth can cause increased pressure in the brain, leading to headache, vomiting, irritability, seizures, and movement problems. Tumors in the brain may also develop.

Individuals with giant congenital melanocytic nevus have an increased risk of developing an aggressive form of cancer called melanoma, which arises from melanocytes. Estimates vary, but it is generally thought that people with giant congenital melanocytic nevus have a 5–10 percent lifetime risk of developing melanoma. Melanoma commonly begins in the nevus, but it can develop when melanocytes that invade other tissues, such as those in the brain and spinal cord, become cancerous. When melanoma occurs in people with giant congenital melanocytic nevus, the survival rate is low. Other types of tumors can also develop in individuals with giant congenital melanocytic nevus, including soft tissue tumors (sarcomas), fatty tumors (lipomas), and tumors of the nerve cells (schwannomas).

Chapter 22

Brain Defects

Chapter Contents

Section 22.1

Agenesis of the Corpus Callosum (ACC)

This section includes text excerpted from "Agenesis of the Corpus
Callosum Information Page," National Institute of Neurological
Disorders and Stroke (NINDS), February 26, 2016.

Agenesis of the corpus callosum (ACC) is one of several disorders of
the corpus callosum, the structure that connects the two hemispheres
(left and right) of the brain. In ACC the corpus callosum is partially or
completely absent. It is caused by a disruption of brain cell migration
during fetal development. ACC can occur as an isolated condition or
in combination with other cerebral abnormalities, including Arnold-
Chiari malformation, Dandy-Walker syndrome (DWS), schizencephaly
(clefts or deep divisions in brain tissue), and holoprosencephaly (failure
of the forebrain to divide into lobes.) Girls may have a gender-spe-
cific condition called Aicardi syndrome, which causes severe cognitive
impairment and developmental delays, seizures, abnormalities in the
vertebra of the spine, and lesions on the retina of the eye.

ACC can also be associated with malformations in other parts of
the body, such as midline facial defects. The effects of the disorder
range from subtle or mild to severe, depending on associated brain
abnormalities. Children with the most severe brain malformations may
have intellectual impairment, seizures, hydrocephalus, and spasticity.

Other disorders of the corpus callosum include dysgenesis, in which
the corpus callosum is developed in a malformed or incomplete way,
and hypoplasia, in which the corpus callosum is thinner than usual.
Individuals with these disorders have a higher risk of hearing deficits
and cardiac abnormalities than individuals with the normal structure.
It is estimated that at least 1 in 4,000 individuals has a disorder of
the corpus callosum.

Treatment

There is no standard course of treatment for ACC. Treatment usually involves management of symptoms and seizures if they occur. Associated difficulties are much more manageable with early recognition

and therapy, especially therapies focusing on left/right coordination. Early diagnosis and interventions are currently the best treatments to improve social and developmental outcomes.

Prognosis

Prognosis depends on the extent and severity of malformations. Intellectual impairment does not worsen. Individuals with a disorder of the corpus callosum typically have delays in attaining developmental milestones such as walking, talking, or reading; challenges with social interactions; clumsiness and poor motor coordination, particularly on skills that require coordination of left and right hands and feet (such as swimming, bicycle riding, and driving; and mental and social processing problems that become more apparent with age, with problems particularly evident from junior high school into adulthood.

Section 22.2

Anencephaly

This section includes text excerpted from "Birth Defects— Facts about Anencephaly," Centers for Disease Control and Prevention (CDC), August 2, 2017.

Anencephaly is a serious birth defect in which a baby is born without parts of the brain and skull. It is a type of neural tube defect (NTD). As the neural tube forms and closes, it helps form the baby's brain and skull (upper part of the neural tube), spinal cord, and back bones (lower part of the neural tube). Anencephaly happens if the upper part of the neural tube does not close all the way. This often results in a baby being born without the front part of the brain (forebrain) and the thinking and coordinating part of the brain (cerebrum). The remaining parts of the brain are often not covered by bone or skin.

Occurrence

Centers for Disease Control and Prevention (CDC) estimates that each year, about 3 pregnancies in every 10,000 in the United States will have anencephaly. This means about 1,206 pregnancies are affected by these conditions each year in the United States.

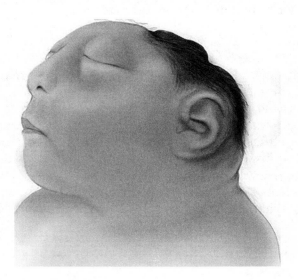

Figure 22.1. *Anencephaly*

Causes and Prevention

The causes of anencephaly among most infants are unknown. Some babies have anencephaly because of a change in their genes or chromosomes. Anencephaly might also be caused by a combination of genes and other factors, such as the things the mother comes in contact with in the environment or what the mother eats or drinks, or certain medicines she uses during pregnancy. Getting enough folic acid before and during early pregnancy can help prevent neural tube defects, such as anencephaly. If you are pregnant or could get pregnant, take 400 micrograms (mcg) of folic acid every day. If you have already had a pregnancy affected by an NTD, you can speak with your doctor about taking a higher dose of folic acid before pregnancy and during early pregnancy.

- Since the United States began fortifying grains with folic acid, there has been a 28 percent decline in pregnancies affected by neural tube defects (spina bifida and anencephaly).

- In order to get the recommended 400 micrograms of folic acid every day, a woman of reproductive age can take a supplement containing folic acid or to eat foods fortified with folic acid, or both, depending on her dietary habits.

Diagnosis

Anencephaly can be diagnosed during pregnancy or after the baby is born.

During Pregnancy

During pregnancy, there are screening tests (prenatal tests) to check for birth defects and other conditions. Anencephaly would result in an abnormal result on a blood or serum screening test or it might be seen during an ultrasound (which creates pictures of the body).

After the Baby Is Born

In some cases, anencephaly might not be diagnosed until after the baby is born. Anencephaly is immediately seen at birth.

Treatments

There is no known cure or standard treatment for anencephaly. Almost all babies born with anencephaly will die shortly after birth.

Section 22.3

Cerebral Palsy

This section includes text excerpted from "Cerebral Palsy—Overview," *Eunice Kennedy Shriver* National Institute of Child Health and Human Development (NICHD), September 13, 2014. Reviewed December 2017.

Cerebral palsy is the term for a group of brain disorders that affect muscles and body movement. The condition is caused by damage to parts of the brain that control muscle movement, balance, and posture. Signs and symptoms of cerebral palsy usually appear in infancy or early childhood and last throughout a person's life. In most cases, the symptoms do not get worse over time. Cerebral palsy is the most common movement disorder in children, according to the Centers for Disease Control and Prevention (CDC). The level and severity of disability caused by the condition differs from person to person. Some people with cerebral palsy may not be able to walk and need intensive, lifelong care, while others can walk and move with little or no help.

What Are the Types of Cerebral Palsy?

There are several types of cerebral palsy, classified by the kind of movement affected, the body parts affected, and how severe the symptoms are. Some types involve intellectual and developmental disabilities (IDDs) as well as movement problems.

- **Spastic cerebral palsy.** This type is the most common form of the disorder. People with spastic cerebral palsy have stiff muscles which cause jerky or repeated movements. There are different forms of spastic cerebral palsy, depending on the body parts affected. These forms are:

- **Spastic hemiplegia or hemiparesis.** This type affects the arm, the hand, and sometimes the leg on only one side of the body. Children with this form may have delays in learning to talk, but intelligence is usually normal.

- **Spastic diplegia or diparesis.** People with this form mostly have muscle stiffness in the legs, while the arms and face are less severely affected. Intelligence and language skills are usually normal.

- **Spastic quadriplegia or quadriparesis.** This is the most severe form of cerebral palsy, involving severe stiffness of the arms and legs and a floppy, or weak, neck. People with spastic quadriplegia are usually unable to walk and often have trouble speaking. This form may involve moderate to severe IDD as well.

- **Dyskinetic cerebral palsy.** This type involves slow and uncontrollable jerky movements of the hands, feet, arms, or legs. The face muscles and tongue may be overactive and cause some children to drool or make faces. People with this type often have trouble sitting straight or walking. People with dyskinetic cerebral palsy do not usually have intellectual problems.

- **Ataxic cerebral palsy.** This form of the disorder affects balance and depth perception. People with ataxic cerebral palsy walk in an unsteady manner and have a hard time with quick or

310

precise movements such as writing, buttoning a shirt, or reaching for a book.

- **Mixed types.** This kind of cerebral palsy includes symptoms that are a mix of the other types.

What Are the Symptoms of Cerebral Palsy?

Even though the symptoms of cerebral palsy often differ from person to person, they can include:

- Ataxia, the loss of muscle coordination when making movements
- Spasticity, stiff or tight muscles; jerky, repeated movements; and stronger-than-normal reflexes (for example, the knee-jerk reflex)
- Weakness in arms or legs
- Walking on the toes
- Walking in a crouched position
- Muscle tone that is either too stiff or too floppy
- Drooling
- Trouble with swallowing or speaking
- Shaking (tremor) of arms, legs, hands, or feet
- Sudden, uncontrolled movements
- In infants and toddlers, delays in motor skills (such as sitting, crawling, walking)
- Trouble with precise movements such as writing or buttoning a shirt

It's important to note that many of these symptoms result from problems with muscles and not from problems with cognition or thinking. For example, a person with cerebral palsy may have trouble speaking because he or she cannot control or move the muscles involved with speaking, not because of brain problems with language.

The symptoms of cerebral palsy vary in type, can range from mild to severe, and can change over time. Symptoms are different for each person, depending on the areas of the brain that have been affected. All people with cerebral palsy have movement and posture problems.

In addition to problems with muscle movement, symptoms occasionally include:

- Intellectual and developmental disabilities

- Seizures

- Feeling unusual physical sensations

- Vision problems

- Hearing problems

What Are the Early Signs of Cerebral Palsy?

The signs of cerebral palsy usually appear in the first few months of life, but many children are not diagnosed until age two or later. In general, early signs of cerebral palsy include:

- **Developmental delays.** The child is slow to reach milestones such as rolling over, sitting, crawling, and walking. Developmental delays are the main clues that a child might have cerebral palsy.

- **Abnormal muscle tone.** Body parts are floppy or too stiff.

- **Abnormal posture.** The child might also use one side of the body more than the other when reaching, crawling, or moving.

Children without cerebral palsy may show some of these signs. If you notice any of these signs, you should talk to your child's healthcare provider. Some age-specific signs may include:

- **Infants younger than 6 months of age**

  - Cannot hold up their head when picked up from lying on their back

  - May feel stiff or floppy

  - When picked up, their legs get stiff or cross

  - When held, they may overextend their back and neck, constantly acting as though they are pushing away from you

- **Infants older than 6 months of age**

  - Cannot roll over

  - Cannot bring their hands to their mouth

  - Have a hard time bringing their hands together

- Reach out with only one hand while holding the other in a fist

- **Infants older than 10 months of age**

  - Crawl in a lopsided way, pushing with one hand and leg while dragging the opposite hand and leg

  - Scoot around on their buttocks or hop on their knees but do not crawl on all fours

  - Cannot stand even when holding onto support

Children without cerebral palsy may show some of these signs. If you notice any of these signs, you should talk to your child's healthcare provider.

How Many People Are Affected?

The Centers for Disease Control and Prevention (CDC) estimates that, worldwide, 1.5–4 of every 1,000 infants are born with cerebral palsy. Cerebral palsy is the most common movement disorder in children. One U.S. study measured the number of 8-year-old children with cerebral palsy in four states: Alabama, Georgia, Missouri, and Wisconsin. Of the 142,338 children surveyed across those states, an average of 3.3 per 1,000 had the disorder. These findings suggest that approximately 1 in 303 8-year-olds in the United States has cerebral palsy.

What Causes Cerebral Palsy?

Cerebral palsy is caused by damage or abnormal development in the parts of the brain that control movement. These events can happen before, during, or shortly after birth or in the first few years of life, when the brain is still developing. In many cases the exact cause of cerebral palsy is not known.

Most children with cerebral palsy (85–90%) were born with the condition; this is called congenital cerebral palsy.

Causes of cerebral palsy that occur before birth include:

- **Damage to the white matter of the brain.** The brain's white matter sends signals throughout the brain and the rest of the body. Damage to white matter can disrupt the signals between the brain and the body that control movement. The white matter in the fetus's brain is more sensitive to injury between 26 weeks and 34 weeks of pregnancy, but damage can happen at any time during pregnancy.

- **Abnormal brain development.** Disruptions in the normal growth process of the brain can cause abnormalities. These abnormalities affect the transmission of brain signals. Infections, fever, trauma, or gene changes (mutations) can cause the brain to develop abnormally.

- **Bleeding in the brain.** A fetus can have a stroke, which is a common cause of brain bleeding. Strokes occur when blood vessels in the brain become blocked or broken, leading to brain damage. Conditions including blood clotting problems, abnormally formed blood vessels, heart defects, and sickle cell disease can also cause bleeding in the brain.

- **Lack of oxygen in the brain.** The brain can become damaged if it does not get enough oxygen for a long time. Very low blood pressure in the mother, a torn uterus, detachment of the placenta, problems with the umbilical cord, or severe trauma to the infant's head during labor and delivery can prevent oxygen from getting to the brain.

A small number of children have what is called acquired cerebral palsy, which means the disorder begins more than 28 days after birth. Causes of acquired cerebral palsy may include:

- Brain damage in the first few months or years of life

- Infections, such as meningitis or encephalitis

- Problems with blood flow to the brain due to stroke, blood clotting problems, abnormal blood vessels, a heart defect that was present at birth, or sickle cell disease

- Head injury from a car accident, a fall, or child abuse

What Are the Risk Factors for Cerebral Palsy?

Some events or medical problems during pregnancy can increase the risk of congenital cerebral palsy. These risk factors include:

- **Low birth weight or preterm birth.** Infants born preterm (defined as before 37 weeks of pregnancy) and infants who weigh less than 5.5 pounds at birth are at greater risk of cerebral palsy than are early term (defined as 37 weeks–38 weeks of pregnancy) and full-term (defined as 39 weeks–40 weeks of pregnancy) infants and those who are heavier at birth. The earlier the birth and the lower the infant's birth weight, the greater the risk.

- **Multiple gestations.** Twins, triplets, and other multiple births are at higher risk of cerebral palsy. The risk is also greater for an infant whose twin or triplet dies before or shortly after birth.

- **Infertility treatments.** Infants born from pregnancies resulting from the use of certain infertility treatments are at higher risk for cerebral palsy than are infants born from pregnancies not related to infertility treatments. Much of this increased risk may be due to the fact that infertility treatments are more likely to result in preterm delivery and multiple gestations.

- **Infections during pregnancy.** Toxoplasmosis, rubella (German measles), cytomegalovirus, and herpes can infect the womb and placenta, leading to brain damage in the fetus.

- **Fever during pregnancy.** Sometimes fever in the mother during pregnancy or delivery can lead to brain damage in the fetus, resulting in cerebral palsy.

- **Blood factor between mother and fetus does not match.** Those who have a certain protein found on red blood cells—abbreviated Rh—are Rh positive; those who do not have the protein are Rh negative. If a mother's Rh factor is different from that of the fetus, her immune system may attack the blood cells of the fetus, including blood cells in the brain, which can lead to brain damage.

- **Exposure to toxic chemicals.** If a mother is exposed to a toxic substance, such as high levels of methylmercury (found in some thermometers and in some seafood), during pregnancy the fetus is at higher risk of cerebral palsy.

- **Maternal medical conditions.**
  - Abnormal thyroid function
  - Intellectual and developmental disability
  - Too much protein in the urine
  - Seizures

- **Complicated labor and delivery.** Infant heart or breathing problems during labor and delivery and immediately after birth increase the risk of cerebral palsy.

- **Jaundice.** Jaundice, which causes an infant's skin, eyes, and mouth to turn a yellowish color, can be a sign that the liver is not working normally. Jaundice occurs when a substance called bilirubin builds up faster than the liver can clear it from the body. This condition is common and is usually not serious. However, in cases of severe, untreated jaundice, the excess bilirubin can damage the brain and cause cerebral palsy.

- **Seizures.** Infants who have seizures are more likely to be diagnosed with cerebral palsy later in childhood.

Some risk factors for acquired cerebral palsy are:

- **Infancy.** Infants are at greater risk than older children for an event that causes brain damage.

- **Preterm or low birthweight.** Children born preterm or at a low birthweight have a higher risk for acquired cerebral palsy.

- **Not getting certain vaccinations.** Childhood vaccinations can prevent brain infections that can cause cerebral palsy.

- **Injury.** Not taking certain safety precautions for infants or lack of adult supervision can lead to injury that can cause cerebral palsy.

How Is Cerebral Palsy Diagnosed?

Most children with cerebral palsy are diagnosed during their first 2 years of life. But if symptoms are mild, a healthcare provider may not be able to make a diagnosis before the age of 4 or 5.

During regular well-baby and well-child visits, a child's healthcare provider will examine:

- Growth and development
- Muscle tone
- Control of movement
- Hearing and vision
- Posture
- Coordination and balance

If a healthcare provider finds signs of cerebral palsy during an examination, he or she may then use one or more brain scanning methods to look for damage in the brain. These methods may include:

- **Ultrasound.** This method is used most commonly in high-risk preterm infants to take pictures of the brain. Ultrasound is not as good as other methods at taking images of the brain, but it is the safest way to look at the brains of preterm infants.

- **Computed tomography (CT).** CT uses X-rays to take pictures of the brain and can show areas that are damaged.

- **Magnetic resonance imaging (MRI).** MRI uses a computer, a magnetic field, and radio waves to create an image of the brain. It can show the location and type of damage in better detail than CT.

- **Electroencephalogram (EEG).** If a child has had seizures, a healthcare provider may order this test to rule out another disorder such as epilepsy. Small disks called electrodes are placed on the scalp to measure the brain's activity.

If a healthcare provider thinks that your child has cerebral palsy, he or she may then refer the child to specialists such as a pediatric neurologist (doctor who specializes in the brain and nervous system), a developmental pediatrician (doctor who specializes in child development), an ophthalmologist (eye doctor), or an otologist (hearing doctor), depending on the specific symptoms. These healthcare providers can help give a more accurate diagnosis and create a treatment plan.

What Are Common Treatments for Cerebral Palsy?

A child may need one or several different types of treatment depending on how severe the symptoms are and what parts of the body are affected. The treatment differs from person to person, depending on each one's specific needs. Although the initial damage of cerebral palsy in the brain cannot be reversed, earlier and aggressive treatments may help to improve function and adjustments for the young nervous system and musculoskeletal system.

Families may also work with their healthcare providers and, during the school years, school staff to develop individual care and treatment programs.

Common types of treatment for cerebral palsy include:

- **Physical therapy and rehabilitation.** A child with cerebral palsy usually starts these therapies in the first few years of life or soon after being diagnosed. Physical therapy is one of the most important parts of treatment. It involves exercises and activities that can maintain or improve muscle strength, balance, and movement. A physical therapist helps the child learn skills such as sitting, walking, or using a wheelchair. Other types of therapy include:

- **Occupational therapy.** This type of therapy helps a child learn to do everyday activities such as dressing and going to school.

- **Recreational therapy.** Participating in art programs, cultural activities, and sports can help improve a child's physical and intellectual skills.

- **Speech and language therapy.** A speech therapist can help a child learn to speak more clearly, help with swallowing problems, and teach new ways to communicate, such as by using sign language or a special communication device.

- **Orthotic devices.** Braces, splints, and casts can be placed on the affected limbs and can improve movement and balance. Other devices that can help with movement and posture include wheelchairs, rolling walkers, and powered scooters.

- **Assistive devices and technologies.** These include special computer-based communication machines, Velcro-fastened shoes, or crutches, which can help make daily life easier.

- **Medication.** Certain medications can relax stiff or overactive muscles and reduce abnormal movement. They may be taken by mouth, injected into affected muscles, or infused into the fluid surrounding the spinal cord through a pump implanted near the spinal cord. For children who have cerebral palsy and epilepsy (seizures), standard epileptic medications should be considered, but these medications may also have negative effects on the developing brain.

- **Surgery.** A child may need surgery if symptoms are severe. For instance, surgery can lengthen stiff, tightly contracted muscles. A surgeon can also place arms or legs in better positions or correct or improve an abnormally curved spine. Sometimes, if other treatments have not worked, a surgeon can cut certain nerves to treat abnormal, spastic movements. Before conducting surgery, it is important for a healthcare provider to assess the procedure's benefits by carefully analyzing biomechanics of the joints and muscles.

Not all therapies are appropriate for everyone with cerebral palsy. It is important for parents, patients, and healthcare providers to work together to come up with the best treatment plan for the patient.

Section 22.4

Chiari Malformation (CM)

This section includes text excerpted from "Chiari Malformation Fact Sheet," National Institute of Neurological Disorders and Stroke (NINDS), June 2017.

What Are Chiari Malformations (CM)?

Chiari malformations (CM) are structural defects in the base of the skull and cerebellum, the part of the brain that controls balance. Normally the cerebellum and parts of the brainstem sit above an opening in the skull that allows the spinal cord to pass through it (called the foramen magnum). When part of the cerebellum extends below the foramen magnum and into the upper spinal canal, it is called a CM.

CM may develop when part of the skull is smaller than normal or misshapen, which forces the cerebellum to be pushed down into the foramen magnum and spinal canal. This causes pressure on the cerebellum and brainstem that may affect functions controlled by these areas and block the flow of cerebrospinal fluid (CSF)—the clear liquid that surrounds and cushions the brain and spinal cord. The CSF also circulates nutrients and chemicals filtered from the blood and removes waste products from the brain.

What Causes These Malformations?

CM has several different causes. Most often it is caused by structural defects in the brain and spinal cord that occur during fetal development. This can be the result of genetic mutations or a maternal diet that lacked certain vitamins or nutrients. This is called primary or congenital CM. It can also be caused later in life if spinal fluid is drained excessively from the lumbar or thoracic areas of the spine either due to traumatic injury, disease, or infection. This is called acquired or secondary CM. Primary CM is much more common than secondary CM.

What Are the Symptoms of a CM?

Headache is the hallmark sign of CM, especially after sudden coughing, sneezing, or straining. Other symptoms may vary among individuals and may include:

- neck pain

- hearing or balance problems

- muscle weakness or numbness

- dizziness

- difficulty swallowing or speaking

- vomiting

- ringing or buzzing in the ears (tinnitus)

- curvature of the spine (scoliosis)

- insomnia

- depression

- problems with hand coordination and fine motor skills

Some individuals with CM may not show any symptoms. Symptoms may change for some individuals, depending on the compression of the tissue and nerves and on the buildup of CSF pressure.

Infants with a CM may have difficulty swallowing, irritability when being fed, excessive drooling, a weak cry, gagging or vomiting, arm weakness, a stiff neck, breathing problems, developmental delays, and an inability to gain weight.

How Are CMs Classified?

Chiari malformations are classified by the severity of the disorder and the parts of the brain that protrude into the spinal canal.

Chiari Malformation Type I

Type 1 happens when the lower part of the cerebellum (called the cerebellar tonsils) extends into the foramen magnum. Normally, only the spinal cord passes through this opening. Type 1—which may not cause symptoms—is the most common form of CM. It is usually first noticed in adolescence or adulthood, often by accident during an examination for another condition. Adolescents and adults who have CM but no symptoms initially may develop signs of the disorder later in life.

Chiari Malformation Type II

Individuals with Type II have symptoms that are generally more severe than in Type 1 and usually appear during childhood. This disorder can cause life-threatening complications during infancy or early childhood, and treating it requires surgery.

In Type II, also called classic CM, both the cerebellum and brainstem tissue protrude into the foramen magnum. Also the nerve tissue that connects the two halves of the cerebellum may be missing or only partially formed. Type II is usually accompanied by a myelomeningocele—a form of spina bifida that occurs when the spinal canal and backbone don't close before birth. (Spina bifida is a disorder characterized by the incomplete development of the brain, spinal cord, and/or their protective covering.) A myelomeningocele usually results in partial or complete paralysis of the area below the spinal opening. The term Arnold-Chiari malformation (named after two pioneering researchers) is specific to Type II malformations.

Chiari Malformation Type III

Type III is very rare and the most serious form of Chiari malformation. In Type III, some of the cerebellum and the brain stem stick out, or herniate, through an abnormal opening in the back of the skull. This can also include the membranes surrounding the brain or spinal cord.

The symptoms of Type III appear in infancy and can cause debilitating and life-threatening complications. Babies with Type III can have many of the same symptoms as those with Type II but can also have additional severe neurological defects such as mental and physical delays, and seizures.

Chiari Malformation Type IV

Type IV involves an incomplete or underdeveloped cerebellum (a condition known as cerebellar hypoplasia). In this rare form of CM, the cerebellum is located in its normal position but parts of it are missing, and portions of the skull and spinal cord may be visible.

What Other Conditions Are Associated with CM?

- **Hydrocephalus** is an excessive buildup of CSF in the brain. A CM can block the normal flow of this fluid and cause pressure within the head that can result in mental defects and/or an enlarged or misshapen skull. Severe hydrocephalus, if left untreated, can be fatal. The disorder can occur with any type of CM, but is most commonly associated with Type II.

- **Spina bifida** is the incomplete closing of the backbone and membranes around the spinal cord. In babies with spina bifida, the bones around the spinal cord do not form properly, causing defects in the lower spine. While most children with this birth defect have such a mild form that they have no neurological problems, individuals with Type II CM usually have myelomeningocele, and a baby's spinal cord remains open in one area of the back and lower spine. The membranes and spinal cord protrude through the opening in the spine, creating a sac on the baby's back. This can cause a number of neurological impairments such as muscle weakness, paralysis, and scoliosis.

- **Syringomyelia** is a disorder in which a CSF-filled tubular cyst, or syrinx, forms within the spinal cord's central canal. The growing syrinx destroys the center of the spinal cord, resulting in pain, weakness, and stiffness in the back, shoulders, arms, or legs. Other symptoms may include a loss of the ability to feel extremes of hot or cold, especially in the hands. Some individuals also have severe arm and neck pain.

- **Tethered cord syndrome** occurs when a child's spinal cord abnormally attaches to the tissues around the bottom of the spine. This means the spinal cord cannot move freely within the spinal canal. As a child grows, the disorder worsens, and can result in permanent damage to the nerves that control the muscles in the lower body and legs. Children who have a myelomeningocele have an increased risk of developing a tethered cord later in life.

- **Spinal curvature** is common among individuals with syringomyelia or CM Type I. The spine either may bend to the left or right (scoliosis) or may bend forward (kyphosis).

How Common Are CM?

In the past, it was estimated that the condition occurs in about one in every 1,000 births. However, the increased use of diagnostic imaging has shown that CM may be much more common. Complicating this estimation is the fact that some children who are born with this condition may never develop symptoms or show symptoms only in adolescence or adulthood. CM occur more often in women than in men and Type II malformations are more prevalent in certain groups, including people of Celtic descent.

How Are CM Diagnosed?

No test is available to determine if a baby will be born with a CM. Since CMs are associated with certain birth defects like spina bifida, children born with those defects are often tested for malformations. However, some malformations can be seen on ultrasound images before birth.

Many people with CMs have no symptoms and their malformations are discovered only during the course of diagnosis or treatment for another disorder. The doctor will perform a physical exam and check the person's memory, cognition, balance (functions controlled by the cerebellum), touch, reflexes, sensation, and motor skills (functions controlled by the spinal cord). The physician may also order one of the following diagnostic tests:

- **Magnetic resonance imaging (MRI)** is the imaging procedure most often used to diagnose a CM. It uses radio waves and a powerful magnetic field to painlessly produce either a detailed three-dimensional picture or a two-dimensional "slice" of body structures, including tissues, organs, bones, and nerves.

- **X-rays** use electromagnetic energy to produce images of bones and certain tissues on film. An X-ray of the head and neck cannot reveal a CM but can identify bone abnormalities that are often associated with the disorder.

- **Computed tomography (CT)** uses X-rays and a computer to produce two-dimensional pictures of bone and blood vessels. CT can identify hydrocephalus and bone abnormalities associated with CM.

How Are CM Treated?

Some CMs do not show symptoms and do not interfere with a person's activities of daily living. In these cases, doctors may only recommend regular monitoring with MRI. When individuals experience pain or headaches, doctors may prescribe medications to help ease symptoms.

Surgery

In many cases, surgery is the only treatment available to ease symptoms or halt the progression of damage to the central nervous system. Surgery can improve or stabilize symptoms in most individuals. More than one surgery may be needed to treat the condition.

The most common surgery to treat CM is posterior fossa decompression. It creates more space for the cerebellum and relieves pressure on the spinal cord. The surgery involves making an incision at the back of the head and removing a small portion of the bone at the bottom of the skull (craniectomy). In some cases the arched, bony roof of the spinal canal, called the lamina, may also be removed (spinal laminectomy). The surgery should help restore the normal flow of CSF, and in some cases it may be enough to relieve symptoms.

Next, the surgeon may make an incision in the dura, the protective covering of the brain and spinal cord. Some surgeons perform a Doppler ultrasound test during surgery to determine if opening the dura is even necessary. If the brain and spinal cord area is still crowded, the surgeon may use a procedure called electrocautery to remove the cerebellar tonsils, allowing for more free space. These tonsils do not have a recognized function and can be removed without causing any known neurological problems.

The final step is to sew a dura patch to expand the space around the tonsils, similar to letting out the waistband on a pair of pants. This patch can be made of artificial material or tissue harvested from another part of an individual's body.

Infants and children with myelomeningocele may require surgery to reposition the spinal cord and close the opening in the back. Findings from the National Institutes of Health (NIH) show that this surgery is most effective when it is done prenatally (while the baby is still in the womb) instead of after birth. The prenatal surgery reduces the occurrence of hydrocephalus and restores the cerebellum and brainstem to a more normal alignment.

Hydrocephalus may be treated with a shunt (tube) system that drains excess fluid and relieves pressure inside the head. A sturdy tube, surgically inserted into the head, is connected to a flexible tube placed under the skin. These tubes drain the excess fluid into either the chest cavity or the abdomen so it can be absorbed by the body.

An alternative surgical treatment in some individuals with hydrocephalus is third ventriculostomy, a procedure that improves the flow of CSF out of the brain. A small hole is made at the bottom of the third ventricle (brain cavity) and the CSF is diverted there to relieve pressure. Similarly, in cases where surgery was not effective, doctors may open the spinal cord and insert a shunt to drain a syringomyelia or hydromyelia (increased fluid in the central canal of the spinal cord).

Section 22.5

Dandy-Walker Syndrome

This section includes text excerpted from documents published by two public domain sources. Text under headings marked 1 are excerpted from "Dandy-Walker Syndrome Information Page," National Institute of Neurological Disorders and Stroke (NINDS), December 19, 2016; Text under headings marked 2 are excerpted from "Dandy-Walker Malformation," Genetics Home Reference (GHR), National Institutes of Health (NIH), December 12, 2017.

What Is Dandy-Walker Syndrome?[1]

Dandy-Walker Syndrome is a congenital brain malformation involving the cerebellum (an area of the back of the brain that coordinates movement) and the fluid-filled spaces around it. The key features of this syndrome are an enlargement of the fourth ventricle (a small channel that allows fluid to flow freely between the upper and lower areas of the brain and spinal cord), a partial or complete absence of the area of the brain between the two cerebellar hemispheres (cerebellar vermis), and cyst formation near the lowest part of the skull. An increase in the size and pressure of the fluid spaces surrounding the brain (hydrocephalus) may also be present.

Symptoms[1]

The syndrome can appear dramatically or develop unnoticed. Symptoms, which often occur in early infancy, include slow motor development and progressive enlargement of the skull. In older children, symptoms of increased intracranial pressure (pressure within the skull) such as irritability and vomiting, and signs of cerebellar dysfunction such as unsteadiness, lack of muscle coordination, or jerky movements of the eyes may occur. Other symptoms include increased head circumference, bulging at the back of the skull, abnormal breathing problems, and problems with the nerves that control the eyes, face and neck. Dandy-Walker Syndrome is sometimes associated with disorders of other areas of the central nervous system, including absence of the area made up of nerve fibers connecting the two cerebral hemispheres (corpus callosum) and malformations of the heart, face, limbs, fingers and toes.

Frequency[2]

Dandy-Walker malformation is estimated to affect 1 in 10,000 to 30,000 newborns.

Genetic Changes[2]

Researchers have found mutations in a few genes that are thought to cause Dandy-Walker malformation, but these mutations account for only a small number of cases. Dandy-Walker malformation has also been associated with many chromosomal abnormalities. This condition can be a feature of some conditions in which there is an extra copy of one chromosome in each cell (trisomy). Dandy-Walker malformation most often occurs in people with trisomy 18 (an extra copy of chromosome 18), but can also occur in people with trisomy 13, trisomy 21, or trisomy 9. This condition can also be associated with missing (deletions) or copied (duplications) pieces of certain chromosomes. Dandy-Walker malformation can also be a feature of genetic syndromes that are caused by mutations in specific genes. However, the brain malformations associated with Dandy-Walker malformation often occur as an isolated feature (not associated with other health problems), and in these cases the cause is frequently unknown. Research suggests that Dandy-Walker malformation could be caused by environmental factors that affect early development before birth. For example, exposure of the fetus to substances that cause birth defects (teratogens) may be involved in the development of this condition. In addition, a mother with diabetes is more likely than a healthy mother to have a child with Dandy-Walker malformation.

Inheritance Pattern[1]

Most cases of Dandy-Walker malformation are sporadic, which means they occur in people with no history of the disorder in their family. A small percentage of cases seem to run in families; however, Dandy-Walker malformation does not have a clear pattern of inheritance. Multiple genetic and environmental factors likely play a part in determining the risk of developing this disorder. First-degree relatives (such as siblings and children) of people with Dandy-Walker malformation have an increased risk of developing the condition compared with people in the general population. When Dandy-Walker malformation is a feature of a genetic condition, it is inherited in the pattern of that condition.

Treatment[1]

Treatment for individuals with Dandy-Walker Syndrome generally consists of treating the associated problems, if needed. A surgical procedure called a shunt may be required to drain off excess fluid within the brain, which will reduce pressure inside the skull and improve symptoms. Treatment may also include various forms of therapy (physical, occupational) and specialized education.

Prognosis[1]

The effect of Dandy-Walker Syndrome on intellectual development is variable, with some children having normal cognition and others never achieving normal intellectual development even when the excess fluid buildup is treated early and correctly. Longevity depends on the severity of the syndrome and associated malformations. The presence of multiple congenital defects may shorten life span.

Section 22.6

Encephalocele

This section includes text excerpted from "Birth Defects—
Facts about Encephalocele," Centers for Disease
Control and Prevention (CDC), November 21, 2017.

Encephalocele is a rare type of birth defect of the neural tube that affects the brain. The neural tube is a narrow channel that folds and closes during the third and fourth weeks of pregnancy to form the brain and spinal cord. Encephalocele is a sac-like protrusion or projection of the brain and the membranes that cover it through an opening in the skull. Encephalocele happens when the neural tube does not close completely during pregnancy. The result is an opening anywhere along the center of the skull from the nose to the back of the neck, but most often at the back of the head (pictured), at the top of the head, or between the forehead and the nose.

Occurrence

Centers for Disease Control and Prevention (CDC) estimates that approximately 1 in 12,200 babies born in the United States each year will have encephalocele. This means that about 340 U.S. babies are born with this condition each year.

Causes

Although the exact cause of encephalocele is unknown, scientists believe that many factors are involved. There is a genetic (inherited) component to the condition, meaning it often occurs in families that have family members with other defects of the neural tube: spina bifida and anencephaly. Some researchers also believe that certain environmental exposures before or during pregnancy might be causes, but more research is needed.

Prevention

Taking 400 micrograms of the B vitamin, folic acid, every day before and during early pregnancy can help prevent some major birth defects of the baby's brain and spine, such as encephalocele. If you are pregnant or thinking about becoming pregnant, talk with your doctor about ways to increase your chances of having a healthy baby.

Diagnosis

Usually encephaloceles are found right after birth, but sometimes a small encephalocele in the nose and forehead region can go undetected. An encephalocele at the back of the skull is more likely to cause nervous system problems, as well as other brain and face defects. Signs of encephalocele can include:

- Buildup of too much fluid in the brain,
- Complete loss of strength in the arms and legs,
- An unusually small head,
- Uncoordinated use of muscles needed for movement, such as those involved in walking and reaching,
- Developmental delay,
- Intellectual disability,
- Vision problems,
- Delayed growth, and
- Seizures.

Treatment

Encephalocele is treated with surgery to place the protruding part of the brain and the membranes covering it back into the skull and close the opening in the skull. However, neurologic problems caused by the encephalocele will still be present. Long-term treatment depends on the child's condition. Multiple surgeries may be needed, depending on the location of the encephalocele and the parts of the head and face that were affected by the encephalocele.

Section 22.7

Hydrocephalus

This section includes text excerpted from "Hydrocephalus Fact
Sheet," National Institute of Neurological Disorders and Stroke
(NINDS), May 2013. Reviewed December 2017.

What Is Hydrocephalus?

The term hydrocephalus is derived from the Greek words "hydro"
meaning water and "cephalus" meaning head. As the name implies, it
is a condition in which the primary characteristic is excessive accumulation of fluid in the brain. Although hydrocephalus was once known
as "water on the brain," the "water" is actually cerebrospinal fluid
(CSF)—a clear fluid that surrounds the brain and spinal cord. The
excessive accumulation of CSF results in an abnormal widening of
spaces in the brain called ventricles. This widening creates potentially
harmful pressure on the tissues of the brain.

The ventricular system is made up of four ventricles connected by
narrow passages. Normally, CSF flows through the ventricles, exits
into cisterns (closed spaces that serve as reservoirs) at the base of
the brain, bathes the surfaces of the brain and spinal cord, and then
reabsorbs into the bloodstream.

CSF has three important life-sustaining functions:

1. To keep the brain tissue buoyant, acting as a cushion or "shock
   absorber";

2. To act as the vehicle for delivering nutrients to the brain and
   removing waste; and

3. To flow between the cranium and spine and compensate for
   changes in intracranial blood volume (the amount of blood
   within the brain).

The balance between production and absorption of CSF is critically
important. Because CSF is made continuously, medical conditions that
block its normal flow or absorption will result in an over-accumulation
of CSF. The resulting pressure of the fluid against brain tissue is what
causes hydrocephalus.

What Are the Different Types of Hydrocephalus?

Hydrocephalus may be congenital or acquired. Congenital hydrocephalus is present at birth and may be caused by either events or influences that occur during fetal development, or genetic abnormalities. Acquired hydrocephalus develops at the time of birth or at some point afterward. This type of hydrocephalus can affect individuals of all ages and may be caused by injury or disease.

Hydrocephalus may also be communicating or noncommunicating. Communicating hydrocephalus occurs when the flow of CSF is blocked after it exits the ventricles. This form is called communicating because the CSF can still flow between the ventricles, which remain open. Noncommunicating hydrocephalus—also called "obstructive" hydrocephalus—occurs when the flow of CSF is blocked along one or more of the narrow passages connecting the ventricles. One of the most common causes of hydrocephalus is aqueductal stenosis. In this case, hydrocephalus results from a narrowing of the aqueduct of Sylvius, a small passage between the third and fourth ventricles in the middle of the brain.

There are two other forms of hydrocephalus which do not fit exactly into the categories mentioned above and primarily affect adults: hydrocephalus ex-vacuo and Normal Pressure Hydrocephalus (NPH).

Hydrocephalus ex-vacuo occurs when stroke or traumatic injury cause damage to the brain. In these cases, brain tissue may actually shrink. NPH is an abnormal increase of cerebrospinal fluid in the brain's ventricles that may result from a subarachnoid hemorrhage, head trauma, infection, tumor, or complications of surgery. However, many people develop NPH when none of these factors are present. An estimated 375,000 older Americans have NPH.

Who Gets This Disorder?

The number of people who develop hydrocephalus or who are currently living with it is difficult to establish since the condition occurs in children and adults, and can develop later in life. Some estimates report one to two of every 1,000 babies are born with hydrocephalus.

What Causes Hydrocephalus?

The causes of hydrocephalus are still not well understood. Hydrocephalus may result from inherited genetic abnormalities (such as the genetic defect that causes aqueductal stenosis) or developmental disorders (such as those associated with neural tube defects including spina bifida and encephalocele). Other possible causes include complications of premature birth such as intraventricular hemorrhage, diseases such as meningitis, tumors, traumatic head injury, or subarachnoid hemorrhage, which block the exit of CSF from the ventricles to the cisterns or eliminate the passageway for CSF within the cisterns.

What Are the Symptoms of Hydrocephalus?

Symptoms of hydrocephalus vary with age, disease progression, and individual differences in tolerance to the condition. For example, an infant's ability to compensate for increased CSF pressure and enlargement of the ventricles differs from an adult's. The infant skull can expand to accommodate the buildup of CSF because the sutures (the fibrous joints that connect the bones of the skull) have not yet closed.

In infancy, the most obvious indication of hydrocephalus is often a rapid increase in head circumference or an unusually large head size. Other symptoms may include vomiting, sleepiness, irritability, downward deviation of the eyes (also called "sun setting"), and seizures.

Older children and adults may experience different symptoms because their skulls cannot expand to accommodate the buildup of CSF. Symptoms may include headache followed by vomiting, nausea, blurred or double vision, sun setting of the eyes, problems with balance, poor coordination, gait disturbance, urinary incontinence, slowing or loss of developmental progress, lethargy, drowsiness, irritability, or other changes in personality or cognition including memory loss.

Symptoms of normal pressure hydrocephalus include problems with walking, impaired bladder control leading to urinary frequency and/or incontinence, and progressive mental impairment and dementia. An individual with this type of hydrocephalus may have a general slowing of movements or may complain that his or her feet feel "stuck." Because some of these symptoms may also be experienced in other disorders such as Alzheimer disease, Parkinson disease, and Creutzfeldt-Jakob disease, normal pressure hydrocephalus is often incorrectly diagnosed and never properly treated. Doctors may use a variety of tests, including brain scans such as computed tomography (CT) and magnetic resonance imaging (MRI), a spinal tap or lumbar catheter, intracranial pressure monitoring, and neuropsychological tests, to help them accurately diagnose normal pressure hydrocephalus and rule out any other conditions.

The symptoms described in this section account for the most typical ways in which progressive hydrocephalus is noticeable, but it is important to remember that symptoms vary significantly from person to person.

How Is Hydrocephalus Diagnosed?

Hydrocephalus is diagnosed through clinical neurological evaluation and by using cranial imaging techniques such as ultrasonography, CT, MRI, or pressure-monitoring techniques. A physician selects the appropriate diagnostic tool based on an individual's age, clinical presentation, and the presence of known or suspected abnormalities of the brain or spinal cord.

What Is the Treatment for Hydrocephalus?

Hydrocephalus is most often treated by surgically inserting a shunt system. This system diverts the flow of CSF from the CNS to another area of the body where it can be absorbed as part of the normal circulatory process. A shunt is a flexible but sturdy plastic tube. A shunt system consists of the shunt, a catheter, and a valve. One end of the catheter is placed within a ventricle inside the brain or in the CSF outside the spinal cord. The other end of the catheter is commonly placed within the abdominal cavity, but may also be placed at other sites in the body such as a chamber of the heart or areas around the lung where the CSF can drain and be absorbed. A valve located along the catheter maintains one-way flow and regulates the rate of CSF flow.

A limited number of individuals can be treated with an alternative procedure called third ventriculostomy. In this procedure, a neuro endoscope—a small camera that uses fiber optic technology to visualize small and difficult to reach surgical areas—allows a doctor to view the ventricular surface. Once the scope is guided into position, a small tool makes a tiny hole in the floor of the third ventricle, which allows the CSF to bypass the obstruction and flow toward the site of resorption around the surface of the brain.

What Are the Possible Complications of a Shunt System?

Shunt systems are imperfect devices. Complications may include mechanical failure, infections, obstructions, and the need to lengthen or replace the catheter. Generally, shunt systems require monitoring and regular medical follow-up. When complications occur, subsequent surgery to replace the failed part or the entire shunt system may be needed.

Some complications can lead to other problems such as overdraining or underdraining. Overdraining occurs when the shunt allows CSF to drain from the ventricles more quickly than it is produced.

Overdraining can cause the ventricles to collapse, tearing blood vessels and causing headache, hemorrhage (subdural hematoma), or slit-like ventricles (slit ventricle syndrome). Underdraining occurs when CSF is not removed quickly enough and the symptoms of hydrocephalus recur. Overdrainage and underdrainage of CSF are addressed by adjusting the drainage pressure of the shunt valve; if the shunt has an adjustable pressure valve these changes can be made by placing a special magnet on the scalp over the valve. In addition to the common symptoms of hydrocephalus, infections from a shunt may also produce symptoms such as a low-grade fever, soreness of the neck or shoulder muscles, and redness or tenderness along the shunt tract. When there is reason to suspect that a shunt system is not functioning properly (for example, if the symptoms of hydrocephalus return), medical attention should be sought immediately.

What Is the Prognosis for Hydrocephalus?

The prognosis for individuals diagnosed with hydrocephalus is difficult to predict, although there is some correlation between the specific cause of the hydrocephalus and the outcome. Prognosis is further clouded by the presence of associated disorders, the timeliness of diagnosis, and the success of treatment. The degree to which relief of CSF pressure following shunt surgery can minimize or reverse damage to the brain is not well understood.

Affected individuals and their families should be aware that hydrocephalus poses risks to both cognitive and physical development. However, many children diagnosed with the disorder benefit from rehabilitation therapies and educational interventions and go on to lead normal lives with few limitations. Treatment by an interdisciplinary team of medical professionals, rehabilitation specialists, and educational experts is critical to a positive outcome. Left untreated, progressive hydrocephalus may be fatal.

The symptoms of normal pressure hydrocephalus usually get worse over time if the condition is not treated, although some people may experience temporary improvements. While the success of treatment with shunts varies from person to person, some people recover almost completely after treatment and have a good quality of life. Early diagnosis and treatment improves the chance of a good recovery.

Section 22.8

Microcephaly

This section includes text excerpted from "Birth Defects—
Facts about Microcephaly," Centers for Disease
Control and Prevention (CDC), November 21, 2017.

Microcephaly is a birth defect where a baby's head is smaller than expected when compared to babies of the same sex and age. Babies with microcephaly often have smaller brains that might not have developed properly.

What Is Microcephaly?

Microcephaly is a condition where a baby's head is much smaller than expected. During pregnancy, a baby's head grows because the baby's brain grows. Microcephaly can occur because a baby's brain has not developed properly during pregnancy or has stopped growing after birth, which results in a smaller head size. Microcephaly can be an isolated condition, meaning that it can occur with no other major birth defects, or it can occur in combination with other major birth defects.

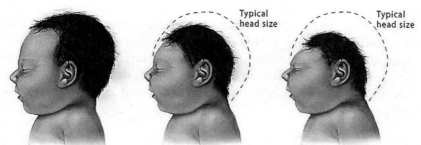

Baby with Typical Head Size   Baby with Microcephaly   Baby with Severe Microcephaly

Figure 22.2. *Typical Head Size, Microcephaly, and Severe Microcephaly Comparison*

What Is Severe Microcephaly?

Severe microcephaly is a more serious, extreme form of this condition where a baby's head is much smaller than expected. Severe microcephaly can result because a baby's brain has not developed properly during pregnancy, or the brain started to develop correctly and then was damaged at some point during pregnancy.

Other Problems

Babies with microcephaly can have a range of other problems, depending on how severe their microcephaly is. Microcephaly has been linked with the following problems:

- Seizures

- Developmental delay, such as problems with speech or other developmental milestones (like sitting, standing, and walking)

- Intellectual disability (decreased ability to learn and function in daily life)

- Problems with movement and balance

- Feeding problems, such as difficulty swallowing

- Hearing loss

- Vision problems

These problems can range from mild to severe and are often lifelong. Because the baby's brain is small and underdeveloped, babies with severe microcephaly can have more of these problems, or have more difficulty with them, than babies with milder microcephaly. Severe microcephaly also can be life-threatening. Because it is difficult to predict at birth what problems a baby will have from microcephaly, babies with microcephaly often need close follow-up through regular check-ups with a healthcare provider to monitor their growth and development.

Occurrence

Microcephaly is not a common condition. State birth defects tracking systems have estimated that microcephaly ranges from 2 babies per 10,000 live births to about 12 babies per 10,000 live births in the Unites States.

Causes and Risk Factors

The causes of microcephaly in most babies are unknown. Some babies have microcephaly because of changes in their genes. Other causes of microcephaly, including severe microcephaly, can include the following exposures during pregnancy:

- Certain infections during pregnancy, such as rubella, toxoplasmosis, or cytomegalovirus

- Severe malnutrition, meaning a lack of nutrients or not getting enough food

- Exposure to harmful substances, such as alcohol, certain drugs, or toxic chemicals

- Interruption of the blood supply to the baby's brain during development

Some babies with microcephaly have been reported among mothers who were infected with Zika virus while pregnant. Centers for Disease Control and Prevention (CDC) scientists announced that enough evidence has accumulated to conclude that Zika virus infection during pregnancy is a cause of microcephaly and other severe fetal brain defects. CDC continues to study birth defects, such as microcephaly, and how to prevent them. If you are pregnant or thinking about becoming pregnant, talk with your doctor about ways to increase your chances of having a healthy baby.

Diagnosis

Microcephaly can be diagnosed during pregnancy or after the baby is born.

During Pregnancy

During pregnancy, microcephaly can sometimes be diagnosed with an ultrasound test (which creates pictures of the body). To see microcephaly during pregnancy, the ultrasound test should be done late in the Second trimester or early in the third trimester.

After the Baby Is Born

To diagnose microcephaly after birth, a healthcare provider will measure the distance around a newborn baby's head, also called the head circumference, during a physical exam. The provider then compares this measurement to population standards by sex and age. Microcephaly is defined as a head circumference measurement that is smaller than a certain value for babies of the same age and sex. This measurement value for microcephaly is usually less than 2 standard deviations (SDs) below the average. The measurement value also may be designated as less than the 3rd percentile. This means the baby's head is extremely small compared to babies of the same age and sex.

Microcephaly can be determined by measuring head circumference (HC) after birth. Although head circumference measurements may be influenced by molding and other factors related to delivery, the measurements should be taken on the first day of life because commonly-used birth head circumference reference charts by age and sex are based on measurements taken before 24 hours of age. The most important factor is that the head circumference is carefully measured and documented. If measurement within the first 24 hours of life is not done, the head circumference should be measured as soon as possible after birth. If the healthcare provider suspects the baby has microcephaly, he or she can request one or more tests to help confirm the diagnosis. For example, special tests like magnetic resonance imaging (MRI) can provide critical information on the structure of the baby's brain that can help determine if the newborn baby had an infection during pregnancy. They also can help the healthcare provider look for other problems that might be present.

Treatment

Microcephaly is a lifelong condition. There is no known cure or standard treatment for microcephaly. Because microcephaly can range from mild to severe, treatment options can range as well. Babies with mild microcephaly often don't experience any other problems besides small head size. These babies will need routine check-ups to monitor their growth and development. For more severe microcephaly, babies will need care and treatment focused on managing their other health problems (mentioned above). Developmental services early in life will often help babies with microcephaly to improve and maximize their physical and intellectual abilities. These services, known as early intervention, can include speech, occupational, and physical therapies. Sometimes medications also are needed to treat seizures or other symptoms.

Chapter 23

Craniofacial Defects

Chapter Contents

Section 23.1

Anophthalmia and Microphthalmia

This section includes text excerpted from "Birth Defects—
Facts about Anophthalmia/Microphthalmia," Centers for
Disease Control and Prevention (CDC), June 27, 2017.

What Is Anophthalmia and Microphthalmia?

Anophthalmia and microphthalmia are birth defects of a baby's
eye(s). Anophthalmia is a birth defect where a baby is born without
one or both eyes. Microphthalmia is a birth defect in which one or both
eyes did not develop fully, so they are small.

- Anophthalmia and microphthalmia develop during pregnancy
  and can occur alone, with other birth defects, or as part of a syndrome. Anophthalmia and microphthalmia often result in blindness or limited vision.

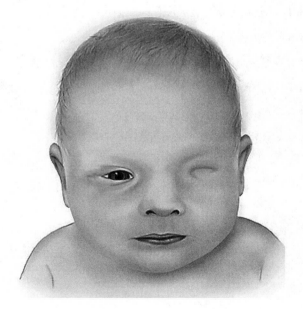

Figure 23.1. *Anophthalmia*

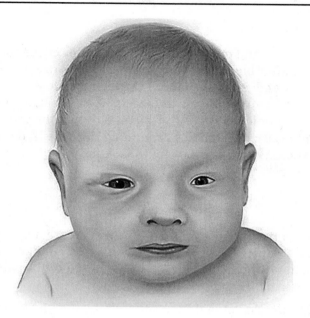

Figure 23.2. *Microphthalmia*

Occurrence

Anophthalmia and microphthalmia are rare. Researchers estimate that about 1 in every 5,300 babies born in the United States will have anophthalmia or microphthalmia. This means about 780 U.S. babies are born with these conditions each year.

Causes and Risk Factors

The causes of anophthalmia and microphthalmia among most infants are unknown. Some babies have anophthalmia or microphthalmia because of a change in their genes or chromosomes. Anophthalmia and microphthalmia can also be caused by taking certain medicines, like isotretinoin (Accutane®) or thalidomide, during pregnancy. These medicines can lead to a pattern of birth defects, which can include anophthalmia or microphthalmia. These defects might also be caused by a combination of genes and other factors, such as the things the mother comes in contact with in the environment or what the mother eats or drinks, or certain medicines she uses during pregnancy.

If you are pregnant or thinking about becoming pregnant, talk with your doctor about ways to increase your chances of having a healthy baby.

Diagnosis

Anophthalmia and microphthalmia can either be diagnosed during pregnancy or after birth. During pregnancy, doctors can often identify anophthalmia and microphthalmia through an ultrasound or a computerized tomography (CT) scan (special X-ray test) and sometimes with certain genetic testing. After birth, a doctor can identify anophthalmia and microphthalmia by examining the baby. A doctor will also perform a thorough physical exam to look for any other birth defects that may be present.

Treatment

There is no treatment available that will create a new eye or that will restore complete vision for those affected by anophthalmia or microphthalmia. A baby born with one of these conditions should be seen by a team of special eye doctors:

- An ophthalmologist, a doctor specially trained to care for eyes

- An ocularist, a healthcare provider who is specially trained in making and fitting prosthetic eyes

- An oculoplastic surgeon, a doctor who specializes in surgery for the eye and eye socket

The eye sockets are critical for a baby's face to grow and develop properly. If a baby has one of these conditions, the bones that shape the eye socket may not grow properly. Babies can be fitted with a plastic structure called a conformer that can help the eye socket and bones to grow properly. As babies get older, these devices will need to be enlarged to help expand the eye socket. Also, as children age, they can be fitted for an artificial eye.

A team of eye specialists should frequently monitor children with these conditions early in life. If other conditions arise, like a cataract or detached retina, children might need surgery to repair these other conditions. If anophthalmia or microphthalmia affects only one eye, the ophthalmologist can suggest ways to protect and preserve sight in the healthy eye. Depending on the severity of anophthalmia and microphthalmia, children might need surgery. It is important to talk to their team of eye specialists to determine the best plan of action.

Babies born with these conditions can often benefit from early intervention and therapy to help their development and mobility.

Section 23.2

Cleft Lip and Palate

This section includes text excerpted from "Birth Defects—
Facts about Cleft Lip and Cleft Palate," Centers for Disease
Control and Prevention (CDC), June 27, 2017.

Cleft lip and cleft palate are birth defects that occur when a baby's
lip or mouth do not form properly during pregnancy. Together, these
birth defects commonly are called "orofacial clefts."

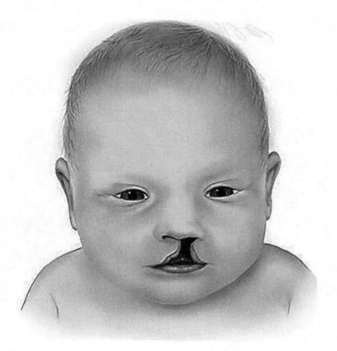

Figure 23.3. *Cleft Lip*

What Is Cleft Lip?

The lip forms between the fourth and seventh weeks of pregnancy.
As a baby develops during pregnancy, body tissue and special cells

from each side of the head grow toward the center of the face and join together to make the face. This joining of tissue forms the facial features, like the lips and mouth. A cleft lip happens if the tissue that makes up the lip does not join completely before birth. This results in an opening in the upper lip. The opening in the lip can be a small slit or it can be a large opening that goes through the lip into the nose. A cleft lip can be on one or both sides of the lip or in the middle of the lip, which occurs very rarely. Children with a cleft lip also can have a cleft palate.

What Is Cleft Palate?

The roof of the mouth (palate) is formed between the sixth and ninth weeks of pregnancy. A cleft palate happens if the tissue that makes up the roof of the mouth does not join together completely during pregnancy. For some babies, both the front and back parts of the palate are open. For other babies, only part of the palate is open.

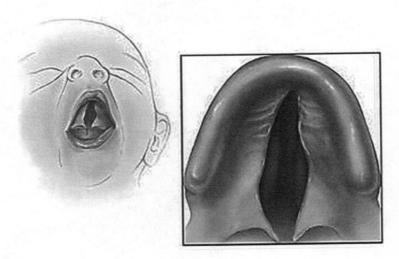

Figure 23.4. *Cleft Palate*

Other Problems

Children with a cleft lip with or without a cleft palate or a cleft palate alone often have problems with feeding and speaking clearly and can have ear infections. They also might have hearing problems and problems with their teeth.

Occurrence

The Centers for Disease Control and Prevention (CDC) estimated that, each year in the United States, about 2,650 babies are born with a cleft palate and 4,440 babies are born with a cleft lip with or without a cleft palate. Isolated orofacial clefts, or clefts that occur with no other major birth defects, are one of the most common types of birth defects in the United States. Depending on the cleft type, the rate of isolated orofacial clefts can vary from 50–80 percent of all clefts.

Causes and Risk Factors

The causes of orofacial clefts among most infants are unknown. Some children have a cleft lip or cleft palate because of changes in their genes. Cleft lip and cleft palate are thought to be caused by a combination of genes and other factors, such as things the mother comes in contact with in her environment, or what the mother eats or drinks, or certain medications she uses during pregnancy.

CDC reported on important findings from research studies about some factors that increase the chance of having a baby with an orofacial cleft:

- **Smoking.** Women who smoke during pregnancy are more likely to have a baby with an orofacial cleft than women who do not smoke.

- **Diabetes.** Women with diabetes diagnosed before pregnancy have an increased risk of having a child with a cleft lip with or without cleft palate, compared to women who did not have diabetes.

- **Use of certain medicines.** Women who used certain medicines to treat epilepsy, such as topiramate (TPM) or valproic acid (VPA), during the first trimester (the first 3 months) of pregnancy have an increased risk of having a baby with cleft lip with or without cleft palate, compared to women who didn't take these medicines.

If you are pregnant or thinking about becoming pregnant, talk with your doctor about ways to increase your chances of having a healthy baby.

Diagnosis

Orofacial clefts, especially cleft lip with or without cleft palate, can be diagnosed during pregnancy by a routine ultrasound. They can also

345

be diagnosed after the baby is born, especially cleft palate. However, sometimes certain types of cleft palate (for example, submucous cleft palate and bifid uvula) might not be diagnosed until later in life.

Management and Treatment

Services and treatment for children with orofacial clefts can vary depending on the severity of the cleft; the child's age and needs; and the presence of associated syndromes or other birth defects, or both.

Surgery to repair a cleft lip usually occurs in the first few months of life and is recommended within the first 12 months of life. Surgery to repair a cleft palate is recommended within the first 18 months of life or earlier if possible. Many children will need additional surgical procedures as they get older. Surgical repair can improve the look and appearance of a child's face and might also improve breathing, hearing, and speech and language development. Children born with orofacial clefts might need other types of treatments and services, such as special dental or orthodontic care or speech therapy.

Because children with orofacial clefts often require a variety of services that need to be provided in a coordinated manner throughout childhood and into adolescence and sometimes adulthood, the American Cleft Palate—Craniofacial Association (ACPA) recommends services and treatment by cleft and craniofacial teams. Cleft and craniofacial teams provide a coordinated approach to care for children with orofacial clefts. These teams usually consist of experienced and qualified physicians and healthcare providers from different specialties. Cleft and craniofacial teams and centers are located throughout the United States and other countries.

With treatment, most children with orofacial clefts do well and lead a healthy life. Some children with orofacial clefts may have issues with self-esteem if they are concerned with visible differences between themselves and other children. Parent to parent support groups can prove to be useful for families of babies with birth defects of the head and face, such as orofacial clefts.

Section 23.3

Craniosynostosis

This section includes text excerpted from "Birth Defects—
Facts about Craniosynostosis," Centers for Disease
Control and Prevention (CDC), June 27, 2017.

What Is Craniosynostosis?

Craniosynostosis is a birth defect in which the bones in a baby's skull join together too early. This happens before the baby's brain is fully formed. As the baby's brain grows, the skull can become more misshapen. The spaces between a typical baby's skull bones are filled with flexible material and called sutures. These sutures allow the skull to grow as the baby's brain grows. Around two years of age, a child's skull bones begin to join together because the sutures become

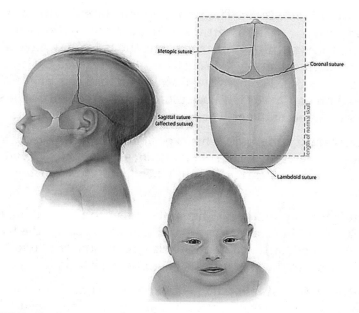

Figure 23.5. *Sagittal Craniosynostosis*

bone. When this occurs, the suture is said to "close." In a baby with craniosynostosis, one or more of the sutures closes too early. This can limit or slow the growth of the baby's brain.

When a suture closes and the skull bones join together too soon, the baby's head will stop growing in only that part of the skull. In the other parts of the skull where the sutures have not joined together, the baby's head will continue to grow. When that happens, the skull will have an abnormal shape, although the brain inside the skull has grown to its usual size. Sometimes, though, more than one suture closes too early. In these instances, the brain might not have enough room to grow to its usual size. This can lead to a buildup of pressure inside the skull.

Types of Craniosynostosis

The types of craniosynostosis depend on what sutures join together early.

- **Sagittal synostosis.** The sagittal suture runs along the top of the head, from the baby's soft spot near the front of the head to the back of the head. When this suture closes too early, the baby's head will grow long and narrow (scaphocephaly). It is the most common type of craniosynostosis.

- **Coronal synostosis.** The right and left coronal sutures run from each ear to the sagittal suture at the top of the head. When one of these sutures closes too early, the baby may have a flattened forehead on the side of the skull that closed early (anterior plagiocephaly). The baby's eye socket on that side might also be raised up and his or her nose could be pulled toward that side. This is the second most common type of craniosynostosis.

- **Bicoronal synostosis.** This type of craniosynostosis occurs when the coronal sutures on both sides of the baby's head close too early. In this case, the baby's head will grow broad and short (brachycephaly).

- **Lambdoid synostosis.** The lambdoid suture runs along the backside of the head. If this suture closes too early, the baby's head may be flattened on the back side (posterior plagiocephaly). This is one of the rarest types of craniosynostosis.

- **Metopic synostosis.** The metopic suture runs from the baby's nose to the sagittal suture at the top of the head. If this suture closes too early, the top of the baby's head shape

348

may look triangular, meaning narrow in the front and broad in the back (trigonocephaly). This is one of the rarest types of craniosynostosis.

Other Problems

Many of the problems a baby can have depend on:

- Which sutures closed early

- When the sutures closed (was it before or after birth and at what age)

- Whether or not the brain has room to grow

Sometimes, if the condition is not treated, the buildup of pressure in the baby's skull can lead to problems, such as blindness, seizures, or brain damage.

Occurrence

In a study of the metropolitan area of Atlanta, Georgia (GA), the Centers for Disease Control and Prevention (CDC) estimated that craniosynostosis affects about 4 in 10,000 live births.

Causes and Risk Factors

The causes of craniosynostosis in most infants are unknown. Some babies have a craniosynostosis because of changes in their genes. In some cases, craniosynostosis occurs because of an abnormality in a single gene, which can cause a genetic syndrome. However, in most cases, craniosynostosis is thought to be caused by a combination of genes and other factors, such as things the mother comes in contact with in her environment, or what the mother eats or drinks, or certain medications she uses during pregnancy.

CDC reported on important findings from research studies about some factors that increase the chance of having a baby with craniosynostosis:

- **Maternal thyroid disease.** Women with thyroid disease or who are treated for thyroid disease while they are pregnant have a higher chance of having an infant with craniosynostosis, compared to women who don't have thyroid disease.

- **Certain medications.** Women who report using clomiphene citrate (a fertility medication) just before or early in pregnancy are more likely to have a baby with craniosynostosis, compared to women who didn't take this medicine.

If you are pregnant or thinking about becoming pregnant, talk with your doctor about ways to increase your chances of having a healthy baby.

Diagnosis

Craniosynostosis usually is diagnosed soon after a baby is born. Sometimes, it is diagnosed later in life.

Usually, the first sign of craniosynostosis is an abnormally shaped skull. Other signs may include:

- No "soft spot" on the baby's skull

- A raised firm edge where the sutures closed early

- Slow growth or no growth in the baby's head size over time

Doctors can identify craniosynostosis during a physical exam. A doctor will feel the baby's head for hard edges along the sutures and unusual soft spots. The doctor also will look for any problems with the shape of the baby's face. If he or she suspects the baby might have craniosynostosis, the doctor usually requests one or more tests to help confirm the diagnosis. For example, a special X-ray test, such as a computed tomography (CT) or computerized axial tomography (CAT) scan, can show the details of the skull and brain, whether certain sutures are closed, and how the brain is growing.

Treatments

Many types of craniosynostosis require surgery. The surgical procedure is meant to relieve pressure on the brain, correct the craniosynostosis, and allow the brain to grow properly. When needed, a surgical procedure is usually performed during the first year of life. But, the timing of surgery depends on which sutures are closed and whether the baby has one of the genetic syndromes that can cause craniosynostosis.

Babies with very mild craniosynostosis might not need surgery. As the baby gets older and grows hair, the shape of the skull can become less noticeable. Sometimes, special medical helmets can be used to help mold the baby's skull into a more regular shape.

Each baby born with craniosynostosis is different, and the condition can range from mild to severe. Most babies with craniosynostosis are otherwise healthy. Some children, however, have developmental delays or intellectual disabilities, because either the craniosynostosis has kept the baby's brain from growing and working normally, or because the baby has a genetic syndrome that caused both craniosynostosis and problems with how the brain works. A baby with craniosynostosis will need to see a healthcare provider regularly to make sure that the brain and skull are developing properly. Babies with craniosynostosis can often benefit from early intervention services to help with any developmental delays or intellectual problems. Some children with craniosynostosis may have issues with self-esteem if they are concerned with visible differences between themselves and other children. Parent to parent support groups also can be useful for new families of babies with birth defects of the head and face, including craniosynostosis.

Section 23.4

Moebius Syndrome

This section contains text excerpted from the following sources: Text in this section begins with excerpts from "Moebius Syndrome," Genetic and Rare Diseases Information Center (GARD), National Center for Advancing Translational Sciences (NCATS), March 3, 2016; Text under the heading "Treatment" is excerpted from "Moebius Syndrome Information Page," National Institute of Neurological Disorders and Stroke (NINDS), December 19, 2016.

Moebius syndrome is a rare neurological condition that primarily affects the muscles that control facial expression and eye movement.

Signs and Symptoms

Signs and symptoms of the condition may include:

- weakness or paralysis of the facial muscles
- feeding, swallowing, and choking problems
- excessive drooling
- crossed eyes
- lack of facial expression

351

- eye sensitivity
- high or cleft palate
- hearing problems
- dental abnormalities
- bone abnormalities in the hands and feet
- speech difficulties

Affected children often experience delayed development of motor skills (such as crawling and walking), although most eventually acquire these skills.

Causes

Moebius syndrome is caused by the absence or underdevelopment of the 6th and 7th cranial nerves, which control eye movement and facial expression. Other cranial nerves may also be affected. There is no cure for Moebius syndrome, but proper care and treatment give many individuals a normal life expectancy.

Inheritance

Most cases of Moebius syndrome are not inherited and occur as isolated cases in individuals with no history of the condition in their family (sporadically). A small percentage of cases of Moebius syndrome have been familial (occurring in more than one individual in a family), but there has not been a consistent pattern of inheritance among all affected families. In some families the pattern has been suggestive of autosomal dominant inheritance, while in other families it has been suggestive of autosomal recessive or X-linked recessive inheritance.

Diagnosis

Making a diagnosis for a genetic or rare disease can often be challenging. Healthcare professionals typically look at a person's medical history, symptoms, physical exam, and laboratory test results in order to make a diagnosis.

Treatment

There is no specific course of treatment for Moebius syndrome. Treatment is supportive and in accordance with symptoms.

Infants may require feeding tubes or special bottles to maintain sufficient nutrition. Surgery may correct crossed eyes and improve limb and jaw deformities. Physical and speech therapy often improves motor skills and coordination, and leads to better control of speaking and eating abilities. Plastic reconstructive surgery may be beneficial in some individuals. Nerve and muscle transfers to the corners of the mouth have been performed to provide limited ability to smile.

Section 23.5

Goldenhar Disease

This section includes text excerpted from "Goldenhar Disease," Genetic and Rare Diseases Information Center (GARD), National Center for Advancing Translational Sciences (NCATS), November 16, 2017.

Goldenhar disease is a condition that is present at birth and mainly affects the development of the eye, ear, and spine. The main sign and symptoms are facial asymmetry (one side of the face is different from the other), a partially formed ear (microtia) or totally absent ear (anotia), noncancerous (benign) growths of the eye (ocular dermoid cysts), and spinal abnormalities. Goldenhar disease may also affect the heart, lungs, kidneys, and central nervous system. It is due to problems that occur when the fetus is forming within the womb of the mother, in structures known as the first and second branchial arch. These structures will develop to form the neck and the head. The cause is still unknown.

Goldenhar syndrome (GS) is part of a group of conditions known as craniofacial microsomia. It is not known whether the conditions included in the group really are different conditions or part of the same problem with different degrees of severity. Treatment is age dependent, with interventions at appropriate stages during the growth and development of the skull and face.

353

Symptoms

The signs and symptoms of Goldenhar disease vary significantly from person to person. Common signs and symptoms of the condition include:

- Microtia (a partially formed or completely absent ear) and other ear abnormalities

- Underdeveloped facial muscles which may be associated with weakness

- Underdeveloped jaw, cheekbone and/or temple bone

- Cleft lip and/or palate

- Abnormalities of the eyes, such as anophthalmia/microphthalmia, epibulbar tumors (noncancerous growths in the eyes), retinal abnormalities, and vision loss

- An unusually large or small mouth

- Dental abnormalities

In most cases, only one side of the face is affected, although approximately 10–33 percent of people with the condition have bilateral (both sides) involvement.

Some people with GS may also experience hearing loss; hydrocephalus (with or without intellectual disability); heart, kidneys, and lung problems; spinal abnormalities; and/or limb malformations.

Cause

The underlying cause of Goldenhar disease is poorly understood. Most cases occur sporadically with no apparent explanation. Some researchers suspect that problems with blood flow or other disruptions during fetal development may contribute to the development of the condition.

Approximately 1–2 percent of affected people have other family members with the condition, which suggests that genes may play a role in some cases.

Most cases of Goldenhar disease occur sporadically in people with no family history of the condition. Rarely (approximately 1–2% of affected people), more than one family member can be affected. In these cases, the condition appears to be passed down through the family in an autosomal dominant manner.

Diagnosis

A diagnosis of Goldenhar disease is based on the presence of characteristic signs and symptoms. These clinical features may be observed on physical examination or may require specialized testing such as imaging studies (i.e., computerized tomography (CT) scan, X-ray, echocardiogram (ECHO), ultrasound). Additional testing including certain genetic tests may also be recommended to rule out conditions that are associated with similar features.

Treatment

The treatment of Goldenhar disease is based on the signs and symptoms present in each person. Ideally, affected children should be managed by an experienced multidisciplinary craniofacial team (MDT). Treatment is age dependent and certain interventions may be recommended at different stages of growth and development.

The following are examples of medical issues that may need to be addressed in a person affected by Goldenhar disease:

- **Feeding issues.** Some people affected by GS may have feeding difficulties caused by the associated craniofacial abnormalities. Interventions may include special bottles, supplemental nasogastric feedings, and gastrostomy tube placement.

- **Breathing problems.** Affected people with an underdeveloped lower jaw may have difficulty breathing or develop sleep apnea. In these cases, referral to appropriate medical specialists is recommended so appropriate care can be provided.

- **Hearing loss.** A hearing evaluation is recommended in all children with Goldenhar disease by six months of age. In those with hearing impairment, hearing aids or other treatments may be recommended.

- **Epibulbar tumors (noncancerous growths in the eyes).** These tumors may need to be surgically removed if they are particularly large or interfere with vision.

- **Craniofacial abnormalities (i.e., cleft lip and/or palate), congenital heart defects (CHDs), kidney problems, and/ or spine abnormalities.** Some of the characteristic symptoms associated with Goldenhar disease may require surgical repair.

- **Speech.** People affected by Goldenhar disease are at an increased risk for a variety of speech problems due to the many

355

associated craniofacial abnormalities. A speech evaluation and/or speech therapy may, therefore, be recommended in some affected people.

Section 23.6

Hemifacial Microsomia (HFM)

This section includes text excerpted from "Hemifacial Microsomia," Genetic and Rare Diseases Information Center (GARD), National Center for Advancing Translational Sciences (NCATS), November 16, 2017.

Hemifacial microsomia (HFM) is a condition in which part of one side of the face is underdeveloped and does not grow normally. The eye, cheekbone, lower jaw, facial nerves, muscles, and neck may be affected. Other findings may include hearing loss from underdevelopment of the middle ear; a small tongue; and macrostomia (large mouth). HFM is the second most common facial birth defect after clefts.

The cause of HFM in most cases is unknown. It usually occurs in people with no family history of HFM, but it is inherited in some cases. HFM is part of a group of conditions known as craniofacial microsomia (CFM). It is not known whether the conditions included in the group really are different conditions or part of the same problem with different degrees of severity. Treatment depends on age and the specific features and symptoms in each person.

Symptoms

People with HFM may have various signs and symptoms, including:

- Facial asymmetry

- Abnormalities of the outer ear such as absence, reduced size (hypoplasia), and/or displacement

- Small and/or flattened maxillary, temporal, and malar bones

- Deafness due to middle ear abnormalities

- Ear tags
- Abnormalities (in shape or number) of the teeth, or significant delay of tooth development
- Narrowed mandible (jaw) or absence of half of the mandible
- Cleft lip and/or palate
- Reduced size of facial muscles
- Abnormalities of the eyes (extremely small or absent)
- Skeletal abnormalities including problems of the spine or ribs
- Absence of check muscles or nerves supplying those muscles (resulting in an uneven smile)

Cause

For most people with HFM, the cause is unknown. It is believed that something occurs in the early stages of development, such as a disturbance of the blood supply to the first and second branchial arches in the first 6–8 weeks of pregnancy.

Studies have suggested multiple possible risk factors for HFM. Environmental risk factors include the use of medications during pregnancy such as accutane, pseudoephedrine, aspirin, or ibuprofen. Other environmental factors include second trimester bleeding, maternal diabetes, being pregnant with multiples, or the use of assisted reproductive technology. A genetic cause is found in some families, such as a chromosome disorder or a genetic syndrome.

Some possible explanations when the cause of HFM is unknown include a very small chromosome deletion or duplication that is not detected, a mutation in an unknown gene, or changes in multiple genes associated with development of the face. It is also possible that a combination of genetic changes and environmental risk factors could cause HFM.

Inheritance

HFM most often occurs in a single individual in a family and is not inherited. If the condition is caused by a chromosomal abnormality, it may be inherited from one affected parent or it may result from a new abnormality in the chromosome and occur in people with no history of the disorder in their family. In a very small number of cases, HFM is inherited in an autosomal dominant pattern, which means one copy of an altered gene in each cell is sufficient to cause the disorder. In rare cases, the condition is inherited in an autosomal recessive pattern, which means both copies of a gene in each cell have mutations. The parents of an individual with an autosomal recessive condition each carry one copy of the mutated gene, but they typically do not show signs and symptoms of the condition. The gene or genes involved in HFM are unknown. In some affected families, people seem to inherit an increased risk of developing HFM, not the condition itself. In these cases, some combination of genetic changes and environmental factors may be involved.

Treatment

Treatment of HFM varies depending on the features present and the severity in each affected person. Various types of surgeries may be needed in many cases.

Some children need breathing support or a tracheostomy soon after birth if the jaw is severely affected. However in most cases, airway problems can be managed without surgery. Those with a jaw deformity and/or clefts may have feeding problems and may need supplemental feedings through a nasogastric tube to support growth and weight gain. Babies born with cleft lip or palate can have surgical repairs done during the first year. Cleft lip repair is typically performed when the child is 3–6 months old, while cleft palate surgery is generally performed when the child is about a year old. A lateral facial cleft, one of the most severe abnormalities associated with the condition, also requires reconstruction in stages.

If eye closure is incomplete due to eyelid abnormalities or facial paralysis is present, a child may need eye protection or surgery. Surgery may also be used for eyelid differences to reposition the lower lids and corners of the eyes. Some children with abnormally shaped or missing ears may choose to have a series of reconstructive surgeries to make the ear appear more normal. Children with skin, cheek and other soft tissue deficiencies may need augmentation procedures such as fat grafting or tissue transfer. Severe bone abnormalities may require surgery as well.

Because multiple body systems may be involved in HFM, affected people should continually be monitored for complications.

Section 23.7

Klippel-Feil Syndrome (KFS)

This section contains text excerpted from the following sources: Text in this section begins with excerpts from "Klippel-Feil Syndrome," Genetics Home Reference (GHR), National Institutes of Health (NIH), November 21, 2017; Text beginning with the heading "Treatment" is excerpted from "Klippel Feil Syndrome Information Page," National Institute of Neurological Disorders and Stroke (NINDS), December 19, 2016.

Klippel Feil syndrome (KFS) is a bone disorder characterized by the abnormal joining (fusion) of two or more spinal bones in the neck (cervical vertebrae). The vertebral fusion is present from birth. Three major features result from this vertebral fusion: a short neck, the resulting appearance of a low hairline at the back of the head, and a limited range of motion in the neck. Most affected people have one or two of these characteristic features. Less than half of all individuals with KFS have all three classic features of this condition.

In people with KFS, the fused vertebrae can limit the range of movement of the neck and back as well as lead to chronic headaches and muscle pain in the neck and back that range in severity. People with minimal bone involvement often have fewer problems compared to individuals with several vertebrae affected. The shortened neck can cause a slight difference in the size and shape of the right and left sides of the face (facial asymmetry). Trauma to the spine, such as a fall or car accident, can aggravate problems in the fused area. Fusion of the vertebrae can lead to nerve damage in the head, neck, or back. Over time, individuals with KFS can develop a narrowing of the spinal canal (spinal stenosis) in the neck, which can compress and damage the spinal cord. Rarely, spinal nerve abnormalities may cause abnormal sensations or involuntary movements in people with KFS. Affected individuals may develop a painful joint disorder called osteoarthritis around the areas of fused bone or experience painful involuntary tensing of the neck muscles (cervical dystonia). In addition to the fused cervical bones, people with this condition may have abnormalities in other vertebrae. Many people with KFS have abnormal side to side curvature of the spine (scoliosis) due to malformation of the vertebrae; fusion of additional vertebrae below the neck may also occur.

People with KFS may have a wide variety of other features in addition to their spine abnormalities. Some people with this condition have hearing difficulties, eye abnormalities, an opening in the roof of the mouth (cleft palate (CL)), genitourinary (GU) problems such as abnormal kidneys, or reproductive organs, heart abnormalities, or lung defects, that can cause breathing problems. Affected individuals may have other skeletal defects including arms or legs of unequal length (limb length discrepancy), which can result in misalignment of the hips or knees. Additionally, the shoulder blades may be under developed so that they sit abnormally high on the back, a condition called Sprengel deformity. Rarely, structural brain abnormalities or a type of birth defect that occurs during the development of the brain and spinal cord (neural tube defect) can occur in people with KFS.

In some cases, KFS occurs as a feature of another disorder or syndrome, such as Wildervanck syndrome or hemifacial microsomia (HFM). In these instances, affected individuals have the signs and symptoms of both KFS and the additional disorder.

Frequency

KFS is estimated to occur in 1 in 40,000–42,000 newborns worldwide. Females seem to be affected slightly more often than males.

Genetic Changes

Mutations in the *GDF6*, *GDF3*, or *MEOX1* gene can cause KFS. These genes are involved in proper bone development. The protein produced from the *GDF6* gene is necessary for the formation of bones and joints, including those in the spine. While the protein produced from the *GDF3* gene is known to be involved in bone development, its exact role is unclear. The protein produced from the *MEOX1* gene, called homeobox protein MOX-1, regulates the process that begins separating vertebrae from one another during early development.

GDF6 and *GDF3* gene mutations that cause KFS likely lead to reduced function of the respective proteins. *MEOX1* gene mutations lead to a complete lack of homeobox protein MOX-1. Although the GDF6, GDF3, and homeobox protein MOX-1 proteins are involved in bone development, particularly formation of vertebrae, it is unclear how a shortage of one of these proteins leads to incomplete separation of the cervical vertebrae in people with KFS.

When KFS is a feature of another disorder, it is caused by mutations in genes involved in the other disorder.

Inheritance Pattern

When KFS is caused by mutations in the *GDF6* or *GDF3* genes, it is inherited in an autosomal dominant pattern, which means one copy of the altered gene in each cell is sufficient to cause the disorder.

When caused by mutations in the *MEOX1* gene, KFS is inherited in an autosomal recessive pattern, which means both copies of the gene in each cell have mutations. The parents of an individual with an autosomal recessive condition each carry one copy of the mutated gene, but they typically do not show signs and symptoms of the condition.

As a feature of another disorder, KFS is inherited in whatever pattern the other disorder follows.

Treatment

Treatment for KFS is symptomatic and may include surgery to relieve cervical or craniocervical instability, and constriction of the spinal cord, and to correct scoliosis. Physical therapy may also be useful.

Prognosis

The prognosis for most individuals with KFS is good if the disorder is treated early and appropriately. Activities that can injure the neck should be avoided.

Section 23.8

Anotia and Microtia

This section includes text excerpted from "Birth Defects—Facts
about Anotia/Microtia," Centers for Disease Control
and Prevention (CDC), June 27, 2017.

What Are Anotia and Microtia?

Anotia and microtia are birth defects of a baby's ear. Anotia happens when the external ear (the part of the ear that can be seen) is missing completely. Microtia happens when the external ear is small and not formed properly.

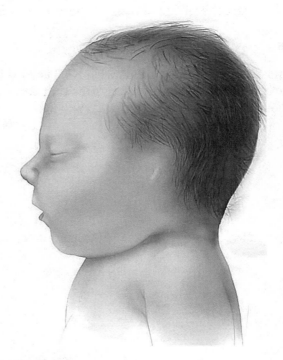

Figure 23.6. *Anotia*

Anotia/microtia usually happens during the first few weeks of pregnancy. These defects can vary from being barely noticeable to being a major problem with how the ear formed. Most of the time, anotia/microtia affects how the baby's ear looks, but usually the parts of the ear inside the head (the inner ear) are not affected. However, some babies with this defect also will have a narrow or missing ear canal.

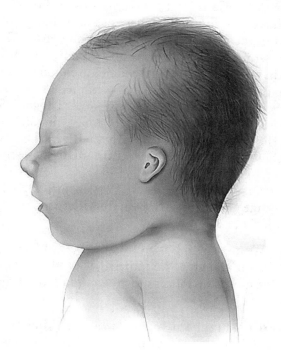

Figure 23.7. *Microtia*

Types of Microtia

There are four types of microtia, ranging from Type 1 to Type 4. Type 1 is the mildest form, where the ear retains its normal shape, but is smaller than usual. Type 4 is the most severe type where all external ear structures are missing—anotia. This condition can affect one or both ears. However, it is more common for babies to have only one affected ear.

Occurrence

Because the severity of microtia ranges from mild to severe, researchers have a hard time estimating how many babies in the

United States are affected. State birth defects tracking systems have estimated that anotia/microtia range from less than 1 in 10,000 live births to about 5 in 10,000 live births.

Causes and Risk Factors

The causes of anotia/microtia among most infants are unknown. Some babies have anotia/microtia because of a change in their genes. In some cases, anotia/microtia occurs because of an abnormality in a single gene, which can cause a genetic syndrome. Another known cause for anotia/microtia is taking a medicine called isotretinoin (Accutane®) during pregnancy. This medicine can lead to a pattern of birth defects, which often includes anotia/microtia. These defects also are thought to be caused by a combination of genes and other factors, such as the things the mother comes in contact with in the environment or what the mother eats or drinks or certain medicines she uses during pregnancy.

Centers for Disease Control and Prevention (CDC) reported on important findings about some factors that increase the risk of having a baby with anotia or microtia:

- **Diabetes.** Women who have diabetes before they get pregnant have been shown to be more at risk for having a baby with anotia/microtia, compared to women who did not have diabetes.

- **Maternal diet.** Pregnant women who eat a diet lower in carbohydrates and folic acid might have an increased risk for having a baby with microtia, compared to all other pregnant women.

If you are pregnant or thinking about becoming pregnant, talk with your doctor about ways to increase your chances of having a healthy baby.

Diagnosis

Anotia/microtia are visible at birth. A doctor will notice the problem by just examining the baby. A computed tomography (CT) or computerized axial tomography (CAT) scan (special X-ray test) of the baby's ear can provide a detailed picture of the ear. This will help the doctor see if the bones or other structures in the ear are affected. A doctor will also perform a thorough physical exam to look for any other birth defects that may be present.

Treatment

Treatment for babies with anotia/microtia depends on the type or severity of the condition. A healthcare provider or hearing specialist called an audiologist will test the baby's hearing to determine any hearing loss in the ear(s) with the defect. Even a hearing loss in one ear can hurt school performance. All treatment options should be discussed and early action may provide better results. Hearing aids may be used to improve a child's hearing ability and to help with speech development.

Surgery is used to reconstruct the external ear. The timing of surgery depends on the severity of the defect and the child's age. Surgery is usually performed between 4 and 10 years of age. Further treatment may be necessary if the child has other birth defects present.

In the absence of other conditions, children with anotia/microtia can develop normally and lead healthy lives. Some children with anotia/microtia may have issues with self-esteem if they are concerned with visible differences between themselves and other children. Parent to parent support groups can prove to be useful for new families of babies with birth defects of the head and face, including anotia/microtia.

Section 23.9

Pierre Robin Sequence (PRS)

This section contains text excerpted from the following sources: Text in this section begins with excerpts from "Pierre Robin Sequence," Genetic and Rare Diseases Information Center (GARD), National Center for Advancing Translational Sciences (NCATS), November 16, 2017; Text beginning with the heading "Frequency" is excerpted from "Isolated Pierre Robin Sequence," Genetics Home Reference (GHR), National Institutes of Health (NIH), November 21, 2017.

Pierre Robin sequence (PRS) is a condition present at birth, in which the infant has a smaller than normal lower jaw (micrognathia), a tongue that is placed further back than normal (glossoptosis), and an opening in the roof of the mouth (cleft palate (CP). This combination of features can lead to difficulty breathing and problems with eating early in life. PRS may occur alone (isolated) or be associated with a variety of other signs and symptoms (described as syndromic). In about 20–40 percent of cases, the condition occurs alone. The exact causes of PRS are unknown. Changes (mutations) in the deoxyribonucleic acid (DNA) near the *SOX9* gene are the most common genetic cause of isolated cases of PRS. Treatment is focused on the specific needs of each patient, but may include surgery to assist with breathing and feeding modifications to prevent choking.

Cause

PRS is a condition with multiple causes. At about 7–10 weeks into a pregnancy, the lower jaw grows rapidly, allowing the tongue to descend from between the two halves of the palate. If, for some reason, the lower jaw does not grow properly, the tongue can prevent the palate from closing, resulting in a cleft palate. The small or displaced lower jaw also causes the tongue to be positioned at the back of the mouth causing breathing difficulties when the child is born. This "sequence of events" is the reason why the condition has been classified as a sequence.

The exact causes of PRS are unknown. Possible mechanisms for the sequence include genetic causes; low volume of amniotic fluid (oligohydramnios), which may limit chin growth; weakness of the facial muscles (myotonia); or connective tissue disease.

The genetic causes for some of the isolated cases (PRS without any associated malformations) may include mutations or deletions of parts of the DNA neighboring the *SOX9* gene (located in chromosome 17 (17q24)). This gene provides instructions for making a protein (protein SOX9) that plays an important role in the formation of many different tissues and organs during embryonic development. The SOX9 protein regulates the activity of other genes, especially those involved in the development of the skeleton, including the jaw.

In about 37 percent of cases, PRS occurs as part of a syndrome with multiple malformations. PRS has been reported as occurring in association with Stickler syndrome (20–25% of these cases), campomelic dysplasia (CMD), trisomy 11q syndrome, deletion 4q syndrome, CHARGE association, velocardiofacial syndrome (VCFS), and Treacher-Collins syndrome (TCS).

Frequency

Isolated PRS affects an estimated 1 in 8,500–14,000 people.

Genetic Changes

Changes in the DNA near the *SOX9* gene are the most common genetic cause of isolated PRS. It is likely that changes in other genes, some of which have not been identified, are also involved in the condition. Doctors speculate that nongenetic factors, for example conditions during pregnancy that restrict growth of the jaw, may cause some cases of isolated PRS.

The *SOX9* gene provides instructions for making a protein that plays a critical role in the formation of many different tissues and organs during embryonic development. The SOX9 protein regulates the activity of other genes, especially those that are important for development of the skeleton, including the mandible.

The genetic changes near the *SOX9* gene that are associated with isolated PRS are thought to disrupt regions of DNA called enhancers, which normally regulate the activity of the *SOX9* gene. These changes reduce *SOX9* gene activity. As a result, the SOX9 protein cannot properly control the genes essential for normal development of the lower jaw, causing micrognathia, and consequently, glossoptosis, airway obstruction, and often cleft palate.

Inheritance Pattern

Isolated PRS is usually not inherited. It typically results from new (de novo) genetic changes and occurs in people with no history of the disorder in their family. When the condition is inherited, it follows an autosomal dominant pattern, which means one copy of the DNA alteration in each cell is sufficient to cause the disorder.

Chapter 24

Digestive Tract Defects

Chapter Contents

Section 24.1

Congenital Diaphragmatic Hernia (CDH)

This section contains text excerpted from the following sources: Text
beginning with the heading "What Is Congenital Diaphragmatic
Hernia?" is excerpted from "Congenital Diaphragmatic Hernia,"
Genetics Home Reference (GHR), National Institutes of Health
(NIH), November 21, 2017; Text beginning with the heading "Causes"
is excerpted from "Congenital Diaphragmatic Hernia," Genetic and
Rare Diseases Information Center (GARD), National Center for
Advancing Translational Sciences (NCATS), November 16, 2017.

What Is Congenital Diaphragmatic Hernia (CDH)?

Congenital diaphragmatic hernia (CDH) is a defect in the diaphragm. The diaphragm, which is composed of muscle and other
fibrous tissue, separates the organs in the abdomen from those in the
chest. Abnormal development of the diaphragm before birth leads to
defects ranging from a thinned area in the diaphragm to its complete
absence. An absent or partially formed diaphragm results in an abnormal opening (hernia) that allows the stomach and intestines to move
into the chest cavity and crowd the heart and lungs. This crowding
can lead to underdevelopment of the lungs (pulmonary hypoplasia),
potentially resulting in life threatening breathing difficulties that are
apparent from birth.

In 5–10 percent of affected individuals, signs, and symptoms of CDH
appear later in life and may include breathing problems or abdominal
pain from protrusion of the intestine into the chest cavity. In about 1
percent of cases, CDH has no symptoms; it may be detected incidentally when medical imaging is done for other reasons.

CDH are often classified by their position. A Bochdalek hernia is a
defect in the side or back of the diaphragm. 80–90 percent of CDH are
of this type. A Morgnani hernia is a defect involving the front part of
the diaphragm. This type of CDH, which accounts for approximately
2 percent of cases, is less likely to cause severe symptoms at birth.
Other types of CDH, such as those affecting the central region of the
diaphragm, or those in which the diaphragm muscle is absent with
only a thin membrane in its place, are rare.

Frequency

CDH affects approximately 1 in 2,500 newborns.

Genetic Changes

CDH has many different causes. In 10–15 percent of affected individuals, the condition appears as a feature of a disorder that affects many body systems, called a syndrome. Donnai Barrow syndrome (DBS), Fryns syndrome (FS), and Pallister Killian mosaic syndrome (PKS) are among several syndromes in which CDH may occur. Some of these syndromes are caused by changes in single genes, and others are caused by chromosomal abnormalities that affect several genes.

About 25 percent of individuals with CDH that is not associated with a known syndrome also have abnormalities of one or more major body systems. Affected body systems can include the heart, brain, skeleton, intestines, genitals, kidneys, or eyes. In these individuals, the multiple abnormalities likely result from a common underlying disruption in development that affects more than one area of the body, but the specific mechanism responsible for this disruption is not clear.

Approximately 50–60 percent of CDH cases are isolated, which means that affected individuals have no other major malformations.

More than 80 percent of individuals with CDH have no known genetic syndrome or chromosomal abnormality. In these cases, the cause of the condition is unknown. Researchers are studying changes in several genes involved in the development of the diaphragm as possible causes of CDH. Some of these genes are transcription factors, which provide instructions for making proteins that help control the activity of particular genes (gene expression). Others provide instructions for making proteins involved in cell structure or the movement (migration) of cells in the embryo. Environmental factors that influence development before birth may also increase the risk of CDH, but these environmental factors have not been identified.

Inheritance Pattern

Isolated CDH is rarely inherited. In almost all cases, there is only one affected individual in a family. When CDH occurs as a feature of a genetic syndrome or chromosomal abnormality, it may cluster in families according to the inheritance pattern for that condition.

CDH is a condition present before birth characterized by abnormal development of the diaphragm. The diaphragm normally separates the organs in the abdomen from those in the chest. The severity of CDH may range from a thinned area in part of the diaphragm, to its complete absence. CDH may allow the stomach and intestines to move through an opening (hernia) into the chest cavity, crowding the heart, and lungs. This can then lead to underdevelopment of the lungs (pulmonary hypoplasia), which may cause life-threatening complications.

CDH may be associated with several syndromes (some caused by genetic mutations or a chromosome abnormality), it may be associated with other birth defects, or it may occur with no other abnormalities. It is rarely inherited. Treatment options depend on the type and severity of the defect and typically include surgery. Prenatal diagnosis and medical advances have increased the survival rate, but various long-term complications affecting health and development may occur.

Causes

CDH can occur as an isolated finding, as part of a genetic syndrome or chromosome abnormality, or with additional birth defects of unknown cause. Some cases have been linked to in utero exposures. In the majority of cases, the cause is not known.

Prognosis

The long-term outlook (prognosis) for those with CDH depends on a number of factors and is hard to predict. A large defect is more likely to result in pulmonary hypoplasia (underdevelopment of the lungs) and death than a small defect. Other factors associated with decreased survival include:

- premature birth
- having a chromosome abnormality or single gene disorder
- the presence of other severe birth defects such as a heart defect
- having a right sided defect or bilateral CDH (on both sides)
- liver herniation
- a lower fetal lung volume

The most serious complication after surgical repair of CDH is persistent pulmonary hypertension of the newborn (PPHN). Other complications that may occur soon after surgery include hemorrhage, chylothorax, and patch infection.

The postnatal survival rate at tertiary centers (providing special-ized care) has improved, with reported rates of 70–92 percent. How-ever, these data represent the survival rate of cases that were full term infants born or transferred to tertiary care centers with available skilled personnel and access to advanced technology.

While reports of normal or near normal long-term outcomes are increasing, many survivors have long-term complications. These may include chronic respiratory disease, recurrent hernia (abnormal open-ing) or patch problems, spine or chest wall abnormalities, gastrointes-tinal difficulties, and neurological impairment.

Section 24.2

Esophageal Atresia

This section includes text excerpted from "Specific Birth Defects— Facts about Esophageal Atresia," Centers for Disease Control and Prevention (CDC), November 21, 2017.

Esophageal atresia is a birth defect in which part of a baby's esopha-gus (the tube that connects the mouth to the stomach) does not develop properly. In a baby with esophageal atresia, the esophagus has two separate sections—the upper and lower esophagus—that do not con-nect. A baby with this birth defect is unable to pass food from the mouth to the stomach, and sometimes difficulty breathing.

Esophageal atresia often occurs with tracheoesophageal fistula, a birth defect in which part of the esophagus is connected to the trachea, or windpipe.

Types of Esophageal Atresia

There are four types of esophageal atresia: Type A, Type B, Type C, and Type D.

- **Type A** is when the upper and lower parts of the esophagus do not connect and have closed ends. In this type, no parts of the esophagus attach to the trachea.

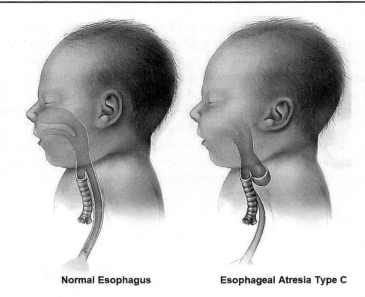

Normal Esophagus   Esophageal Atresia Type C

Figure 24.1. *Normal Esophagus versus Esophageal Atresia*

- **Type B** is very rare. In this type the upper part of the esophagus is attached to the trachea, but the lower part of the esophagus has a closed end.

- **Type C** is the most common type. In this type the upper part of the esophagus has a closed end and the lower part of the esophagus is attached to the trachea.

- **Type D** is the rarest and most severe. In this type the upper and lower parts of the esophagus are not connected to each other, but each is connected separately to the trachea.

Occurrence

Researchers estimates that each year, esophageal atresia affects about 1 in 4,300 pregnancies in the United States. This birth defect can occur alone, but often occurs with other birth defects.

Causes

The causes of esophageal atresia in most babies are unknown. Researchers believe that some instances of esophageal atresia may be caused by abnormalities in the baby's genes. Nearly half of all babies born with esophageal atresia have one or more additional birth defects, such as other problems with the digestive system (intestines and anus), heart, kidneys, or the ribs, or spinal column.

Centers for Disease Control and Prevention (CDC) reported on important findings about some factors that increase the risk of having a baby with esophageal atresia:

- **Paternal age.** Older age of the father is related to an increased chance of having a baby born with esophageal atresia.

- **Assisted reproductive technology (ART).** Women who used ART to become pregnant have an increased risk of having a baby with esophageal atresia compared to women who did not use ART.

If you are pregnant or thinking about becoming pregnant, talk with your doctor about ways to increase your chances of having a healthy baby.

Diagnosis

Esophageal atresia is rarely diagnosed during pregnancy. Esophageal atresia is most commonly detected after birth when the baby first tries to feed and has choking or vomiting, or when a tube inserted in the baby's nose or mouth cannot pass down into the stomach. An X-ray can confirm that the tube stops in the upper esophagus.

Treatment

Once a diagnosis has been made, surgery is needed to reconnect the two ends of the esophagus so that the baby can breathe and feed properly. Multiple surgeries and other procedures or medications may be needed, particularly if the baby's repaired esophagus becomes too narrow for food to pass through it; if the muscles of the esophagus don't work well enough to move food into the stomach; or if digested food in the stomach consistently moves back up into the esophagus.

Section 24.3

Gastroschisis

This section includes text excerpted from "Birth Defects—Facts about Gastroschisis," Centers for Disease Control and Prevention (CDC), November 21, 2017.

Gastroschisis is a birth defect of the abdominal wall. The baby's intestines are found outside of the baby's body, exiting through a hole beside the belly button.

What Is Gastroschisis?

Gastroschisis is a birth defect of the abdominal (belly) wall. The baby's intestines are found outside of the baby's body, exiting through a hole beside the belly button. The hole can be small or large and sometimes other organs, such as the stomach and liver, can also be found outside of the baby's body.

Gastroschisis occurs early during pregnancy when the muscles that make up the baby's abdominal wall do not form correctly. A hole occurs which allows the intestines and other organs to extend outside of the body, usually to the right side of belly button. Because the intestines

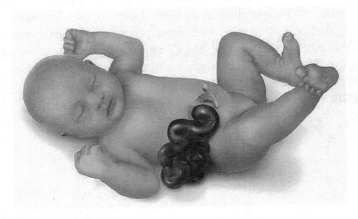

Figure 24.2. *Gastroschisis*

are not covered in a protective sac and are exposed to the amniotic fluid, the intestines can become irritated, causing them to shorten, twist, or swell.

Other Problems

Soon after the baby is born, surgery will be needed to place the abdominal organs inside the baby's body and repair the hole in the abdominal wall. Even after the repair, infants with gastroschisis can have problems with nursing and eating, digestion of food, and absorption of nutrients.

Occurrence

The Centers for Disease Control and Prevention (CDC) estimates that about 1,871 babies are born each year in the United States with gastroschisis, but several studies show that recently this birth defect has become more common, particularly among younger mothers.

Causes and Risk Factors

The causes of gastroschisis among most infants are unknown. Some babies have gastroschisis because of a change in their genes or chromosomes. Gastroschisis might also be caused by a combination of genes and other factors, such as the things the mother comes in contact with in the environment or what the mother eats or drinks, or certain medicines she uses during pregnancy.

CDC researchers have reported important findings about some factors that affect the risk of having a baby with gastroschisis:

- **Younger age.** Teenage mothers were more likely to have a baby with gastroschisis than older mothers.

- **Alcohol and tobacco.** Women who consumed alcohol or were a smoker were more likely to have a baby with gastroschisis.

If you are pregnant or thinking about getting pregnant, talk with your doctor about ways to increase your chance of having a healthy baby.

Diagnosis

Gastroschisis can be diagnosed during pregnancy or after the baby is born.

During Pregnancy

During pregnancy, there are screening tests (prenatal tests) to check for birth defects and other conditions. Gastroschisis might result in an abnormal result on a blood or serum screening test or it might be seen during an ultrasound (which creates pictures of the baby's body while inside the womb).

After the Baby Is Born

Gastroschisis is immediately seen at birth.

Treatment

Soon after the baby is born, surgery will be needed to place the abdominal organs inside the baby's body and repair the defect.

If the gastroschisis defect is small (only some of the intestine is outside of the belly), it is usually treated with surgery soon after birth to put the organs back into the belly and close the opening. If the gastroschisis defect is large (many organs outside of the belly), the repair might done slowly, in stages. The exposed organs might be covered with a special material and slowly moved back into the belly. After all of the organs have been put back in the belly, the opening is closed.

Babies with gastroschisis often need other treatments as well, including receiving nutrients through an intravenous (IV) line, antibiotics to prevent infection, and careful attention to control their body temperature.

Section 24.4

Hirschsprung Disease (HD)

This section includes text excerpted from "Digestive Diseases—Hirschsprung Disease," National Institute of Diabetes and Digestive and Kidney Diseases (NIDDK), September 2015.

What Is Hirschsprung Disease (HD)?

Hirschsprung disease (HD) is a birth defect in which nerve cells are missing at the end of a child's bowel. Normally, the bowel contains many nerve cells all along its length that control how the bowel works. When the bowel is missing nerve cells, it does not work well.

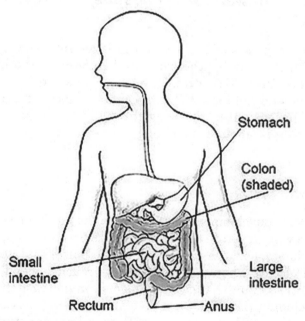

Figure 24.3. Gastrointestinal (GI) Tract

The large intestine, which includes the colon and rectum, is the last part of the gastrointestinal (GI) tract.

This damage causes blockages in the bowel because the stool does not move through the bowel normally.

Most often, the areas missing the nerve cells are the rectum and the sigmoid colon. However, some children are missing the nerve cells for the entire colon or part of the small intestine.

- In short-segment HD, nerve cells are missing from the last part of the large intestine.

- In long-segment HD, nerve cells are missing from most or all of the large intestine and sometimes the last part of the small intestine.

- Rarely, nerve cells are missing in the entire large and small intestine.

In a child with HD, stool moves through the bowel until it reaches the part lacking nerve cells. At that point, the stool moves slowly or stops.

What Are the Bowel, Large Intestine, Colon, Rectum, and Anus?

The bowel consists of the small and large intestines. The large intestine, which includes the colon and rectum, is the last part of the gastrointestinal (GI) tract. The large intestine's main job is to absorb water and hold stool. The rectum connects the colon to the anus. Stool passes out of the body through the anus. At birth, the large intestine is about 2 feet long. An adult's large intestine is about 5 feet long.

What Causes HD?

During early development of the baby in the mother's womb, nerve cells stop growing toward the end of a child's bowel causing HD. Most of these cells start at the beginning of the bowel and grow toward the end. HD occurs when these cells do not reach the end of a child's bowel. Scientists know that genetic defects can increase the chance of a child developing HD. However, no testing exists that can diagnose a child while the mother is pregnant. Researchers are studying if the mother's health history or lifestyle during pregnancy increases the chance of her baby developing HD.

Who Gets HD?

HD occurs in approximately 1 in 5,000 newborns. Children with Down syndrome (DS) and other medical problems, such as congenital heart defects (CHDs), are at much greater risk. For example, about one in 100 children with DS also has HD.

HD is congenital, or present at birth; however, symptoms may or may not be obvious at birth. If you have a child with HD, your chances of having more children with HD are greater than people who don't have a child with HD. Also, if a parent has HD, the chance of their child having HD is higher.

What Are the Signs and Symptoms of HD?

The main signs and symptoms of HD are constipation or intestinal obstruction, usually appearing shortly after birth. Many healthy infants and children have difficulty passing stool or infrequent bowel movements. However, unlike healthy children and infants, kids with HD typically do not respond to constipation medicines given by mouth. Most often, an infant or a child with HD will have other symptoms, including:

- growth failure
- swelling of the abdomen, or belly
- unexplained fever
- vomiting

The symptoms can vary; however, how they vary does not depend on how much of the intestine is missing nerve cells. No matter where in the intestine the nerve cells are missing, once the stool reaches this area, the blockage forms and the child develops symptoms.

Symptoms in Newborns

An early symptom in some newborns is failure to have a first bowel movement within 48 hours after birth. Other symptoms may include:

- green or brown vomit
- explosive stools after a doctor inserts a finger into the newborn's rectum
- swelling of the abdomen
- diarrhea, often with blood

381

Symptoms in Toddlers and Older Children

Symptoms of HD in toddlers and older children may include:

- not being able to pass stools without enemas or suppositories. An enema involves flushing liquid into the child's anus using a special wash bottle. A suppository is a pill placed into the child's rectum.

- swelling of the abdomen.

- diarrhea, often with blood.

- slow growth.

How Does a Doctor Know If My Child Has HD?

A doctor will know if your child has HD based on:

- a physical exam
- a medical and family history
- symptoms
- test results

If your doctor suspects HD, he or she may refer your child to a pediatric gastroenterologist—a doctor who specializes in digestive diseases in children—for additional evaluation.

Physical Exam

During a physical exam, a doctor usually:

- reviews your child's height and weight
- examines your child's abdomen for swelling and examines his or her body for signs of poor nutrition
- uses a stethoscope to listen to sounds within abdomen
- taps on specific areas of your child's body
- performs a rectal exam—explosive stool after a rectal exam may be a sign of HD

Medical and Family History

A doctor will ask you to provide your child's medical and family history to help diagnose HD. The doctor will ask questions about your child's bowel movements. The doctor will also ask about vomiting, swelling of the abdomen, and unexplained fever. The doctor is less likely to diagnose HD if problems with bowel movements began after 1 year of age.

Medical Tests

A doctor who suspects HD will do one or more of the following tests:

- **Rectal biopsy.** A rectal biopsy is a procedure that involves taking a small piece of tissue from the rectum for examination with a microscope. The doctor can perform two types of procedures:

  - **Rectal "suction" biopsy.** During this biopsy, a pediatric gastroenterologist or a pediatric surgeon will insert a small instrument into the child's anus and remove a small piece of tissue from the lining of his or her rectum. The biopsy is not painful and babies may even fall asleep during the procedure. In most cases, doctors do not use pain medicine or anesthesia. However, for older children doctors sometimes will use medicine to relieve anxiety or reduce the memory of the test.

  - **"Full thickness" rectal biopsy.** A pediatric surgeon performs this procedure, in which he or she will remove a thicker piece of tissue. The child will receive anesthesia.

A doctor will examine the tissue under a microscope. The rectal biopsy is the best test to diagnose or rule out HD.

- **Abdominal X-ray.** An X-ray is a picture created by using radiation and recorded on film or on a computer. The amount of radiation is small. An X-ray technician performs the X-ray at a hospital or an outpatient center, and a radiologist—a doctor who specializes in medical imaging—interprets the images. The child does not need anesthesia. The child will lie on a table or stand during the X-ray. The technician may ask the child to change positions for additional pictures. An X-ray of the abdomen may show intestinal obstruction.

- **Anorectal Manometry (ARM).** Anorectal manometry (ARM) is a test that uses pressure sensors and balloons to measure how well the child's rectum is working. A doctor performs ARM in a hospital. During the procedure, the doctor inflates a small balloon inside the child's rectum. Normally, the child's rectal

muscles will relax. If his or her muscles don't relax, the doctor
may suspect HD.

- **Lower gastrointestinal (GI) series.** A lower GI series is an
  X-ray exam that doctors use to look at the large intestine. An
  X-ray technician and a radiologist perform the test at a hospital
  or an outpatient center, and a radiologist interprets the images.
  A child does not need anesthesia and does not need a bowel prep
  for the test.

For the test, the child will lie on a table while the radiologist inserts
a flexible tube into the child's anus. The radiologist fills the child's large
intestine with barium or another contrast material. A technician performs
this test on newborns, toddlers, and older children. A lower GI series can
show changes in the bowel and help doctors diagnose obstructions.

In most cases, doctors diagnose HD in infancy; however, sometimes
doctors diagnose HD in older children.

How Is HD Treated?

HD is a life-threatening illness, and treatment requires surgery.
Children who have surgery for HD most often feel better after surgery.
If growth was slow because of HD, growth typically improves after
surgery.

For treatment, a pediatric surgeon will perform a pull through
procedure or an ostomy surgery. During either procedure, the surgeon
may remove all or part of the colon, called a colectomy.

Pull Through Procedure

During a pull through procedure, a surgeon removes the part of the
large intestine that is missing nerve cells and connects the healthy
part to the anus. A surgeon most often does a pull through procedure
soon after diagnosis.

Ostomy Surgery

Ostomy surgery is a surgical procedure that reroutes the normal
movement of the stool out of the body when a part of the bowel is
removed. Creating an ostomy means bringing part of the intestine
through the abdominal wall so that stool can leave the body without
passing through the anus. The opening in the abdomen through which
stool leaves the body is called a stoma.

A removable external collection pouch, called an ostomy pouch or ostomy appliance, is attached to the stoma and worn outside the body to collect the stool. The child or caregiver will need to empty the pouch several times each day.

Although most children with HD do not need ostomy surgery, a child sick from HD may need ostomy surgery to get better before undergoing the pull through procedure. This gives the inflamed areas of the intestine time to heal. In most cases, an ostomy is temporary and the child will have a second surgery to close the ostomy and reattach the intestine. However, sometimes children with HD have a permanent ostomy, especially if a long segment of the bowel is missing nerve cells or the child has repeated episodes of bowel inflammation, which healthcare providers call enterocolitis.

Ostomy surgeries include the following:

- **Ileostomy surgery** is when the surgeon connects the small intestine to the stoma.

- **Colostomy surgery** is when the surgeon connects part of the large intestine to the stoma.

What Can I Expect as My Child Recovers from Surgery?

After surgery, your child will need time to adjust to the new structure of his or her large intestine.

After the Pull Through Procedure

Most children feel better after the pull through procedure. However, some children can have complications or problems after surgery. Problems can include:

- narrowing of the anus

- constipation

- diarrhea

- leaking stool from the anus

- delayed toilet training

- enterocolitis

Typically, these problems improve over time with guidance from your child's doctors. Most children eventually have normal bowel movements.

After Ostomy Surgery

Infants will feel better after ostomy surgery because they will be able to pass gas and stool easily.

Older children will feel better as well, although they must adjust to living with an ostomy. They will need to learn how to take care of the stoma and how to change the ostomy pouch. With a few lifestyle changes, children with ostomies can lead normal lives. However, they may worry about being different from their friends. A special nurse, called an ostomy nurse, can answer questions and show your child how to care for an ostomy.

Enterocolitis

Adults and children with HD can suffer from enterocolitis before or after surgery. Symptoms of enterocolitis may include:

- a swollen abdomen
- bleeding from the rectum
- diarrhea
- fever
- lack of energy
- vomiting

A child with enterocolitis needs to go to the hospital, because enterocolitis can be life-threatening. Doctors can treat some children with enterocolitis with a special antibiotic by mouth, often in combination with rectal irrigation at home and in the doctor's office. During rectal irrigation, a doctor inserts a small amount of mild salt water into the child's rectum and allows it to come back out.

Doctors will admit children with more severe symptoms of enterocolitis to the hospital for monitoring, rectal irrigation, and intravenous (IV) antibiotics and IV fluid. Doctors give IV antibiotics and fluids through a tube inserted into a vein in the child's arm. In severe or repeated cases of enterocolitis, a child may need a temporary ostomy to let the intestine heal or a revision of the pull through surgery.

Eating, Diet, and Nutrition

If a surgeon removes the child's colon or bypasses it because of an ostomy, the child will need to drink more liquids to make up for water loss and prevent dehydration. They also need twice as much salt as a healthy child. A doctor can measure the sodium in a child's urine and adjust his or her diet to ensure adequate salt replacement.

Some infants may need tube feedings for a while. A feeding tube is a passageway for the infant to receive infant formula or liquid food directly into his or her stomach or small intestine. The doctor will pass the feeding tube through the nose. In some cases the doctor will recommend a more permanent feeding tube that he or she puts in place surgically in the child's abdomen.

Section 24.5

Imperforate Anus

This section includes text excerpted from "Imperforate Anus," Genetic and Rare Diseases Information Center (GARD), National Center for Advancing Translational Sciences (NCATS), November 16, 2017.

Imperforate anus is a birth defect where the opening to the anus is missing or blocked. The anus is the opening to the end part of the intestines, known as rectum through which stools leave the body. Imperforate anus may end in a pouch, or open in other structures or be too narrow (stenotic or atresic).

Symptoms

Symptoms may include absence of the first stools within 24–48 hours after birth, no anal opening or anal opening in an abnormal place, or stool passing out from the vagina, base of penis, scrotum, or urethra, and swollen belly area.

Causes

Although the exact cause of imperforate anus is not fully understood, it is believed to be due to the abnormal development of the rectum when the embryo is forming inside the womb. Many forms of imperforate anus occur with other birth defects. Imperforate anus may also be part of a syndrome with multiple malformations.

Treatment

Treatment may include colostomy, and surgery to correct the defect. Prognosis depends on the severity and type of imperforate anus and in the presence of other malformations.

Section 24.6

Jejunal Atresia

This section includes text excerpted from "Jejunal Atresia," Genetic and Rare Diseases Information Center (GARD), National Center for Advancing Translational Sciences (NCATS), November 16, 2017.

Jejunal atresia is a birth defect in a newborn characterized by partial or complete absence of the membrane connecting the small intestines to the abdominal wall (the mesentery). It causes a portion of the small intestines (the jejunum) to twist around an artery that supplies blood to the colon (the marginal artery). This leads to an intestinal blockage or "atresia." Common symptoms in the newborn include feeding difficulties, failure to thrive, vomiting bile (a yellowish green fluid), abdominal swelling, and/or absence of bowel movements after birth. It typically occurs sporadically in people with no family history of the condition; however, more than one family member can rarely be affected, suggesting that there may be a genetic component in some cases. Jejunal atresia is typically treated with surgery.

Symptoms

Signs and symptoms of jejunal atresia vary but may include:

- Feeding difficulties
- Failure to thrive

- Vomiting bile (a bitter tasting, yellowish green fluid)
- Abdominal swelling, especially the upper middle part just below the breastbone
- Absence of bowel movements after birth

Cause

Jejunal atresia occurs when the membrane that attaches the small intestines to the abdominal wall (called the mesentery) is partially or completely absent. As a result, a portion of the small intestines (the jejunum) twists around an artery that supplies blood to the colon (the marginal artery). This leads to an intestinal blockage or "atresia."

Scientists suspect that it may be a consequence of disruption of blood flow in the developing fetus, leading to the death of cells and tissue in the affected area (necrosis). There may be various reasons that blood flow becomes disrupted.

Because jejunal atresia rarely occurs in more than one family member, there may be a genetic component or predisposition in some cases.

Inheritance

Most cases of jejunal atresia occur sporadically in people with no family history of the condition. However, it can rarely affect more than one family member. In these families, jejunal atresia is likely due to a genetic cause and appears to be inherited in an autosomal recessive or multifactorial manner.

Diagnosis

In some cases, jejunal atresia may be diagnosed before birth on a prenatal ultrasound or fetal magnetic resonance imaging (MRI). This is helpful because infants can be treated promptly after birth, reducing the risk of complications. Ultrasound findings that may suggest intestinal atresia include dilated loops of bowel, hyperechoic bowel (it appears brighter than it should), and accumulation of fluid (ascites). Because prenatal ultrasound is not always accurate, X-rays and imaging studies with contrast should be obtained after birth to confirm the diagnosis.

After birth, a diagnosis is often suspected based on the presence of characteristic signs and symptoms, which suggest intestinal obstruction. These may include abdominal distension, vomiting bile, and failure to pass stool. Imaging studies can then be ordered to confirm the diagnosis.

Treatment

Jejunal atresia is typically treated with surgery as soon as possible. Total parenteral nutrition (TPN) is generally necessary for a period of time following surgery until normal meals are tolerated.

Prognosis

The long-term outlook (prognosis) for people with intestinal atresia is usually good, and in general, children do well postoperatively. Overall survival rates (including preterm babies) have reached 90 percent, with a surgical mortality of less than 1 percent. Most of the mortality occurs in infants with medical conditions such as prematurity or respiratory distress syndrome (RDS), associated anomalies, and complications related to short bowel syndrome (SBS).

Section 24.7

Megacystis Microcolon Intestinal Hypoperistalsis Syndrome (MMIHS)

This section includes text excerpted from "Megacystis Microcolon Intestinal Hypoperistalsis Syndrome," Genetic and Rare Diseases Information Center (GARD), National Center for Advancing Translational Sciences (NCATS), November 16, 2017.

Megacystis microcolon intestinal hypoperistalsis syndrome (MMIHS) is a rare congenital condition characterized by abdominal distension caused by a largely dilated nonobstructed urinary bladder (megacystis); very small colon (microcolon); and decreased or absent intestinal movements (intestinal peristalsis). Usual clinical presentation is similar to other neonatal intestinal obstructions: bile stained vomiting and failure to pass meconium (the first bowel movement the baby has). Other intestinal anomalies may be present like intestinal malrotation. Many problems with the urinary tract result from the bladder dysfunction. It is part of a group of conditions caused by changes (mutations) in the (Actin, gamma-enteric smooth muscle)

ACTG2 gene and is inherited in an autosomal dominant manner. However medical scientists believe that many cases of MMIHS are caused by de novo mutations in the *ACTG2* gene (meaning the mutation in the gene happened by mistake during the making of the sperm or egg). There is currently no cure for MMIHS and treatment is supportive. In the majority of patients total parenteral nutrition is required.

Symptoms

MMIHS is primarily characterized by abdominal distention caused by an enlarged bladder (megacystis) and intestinal pseudoobstruction. The enlarged bladder may be detected prenatally. Children with MMIHS may have various abnormalities of the digestive tract, including microcolon (very small colon), malrotation of the gut, decreased or absent intestinal movements, and short bowel. Additional abnormalities of the urinary tract that have been described include renal dysplasia, hydronephrosis, and enlargement of the ureter. Abnormalities that have been reported in some cases include undescended testes, or bilateral streak gonads (underdeveloped gonads), heart anomalies, umbilical hernia, or omphalocele.

Cause

This condition is part of a group of disorders caused by mutations in the *ACTG2* gene. ACTG2 related disorders are inherited in an autosomal dominant manner.

Inheritance

The MMIHS is inherited in an autosomal dominant manner. This means that having a change (mutation) in only one copy of the responsible gene in each cell is enough to cause features of the condition. There is nothing that either parent can do, before or during a pregnancy, to cause a child to have this condition.

In some cases, an affected person inherits the mutation from an affected parent. In other cases, the mutation occurs for the first time in a person with no family history of the condition. This is called a de novo mutation. While the exact proportion of inherited versus de novo mutations is unknown, current data suggest that de novo mutations are common.

When a person with a mutation that causes an autosomal dominant condition has children, each child has a 50 percent (1 in 2) chance to inherit that mutation. However, the severity of signs and symptoms can vary within a family. If the mutation in a family member with MMIHS has been identified, prenatal testing for pregnancies at increased risk is possible.

Diagnosis

Making a diagnosis for a genetic or rare disease can often be challenging. Healthcare professionals typically look at a person's medical history, symptoms, physical exam, and laboratory test results in order to make a diagnosis. If you have questions about getting a diagnosis, you should contact a healthcare professional.

Prognosis

Survival in MMIHS seems to have improved, thanks to more specialized care, innovations in parenteral nutrition, and introduction of multivisceral transplantation. Long-term survival usually requires total parenteral nutrition and urinary catheterization or diversion. Most long-term survivors have ileostomies. In families with an inherited MMIHS causing mutation, some family members with a mutation have milder features, living into adolescence and early adulthood.

While there are reports of longer survival, the prognosis and life expectancy remains poor, and it is still fatal in many cases. The main causes of death include sepsis, malnutrition, or multiple organ failure.

Section 24.8

Omphalocele

This section includes text excerpted from "Birth Defects—
Facts about Omphalocele," Centers for Disease Control and
Prevention (CDC), June 27, 2017.

What Is Omphalocele?

Omphalocele, also known as exomphalos, is a birth defect of the abdominal (belly) wall. The infant's intestines, liver, or other organs stick outside of the belly through the belly button. The organs are covered in a thin, nearly transparent sac that hardly ever is open or broken.

As the baby develops during weeks six through ten of pregnancy, the intestines get longer and push out from the belly into the umbilical cord. By the eleventh week of pregnancy, the intestines normally go back into the belly. If this does not happen, an omphalocele occurs. The omphalocele can be small, with only some of the intestines outside of the belly, or it can be large, with many organs outside of the belly.

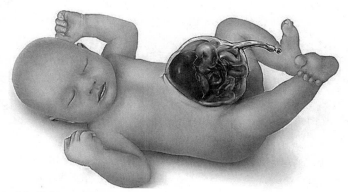

Figure 24.4. Omphalocele

Other Problems

Because some or all of the abdominal (belly) organs are outside of the body, babies born with an omphalocele can have other problems. The abdominal cavity, the space in the body that holds these organs, might not grow to its normal size. Also, infection is a concern, especially if the sac around the organs is broken. Sometimes, an organ might become pinched or twisted, and loss of blood flow might damage the organ.

Occurrence

The Centers for Disease Control and Prevention (CDC) estimates that each year about 775 babies in the United States are born with an omphalocele. In other words, about 1 out of every 5,386 babies born in the United States each year is born with an omphalocele. Many babies born with an omphalocele also have other birth defects, such as heart defects, neural tube defects, and chromosomal abnormalities.

Causes and Risk Factors

The causes of omphalocele among most infants are unknown. Some babies have omphalocele because of a change in their genes or chromosomes. Omphalocele might also be caused by a combination of genes and other factors, such as the things the mother comes in contact with in the environment or what the mother eats or drinks, or certain medicines she uses during pregnancy.

CDC researchers have reported important findings about some factors that can affect the risk of having a baby with an omphalocele:

- **Alcohol and tobacco.** Women who consumed alcohol or were heavy smokers (more than 1 pack a day) were more likely to have a baby with omphalocele.

- **Certain medications.** Women who used selective serotonin reuptake inhibitors (SSRIs) during pregnancy were more likely to have a baby with an omphalocele.

- **Obesity.** Women who were obese or overweight before pregnancy were more likely to have a baby with an omphalocele.

If you are pregnant or thinking about getting pregnant, talk with your doctor about ways to increase your chances of having a healthy baby.

Diagnosis

An omphalocele can be diagnosed during pregnancy or after a baby is born.

During Pregnancy

During pregnancy, there are screening tests (prenatal tests) to check for birth defects and other conditions. An omphalocele might result in an abnormal result on a blood or serum screening test or it might be seen during an ultrasound (which creates pictures of the baby).

After a Baby Is Born

In some cases, an omphalocele might not be diagnosed until after a baby is born. An omphalocele is seen immediately at birth.

Treatment

Treatment for infants with an omphalocele depends on a number of factors, including:

- the size of the omphalocele,

- the presence of other birth defects or chromosomal abnormalities, and

- the baby's gestational age.

If the omphalocele is small (only some of the intestine is outside of the belly), it usually is treated with surgery soon after birth to put the intestine back into the belly and close the opening. If the omphalocele is large (many organs outside of the belly), the repair might be done in stages. The exposed organs might be covered with a special material, and slowly, over time, the organs will be moved back into the belly. When all the organs have been put back in the belly, the opening is closed.

Chapter 25

Fetal Alcohol Spectrum Disorders (FASDs)

Fetal alcohol spectrum disorders (FASDs) are a group of conditions that can occur in a person whose mother drank alcohol during pregnancy. These effects can include physical problems and problems with behavior and learning. Often, a person with an FASD has a mix of these problems.

Cause and Prevention

FASDs are caused by a woman drinking alcohol during pregnancy. Alcohol in the mother's blood passes to the baby through the umbilical cord. When a woman drinks alcohol, so does her baby. There is no known safe amount of alcohol during pregnancy or when trying to get pregnant. There is also no safe time to drink during pregnancy. Alcohol can cause problems for a developing baby throughout pregnancy, including before a woman knows she's pregnant. All types of alcohol are equally harmful, including all wines and beer.

To prevent FASDs, a woman should not drink alcohol while she is pregnant, or when she might get pregnant. This is because a woman

This chapter includes text excerpted from "Fetal Alcohol Spectrum Disorders (FASDs)—Facts about FASDs," Centers for Disease Control and Prevention (CDC), June 6, 2017.

could get pregnant and not know for up to 4 to 6 weeks. In the United States, nearly half of pregnancies are unplanned. If a woman is drinking alcohol during pregnancy, it is never too late to stop drinking. Because brain growth takes place throughout pregnancy, the sooner a woman stops drinking the safer it will be for her and her baby. FASDs are completely preventable if a woman does not drink alcohol during pregnancy—so why take the risk?

Signs and Symptoms

FASDs refer to the whole range of effects that can happen to a person whose mother drank alcohol during pregnancy. These conditions can affect each person in different ways, and can range from mild to severe.

A person with an FASD might have:

- Abnormal facial features, such as a smooth ridge between the nose and upper lip (this ridge is called the philtrum)

- Small head size

- Shorter-than-average height

- Low body weight

- Poor coordination

- Hyperactive behavior

- Difficulty with attention

- Poor memory

- Difficulty in school (especially with math)

- Learning disabilities

- Speech and language delays

- Intellectual disability or low intelligence quotient (IQ)

- Poor reasoning and judgment skills

- Sleep and sucking problems as a baby

- Vision or hearing problems

- Problems with the heart, kidneys, or bones

Types of FASDs

Different terms are used to describe FASDs, depending on the type of symptoms.

- **Fetal Alcohol Syndrome (FAS).** FAS represents the most involved end of the FASD spectrum. Fetal death is the most extreme outcome from drinking alcohol during pregnancy. People with FAS might have abnormal facial features, growth problems, and central nervous system (CNS) problems. People with FAS can have problems with learning, memory, attention span, communication, vision, or hearing. They might have a mix of these problems. People with FAS often have a hard time in school and trouble getting along with others.

- **Alcohol-Related Neurodevelopmental Disorder (ARND).** People with ARND might have intellectual disabilities and problems with behavior and learning. They might do poorly in school and have difficulties with math, memory, attention, judgment, and poor impulse control.

- **Alcohol-Related Birth Defects (ARBD).** People with ARBD might have problems with the heart, kidneys, or bones or with hearing. They might have a mix of these.

- **Neurobehavioral Disorder Associated with Prenatal Alcohol Exposure (ND-PAE).** ND-PAE was first included as a recognized condition in the *Diagnostic and Statistical Manual 5* (DSM 5) of the American Psychiatric Association (APA) in 2013. A child or youth with ND-PAE will have problems in three areas: (1) thinking and memory, where the child may have trouble planning or may forget material he or she has already learned, (2) behavior problems, such as severe tantrums, mood issues (for example, irritability), and difficulty shifting attention from one task to another, and (3) trouble with day-to-day living, which can include problems with bathing, dressing for the weather, and playing with other children. In addition, to be diagnosed with ND-PAE, the mother of the child must have consumed more than minimal levels of alcohol before the child's birth, which APA defines as more than 13 alcoholic drinks per month of pregnancy (that is, any 30-day period of pregnancy) or more than 2 alcoholic drinks in one sitting.

Diagnosis

The term FASDs is *not* meant for use as a clinical diagnosis. Centers for Disease Control and Prevention (CDC) worked with a group of experts and organizations to review the research and develop guidelines for diagnosing FAS. The guidelines were developed for FAS only. CDC and its partners are working to put together diagnostic criteria for other FASDs, such as ARND.

Diagnosing FAS can be hard because there is no medical test, like a blood test, for it. And other disorders, such as ADHD (attention deficit hyperactivity disorder) and Williams syndrome, have some symptoms like FAS.

To diagnose FAS, doctors look for:

- Abnormal facial features (e.g., smooth ridge between nose and upper lip)

- Lower-than-average height, weight, or both

- Central nervous system problems (e.g., small head size, problems with attention and hyperactivity, poor coordination)

- Prenatal alcohol exposure; although confirmation is not required to make a diagnosis

Treatment

FASDs last a lifetime. There is no cure for FASDs, but research shows that early intervention treatment services can improve a child's development.

There are many types of treatment options, including medication to help with some symptoms, behavior and education therapy, parent training, and other alternative approaches. No one treatment is right for every child. Good treatment plans will include close monitoring, follow-ups, and changes as needed along the way.

Also, "protective factors" can help reduce the effects of FASDs and help people with these conditions reach their full potential.

Protective factors include:

- Diagnosis before six years of age

- Loving, nurturing, and stable home environment during the school years

- Absence of violence

- Involvement in special education and social services

Chapter 26

Fetal Tumors

Cystic Hygroma

A cystic hygroma is a fluid-filled sac that results from a blockage in the lymphatic system. It is most commonly located in the neck or head area, but can be located anywhere in the body. It may be discovered in a fetus during a pregnancy ultrasound, or it may be apparent at birth as a soft bulge under the skin. When it is identified on pregnancy ultrasound, there is an increased risk for miscarriage. In some cases, it is not discovered until a person is older. Symptoms can vary depending on its size and specific location, and it can potentially cause problems with nearby structures or organs.

Causes

A cystic hygroma may be caused by genetic or environmental factors that cause abnormal development of the lymphatic vascular system during embryonic growth. It may occur on its own or as part of a genetic syndrome with other features, such as Turner syndrome, Down

---

This chapter contains text excerpted from the following sources: Text under the heading "Cystic Hygroma" is excerpted from "Cystic Hygroma," Genetic and Rare Diseases Information Center (GARD), National Center for Advancing Translational Sciences (NCATS), August 15, 2017; Text under the heading "Sacrococcygeal Teratoma" is excerpted from "Sacrococcygeal Teratoma," Genetic and Rare Diseases Information Center (GARD), National Center for Advancing Translational Sciences (NCATS), February 17, 2016.

syndrome or Noonan syndrome. In adults it may result from trauma, or from earlier respiratory infections. In many cases, the cause is not known.

Symptoms

The signs and symptoms of a cystic hygroma can vary depending on its size and location. Regardless of size, a cystic hygroma can potentially cause functional impairment of nearby structures or organs, as well as disfigurement of affected areas. When identified after birth, it most often looks like a soft bulge under the skin. The overlying skin may have a bluish tint. The cystic hygroma typically grows as the child grows, and may become apparent after a sudden increase in size, due to an infection or bleeding within the cyst. Feeding difficulties and failure to thrive may be present. Rarely, a child with a cystic hygroma may have symptoms of obstructive sleep apnea. Other symptoms or complications may include airway obstruction, hemorrhage, infection, or deformation of surrounding bony structures or teeth (if it is left untreated).

Treatment

Treatment involves removing the cystic hygroma, although removing all of it may not be possible. Other treatments that have been tried with limited success include chemotherapy, injection of sclerosing medicines, radiation therapy, and steroids.

Treatment options for a cystic hygroma depend on the size, location and symptoms present. Options may include surgery (recommended when possible), percutaneous drainage, sclerotherapy, laser therapy, radiofrequency ablation, or medical therapy. These different treatment options may be used in various combinations. When surgery removes all abnormal tissue, the chance of complete recovery is good. If complete removal is not obtained, the cystic hygroma will often return. In very rare cases, a cystic hygroma will shrink or go away without treatment.

Prognosis

The long-term outlook (prognosis) associated with a cystic hygroma may depend on when the cystic hygroma is detected, the size and location of the lesion, whether complications arise, and whether an underlying syndrome or chromosome abnormality is present. If surgery to remove the lesion is successful and all affected tissue is removed, the prognosis reportedly is good. If residual tissue is left behind, the recurrence rate is approximately 15 percent.

Cystic hygromas detected prenatally on ultrasound are associated with an increased risk for chromosome abnormalities (particularly Down syndrome) and birth defects (particularly heart defects). Both of these increase the risk for miscarriage, hydrops, fetal demise, and neonatal death. Increasing size is associated with an increasing risk of an underlying abnormality. As a person with a cystic hygroma ages, morbidity is often related to cosmetic disfigurement and how the cystic hygroma affects other critical structures, such as nerves, blood vessels, lymphatics, and the airway. Quality of life can be significantly impaired in many cases. Recurrent inflammation can lead to cellulitis, which can cause pain and disfigurement of the affected area. Bleeding in the lesion can cause rapid pain, hardening, and swelling or enlargement of the affected area. Complications from surgery may also occur, and depending on the location may include damage to neurovascular structures (including cranial nerves), chylous fistula or chylothorax (leakage of lymphatic fluid), or hemorrhage. Specific possible complications, and areas of the head or body affected, will vary from person to person.

Some studies have reported an associated mortality rate of up to 2–6 percent, usually due to pneumonia, bronchiectasis, or airway compromise.

Sacrococcygeal Teratoma

A sacrococcygeal teratoma is a tumor that grows at the base of the spine in a developing fetus. It occurs in one in 40,000 newborns and girls are four times more likely to be affected than boys. Though it is usually benign, there is a possibility that the teratoma could become malignant. As such, the recommended treatment of a teratoma is complete removal of the tumor by surgery, performed soon after the birth. If not all of the tumor is removed during the initial surgery, the teratoma may grow back (recur) and additional surgeries may be needed. Studies have found that sacrococcygeal teratomas recur in up to 22 percent of cases.

Treatment

The treatment for sacrococcygeal teratoma (SCT) typically involves surgery to remove the tumor. Surgery occurs either in the prenatal period or shortly after delivery. The timing is dependent on the size of the tumor and the associated symptoms.

Chapter 27

Heart Defects

Chapter Contents

Section 27.1

Aortic Valve Stenosis (AVS)

This section includes text excerpted from "Aortic Valve Stenosis,"
Genetic and Rare Diseases Information Center (GARD), National
Center for Advancing Translational Sciences (NCATS), July 5, 2013.
Reviewed December 2017.

What Is Aortic Valve Stenosis (AVS)?

Aortic valve stenosis (AVS) is a condition characterized by narrowing of the heart's aortic valve opening. This narrowing prevents the valve from opening fully, which obstructs blood flow from the heart into the aorta, and onward to the rest of the body. AVS can range from mild to severe.

Signs and symptoms typically develop when the narrowing of the opening is severe and may include chest pain (angina) or tightness; shortness of breath or fatigue (especially during exertion); feeling faint or fainting; heart palpitations; and heart murmur. Individuals with less severe congenital AVS (present at birth) may not develop symptoms until adulthood. Individuals with severe cases may faint without warning. The condition can eventually lead to heart failure.

AVS can have several causes including abnormal development before birth (such as having 1 or 2 valve leaflets instead of 3); calcium buildup on the valve in adulthood; and rheumatic fever. Treatment may include medications to ease the symptoms, but surgery to repair or replace the valve is the only way to eliminate the condition.

What Causes AVS?

Aortic valve stenosis can be congenital (present at birth) or can develop later in life. When the condition is congenital, it is typically due to abnormal development of the aortic valve—either it forms abnormally narrow, or it is made up of one flap or leaflet (called a unicuspid valve, which is very rare) or two leaflets (bicuspid valve) instead of the usual three. Having a bicuspid valve can run in families. A bicuspid valve may not cause any problems until adulthood, when the valve begins to narrow or leak. In most cases, the exact underlying cause of congenital aortic valve stenosis is unknown. Aortic valve stenosis can also be caused by the buildup of calcium deposits on the heart valve with increasing age. This cause is most common in people older than 65. Rheumatic fever can also cause the condition because it may result in scar tissue forming on the valve, causing the leaflets to stiffen and fuse. Rheumatic fever can also cause a rough surface on the valve, which can lead to accumulation of calcium deposits later in life.

What Is Supravalvular Aortic Stenosis (SVAS)?

Supravalvular aortic stenosis (SVAS) is a type of heart defect that develops before birth. It is characterized by a narrowing (stenosis) of the section of the aorta just above the valve that connects the aorta to the heart (aortic valve). The severity of SVAS varies from person to person; some individuals may die in infancy while others never experience symptoms. If symptoms develop, they may include shortness of breath, chest pain, murmur, and/or eventual heart failure. Some affected individuals also have defects in other blood vessels, such as the pulmonary artery. SVAS can be caused by mutations in the *ELN* gene and be inherited in an autosomal dominant manner, although some individuals that inherit the mutated gene never develop features of the condition called reduced penetrance. SVAS can also be associated with Williams syndrome. Treatment may include surgery to repair the condition in severe cases.

What Syndromes or Related Abnormalities Have Been Associated with Aortic Stenosis in a Fetus?

AVS is not usually associated with malformations outside the heart, although it can sometimes occur with other abnormalities and/or be part of several syndromes. It is often associated with the presence of a unicuspid or bicuspid aortic valve (the presence of 1 or 2 valve leaflets instead of the usual 3). Bicuspid aortic valve (BAV) is now believed to be the most common congenital heart defect with a prevalence of 1–2 percent in the general population. Although BAV is usually an isolated defect, it may be associated with other cardiovascular syndromes or abnormalities with at least a third of affected individuals likely to develop serious complications that will eventually require valve surgery. Studies have suggested that BAV can be inherited in an autosomal dominant pattern, although whether it is present, and how severe the defect is, can vary among family members. BAV is a common congenital heart defect in individuals with a chromosomal disorder called Turner syndrome, but most individuals with BAV do not have Turner syndrome. A single, specific genetic cause of AVS has not been identified.

Some fetuses diagnosed with AVS will eventually progress to having hypoplastic left heart syndrome (HLHS). Those with severe AVS can also develop endocardial fibroelastosis, depending on the time of onset during fetal development.

SVAS can either be isolated or can occur as part of Williams syndrome. Isolated SVAS can be caused by mutations in the *ELN* gene and may be inherited in an autosomal dominant manner. Some individuals with SVAS have associated abnormalities such as peripheral pulmonary artery stenosis. Individuals with Williams syndrome have a deletion of the region of chromosome 7 that normally contains the *ELN* gene.

Aortic stenosis has also been reported in individuals with other disorders including Alagille syndrome and Shone's complex.

Is Aortic Stenosis Associated with Assisted Reproductive Technology (ART)?

Assisted reproductive technology (ART) is known to be associated with an increase in the overall risk of congenital anomalies. However, little specific information exists on the risk of congenital heart defects for fetuses conceived following ART. Although some studies have reported an increased frequency of congenital heart defects in general in IVF pregnancies, this may be due, in part, to an increased frequency of multiple gestation pregnancies (such as twins or triplets) seen among these individuals, as multiple gestation pregnancies are at increased risk for congenital abnormalities.

What Kinds of Tests Are Available for a Fetus Diagnosed with Aortic Stenosis?

AVS is not usually associated with malformations outside the heart, although it can sometimes occur with other abnormalities and/or be part of several syndromes or chromosomal abnormalities. Further testing for a fetus with AVS often depends on the severity of the condition, whether other abnormalities are detected, and the nature of other abnormalities that are detected. Examples of types of testing that may be available include ultrasounds, amniocentesis to detect a chromosome abnormality or to look for a specific genetic disorder, and/

or fetal echocardiogram to monitor and/or look for any other cardiac abnormalities. Individuals interested in further testing for a fetus diagnosed with aortic stenosis should speak with a perinatologist, pediatric cardiologist, and/or genetics professional.

Do I Have an Increased Risk to Have a Child with Congenital Abnormalities If There Were Abnormalities in a Previous Pregnancy?

There are many factors that influence the recurrence risk of congenital abnormalities, including the nature of the abnormalities and the underlying cause. Congenital abnormalities can be inherited in a specific manner, can be due to an exposure during pregnancy, or can occur sporadically by chance. Unfortunately, in some cases the cause and recurrence risk are unknown. If the congenital abnormalities are known to be associated with a specific underlying condition that was diagnosed, the recurrence risk for associated abnormalities might be that of the specific condition.

Recurrence risks also depend upon whether a subsequent pregnancy is conceived with an egg and sperm from the same individuals as in the previous pregnancy. For example, if congenital abnormalities are due to an autosomal recessive genetic condition, the risk for the same two parents to have an affected child with each pregnancy would be 1 in 4 (25%). However, if the pregnancy is achieved with a different partner, the risk for recurrence would likely be significantly reduced. Likewise, if an affected pregnancy is conceived with egg or sperm donation, estimated recurrence risks in a subsequent pregnancy might depend on whether the same egg and/or sperm donors were used.

Speaking with a genetics professional for individuals interested in obtaining a personal risk assessment is recommended.

Section 27.2

Atrial Septal Defect (ASD)

This section includes text excerpted from "Congenital Heart Defects
(CHDs)—Facts about Atrial Septal Defect," Centers for Disease
Control and Prevention (CDC), November 8, 2016.

What Is Atrial Septal Defect (ASD)?

An atrial septal defect ASD is a birth defect of the heart in which
there is a hole in the wall (septum) that divides the upper chambers
of the heart (atria). A hole can vary in size and may close on its own
or may require surgery. An ASD is one type of congenital heart defect.
Congenital means present at birth.

As a baby develops during pregnancy, there are normally several
openings in the wall dividing the upper chambers of the heart (atria).
These usually close during pregnancy or shortly after birth.

If one of these openings does not close, a hole is left, and it is called
an ASD. The hole increases the amount of blood that flows through
the lungs and over time, it may cause damage to the blood vessels
in the lungs. Damage to the blood vessels in the lungs may cause
problems in adulthood, such as high blood pressure in the lungs and
heart failure. Other problems may include abnormal heartbeat, and
increased risk of stroke.

Occurrence

The Centers for Disease Control and Prevention (CDC) estimated
that each year about 1,966 babies in the United States are born with
an ASD. It can also occur with other heart defects.

Causes and Risk Factors

The causes of heart defects such as ASD among most babies are
unknown. Some babies have heart defects because of changes in their
genes or chromosomes. These types of heart defects also are thought
to be caused by a combination of genes and other risk factors, such as

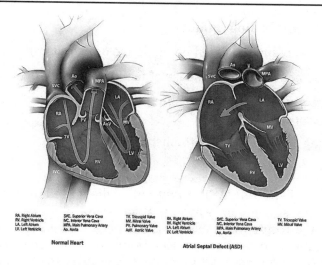

RA. Right Atrium   SVC. Superior Vena Cava   TV. Tricuspid Valve   RA. Right Atrium   SVC. Superior Vena Cava   TV. Tricuspid Valve
RV. Right Ventricle   IVC. Inferior Vena Cava   MV. Mitral Valve   RV. Right Ventricle   IVC. Inferior Vena Cava   MV. Mitral Valve
LA. Left Atrium   MPA. Main Pulmonary Artery   PV. Pulmonary Valve   LA. Left Atrium   MPA. Main Pulmonary Artery
LV. Left Ventricle   Ao. Aorta   AoV. Aortic Valve   LV. Left Ventricle   Ao. Aorta

Normal Heart   **Atrial Septal Defect (ASD)**

Figure 27.1. *Normal Heart and Atrial Septal Defect (ASD)*

things the mother comes in contact with in the environment or what the mother eats or drinks or the medicines the mother uses.

Diagnosis

An ASD may be diagnosed during pregnancy or after the baby is born. In many cases, it may not be diagnosed until adulthood.

During Pregnancy

During pregnancy, there are screening tests (prenatal tests) to check for birth defects and other conditions. An ASD might be seen during an ultrasound (which creates pictures of the body), but it depends on the size of the hole and its location. If an ASD is suspected, a specialist will need to confirm the diagnosis.

After the Baby Is Born

An ASD is present at birth, but many babies do not have any signs or symptoms. Signs and symptoms of a large or untreated ASD may include the following:

- Frequent respiratory or lung infections
- Difficulty breathing

411

- Tiring when feeding (infants)

- Shortness of breath when being active or exercising

- Skipped heartbeats or a sense of feeling the heartbeat

- A heart murmur, or a whooshing sound that can be heard with a stethoscope

- Swelling of legs, feet, or stomach area

- Stroke

It is possible that an ASD might not be diagnosed until adulthood. One of the most common ways an atrial septal defect is found is by detecting a murmur when listening to a person's heart with a stethoscope. If a murmur is heard or other signs or symptoms are present, the healthcare provider might request one or more tests to confirm the diagnosis. The most common test is an echocardiogram (ECHO) which is an ultrasound of the heart.

Treatment

Treatment for an ASD depends on the age of diagnosis, the number of or seriousness of symptoms, size of the hole, and presence of other conditions. Sometimes surgery is needed to repair the hole. Sometimes medications are prescribed to help treat symptoms. There are no known medications that can repair the hole.

If a child is diagnosed with an ASD, the healthcare provider may want to monitor it for a while to see if the hole closes on its own. During this period of time, the healthcare provider might treat symptoms with medicine. A healthcare provider may recommend surgery for a child with a large ASD, even if there are few symptoms, to prevent problems later in life. Surgery may also be recommended for an adult who has many or severe symptoms. Surgery involves fixing the hole and may be done through cardiac catheterization or open-heart surgery. After surgery, follow-up care will depend on the size of the defect, person's age, and whether the person has other birth defects.

Section 27.3

Coarctation of the Aorta

This section includes text excerpted from "Congenital Heart Defects (CHDs)—Facts about Coarctation of the Aorta," Centers for Disease Control and Prevention (CDC), September 26, 2016.

What Is Coarctation of the Aorta?

Coarctation of the aorta is a birth defect in which a part of the aorta is narrower than usual. If the narrowing is severe enough and if it is not diagnosed, the baby may have serious problems and may need surgery or other procedures soon after birth. For this reason, coarctation of the aorta is often considered a critical congenital heart defect (CCHD). The defect occurs when a baby's aorta does not form correctly as the baby grows and develops during pregnancy. The narrowing of the aorta usually happens in the part of the blood vessel just after the arteries branch off to take blood to the head and arms, near the patent ductus arteriosus, although sometimes the narrowing occurs before or after the ductus arteriosus. In some babies with coarctation, it is thought that some tissue from the wall of ductus arteriosus blends into the tissue of the aorta. When the tissue tightens and allows the ductus arteriosus to close normally after birth, this extra tissue may also tighten and narrow the aorta

The narrowing, or coarctation, blocks normal blood flow to the body. This can back up flow into the left ventricle of the heart, making the muscles in this ventricle work harder to get blood out of the heart. Since the narrowing of the aorta is usually located after arteries branch to the upper body, coarctation in this region can lead to normal or high blood pressure and pulsing of blood in the head and arms and low blood pressure and weak pulses in the legs and lower body.

If the condition is very severe, enough blood may not be able to get through to the lower body. The extra work on the heart can cause the walls of the heart to become thicker in order to pump harder. This eventually weakens the heart muscle. If the aorta is not widened, the heart may weaken enough that it leads to heart failure. Coarctation of the aorta often occurs with other congenital heart defects.

413

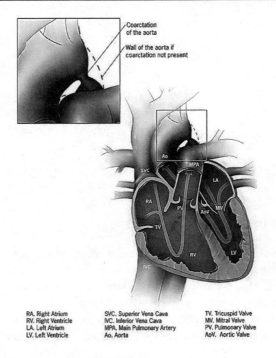

RA. Right Atrium	SVC. Superior Vena Cava	TV. Tricuspid Valve
RV. Right Ventricle	IVC. Inferior Vena Cava	MV. Mitral Valve
LA. Left Atrium	MPA. Main Pulmonary Artery	PV. Pulmonary Valve
LV. Left Ventricle	Ao. Aorta	AoV. Aortic Valve

Figure 27.2. *Coarctation of the Aorta*

Occurrence

The Centers for Disease Control and Prevention (CDC) estimates that about 4 out of every 10,000 babies are born each year in the United States with coarctation of the aorta.

Causes and Risk Factors

The causes of heart defects, including coarctation of the aorta, among most babies are unknown. Some babies have heart defects because of changes in their genes or chromosomes. Heart defects, like coarctation of the aorta, are also thought to be caused by a combination of genes and other risk factors, such as things the mother comes in contact with in the environment, what the mother eats or drinks, or medicines the mother uses.

Diagnosis

Coarctation of the aorta is usually diagnosed after the baby is born. How early in life the defect is diagnosed usually depends on how mild or severe the symptoms are. Those with severe narrowing will have symptoms early in life, while babies with mild narrowing may never have problems, or signs may not be detected until later in life.

In babies with a more serious condition, early signs usually include:

- pale skin
- irritability
- heavy sweating
- difficulty breathing

Detection of the defect is often made during a physical exam. In infants and older individuals, the pulse will be noticeably weaker in the legs or groin than it is in the arms or neck, and a heart murmur—an abnormal whooshing sound caused by disrupted blood flow—may be heard through a doctor's stethoscope. Older children and adults with coarctation of the aorta often have high blood pressure in the arms.

Once suspected, an echocardiogram (ECHO) is the most commonly used test to confirm the diagnosis. An echocardiogram is an ultrasound of the heart that can show problems with the structure of the heart and the blood flow through it, and how well the heart is working. It will show the location and severity of the coarctation and whether any other heart defects are present. Other tests to measure the function of the heart may be used including chest X-ray, electrocardiogram (EKG), magnetic resonance imaging (MRI), and cardiac catheterization.

Coarctation of the aorta is often considered a critical congenital heart defect (CCHD) because if the narrowing is severe enough and it is not diagnosed, the baby may have serious problems soon after birth. CCHDs also can be detected with newborn pulse oximetry screening. Pulse oximetry is a simple bedside test to determine the amount of oxygen in a baby's blood. Low levels of oxygen in the blood can be a sign of a CCHD. Newborn screening using pulse oximetry can identify some infants with a CCHD, like coarctation of the aorta, before they show any symptoms.

Treatment

No matter what age the defect is diagnosed, the narrow aorta will need to be widened once symptoms are present. This can be done with surgery or a procedure called balloon angioplasty. A balloon angioplasty is a procedure that uses a thin, flexible tube, called a catheter, which is inserted into a blood vessel and directed to the aorta. When the catheter reaches the narrow area of the aorta, a balloon at the tip is inflated to expand the blood vessel. Sometimes a mesh-covered tube (stent) is inserted to keep the vessel open. The stent is used more often to initially widen the aorta or re-widen it if the aorta narrows again after surgery has been performed. During surgery to correct a coarctation, the narrow portion is removed and the aorta is reconstructed or patched to allow blood to flow normally through the aorta.

Even after surgery, children with a coarctation of the aorta often have high blood pressure that is treated with medicine. It is important for children and adults with coarctation of the aorta to follow up regularly with a cardiologist (a heart doctor) to monitor their progress and check for other health conditions that might develop as they get older.

Section 27.4

dextro-Transposition of the Great Arteries (d-TGA)

This section includes text excerpted from "Congenital Heart Defects (CHDs)—Facts about dextro-Transposition of the Great Arteries (d-TGA)," Centers for Disease Control and Prevention (CDC), November 14, 2016.

What Is dextro-Transposition of the Great Arteries (d-TGA)?

dextro-Transposition of the Great Arteries or d-TGA is a birth defect of the heart in which the two main arteries carrying blood out of the heart—the main pulmonary artery and the aorta—are switched in position, or "transposed." Because a baby with this defect may need surgery or other procedures soon after birth, d-TGA is considered a congenital birth defect. Congenital means present at birth.

In transposition of the great arteries, the aorta is in front of the pulmonary artery and is either primarily to the right (dextro) or to the left (levo) of the pulmonary artery. d-TGA is often simply called "TGA." However, "TGA" is a broader term that includes both dextro-TGA (d-TGA) and a rarer heart defect called levo-TGA (l-TGA), or congenitally corrected TGA, which is not discussed here.

In a baby without a congenital heart defect, the right side of the heart pumps oxygen-poor blood from the heart to the lungs through the pulmonary artery. The left side of the heart pumps oxygen-rich blood to the rest of the body through the aorta. The aorta is usually behind the pulmonary artery.

In babies with d-TGA, oxygen-poor blood from the body enters the right side of the heart. But, instead of going to the lungs, the blood is pumped directly back out to the rest of the body through the aorta. Oxygen-rich blood from the lungs entering the heart is pumped straight back to the lungs through the main pulmonary artery.

Often, babies with d-TGA have other heart defects, such as a hole between the lower chambers of the heart (a ventricular septal defect) or the upper chambers of the heart (an atrial septal defect) that allow blood to mix so that some oxygen-rich blood can be pumped to the rest of the body. The patent ductus arteriosus also allows some oxygen-rich blood to be pumped to the rest of the body.

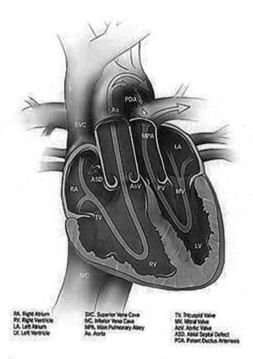

Figure 27.3. *dextro-Transposition of the Great Arteries (d-TGA)*

Occurrence

The Centers for Disease Control and Prevention (CDC) estimates that about 1,250 babies are born with TGA each year in the United States. This means that every 1 in 3,300 babies born in the United States is affected by this defect.

Causes and Risk Factors

The causes of congenital heart defects, such as d-TGA, among most babies are unknown. Some babies have congenital heart defects because of changes in their genes or chromosomes. Heart defects are also thought to be caused by the combination of genes and other risk factors such as things the mother comes in contact with in her environment, or what the mother eats or drinks, or certain medications she uses.

Diagnosis

This defect may be diagnosed during pregnancy or soon after the baby is born.

During Pregnancy

During pregnancy, there are screening tests that the mother can have (also called prenatal tests) to check for birth defects and other conditions. d-TGA may be diagnosed during pregnancy with an ultrasound test (which creates pictures of the baby). Some findings from the ultrasound may make the healthcare provider suspect a baby could have d-TGA. If so, the healthcare provider can request a fetal echocardiogram to confirm the diagnosis. A fetal echocardiogram is a more detailed ultrasound of the baby's heart. This test can show problems with the structure of the heart and how the heart is working with this defect.

After the Baby Is Born

Symptoms occur at birth or very soon afterwards. How severe the symptoms are will depend on whether there is a way for blood to mix and for oxygen-rich blood to get out to the rest of the body. For example, if an infant with d-TGA has another defect, like an atrial septal defect (ASD), the ASD forms a passageway for some oxygen-rich blood to be pumped to the rest of the body. This infant with both d-TGA and an

ASD may not have as severe symptoms as infants whose hearts don't have any mixing of blood. Infants with d-TGA can have a bluish looking skin color—called cyanosis—because their blood doesn't carry enough oxygen. Infants with d-TGA or other conditions causing cyanosis can have symptoms such as:

- Problems breathing

- Pounding heart

- Weak pulse

- Ashen or bluish skin color

- Poor feeding

Because the infant might be bluish in color and have trouble breathing, d-TGA is usually diagnosed within the first week of life. The healthcare provider can request one or more tests to confirm the diagnosis. The most common test is an echocardiogram (ECHO). An echocardiogram is an ultrasound of the heart that can show problems with the structure of the heart, like incorrect positioning of the two large arteries, and any irregular blood flow. An electrocardiogram (EKG), which measures the electrical activity of the heart, chest X-rays, and other medical tests may also be used to make the diagnosis.

d-TGA is a that also can be detected with newborn pulse oximetry screening. Pulse oximetry is a simple bedside test to determine the amount of oxygen in a baby's blood. Low levels of oxygen in the blood can be a sign of a critical congenital heart defect (CCHD). Newborn screening using pulse oximetry can identify some infants with a CCHD, like d-TGA, before they show any symptoms.

Treatments

Surgery is required for all babies born with d-TGA. Other procedures may be done before surgery in order to maintain, enlarge, or create openings that will allow oxygen-rich blood to get out to the body.

There are two types of surgery to repair d-TGA:

- **Arterial switch operation.** This is the most common procedure and it is usually done in the first month of life. It restores usual blood flow through the heart and out to the rest of the body. During this surgery, the arteries are switched to their usual positions—the pulmonary artery arising from the right ventricle and the aorta from the left ventricle. The coronary arteries (small arteries that provide blood to the heart muscle) also must be moved and reattached to the aorta.

- **Atrial switch operation.** This procedure is less commonly performed. During this surgery, the arteries are left in place, but a tunnel (baffle) is created between the top chambers (atria) of the heart. This tunnel allows oxygen-poor blood to move from the right atrium to the left ventricle and out the pulmonary artery to the lungs. Returning oxygen-rich blood moves through the tunnel from the left atrium to the right ventricle and out the aorta to the body. Although this repair helps blood to go to the lungs and then out to the body, it also makes extra work for the right ventricle to pump blood to the entire body. Therefore, this repair can lead to difficulties later in life.

After surgery, medications may be needed to help the heart pump better, control blood pressure, help get rid of extra fluid in the body, and slow down the heart if it is beating too fast. If the heart is beating too slowly, a pacemaker can be used.

Infants who have these surgeries are not cured; they may have lifelong complications. A child or adult with d-TGA will need regular follow-up visits with a cardiologist (a heart doctor) to monitor their progress and avoid complications or other health problems. With proper treatment, most babies with d-TGA grow up to lead healthy, productive lives.

Section 27.5

Hypoplastic Left Heart Syndrome (HLHS)

This section includes text excerpted from "Congenital Heart Defects (CHDs)—Facts about Hypoplastic Left Heart Syndrome," Centers for Disease Control and Prevention (CDC), November 8, 2016.

What Is Hypoplastic Left Heart Syndrome (HLHS)?

Hypoplastic left heart syndrome (HLHS) is a birth defect that affects normal blood flow through the heart. As the baby develops during pregnancy, the left side of the heart does not form correctly. HLHS is one type of congenital heart defect. Congenital means present at birth.

HLHS affects a number of structures on the left side of the heart that do not fully develop, for example:

- The left ventricle is underdeveloped and too small.

- The mitral valves is not formed or is very small.

- The aortic valve is not formed or is very small.

- The ascending portion of the aorta is underdeveloped or is too small.

- Often, babies with hypoplastic left heart syndrome also have an atrial septal defect, which is a hole between the left and right upper chambers (atria) of the heart.

In a baby without a congenital heart defect, the right side of the heart pumps oxygen-poor blood from the heart to the lungs. The left side of the heart pumps oxygen-rich blood to the rest of the body. When a baby is growing in a mother's womb during pregnancy, there are two small openings between the left and right sides of the heart: the patent ductus arteriosus and the patent foramen ovale. Normally, these openings will close a few days after birth.

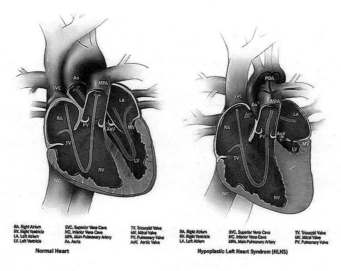

Figure 27.4. *Normal Heart and Hypoplastic Left Heart Syndrome*

In babies with HLHS, the left side of the heart cannot pump oxygen-rich blood to the body properly. During the first few days of life for a baby with HLHS, the oxygen-rich blood bypasses the poorly functioning left side of the heart through the patent ductus arteriosus and the patent foramen ovale. The right side of the heart then pumps blood to both the lungs and the rest of the body. However, among babies with HLHS, when these openings close, it becomes hard for oxygen-rich blood to get to the rest of the body.

Occurrence

The Centers for Disease Control and Prevention (CDC) estimates that each year about 960 babies in the United States are born with HLHS. In other words, about 1 out of every 4,344 babies born in the United States each year is born with HLHS.

Causes and Risk Factors

The causes of heart defects such as HLHS among most babies are unknown. Some babies have heart defects because of changes in their genes or chromosomes. These types of heart defects also are thought to be caused by a combination of genes and other risk factors, such as things the mother comes in contact with in the environment or what the mother eats or drinks or the medicines the mother uses.

Diagnosis

Hypoplastic left heart syndrome may be diagnosed during pregnancy or soon after the baby is born.

During Pregnancy

During pregnancy, there are screening tests (also called prenatal tests,) to check for birth defects and other conditions. HLHS may be diagnosed during pregnancy with an ultrasound, (which creates pictures of the body). Some findings from the ultrasound may make the healthcare provider suspect a baby may have HLHS. If so, the healthcare provider can request a fetal echocardiogram (ECHO), an ultrasound of the baby's heart, to confirm the diagnosis. This test can show problems with the structure of the heart and how the heart is working with this defect.

After the Baby Is Born

Babies with HLHS might not have trouble for the first few days of life while the patent ductus arteriosus (PDA) and the patent foramen ovale (PFO) (the normal openings in the heart) are open, but quickly develop signs after these openings are closed, including:

- Problems breathing,
- Pounding heart,
- Weak pulse, or
- Ashen or bluish skin color.

During a physical examination, a doctor can see these signs or might hear a heart murmur (an abnormal whooshing sound caused by blood not flowing properly). If a murmur is heard or other signs are present, the healthcare provider might request one or more tests to make a diagnosis, the most common being an echocardiogram. Echocardiography also is useful for helping the healthcare provider follow the child's health over time.

Treatment

Treatments for some health problems associated with HLHS might include:

Medicines

Some babies and children will need medicines to help strengthen the heart muscle, lower their blood pressure, and help the body get rid of extra fluid.

Nutrition

Some babies with hypoplastic left heart syndrome become tired while feeding and do not eat enough to gain weight. To make sure babies have a healthy weight gain, a special high-calorie formula might be prescribed. Some babies become extremely tired while feeding and might need to be fed through a feeding tube.

Surgery

Soon after a baby with HLHS is born, multiple surgeries done in a particular order are needed to increase blood flow to the body and bypass the poorly functioning left side of the heart. The right ventricle becomes the main pumping chamber to the body. These surgeries do not cure HLHS, but help restore heart function. Sometimes medicines are given to help treat symptoms of the defect before or after surgery. Surgery for HLHS usually is done in three separate stages:

1. **Norwood procedure.** This surgery usually is done within the first 2 weeks of a baby's life. Surgeons create a "new" aorta and connect it to the right ventricle. They also place a tube from either the aorta or the right ventricle to the vessels supplying the lungs (pulmonary arteries). Thus, the right ventricle can pump blood to both the lungs and the rest of the body. This can be a very challenging surgery. After this procedure, an infant's skin still might look bluish because oxygen-rich and oxygen-poor blood still mix in the heart.

2. **Bidirectional Glenn Shunt Procedure.** This usually is performed when an infant is 4–6 months of age. This procedure creates a direct connection between the pulmonary artery and the vessel (the superior vena cava) returning oxygen-poor blood from the upper part of the body to the heart. This reduces the work the right ventricle has to do by allowing blood returning from the body to flow directly to the lungs.

3. **Fontan procedure.** This procedure usually is done sometime during the period when an infant is 18 months–3 years of age. Doctors connect the pulmonary artery and the vessel (the inferior vena cava) returning oxygen-poor blood from the lower part of the body to the heart, allowing the rest of the blood coming back from the body to go to the lungs. Once this procedure is complete, oxygen-rich and oxygen-poor blood no longer mix in the heart and an infant's skin will no longer look bluish.

Infants who have these surgeries are not cured; they may have lifelong complications.

Infants with HLHS will need regular follow-up visits with a cardiologist (a heart doctor) to monitor their progress. If the HLHS defect is very complex, or the heart becomes weak after the surgeries, a heart transplant may be needed. Infants who receive a heart transplant will need to take medicines for the rest of their lives to prevent their body from rejecting the new heart.

Section 27.6

Patent Ductus Arteriosus (PDA)

This section includes text excerpted from "What Is Patent Ductus Arteriosus?" National Heart, Lung, and Blood Institute (NHLBI), September 26, 2011. Reviewed December 2017.

How the Heart Works

To understand patent ductus arteriosus (PDA), it helps to know how a normal heart works. Your child's heart is a muscle about the size of his or her fist. It works like a pump and beats about 100,000 times a day.

The heart has two sides, separated by an inner wall called the septum. The right side of the heart pumps blood to the lungs to pick up oxygen. Then, oxygen-rich blood returns from the lungs to the left side of the heart, and the left side pumps it to the body.

The heart has four chambers and four valves and is connected to various blood vessels. Veins are the blood vessels that carry blood from the body to the heart. Arteries are the blood vessels that carry blood away from the heart to the body.

Heart Chambers

The heart has four chambers or "rooms."

- The atria are the two upper chambers that collect blood as it flows into the heart.

- The ventricles are the two lower chambers that pump blood out of the heart to the lungs or other parts of the body.

Heart Valves

Four valves control the flow of blood from the atria to the ventricles and from the ventricles into the two large arteries connected to the heart.

- The tricuspid valve is in the right side of the heart, between the right atrium and the right ventricle.

- The pulmonary valve is in the right side of the heart, between the right ventricle and the entrance to the pulmonary artery. This artery carries blood from the heart to the lungs.

- The mitral valve is in the left side of the heart, between the left atrium and the left ventricle.

- The aortic valve is in the left side of the heart, between the left ventricle and the entrance to the aorta. This artery carries blood from the heart to the body.

Valves are like doors that open and close. They open to allow blood to flow through to the next chamber or to one of the arteries. Then they shut to keep blood from flowing backward.

When the heart's valves open and close, they make a "lub-DUB" sound that a doctor can hear using a stethoscope.

- The first sound—the "lub"—is made by the mitral and tricuspid valves closing at the beginning of systole. Systole is when the ventricles contract, or squeeze, and pump blood out of the heart.

- The second sound—the "DUB"—is made by the aortic and pulmonary valves closing at the beginning of diastole. Diastole is when the ventricles relax and fill with blood pumped into them by the atria.

Arteries

The arteries are major blood vessels connected to your heart.

- The pulmonary artery carries blood from the right side of the heart to the lungs to pick up a fresh supply of oxygen.

- The aorta is the main artery that carries oxygen-rich blood from the left side of the heart to the body.

- The coronary arteries are the other important arteries attached to the heart. They carry oxygen-rich blood from the aorta to the heart muscle, which must have its own blood supply to function.

Veins

The veins also are major blood vessels connected to your heart.

- The pulmonary veins carry oxygen-rich blood from the lungs to the left side of the heart so it can be pumped to the body.

- The superior and inferior vena cavae are large veins that carry oxygen-poor blood from the body back to the heart.

What Is PDA?

PDA is a heart problem that occurs soon after birth in some babies. In PDA, abnormal blood flow occurs between two of the major arteries connected to the heart.

Before birth, the two major arteries—the aorta and the pulmonary artery—are connected by a blood vessel called the ductus arteriosus. This vessel is an essential part of fetal blood circulation.

Within minutes or up to a few days after birth, the vessel is supposed to close as part of the normal changes occurring in the baby's circulation.

In some babies, however, the ductus arteriosus remains open (patent). This opening allows oxygen-rich blood from the aorta to mix with oxygen-poor blood from the pulmonary artery. This can put strain on the heart and increase blood pressure in the lung arteries.

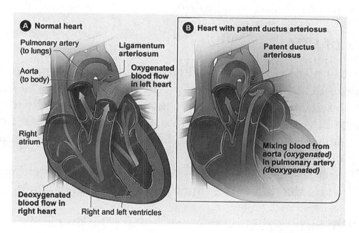

Figure 27.5. *Normal Heart and Heart with Patent Ductus Arteriosus*

Figure A shows the interior of a normal heart and normal blood flow. Figure B shows a heart with patent ductus arteriosus (PDA). The defect connects the aorta with the pulmonary artery. This allows oxygen-rich blood from the aorta to mix with oxygen-poor blood in the pulmonary artery.

The Heart with PDA

The ductus arteriosus is a blood vessel that connects the aorta and pulmonary artery in unborn babies. This vessel allows blood to be pumped from the right side of the heart into the aorta, without stopping at the lungs for oxygen.

While a baby is in the womb, only a small amount of his or her blood needs to go to the lungs. This is because the baby gets oxygen from the mother's bloodstream.

After birth, the baby no longer is connected to the mother's bloodstream. Thus, the baby's blood must travel to his or her own lungs to get oxygen. As the baby begins to breathe on his or her own, the pulmonary artery opens to allow blood into the lungs. Normally, the ductus arteriosus closes because the infant no longer needs it.

Once the ductus arteriosus closes, blood leaving the right side of the heart no longer goes into the aorta. Instead, the blood travels through the pulmonary artery to the lungs. There, the blood picks up oxygen. The oxygen-rich blood returns to the left side of the heart and is pumped to the rest of the body.

Sometimes the ductus arteriosus remains open (patent) after birth. A PDA allows blood to flow from the aorta into the pulmonary artery and to the lungs. The extra blood flowing into the lungs strains the heart. It also increases blood pressure in the lung's arteries.

Effects of PDA

Full-term infants. A small PDA might not cause any problems, but a large PDA likely will cause problems. The larger the PDA, the greater the amount of extra blood that passes through the lungs.

A large PDA that remains open for an extended time can cause the heart to enlarge, forcing it to work harder. Also, fluid can buildup in the lungs.

A PDA can slightly increase the risk of infective endocarditis (IE). IE is an infection of the inner lining of the heart chambers and valves.

In PDA, increased blood flow can irritate the lining of the pulmonary artery, where the ductus arteriosus connects. This irritation makes it easier for bacteria in the bloodstream to collect and grow, which can lead to IE.

Premature infants. PDA can be more serious in premature infants than in full-term infants. Premature babies are more likely to have lung damage from the extra blood flowing from the PDA into the lungs. These infants may need to be put on ventilators. Ventilators are machines that support breathing.

Increased blood flow through the lungs also can reduce blood flow to the rest of the body. This can damage other organs, especially the intestines and kidneys.

What Causes PDA?

If your child has PDA, you may think you did something wrong during your pregnancy to cause the problem. However, the cause of patent ductus arteriosus isn't known.

Genetics may play a role in causing the condition. A defect in one or more genes might prevent the ductus arteriosus from closing after birth.

Who Is at Risk for PDA?

PDA is a relatively common congenital heart defect in the United States.

The condition occurs more often in premature infants (on average, occurring in about 8 of every 1,000 births). However, PDA also occurs in full-term infants (on average, occurring in about 2 of every 1,000 births).

PDA also is more common in:

- Infants who have genetic conditions such as Down syndrome

- Infants whose mothers had German measles (rubella) during pregnancy

PDA is twice as common in girls as it is in boys.

What Are the Signs and Symptoms of PDA?

A heart murmur may be the only sign that a baby has PDA. A heart murmur is an extra or unusual sound heard during the heartbeat. Heart murmurs also have other causes besides PDA, and most murmurs are harmless.

Some infants may develop signs or symptoms of volume overload on the heart and excess blood flow in the lungs. Signs and symptoms may include:

- Fast breathing, working hard to breathe, or shortness of breath. Premature infants may need increased oxygen or help breathing from a ventilator.

- Poor feeding and poor weight gain.

- Tiring easily.

- Sweating with exertion, such as while feeding.

How Is PDA Diagnosed?

In full-term infants, PDA usually is first suspected when the baby's doctor hears a heart murmur during a regular checkup.

A heart murmur is an extra or unusual sound heard during the heartbeat. Heart murmurs also have other causes besides PDA, and most murmurs are harmless.

If a PDA is large, the infant also may develop symptoms of volume overload and increased blood flow to the lungs. If a PDA is small, it may not be diagnosed until later in childhood.

If your child's doctor thinks your child has PDA, he or she may refer you to a pediatric cardiologist. This is a doctor who specializes in diagnosing and treating heart problems in children.

Premature babies who have PDA may not have the same signs as full-term babies, such as heart murmurs. Doctors may suspect PDA in premature babies who develop breathing problems soon after birth. Tests can help confirm a diagnosis.

Diagnostic Tests

Echocardiography (ECHO)

ECHO is a painless test that uses sound waves to create a moving picture of your baby's heart. During ECHO, the sound waves bounce off your child's heart. A computer converts the sound waves into pictures of the heart's structures.

The test allows the doctor to clearly see any problems with the way the heart is formed or the way it's working. ECHO is the most important test available to your baby's cardiologist to both diagnose a heart problem and follow the problem over time.

In babies who have PDA, aECHO shows how big the PDA is and how well the heart is responding to it. When medical treatments are used to try to close a PDA, echo is used to see how well the treatments are working.

Electrocardiogram (EKG)

An EKG is a simple, painless test that records the heart's electrical activity. For babies who have PDA, an EKG can show whether the heart is enlarged. The test also can show other subtle changes that can suggest the presence of a PDA.

How Is PDA Treated?

PDA is treated with medicines, catheter-based procedures, and surgery. The goal of treatment is to close the PDA. Closure will help prevent complications and reverse the effects of increased blood volume.

Small PDAs often close without treatment. For full-term infants, treatment is needed if the PDA is large or causing health problems. For premature infants, treatment is needed if the PDA is causing breathing problems or heart problems.

Talk with your child's doctor about treatment options and how your family prefers to handle treatment decisions.

Medicines

Your child's doctor may prescribe medicines to help close your child's PDA.

Indomethacin is a medicine that helps close PDAs in premature infants. This medicine triggers the PDA to constrict or tighten, which closes the opening. Indomethacin usually doesn't work in full-term infants.

Ibuprofen also is used to close PDAs in premature infants. This medicine is similar to indomethacin.

Catheter-Based Procedures

Catheters are thin, flexible tubes that doctors use as part of a procedure called cardiac catheterization. Catheter-based procedures often are used to close PDAs in infants or children who are large enough to have the procedure.

Your child's doctor may refer to the procedure as "transcatheter device closure." The procedure sometimes is used for small PDAs to prevent the risk of infective endocarditis (IE). IE is an infection of the inner lining of the heart chambers and valves.

Your child will be given medicine to help him or her relax or sleep during the procedure. The doctor will insert a catheter in a large blood vessel in the groin (upper thigh). He or she will then guide the catheter to your child's heart.

A small metal coil or other blocking device is passed through the catheter and placed in the PDA. This device blocks blood flow through the vessel.

Catheter-based procedures don't require the child's chest to be opened. They also allow the child to recover quickly.

These procedures often are done on an outpatient basis. You'll most likely be able to take your child home the same day the procedure is done.

Complications from catheter-based procedures are rare and short term. They can include bleeding, infection, and movement of the blocking device from where it was placed.

Surgery

Surgery to correct a PDA may be done if:

- A premature or full-term infant has health problems due to a PDA and is too small to have a catheter-based procedure

- A catheter-based procedure doesn't successfully close the PDA

- Surgery is planned for treatment of related congenital heart defects

Often, surgery isn't done until after 6 months of age in infants who don't have health problems from their PDAs. Doctors sometimes do surgery on small PDAs to prevent the risk of IE.

For the surgery, your child will be given medicine so that he or she will sleep and not feel any pain. The surgeon will make a small incision (cut) between your child's ribs to reach the PDA. He or she will close the PDA using stitches or clips.

Complications from surgery are rare and usually short term. They can include hoarseness, a paralyzed diaphragm (the muscle below the lungs), infection, bleeding, or fluid buildup around the lungs.

After Surgery

After surgery, your child will spend a few days in the hospital. He or she will be given medicine to reduce pain and anxiety. Most children go home 2 days after surgery. Premature infants usually have to stay in the hospital longer because of their other health issues.

The doctors and nurses at the hospital will teach you how to care for your child at home. They will talk to you about:

- Limits on activity for your child while he or she recovers

- Follow up appointments with your child's doctors

- How to give your child medicines at home, if needed

When your child goes home after surgery, you can expect that he or she will feel fairly comfortable. However, you child may have some short-term pain.

Your child should begin to eat better and gain weight quickly. Within a few weeks, he or she should fully recover and be able to take part in normal activities.

Long-term complications from surgery are rare. However, they can include narrowing of the aorta, incomplete closure of the PDA, and reopening of the PDA.

Living with PDA

Most children who have PDAs live healthy, normal lives after treatment. Full-term infants will likely have normal activity levels, appetite, and growth after PDA treatment, unless they had other congenital heart defects.

For premature infants, the outlook after PDA treatment depends on other factors, such as:

- How early the child was born

- Whether the child has other illnesses or conditions, such as other congenital heart defects

Ongoing Care

Children who have PDAs are at slightly increased risk for infective endocarditis (IE). IE is an infection of the inner lining of the heart chambers and valves.

Your child's doctor will tell you whether your child needs antibiotics before certain medical procedures to help prevent IE. According to the most recent American Heart Association (AHA) guidelines, most children who have PDAs don't need antibiotics.

Section 27.7

Pulmonary Atresia

This section includes text excerpted from "Congenital
Heart Defects (CHDs)—Facts about Pulmonary Atresia," Centers for
Disease Control and Prevention (CDC), February 11, 2016.

What Is Pulmonary Atresia?

Pulmonary atresia is a birth defect of the pulmonary valve, which is
the valve that controls blood flow from the right ventricle (lower right
chamber of the heart) to the main pulmonary artery (the blood vessel
that carries blood from the heart to the lungs). Pulmonary atresia is
when this valve didn't form at all, and no blood can go from the right
ventricle of the heart out to the lungs. Because a baby with pulmonary
atresia may need surgery or other procedures soon after birth, this
birth defect is considered a critical congenital heart defect (critical
CHD). Congenital means present at birth.

In a baby without a congenital heart defect, the right side of
the heart pumps oxygen-poor blood from the heart to the lungs
through the pulmonary artery. The blood that comes back from
the lungs is oxygen-rich and can then be pumped to the rest of the
body. In babies with pulmonary atresia, the pulmonary valve that
usually controls the blood flowing through the pulmonary artery is
not formed, so blood is unable to get directly from the right ventricle
to the lungs.

In pulmonary atresia, since blood cannot directly flow from
the right ventricle of the heart out to the pulmonary artery, blood
must use other routes to bypass the unformed pulmonary valve.
The foramen ovale, a natural opening between the right and left
upper chambers of the heart during pregnancy that usually closes
after the baby is born, often remains open to allow blood flow to the
lungs. Additionally, doctors may give medicine to the baby to keep
the baby's patent ductus arteriosus open after the baby's birth. The
patent ductus arteriosus is the blood vessel that allows blood to move
around the baby's lungs before the baby is born and it also usually
closes after birth.

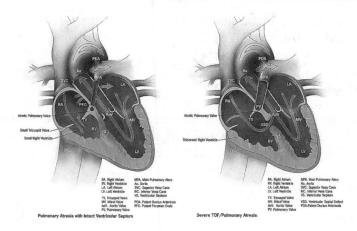

Figure 27.6. *Pulmonary Atresia with Intact Ventricular Septum and TOF/ Pulmonary Atresia*

Types of Pulmonary Atresia

There are typically two types of pulmonary atresia, according to whether or not a baby also has a ventricular septal defect (a hole in the wall that separates the two lower chambers, or ventricles, of the heart):

- **Pulmonary atresia with an intact ventricular septum.** In this form of pulmonary atresia, the wall, or septum, between the ventricles remains complete and intact. During pregnancy when the heart is developing, very little blood flows into or out of the right ventricle (RV), and therefore the RV doesn't fully develop and remains very small. If the RV is underdeveloped, the heart can have problems pumping blood to the lungs and the body. The artery which usually carries blood out of the right ventricle, the main pulmonary artery (MPA), remains very small, since the pulmonary valve (PV) doesn't form.

- **Pulmonary atresia with a ventricular septal defect (VSD).** In this form of pulmonary atresia, a VSD allows blood to flow into and out of the RV. Therefore, blood flowing into the RV can help the ventricle develop during pregnancy, so it is typically not as small as in pulmonary atresia with an intact ventricular septum. Pulmonary atresia with a VSD is similar to another condition called tetralogy of Fallot. However, in tetralogy of Fallot (TOF), the pulmonary valve (PV) does form, although it is small

435

and blood has trouble flowing through it—this is called pulmonary valve stenosis (PVS). Thus, pulmonary atresia with a VSD is like a very severe form of TOF.

Occurrence

In a study using data from birth defects tracking systems across the United States, researchers estimated that about 1 out of every 10,000 babies is born with pulmonary atresia.

Causes and Risk Factors

The causes of heart defects, such as pulmonary atresia, among most babies are unknown. Some babies have heart defects because of changes in their genes or chromosomes. Heart defects also are thought to be caused by a combination of genes and other factors, such as the things the mother comes in contact with in the environment, or what the mother eats or drinks, or certain medicines she uses.

Diagnosis

Pulmonary atresia may be diagnosed during pregnancy or soon after a baby is born.

During Pregnancy

During pregnancy, there are screening tests (also called prenatal tests) to check for birth defects and other conditions. Pulmonary atresia might be seen during an ultrasound (which creates pictures of the body). Some findings from the ultrasound may make the healthcare provider suspect a baby may have pulmonary atresia. If so, the healthcare provider can request a fetal echocardiogram to confirm the diagnosis. A fetal echocardiogram is an ultrasound specifically of the baby's heart and major blood vessels that is performed during the pregnancy. This test can show problems with the structure of the heart and how well the heart is working.

After the Baby Is Born

Babies born with pulmonary atresia will show symptoms at birth or very soon afterwards. They may have a bluish looking skin color, called cyanosis, because their blood doesn't carry enough oxygen. Infants with pulmonary atresia can have additional symptoms such as:

- Problems breathing

- Ashen or bluish skin color

- Poor feeding

- Extreme sleepiness

During a physical examination, a doctor can see the symptoms, such as bluish skin or problems breathing. Using a stethoscope, a doctor will check for a heart murmur (an abnormal "whooshing" sound caused by blood not flowing properly). However, it is not uncommon for a heart murmur to be absent right at birth.

If a doctor suspects that there might be a problem, the doctor can request one or more tests to confirm the diagnosis of pulmonary atresia. The most common test is an echocardiogram (ECHO). This test is an ultrasound of the baby's heart that can show problems with the structure of the heart, like holes in the walls between the chambers, and any irregular blood flow. Cardiac catheterization (inserting a thin tube into a blood vessel and guiding it to the heart) also can confirm the diagnosis by looking at the inside of the heart and measuring the blood pressure and oxygen levels. An electrocardiogram (EKG), which measures the electrical activity of the heart, and other medical tests may also be used to make the diagnosis.

Pulmonary atresia is a critical congenital heart defect (CCHD) that may be detected with newborn screening using pulse oximetry (also known as pulse ox). Pulse oximetry is a simple bedside test to estimate the amount of oxygen in a baby's blood. Low levels of oxygen in the blood can be a sign of a critical CHD. Newborn screening using pulse oximetry can identify some infants with a critical CHD, like pulmonary atresia, before they show any symptoms.

Treatment

Most babies with pulmonary atresia will need medication to keep the ductus arteriosus open after birth. Keeping this blood vessel open will help with blood flow to the lungs until the pulmonary valve can be repaired.

Treatment for pulmonary atresia depends on its severity.

- In some cases, blood flow can be improved by using cardiac catheterization (inserting a thin tube into a blood vessel and guiding it to the heart). During this procedure, doctors can expand the valve using a balloon or they may need to place a stent (a small tube) to keep the ductus arteriosus open.

437

- In most cases of pulmonary atresia, a baby may need surgery soon after birth. During surgery, doctors widen or replace the pulmonary valve and enlarge the passage to the pulmonary artery. If a baby has a ventricular septal defect (VSD), the doctor also will place a patch over the VSD to close the hole between the two lower chambers of the heart. These actions will improve blood flow to the lungs and the rest of the body. If a baby with pulmonary atresia has an underdeveloped right ventricle, he or she might need staged surgical procedures, similar to surgical repairs for hypoplastic left heart syndrome.

Most babies with pulmonary atresia will need regular follow-up visits with a cardiologist (a heart doctor) to monitor their progress and check for other health conditions that might develop as they get older. As adults, they may need more surgery or medical care for other possible problems.

Section 27.8

Tetralogy of Fallot (TOF)

This section includes text excerpted from "Congenital Heart Defects (CHDs)—Facts about Tetralogy of Fallot," Centers for Disease Control and Prevention (CDC), March 4, 2016.

Tetralogy of Fallot (TOF) is a birth defect that affects normal blood flow through the heart. It happens when a baby's heart does not form correctly as the baby grows and develops in the mother's womb during pregnancy.

What Is Tetralogy of Fallot (TOF)?

TOF is made up of the following four defects of the heart and its blood vessels:

1. A hole in the wall between the two lower chambers or ventricles of the heart. This condition also is called a ventricular septal defect (VSD).

2. A narrowing of the pulmonary valve and main pulmonary artery. This condition also is called pulmonary stenosis.

3. The aortic valves, which opens to the aorta, is enlarged and seems to open from both ventricles, rather than from the left ventricle only, as in a normal heart. In this defect, the aortic valve sits directly on top of the VSD.

4. The muscular wall of the lower right chamber of the heart (right ventricle) is thicker than normal. This also is called ventricular hypertrophy.

Because a baby with TOF may need surgery or other procedures soon after birth, this birth defect is considered a critical congenital heart defect (CCHD). Congenital means present at birth.

This heart defect can cause oxygen in the blood that flows to the rest of the body to be reduced. Infants with TOF can have a bluish-looking skin color, called cyanosis, because their blood doesn't carry enough oxygen. At birth, infants might not have blue-looking skin, but later might develop sudden episodes of bluish skin during crying or feeding. These episodes are called tet spells.

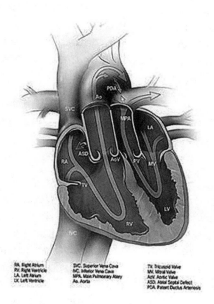

Figure 27.7. *Heart with Tetralogy of Fallot (TOF)*

Infants with TOF or other conditions causing cyanosis can have problems including:

- A higher risk of getting an infection of the layers of the heart, called endocarditis.

- A higher risk of having irregular heart rhythms, called arrhythmia.

- Dizziness, fainting, or seizures, because of the low oxygen levels in their blood.

- Delayed growth and development.

Occurrence

The Centers for Disease Control and Prevention (CDC) estimates that each year about 1,660 babies in the United States are born with TOF. In other words, about 1 in every 2518 babies born in the United States each year are born with TOF.

Causes and Risk Factors

The causes of heart defects (such as TOF) among most babies are unknown. Some babies have heart defects because of changes in their genes or chromosomes. Heart defects such as TOF also are thought to be caused by a combination of genes and other risk factors, such as the things the mother or fetus come in contact with in the environment or what the mother eats or drinks or the medicines she uses.

Diagnosis

TOF may be diagnosed during pregnancy or soon after a baby is born.

During Pregnancy

During pregnancy, there are screening tests (also called prenatal tests) to check for birth defects and other conditions. TOF might be seen during an ultrasound (which creates pictures of the body). Some findings from the ultrasound may make the healthcare provider suspect a baby may have TOF. If so, the healthcare provider can request a fetal echocardiogram to confirm the diagnosis. A fetal echocardiogram is an ultrasound of the heart of the fetus. This test can show problems with the structure of the heart and how the heart is working with this defect.

After a Baby Is Born

TOF usually is diagnosed after a baby is born, often after the infant has an episode of turning blue during crying or feeding (a tet spell). Some findings on a physical exam may make the healthcare provider think a baby may have TOF, including bluish-looking skin or a heart murmur (a "whooshing" sound caused by blood not flowing properly through the heart). However, it is not uncommon for a heart murmur to be absent right at birth.

The healthcare provider can request one or more tests to confirm the diagnosis. The most common test is an echocardiogram (ECHO). An echocardiogram is an ultrasound of the heart that can show problems with the structure of the heart and how the heart is working (or not) with this defect. Echocardiography also is useful for helping the doctor follow the child's health over time.

TOF is a critical congenital heart defect (CCHD) that may be detected with newborn screening using pulse oximetry (also known as pulse ox). Pulse oximetry is a simple bedside test to estimate the amount of oxygen in a baby's blood. Low levels of oxygen in the blood can be a sign of a critical CHD. Newborn screening using pulse oximetry can identify some infants with a critical CHD, like pulmonary atresia, before they show any symptoms.

Treatment

TOF can be treated by surgery soon after the baby is born. During surgery, doctors widen or replace the pulmonary valve and enlarge the passage to the pulmonary artery. They also will place a patch over the ventricular septal defect to close the hole between the two lower chambers of the heart. These actions will improve blood flow to the lungs and the rest of the body.

Most infants will live active, healthy lives after surgery. However, they will need regular follow-up visits with a cardiologist (a heart doctor) to monitor their progress and check for other health conditions that might develop as they get older. As adults, they may need more surgery or medical care for other possible problems.

Section 27.9

Total Anomalous Pulmonary Venous Return (TAPVR)

This section includes text excerpted from "Congenital
Heart Defects (CHDs)—Facts about Total Anomalous Pulmonary
Venous Return or TAPVR," Centers for Disease Control and
Prevention (CDC), February 11, 2016.

Total anomalous pulmonary venous return (TAPVR) is a birth defect of the heart. In a baby with TAPVR, oxygen-rich blood does not return from the lungs to the left atrium. Instead, the oxygen-rich blood returns to the right side of the heart. Here, oxygen-rich blood mixes with oxygen-poor blood. This causes the baby to get less oxygen than is needed to the body. To survive with this defect, babies with TAPVR usually have a hole between the right atrium and the left atrium (an atrial septal defect) that allows the mixed blood to get to the left side of the heart and pumped out to the rest of the body. Some children can have other heart defects along with TAPVR, aside from the atrial septal defect. Because a baby with this defect may need surgery or other procedures soon after birth, TAPVR is considered a critical congenital heart defect. Congenital means present at birth. In a related defect, partial anomalous pulmonary venous return (PAPVR), not all of the veins have an abnormal connection. There are some abnormal connections, but one or more of the veins return normally to the left atrium. Therefore, PAPVR is not as critical as TAPVR.

In a baby without a congenital heart defect, the right side of the heart pumps oxygen-poor blood from the heart to the lungs through the pulmonary artery. The blood that comes back from the lungs is oxygen-rich, and it moves through the pulmonary veins to the left atrium. The left side of the heart pumps oxygen-rich blood to the rest of the body through the aorta.

Types of TAPVR

There are different types of TAPVR, based on where the pulmonary veins connect:

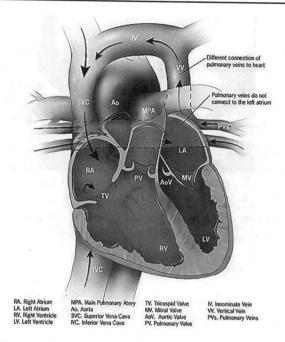

Figure 27.8. *Total Anomalous Pulmonary Venous Return (TAPVR)*

- **Supracardiac.** In supracardiac TAPVR, the pulmonary veins come together and form an abnormal connection above the heart to the superior vena cava, which is a main blood vessel that brings oxygen-poor blood from the upper part of the body to the heart. In this type of TAPVR, a mixture of oxygen-poor and oxygen-rich blood returns to the right atrium through the superior vena cava.

- **Cardiac.** In cardiac TAPVR, the pulmonary veins meet behind the heart and connect to the right atrium. The coronary sinus, which is a vein that helps bring oxygen-poor blood from the heart muscle back to the heart, helps connect the pulmonary veins to the right atrium in this type of TAPVR.

- **Infracardiac.** In infracardiac TAPVR, the pulmonary veins come together and form abnormal connections below the heart. A mixture of oxygen-poor blood and oxygen-rich blood returns to the right atrium from the veins of the liver and the inferior vena cava, which is the main blood vessel that brings oxygen-poor blood from the lower part of the body to the heart.

Occurrence

In a study, using data from the Metropolitan Atlanta Congenital Defects Program (MACDP), researchers estimated that, together, TAPVR and PAPVR occur in about 1 out of every 10,000 births.

Causes and Risk Factors

The causes of heart defects, such as TAPVR, among most babies are unknown. Some babies have heart defects because of changes in their genes or chromosomes. Heart defects also are thought to be caused by a combination of genes and other risk factors, such as the things the mother or fetus come in contact with in the environment or what the mother eats or drinks or the medicines she uses.

Diagnosis

TAPVR and PAPVR might be diagnosed during pregnancy, but more often these defects are diagnosed soon after a baby is born.

During Pregnancy

During pregnancy, there are screening tests (also called prenatal tests) to check for birth defects and other conditions. TAPVR might be diagnosed during pregnancy with an ultrasound (which creates pictures of the body). Some findings from the ultrasound may make the healthcare provider suspect a baby could have TAPVR. If so, the healthcare provider can request a fetal echocardiogram to confirm the diagnosis. A fetal echocardiogram is an ultrasound specifically of the baby's heart and major blood vessels that is performed during the pregnancy. This test can show problems with the structure of the heart and how well the heart is working. However, TAPVR defect is not commonly detected during pregnancy. It is hard for doctors to see the pulmonary veins on the prenatal screening tests since not much blood goes to the lungs before the baby is born. It is easier to detect this defect after birth when the blood is flowing to the lungs and returning to the heart.

After a Baby Is Born

Symptoms usually occur at birth or very soon afterwards. Infants with TAPVR can have a bluish looking skin color, called cyanosis, because their blood doesn't carry enough oxygen. Infants with

TAPVR or other conditions causing cyanosis can have symptoms such as:

- Problems breathing
- Pounding heart
- Weak pulse
- Ashen or bluish skin color
- Poor feeding
- Extreme sleepiness

Using a stethoscope, a doctor will often hear a heart murmur (an abnormal "whooshing" sound caused by blood flowing through the atrial septal defect). However, it is not uncommon for a heart murmur to be absent right at birth.

If a doctor suspects that there might be a problem, the doctor can request one or more tests to confirm the diagnosis of TAPVR. The most common test is an echocardiogram. This is an ultrasound of the heart that can show problems with the structure of the heart, like holes in the walls between the chambers, and any irregular blood flow. Cardiac catheterization also can confirm the diagnosis by showing that the blood vessels are abnormally attached. An electrocardiogram (EKG), which measures the electrical activity of the heart, chest X-rays, and other medical tests may also be used to make the diagnosis.

TAPVR is a critical congenital heart defect (CCHD) that also can be detected with newborn pulse oximetry screening. Pulse oximetry is a simple bedside test to determine the amount of oxygen in a baby's blood. Low levels of oxygen in the blood can be a sign of a CCHD. Newborn screening using pulse oximetry can identify some infants with a CCHD, like TAPVR, before they show any symptoms.

Treatment

Babies with TAPVR will need surgery to repair the defect. The age at which the surgery is done depends on how sick the child is and the specific structure of the abnormal connections between the pulmonary veins and the right atrium. The goal of the surgical repair of TAPVR is to restore normal blood flow through the heart. To repair this defect, doctors usually connect the pulmonary veins to the left atrium, close off any abnormal connections between blood vessels, and close the atrial septal defect.

445

Infants whose defects are surgically repaired are not cured; they may have lifelong complications. A child or adult with TAPVR will need regular follow-up visits with a cardiologist (a heart doctor) to monitor their progress, avoid complications, and check for other health conditions that might develop as they get older.

Section 27.10

Tricuspid Atresia

This section includes text excerpted from "Congenital Heart Defects (CHDs)—Facts about Tricuspid Atresia," Centers for Disease Control and Prevention (CDC), March 4, 2016.

What Is Tricuspid Atresia?

Tricuspid atresia is a birth defect of the tricuspid valve, which is the valve that controls blood flow from the right atrium (upper right chamber of the heart) to the right ventricle (lower right chamber of the heart). Tricuspid atresia occurs when this valve does not form at all, and no blood can go from the right atrium through the right ventricle to the lungs for oxygen. Because a baby with tricuspid atresia may need surgery or other procedures soon after birth, this birth defect is considered a critical congenital heart defect. Congenital means present at birth.

In a baby without a congenital heart defect, the right side of the heart pumps oxygen-poor blood from the heart to the lungs through the main pulmonary artery. The blood that comes back from the lungs is oxygen-rich and can then be pumped to the rest of the body through the aorta. In babies with tricuspid atresia, the tricuspid valve that controls blood flow from the right atrium to the right ventricle is not formed, so blood is unable to get to the right ventricle and out to the lungs. For this reason, the right ventricle can be underdeveloped. The main pulmonary artery may also be small with very little blood going through it to the lungs.

In tricuspid atresia, since blood cannot directly flow from the right atrium to the right ventricle, blood must use other routes to bypass the unformed tricuspid valve. Babies born with tricuspid atresia often also have an atrial septal defect, which is a hole between the right and left atria, or a ventricular septal defect, which is a hole between the right and left ventricles. These defects allow oxygen-rich blood to mix with oxygen-poor blood, so that oxygen-rich blood has a way to get pumped to the rest of the body.

Doctors may give the baby medicine to keep the baby's patent ductus arteriosus open after the baby's birth. The PDA is the blood vessel that allows blood to move around the baby's lungs before the baby is born, and it usually closes after birth. Keeping this connection open allows blood to get to the lungs for oxygen and bypass the small right side of the heart.

Some babies with tricuspid atresia can also have other heart defects, including transposition of the great arteries (TGA). In TGA, the main connections (arteries) from the heart are reversed. The main pulmonary artery, which normally carries oxygen-poor blood from the right side of the heart to the lungs, now arises from the left side and carries oxygen-rich blood returning from the lungs back to the lungs.

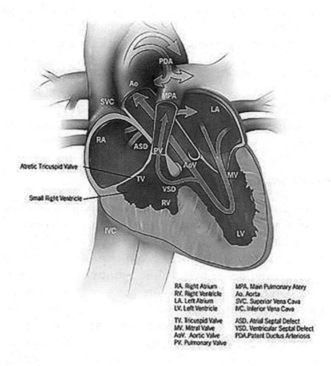

Figure 27.9. *Tricuspid Atresia*

The aorta, which normally carries blood from the left side of the heart to the body, now arises from the right side and carries oxygen-poor blood back out to the body. When a baby has both tricuspid atresia and TGA, blood is able to get to the lungs because the main pulmonary artery arises from the developed left ventricle. However, blood cannot get out to the body because the aorta arises from the poorly formed right ventricle and is small.

Occurrence

In a study using data from birth defects surveillance systems across the United States, researchers estimated that about 1 out of every 10,000 babies is born with tricuspid atresia.

Causes and Risk Factors

The causes of heart defects, such as tricuspid atresia, among most babies are unknown. Some babies have heart defects because of changes in their genes or chromosomes. Heart defects also are thought to be caused by a combination of genes and other factors, such as the things the mother comes in contact with in the environment, or what the mother eats or drinks, or certain medicines she uses.

Diagnosis

Tricuspid atresia may be diagnosed during pregnancy or soon after a baby is born.

During Pregnancy

During pregnancy, there are screening tests (also called prenatal tests) to check for birth defects and other conditions. Tricuspid atresia might be seen during an ultrasound (which creates pictures of the body). Some findings from the ultrasound may make the healthcare provider suspect that a baby might have tricuspid atresia. If so, the healthcare provider can request a fetal echocardiogram to confirm the diagnosis. A fetal echocardiogram is an ultrasound specifically of the baby's heart and major blood vessels that is performed during the pregnancy. This test can show problems with the structure of the heart and how the heart is working with this defect.

After a Baby Is Born

Babies born with tricuspid atresia will show symptoms at birth or very soon afterwards. They may have a bluish looking skin color, called cyanosis, because their blood doesn't carry enough oxygen. Infants with tricuspid atresia can have additional symptoms such as:

- Problems breathing
- Ashen or bluish skin color
- Poor feeding
- Extreme sleepiness

During a physical examination, a doctor can see the symptoms, such as bluish skin or problems breathing. Using a stethoscope, a doctor will check for a heart murmur (an abnormal "whooshing" sound caused by blood not flowing properly), or other sounds that may indicate a heart problem. However, it is not uncommon for a heart murmur to be absent right at birth.

If a doctor suspects that there might be a problem, the doctor can request one or more tests to confirm the diagnosis of tricuspid atresia. The most common test is an echocardiogram (ECHO). This is an ultrasound of the heart that can show problems with the structure of the heart, like holes in the walls between the chambers, and any irregular blood flow. Cardiac catheterization (inserting a thin tube into a blood vessel and guiding it to the heart) also can confirm the diagnosis by looking at the inside of the heart and measuring the blood pressure and oxygen. An electrocardiogram (EKG), which measures the electrical activity of the heart, and other medical tests may also be used to make the diagnosis.

Tricuspid atresia is a critical congenital heart defect (CCHD) that also can be detected with newborn screening using pulse oximetry (also known as pulse ox). Pulse oximetry is a simple, painless bedside test to estimate the amount of oxygen in a baby's blood. The test is done using a machine called a pulse oximeter, with sensors placed on the baby's skin. Low levels of oxygen in the blood can be a sign of a CCHD. Newborn screening using pulse oximetry can identify some infants with a CCHD, like tricuspid atresia, before they show any symptoms.

Treatment

Medicines

Some babies and children will need medicines to help strengthen the heart muscle, lower their blood pressure, and help the body get rid of extra fluid.

Nutrition

Some babies with tricuspid atresia become tired while feeding and do not eat enough to gain weight. To make sure babies have a healthy weight gain, a special high-calorie formula might be prescribed. Some babies become extremely tired while feeding and might need to be fed through a feeding tube.

Surgery

Surgical treatment for tricuspid atresia depends on its severity and presence of other heart defects. Soon after a baby with tricuspid atresia is born, one or more surgeries may be needed to increase blood flow to the lungs and bypass the poorly functioning right side of the heart. Other surgeries or procedures may be needed later. These surgeries, described below, do not cure tricuspid atresia, but they help restore heart function. Sometimes medicines are given to help treat symptoms of the defect before or after surgery.

- **Septostomy.** A septostomy may be done within the first few days or weeks of a baby's life, and creates or enlarges the atrial septal defect, the hole between the right and left upper chambers (atria). This is done so that more oxygen-poor blood can mix with oxygen-rich blood, so that more oxygen-rich blood can get to the body.

- **Banding.** If the baby has other heart defects along with tricuspid atresia, sometimes there is too much blood flowing to the lungs and not enough going out to the rest of the body. Too much blood in the lungs can damage them. If this is the problem, surgery may be done within the first few weeks of a baby's life to place a band around the artery going to the lungs (main pulmonary artery) to control the blood flow to the lungs. This banding is a temporary procedure and will likely be removed.

- **Shunt procedure.** This surgery usually is done within the first two weeks of a baby's life. Surgeons create a bypass (shunt) from the aorta to the main pulmonary artery, allowing blood to get to the lungs. If the aorta is small, as occurs when the baby also has transposition of the great arteries, the surgeon will also enlarge the aorta at this time. After this procedure, an infant's skin still might look bluish because oxygen-rich and oxygen-poor blood still mix in the heart.

- **Bidirectional Glenn procedure.** This usually is performed when an infant is 4–6 months of age. This procedure creates a direct connection between the main pulmonary artery and the superior vena cava, the vessel returning oxygen-poor blood from the upper part of the body to the heart. This allows blood returning from the body to flow directly to the lungs and bypass the heart.

- **Fontan procedure.** This procedure usually is done sometime around two years of age. Doctors connect the main pulmonary artery and the inferior vena cava, the vessel returning oxygen-poor blood from the lower part of the body to the heart, allowing the rest of the blood coming back from the body to go to the lungs. Once this procedure is complete, oxygen-rich and oxygen-poor blood no longer mix in the heart and an infant's skin will no longer look bluish.

Infants who have these surgeries are not cured; they might have lifelong complications. If the tricuspid atresia is very complex, or the heart becomes weak after the surgeries, a heart transplant might be needed. An infant or child who receives a heart transplant will need to take medicines for the rest of his or her life to prevent the body from rejecting the new heart.

Babies born with tricuspid atresia will need regular follow-up visits with a cardiologist (a heart doctor) to monitor their progress and check for other health conditions that might develop as they get older. As adults, they may need more surgery or medical care for other possible problems.

Section 27.11

Truncus Arteriosus

This section includes text excerpted from "Congenital
Heart Defects (CHDs)—Facts about Truncus Arteriosus,"
Centers for Disease Control and Prevention (CDC), March 4, 2016.

What Is Truncus Arteriosus?

Truncus arteriosus is a birth defect of the heart. It occurs when the blood vessel coming out of the heart in the developing baby fails to separate completely during development, leaving a connection between the aorta and pulmonary artery. There are several different types of truncus, depending on how the arteries remain connected. There is

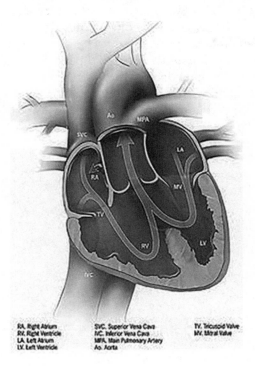

Figure 27.10. *Truncus Arteriosus*

also usually a hole between the bottom two chambers of the heart (ventricles) called a ventricular septal defect. Because a baby with this defect may need surgery or other procedures soon after birth, truncus arteriosus is considered a congenital heart defect. Congenital means present at birth.

In a baby without a congenital heart defect, the right side of the heart pumps oxygen-poor blood through the pulmonary artery to the lungs. The left side of the heart pumps oxygen-rich blood through the aorta to the rest of the body.

In babies with a truncus arteriosus, oxygen-poor blood and oxygen-rich blood are mixed together as blood flows to the lungs and the rest of the body. As a result, too much blood goes to the lungs and the heart works harder to pump blood to the rest of the body. Also, instead of having both an aortic valve and a pulmonary valve, babies with truncus arteriosus have a single common valve (truncal valve) controlling blood flow out of the heart. The truncal valve is often abnormal. The valve can be thickened and narrowed, which can block the blood as it leaves the heart. It can also leak, causing blood that leaves the heart to leak back into the heart across the valve.

Occurrence

Truncus arteriosus occurs in less than 1 out of every 10,000 live births. It can occur by itself or as part of certain genetic disorders. There are about 300 cases of truncus arteriosus per year in the United States.

Causes and Risk Factors

The causes of heart defects, such as truncus arteriosus, among most babies are unknown. Some babies have congenital heart defects because of changes in their genes or chromosomes. Congenital heart defects are also thought to be caused by the combination of genes and other risk factors such as things the mother comes in contact with in her environment, or what the mother eats or drinks, or certain medications she uses.

Diagnosis

Truncus arteriosus may be diagnosed during pregnancy or soon after the baby is born.

During Pregnancy

During pregnancy, there are screening tests (also called prenatal tests) to check for birth defects and other conditions. Some heart defects might be seen during an ultrasound (which creates pictures of the body). If a healthcare provider suspect a baby might have truncus arteriosus, the healthcare provider can request a fetal echocardiogram to confirm the diagnosis. A fetal echocardiogram is a more detailed ultrasound of the baby's heart. This test can show problems with the structure of the heart, like a single large vessel coming from the heart, and how the heart is working with this defect.

After a Baby Is Born

Infants with truncus arteriosus usually are in distress in the first few days of life because of the high amount of blood going to the lungs which makes the heart work harder. Infants with truncus arteriosus can have a bluish looking skin color, called cyanosis, because their blood doesn't carry enough oxygen. Infants with truncus arteriosus or other conditions causing cyanosis can have symptoms such as:

- Problems breathing
- Pounding heart
- Weak pulse
- Ashen or bluish skin color
- Poor feeding
- Extreme sleepiness

If a healthcare provider suspects a baby might have truncus arteriosus, the healthcare provider can request an echocardiogram (ECHO) to confirm the diagnosis. An ECHO is an ultrasound of the heart that can show problems with the structure of the heart, like the single large vessel coming from the heart or misshapen truncal valve. It can also show how the heart is working (or not) with this defect, like if the blood is leaking back into the heart or if it is moving through a hole between the ventricles. ECHOs are also useful for helping the doctor follow the child's health over time.

Truncus arteriosus is a that also can be detected with newborn pulse oximetry screening. Pulse oximetry is a simple bedside test to determine the amount of oxygen in a baby's blood. Low levels of oxygen in the blood can be a sign of a CCHD. Newborn screening using pulse oximetry can identify some infants with a CCHD, like truncus arteriosus, before they show any symptoms.

Treatment

Medications

Some babies with truncus arteriosus also will need medicines to help strengthen the heart muscle, lower their blood pressure, and help their body get rid of extra fluid.

Nutrition

Some babies with truncus arteriosus might become tired while feeding and might not eat enough to gain weight. To make sure babies have a healthy weight gain, a special high-calorie formula might be prescribed. Some babies become extremely tired while feeding and might need to be fed through a feeding tube.

Surgery

Surgery is needed to repair the heart and blood vessels. This is usually done in the first few months of life. Options for repair depend on how sick the child is and the specific structure of the defect. The goal of the surgery to repair truncus arteriosus is to create a separate flow of oxygen-poor blood to the lungs and oxygen-rich blood to the body. Usually, surgery to repair this defect involves the following steps:

- Close the hole between the bottom chambers of the heart (ventricular septal defect (VSD)) usually with a patch.

- Use the original single blood vessel to create a new aorta to carry oxygen-rich blood from the left ventricle out to the body.

- Use an artificial tube (conduit) with an artificial valve to connect the right ventricle to the arteries going to the lungs in order to carry oxygen-poor blood to the lungs.

Most babies with truncus arteriosus survive the surgical repair, but may need more surgery or other procedures as they get older. For example, the artificial tube doesn't grow, so it will need to be replaced as the child grows. There also may be blockages to blood flow which may need to be relieved, or problems with the truncal valve. Thus, a person born with truncus arteriosus will need regular follow-up visits with a cardiologist (a heart doctor) to monitor their progress and avoid complications or other health problems.

Section 27.12

Ventricular Septal Defect (VSD)

This section includes text excerpted from "Congenital Heart Defects (CHDs)—Facts about Ventricular Septal Defect," Centers for Disease Control and Prevention (CDC), November 8, 2016.

What Is a Ventricular Septal Defect (VSD)?

A ventricular septal defect (VSD) happens during pregnancy if the wall that forms between the two ventricles does not fully develop, leaving a hole. A VSD is one type of congenital heart defect. Congenital means present at birth.

In a baby without a congenital heart defect, the right side of the heart pumps oxygen-poor blood from the heart to the lungs, and the left side of the heart pumps oxygen-rich blood to the rest of the body.

In babies with a VSD, blood often flows from the left ventricle through the VSD to the right ventricle and into the lungs. This extra blood being pumped into the lungs forces the heart and lungs to work harder. Over time, if not repaired, this defect can increase the risk for other complications, including heart failure, high blood pressure in the lungs (called pulmonary hypertension), irregular heart rhythms (called arrhythmia), or stroke.

Types of VSD

An infant with a VSD can have one or more holes in different places of the septum. There are several names for these holes. Some common locations and names are:

- **Conoventricular VSD.** In general, this is a hole where portions of the ventricular septum should meet just below the pulmonary and aortic valves.

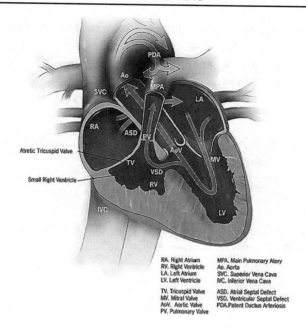

RA. Right Atrium
RV. Right Ventricle
LA. Left Atrium
LV. Left Ventricle

TV. Tricuspid Valve
MV. Mitral Valve
AoV. Aortic Valve
PV. Pulmonary Valve

MPA. Main Pulmonary Atery
Ao. Aorta
SVC. Superior Vena Cava
IVC. Inferior Vena Cava

ASD. Atrial Septal Defect
VSD. Ventricular Septal Defect
PDA.Patent Ductus Arteriosis

Figure 27.11. *Ventricular Septal Defect*

- **Perimembranous VSD.** This is a hole in the upper section of the ventricular septum.

- **Inlet VSD.** This is a hole in the septum near to where the blood enters the ventricles through the tricuspid and mitral valves. This type of VSD also might be part of another heart defect called an atrioventricular septal defect (AVSD).

- **Muscular VSD.** This is a hole in the lower, muscular part of the ventricular septum and is the most common type of VSD.

Occurrence

In a study in Atlanta, the Centers for Disease Control and Prevention (CDC) estimated that 42 of every 10,000 babies born had a VSD.

Causes and Risk Factors

The causes of heart defects (such as a VSD) among most babies are unknown. Some babies have heart defects because of changes in their genes or chromosomes. Heart defects also are thought to be caused by a combination of genes and other risk factors, such as the things the mother comes in contact with in the environment or what the mother eats or drinks or the medicines the mother uses.

Diagnosis

A VSD usually is diagnosed after a baby is born. The size of the VSD will influence what symptoms, if any, are present, and whether a doctor hears a heart murmur during a physical examination. Signs of a VSD might be present at birth or might not appear until well after birth. If the hole is small, it usually will close on its own and the baby might not show any signs of the defect. However, if the hole is large, the baby might have symptoms, including:

- Shortness of breath,
- Fast or heavy breathing,
- Sweating,
- Tiredness while feeding, or
- Poor weight gain.

During a physical examination the doctor might hear a distinct whooshing sound, called a heart murmur. If the doctor hears a heart murmur or other signs are present, the doctor can request one or more tests to confirm the diagnosis. The most common test is an echocardiogram (ECHO), which is an ultrasound of the heart that can show problems with the structure of the heart, show how large the hole is, and show how much blood is flowing through the hole.

Treatment

Treatments for a VSD depend on the size of the hole and the problems it might cause. Many VSDs are small and close on their own; if the hole is small and not causing any symptoms, the doctor will check the infant regularly to ensure there are no signs of heart failure and that the hole closes on its own. If the hole does not close on its own or if it is large, further actions might need to be taken.

Depending on the size of the hole, symptoms, and general health of the child, the doctor might recommend either cardiac catheterization or open-heart surgery to close the hole and restore normal blood flow. After surgery, the doctor will set up regular follow-up visits to make sure that the VSD remains closed. Most children who have a VSD that closes (either on its own or with surgery) live healthy lives.

Medicines

Some children will need medicines to help strengthen the heart muscle, lower their blood pressure, and help the body get rid of extra fluid.

Nutrition

Some babies with a VSD become tired while feeding and do not eat enough to gain weight. To make sure babies have a healthy weight gain, a special high-calorie formula might be prescribed. Some babies become extremely tired while feeding and might need to be fed through a feeding tube.

Chapter 28

Kidney Defects

Chapter Contents

Section 28.1

Ectopic Kidneys

This section includes text excerpted from "Ectopic Kidney," National
Institute of Diabetes and Digestive and Kidney Diseases (NIDDK),
June 2012. Reviewed December 2017.

What Are the Kidneys and What Do They Do?

The kidneys are two bean-shaped organs, each about the size of a
fist. They are located near the middle of the back, just below the rib
cage, one on each side of the spine. Every minute, a person's kidneys
filter about 3 ounces of blood, removing wastes and extra water. The
wastes and extra water make up the 1–2 quarts of urine a person produces each day. The urine flows to the bladder through tubes called
ureters where it is stored until being released through urination.

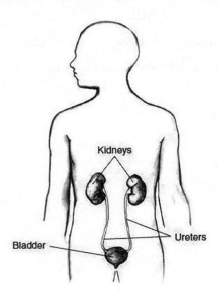

Figure 28.1. *Kidneys*

*The kidneys remove wastes and extra water from the blood to form urine. Urine flows
from the kidneys to the bladder through the ureters.*

What Is an Ectopic Kidney?

An ectopic kidney is a birth defect in which a kidney is located below, above, or on the opposite side of its usual position. About one in 900 people has an ectopic kidney.

What Causes an Ectopic Kidney?

During fetal development, a baby's kidneys first appear as buds inside the pelvis—the bowl shaped bone that supports the spine and holds up the digestive, urinary, and reproductive organs—near the bladder. As the kidneys develop, they move gradually toward their usual position in the back near the rib cage. Sometimes, one of the kidneys remains in the pelvis or stops moving before it reaches its usual position. In other cases, the kidney moves higher than the usual position. Rarely does a child have two ectopic kidneys.

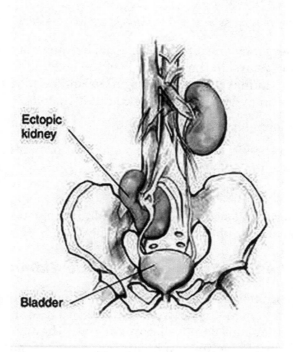

Figure 28.2. *Ectopic Kidney*

An ectopic kidney may remain in the pelvis, near the bladder.

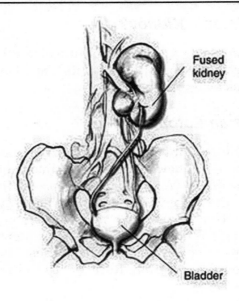

Figure 28.3. *Fused Kidney*

An ectopic kidney may cross over and become fused with the other kidney.

Most kidneys move toward the rib cage, but one may cross over so that both kidneys are on the same side of the body. When a crossover occurs, the two kidneys often grow together and become fused.

Factors that may lead to an ectopic kidney include:

- poor development of a kidney bud

- a defect in the kidney tissue responsible for prompting the kidney to move to its usual position

- genetic abnormalities

- the mother being sick or being exposed to an agent, such as a drug or chemical, that causes birth defects

What Are the Symptoms of an Ectopic Kidney?

An ectopic kidney may not cause any symptoms and may function normally, even though it is not in its usual position. Many people have an ectopic kidney and do not discover it until they have tests done for other reasons. Sometimes, a healthcare provider may discover an ectopic kidney after feeling a lump in the abdomen during an examination. In other cases, an ectopic kidney may cause abdominal pain or urinary problems.

What Are the Possible Complications of an Ectopic Kidney?

Possible complications of an ectopic kidney include problems with urine drainage from that kidney. Sometimes, urine can even flow backwards from the bladder to the kidney, a problem called vesicoureteral reflux (VUR).

Abnormal urine flow and the placement of the ectopic kidney can lead to various problems:

- **Infection.** Normally, urine flow washes out bacteria and keeps them from growing in the kidneys and urinary tract. When a kidney is out of the usual position, urine may get trapped in the ureter or in the kidney itself. Urine that remains in the urinary tract gives bacteria the chance to grow and spread. Symptoms of a urinary tract infection include frequent or painful urination, back or abdominal pain, fever, chills, and cloudy or foul smelling urine.

- **Stones.** Urinary stones form from substances found in the urine, such as calcium and oxalate. When urine remains in the urinary tract for too long, the risk that these substances will have time to form stones is increased. Symptoms of urinary stones include extreme pain in the back, side, or pelvis; blood in the urine; fever or chills; vomiting; and a burning feeling during urination.

- **Kidney damage.** If urine backs up all the way to the kidney, damage to the kidney can occur. As a result, the kidney can't filter wastes and extra water from the blood. One ectopic kidney, even when it has no function, will not cause kidney failure. The other kidney can usually perform the functions of two healthy kidneys. Total kidney failure happens only in rare cases when both kidneys are damaged.

- **Trauma.** If the ectopic kidney is in the lower abdomen or pelvis, it may be susceptible to injury from blunt trauma. People with an ectopic kidney who want to participate in body contact sports may want to wear protective gear.

How Is an Ectopic Kidney Diagnosed?

A healthcare provider may use one or more of the following imaging tests to diagnose an ectopic kidney:

- **Ultrasound.** An ultrasound uses a device, called a transducer, that bounces safe, painless sound waves off organs to create an image of their structure. The procedure is performed in a health-care provider's office, outpatient center, or hospital by a specially trained technician, and the images are interpreted by a radiologist—a doctor who specializes in medical imaging; anesthesia is not needed. The images can show the location of the kidneys.

- **Intravenous pyelogram (IVP).** An IVP is an X-ray of the urinary tract. A special dye, called contrast medium, is injected into a vein in the person's arm, travels through the body to the kidneys, and makes urine visible on the X-ray. The procedure is performed in a healthcare provider's office, outpatient center, or hospital by an X-ray technician, and the images are interpreted by a radiologist; anesthesia is not needed. An IVP can show a blockage in the urinary tract. In children, ultrasounds are usually done instead of IVPs.

- **Voiding cystourethrogram (VCUG).** A VCUG is an X-ray image of the bladder and urethra taken while the bladder is full and during urination, also called voiding. The bladder and urethra are filled with contrast medium to make the structures clearly visible on the X-ray images. The X-ray machine captures images of the contrast medium while the bladder is full and when the person urinates. The procedure is performed in a healthcare provider's office, outpatient center, or hospital by an X-ray technician supervised by a radiologist, who then interprets the images. Anesthesia is not needed, but sedation may be used for some people. The test can show abnormalities of the inside of the urethra and bladder and whether urine is backing up toward the kidneys during urination.

- **Radionuclide scan.** A radionuclide scan is an imaging technique that relies on the detection of small amounts of radiation after injection of radioactive chemicals. Because the dose of the radioactive chemicals is small, the risk of causing damage to cells is low. Special cameras and computers are used to create images of the radioactive chemicals as they pass through the kidneys. The procedure is performed in a healthcare provider's office, outpatient center, or hospital by a specially trained technician, and the images are interpreted by a radiologist; anesthesia is not needed. This test can show the location of an ectopic kidney and whether the ureters are blocked.

- **Magnetic resonance imaging (MRI).** MRI machines use radio waves and magnets to produce detailed pictures of the body's internal organs and soft tissues without using X-rays. An MRI may include the injection of contrast medium. With most MRI machines, the person lies on a table that slides into a tunnel shaped device that may be open ended or closed at one end; some newer machines are designed to allow the person to lie in a more open space. The procedure is performed in an outpatient center or hospital by a specially trained technician, and the images are interpreted by a radiologist; anesthesia is not needed though light sedation may be used for people with a fear of confined spaces. MRIs can show the location of the kidneys.

In addition to imaging tests, blood tests may be done to determine how well the kidneys are working. These tests are almost always normal in people with an ectopic kidney, even if it is badly damaged, because the other kidney usually has completely normal function.

How Is an Ectopic Kidney Treated?

No treatment for an ectopic kidney is needed if urinary function is normal and no blockage of the urinary tract is present. If tests show an obstruction, surgery may be needed to correct the position of the kidney to allow for better drainage of urine. Reflux can be corrected by surgery to alter the ureter or injection of a gel like liquid into the bladder wall near the opening of the ureter. If extensive kidney damage has occurred, surgery may be needed to remove the kidney. As long as the other kidney is working properly, losing one kidney should have no adverse health effects.

With the right testing and treatment, if needed, an ectopic kidney should cause no serious long-term health problems.

Eating, Diet, and Nutrition

Eating, diet, and nutrition have not been shown to play a role in causing or preventing an ectopic kidney.

Section 28.2

Horseshoe Kidney (Renal Fusion)

"Horseshoe Kidney (Renal Fusion)," © 2017 Omnigraphics.
Reviewed December 2017.

What Is Horseshoe Kidney?

Horseshoe kidney, a congenital disorder, happens when two kidneys fuse together forming a 'U' shape at the lower end or base. The 'U' shape looks like a horseshoe. The condition occurs during fetal development as the kidneys move to their normal position. About 1 in 500 children (mostly males) seems to be affected by horseshoe kidney. This condition leaves the kidneys susceptible to trauma and also involves risk factors for development of renal calculi or kidney cancer and is the most common type of renal fusion anomaly. The exact cause of the horseshoe kidney is unclear; however, problems with chromosomes can be a cause. Some genetic disorders such as Turner syndrome and Edwards syndrome can co-occur with the condition. Few other conditions that can occur along with horseshoe kidney include complications in the cardiovascular system, the central nervous system, or the genitourinary system, such as:

- Renal cancer, or polycystic kidney disease

- Kidney stones that lead to urinary tract obstruction

- Hydronephrosis, enlargement of kidneys due to urinary tract obstruction

- Wilms tumor, a tumor of the kidneys

- Cardiovascular or gastrointestinal complications

Symptoms of Horseshoe Kidney

In most cases, a child shows no symptoms. However, some kids may have pain in the belly or nausea, and other symptoms can include:

- Kidney stones

- Urinary tract infections

- Fever

- A sudden urge to urinate

- Foul-smelling urine

- Pain while urinating

- Incontinence (loss of control of urine)

- Problems urinating

Certain symptoms of horseshoe kidney may resemble other medical conditions; therefore, consulting a healthcare provider is mandatory. Horseshoe kidneys are more prone to get cancerous tumors than normal kidneys, even though kidney cancer is rare in children. Some symptoms of kidney tumor are mass in the belly, hematuria (blood in the urine), and flank pain.

Diagnosis of Horseshoe Kidney

Healthcare providers usually find horseshoe kidney while treating other conditions. The healthcare provider begins by asking questions about the child's symptoms, health history, and family history. The doctor may order diagnostic tests, including:

- **Renal ultrasound.** Images of blood vessels, tissues, and organs are taken using sound waves and computers during this painless test. A healthcare provider uses a device called a "transducer" that helps send the picture of the kidney to a video screen.

- **Blood test.** This is done to see if the kidneys are functioning properly.

- **Urine test.** This is done to detect chemicals in urine and signs of infection.

- **Voiding cystourethrogram (VCUG).** A type of X-ray that examines the urinary tract. The results of the X-ray would help understand if there is a reverse flow of urine into the ureters and kidneys.

- **Intravenous pyelogram (IVP).** An imaging technique that uses an X-ray to view the urinary tract. An intravenous contrast of dye is given so that the tract can be seen on film. IVP helps show the rate and path of urine flow through the tract.

Treatment of Horseshoe Kidney

A child with no symptoms may not need any treatment. There is no specific cure for horseshoe kidneys; however, the symptoms and related problems can be treated. The type of treatment will depend on the child's age, symptoms, severity of the condition, and general health. The healthcare provider will determine the treatment based on the extent of the disorder; the child's tolerance for medications, procedures, or therapies; and the parent's expectation and preference.

Possible Complications of Horseshoe Kidney

Some children with horseshoe kidneys may develop problems with their heart and blood vessels, nervous system, or genitourinary system. Children with this condition have kidneys placed closer to the front of the body than normal kidneys and hence are at risk for kidney injury. The healthcare provider may advise that the child wear a medical bracelet and avoid contact sports.

References

1. "What Is Horseshoe Kidney (Renal Fusion)?" Urology Care Foundation, n.d.

2. "Horseshoe Kidney (Renal Fusion) in Children," AdventistHealth.org, n.d.

3. "Horseshoe Kidney," Stanford Children's Health, n.d.

4. Gaillard, Frank; et al. "Horseshoe Kidney," Radiopaedia, n.d.

Section 28.3

Hydronephrosis

This section includes text excerpted from "Urine Blockage in Newborns," National Institute of Diabetes and Digestive and Kidney Diseases (NIDDK), September 2013. Reviewed December 2017.

Hydronephrosis is the most common problem found during prenatal ultrasound of a baby in the womb. The swelling may be easy to see or barely detectable. The results of hydronephrosis may be mild or severe, yet the long-term outcome for the child's health cannot always be predicted by the severity of swelling. Urine blockage may damage the developing kidneys and reduce their ability to filter. In the most severe cases of urine blockage, where little or no urine leaves the baby's bladder, the amount of amniotic fluid is reduced to the point that the baby's lung development is threatened. After birth, urine blockage may raise a child's risk of developing a urinary tract infection (UTI). Recurring UTIs can lead to more permanent kidney damage.

How Is Urine Blockage in Newborns Diagnosed?

Defects of the urinary tract may be diagnosed before or after the baby is born.

Diagnosis before Birth

Tests during pregnancy can help determine if the baby is developing normally in the womb.

- **Ultrasound.** Ultrasound uses a device called a transducer that bounces safe, painless sound waves off organs to create an image of their structure. A prenatal ultrasound can show internal organs within the baby. The procedure is performed in a health-care provider's office, outpatient center, or hospital by a specially trained technician, and the images are interpreted by:

  - a radiologist—a doctor who specializes in medical imaging, or

  - an obstetrician—a doctor who delivers babies.

471

The images can show enlarged kidneys, ureters, or bladders in babies

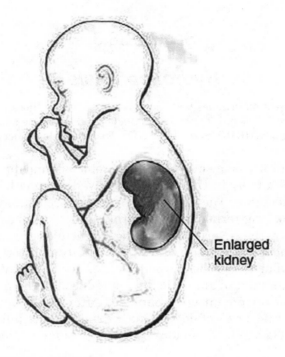

Figure 28.4. *Enlarged Kidney*

- **Amniocentesis.** Amniocentesis is a procedure in which amniotic fluid is removed from the mother's womb for testing. The procedure can be performed in the healthcare provider's office, and local anesthetic may be used. The healthcare provider inserts a thin needle through the abdomen into the uterus to obtain a small amount of amniotic fluid. Cells from the fluid are grown in a lab and then analyzed. The healthcare provider usually uses ultrasound to find the exact location of the baby. The test can show whether the baby has certain birth defects and how well the baby's lungs are developing.

- **Chorionic villus sampling (CVS).** CVS is the removal of a small piece of tissue from the placenta for testing. The procedure can be performed in the healthcare provider's office; anesthesia is not needed. The healthcare provider uses ultrasound to guide a thin tube or needle through the vagina or abdomen into the placenta. Cells are removed from the placenta and then analyzed. The test can show whether the baby has certain genetic defects.

Most healthy women do not need all of these tests. Ultrasound exams during pregnancy are routine. Amniocentesis and CVS are recommended only when a risk of genetic problems exists because of family history or a problem is detected during an ultrasound. Amniocentesis and CVS carry a slight risk of harming the baby and mother or ending the pregnancy in miscarriage, so the risks should be carefully considered.

Diagnosis after Birth

Different imaging techniques can be used in infants and children to determine the cause of urine blockage.

- **Ultrasound.** Ultrasound can be used to view the child's urinary tract. For infants, the image is clearer than could be achieved while the baby was in the womb.

- **Voiding cystourethrogram (VCUG).** VCUG is an X-ray image of the bladder and urethra taken while the bladder is full and during urination, also called voiding. The procedure is performed in an outpatient center or hospital by an X-ray technician supervised by a radiologist, who then interprets the images. While anesthesia is not needed, sedation may be used for some children. The bladder and urethra are filled with a special dye, called contrast medium, to make the structures clearly visible on the X-ray images. The X-ray machine captures images of the contrast medium while the bladder is full and when the child urinates. The test can show reflux or blockage of the bladder due to an obstruction, such as PUV.

- **Radionuclide scan.** A radionuclide scan is an imaging technique that detects small amounts of radiation after a person is injected with radioactive chemicals. The dose of the radioactive chemicals is small; therefore, the risk of causing damage to cells is low. Radionuclide scans are performed in an outpatient center or hospital by a specially trained technician, and the images are interpreted by a radiologist. Anesthesia is not needed. Special cameras and computers are used to create images of the radioactive chemicals as they pass through the kidneys. Radioactive chemicals injected into the blood can provide information about kidney function.

How Is Urine Blockage in Newborns Treated?

Treatment for urine blockage depends on the cause and severity of the blockage. Hydronephrosis discovered before the baby is born rarely requires immediate action, especially if it is only on one side. The condition often goes away without any treatment before or after birth. The healthcare provider should keep track of the condition with frequent ultrasounds.

Surgery

If the urine blockage threatens the life of the unborn baby, a fetal surgeon may recommend surgery to insert a shunt or correct the problem causing the blockage. A shunt is a small tube that can be inserted into the baby's bladder to release urine into the amniotic sac. The procedure is similar to amniocentesis, in that a needle is inserted through the mother's abdomen. Ultrasound guides placement of the shunt, which is attached to the end of the needle. Alternatively, an endoscope—a small, flexible tube with a light—can be used to place a shunt or to repair the problem causing the blockage. Fetal surgery carries many risks, so it is performed only in special circumstances, such as when the amniotic fluid is absent and the baby's lungs are not developing or when the kidneys are severely damaged.

If the urinary defect does not correct itself after the child is born, and the child continues to have urine blockage, surgery may be needed to remove the obstruction and restore urine flow. The decision to operate depends on the degree of blockage. After surgery, a small tube, called a stent, may be placed in the ureter or urethra to keep it open temporarily while healing occurs.

Antibiotics

Antibiotics are bacteria-fighting medications. A child with possible urine blockage or VUR may be given antibiotics to prevent urinary tract infections (UTIs) from developing until the urinary defect corrects itself or is corrected with surgery.

Intermittent Catheterization

Intermittent catheterization may be used for a child with urinary retention due to a nerve disease. The parent or guardian, and later the child, is taught to drain the bladder by inserting a thin tube, called a catheter, through the urethra to the bladder. Emptying the bladder in this way helps to decrease kidney damage, urine leakage, and UTIs.

Eating, Diet, and Nutrition

Researchers have not found that a mother's eating, diet, and nutrition play a role in causing or preventing urine blockage in newborns.

Section 28.4

Kidney Dysplasia

This section includes text excerpted from "Kidney Dysplasia," National Institute of Diabetes and Digestive and Kidney Diseases (NIDDK), July 2015.

What Is Kidney Dysplasia?

Kidney dysplasia is a condition in which the internal structures of one or both of a fetus' kidneys do not develop normally while in the womb. During normal development, two thin tubes of muscle called ureters grow into the kidneys and branch out to form a network of tiny structures called tubules. The tubules collect urine as the fetus grows in the womb. In kidney dysplasia, the tubules fail to branch out completely. Urine that would normally flow through the tubules has nowhere to go. Urine collects inside the affected kidney and forms fluid filled sacs called cysts. The cysts replace normal kidney tissue and prevent the kidney from functioning.

Kidney dysplasia can affect one kidney or both kidneys. Babies with severe kidney dysplasia affecting both kidneys generally do not survive birth. Those who do survive may need the following early in life:

- Blood filtering treatments called dialysis

- a kidney transplant

- Children with dysplasia in only one kidney have normal kidney function if the other kidney is unaffected. Those with mild dysplasia of both kidneys may not need dialysis or a kidney transplant for several years.

Kidney dysplasia is also called renal dysplasia or multicystic dysplastic kidney.

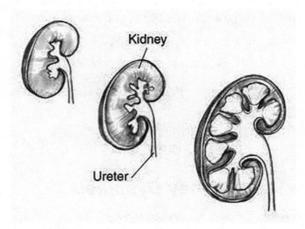

Figure 28.5. *The Formation of Tubules*

During normal development, two thin tubes of muscle called ureters grow into the kidneys and branch out to form a network of tiny structures called tubules.

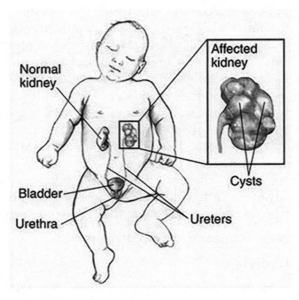

Figure 28.6. *Kidney Dysplasia in One Kidney*

What Are the Kidneys and What Do They Do?

The kidneys are two bean shaped organs, each about the size of a fist. They are located just below the rib cage, one on each side of the spine. Every day, the two kidneys filter about 120–150 quarts of blood to produce about 1–2 quarts of urine, which is composed of wastes and extra fluid. Children produce less urine than adults—the amount they produce depends on their age.

The urine flows from the kidneys to the bladder through the two ureters, one on each side of the bladder. The bladder stores urine. The muscles of the bladder wall remain relaxed while the bladder fills with urine. As the bladder fills to capacity, signals sent to the brain tell a person to find a toilet soon. When the bladder empties, urine flows out of the body through a tube called the urethra, located at the bottom of the bladder.

The kidneys, ureters, bladder, and urethra are parts of the urinary tract.

What Causes Kidney Dysplasia?

Genetic factors can cause kidney dysplasia. Genes pass information from both parents to the child and determine the child's traits. Sometimes, parents may pass a gene that has changed, or mutated, causing kidney dysplasia.

Genetic syndromes that affect multiple body systems can also cause kidney dysplasia. A syndrome is a group of symptoms or conditions that may seem unrelated yet are thought to have the same genetic cause. A baby with kidney dysplasia due to a genetic syndrome might also have problems of the digestive tract, nervous system, heart and blood vessels, muscles and skeleton, or other parts of the urinary tract.

A baby may also develop kidney dysplasia if his or her mother takes certain prescription medications during pregnancy, such as some used to treat seizures and high blood pressure. A mother's use of illegal drugs, such as cocaine, during pregnancy may also cause kidney dysplasia in her unborn child.

How Common Is Kidney Dysplasia?

Kidney dysplasia is a common condition. Scientists estimate that kidney dysplasia affects about 1 in 4,000 babies. This estimate may be low because some people with kidney dysplasia are never diagnosed with the condition. About half of the babies diagnosed with this condition have other urinary tract defects.

Who Is More Likely to Develop Kidney Dysplasia?

Babies who are more likely to develop kidney dysplasia include those:

- whose parents have the genetic traits for the condition.
- with certain genetic syndromes affecting multiple body systems.
- whose mothers used certain prescription medications or illegal drugs during pregnancy.

What Are the Signs of Kidney Dysplasia?

Many babies with kidney dysplasia in only one kidney have no signs of the condition. In some cases, the affected kidney may be enlarged at birth and may cause pain.

What Are the Complications of Kidney Dysplasia?

The complications of kidney dysplasia can include:

- **Hydronephrosis of the working kidney.** A baby with kidney dysplasia in only one kidney might have other urinary tract defects. When other defects in the urinary tract block the flow of urine, the urine backs up and causes the kidneys and ureters to swell, a condition called hydronephrosis. If left untreated, hydronephrosis can damage the working kidney and reduce its ability to filter blood. Kidney damage may lead to chronic kidney disease (CKD) and kidney failure.
- **A urinary tract infection (UTI).** A urine blockage may increase a baby's chance of developing a UTI. Recurring UTIs can also lead to kidney damage.
- **High blood pressure.**
- **Kidney cancer.** A slightly increased chance of developing kidney cancer.

How Is Kidney Dysplasia Diagnosed?

Healthcare providers may be able to diagnose kidney dysplasia during a woman's pregnancy using a fetal ultrasound, also called a fetal sonogram. Ultrasound uses a device, called a transducer, that bounces safe, painless sound waves off organs to create an image of their structure. Fetal ultrasound is a test done during pregnancy to create images of the fetus in the womb. A specially trained technician performs the procedure in a healthcare provider's office, an outpatient center, or a hospital, and an obstetrician, or a radiologist interprets the images. An obstetrician is a doctor who specializes in pregnancy and childbirth. A radiologist is a doctor who specializes in medical imaging. The patient—in this case, the fetus' mother—does not need anesthesia for this procedure. The images can show defects in the fetus' kidneys and other parts of the urinary tract.

Healthcare providers do not always diagnose kidney dysplasia before a baby is born. After birth, healthcare providers often diagnose kidney dysplasia during an evaluation of the child for a UTI or another medical condition. A healthcare provider uses ultrasound to diagnose kidney dysplasia after the baby is born.

How Is Kidney Dysplasia Treated?

If the condition is limited to one kidney and the baby has no signs of kidney dysplasia, no treatment may be necessary. However, the baby should have regular checkups that include:

- checking blood pressure.

- testing blood to measure kidney function.

- testing urine for albumin, a protein most often found in blood. Albumin in the urine may be a sign of kidney damage.

- performing periodic ultrasounds to monitor the damaged kidney and to make sure the functioning kidney continues to grow and remains healthy.

How Can Kidney Dysplasia Be Prevented?

Researchers have not found a way to prevent kidney dysplasia caused by genetic factors or certain genetic syndromes. Pregnant women can prevent kidney dysplasia by avoiding the use of certain prescription medications or illegal drugs during pregnancy. Pregnant women should talk with their healthcare provider before taking any medications during pregnancy.

What Is the Long-Term Outlook for a Child with Kidney Dysplasia in Only One Kidney?

The long-term outlook for a child with kidney dysplasia in only one kidney is generally good. A person with one working kidney, a condition called solitary kidney, can grow normally and may have few, if any, health problems.

The affected kidney may shrink as the child grows. By age 10, the affected kidney may no longer be visible on X-ray or ultrasound. Children and adults with only one working kidney should have regular checkups to test for high blood pressure and kidney damage. A child with urinary tract problems that lead to failure of the working kidney may eventually need dialysis or a kidney transplant.

What Is the Long-Term Outlook for a Child with Kidney Dysplasia in Both Kidneys?

The long-term outlook for a child with kidney dysplasia in both kidneys is different from the long-term outlook for a child with one dysplastic kidney. A child with kidney dysplasia in both kidneys:

- is more likely to develop CKD.

- needs close follow-up with a pediatric nephrologist—a doctor who specializes in caring for children with kidney disease. Children who live in areas that don't have a pediatric nephrologist available can see a nephrologist who cares for both children and adults.

- may eventually need dialysis or a kidney transplant.

Eating, Diet, and Nutrition

Researchers have not found that eating, diet, and nutrition play a role in causing or preventing kidney dysplasia.

Section 28.5

Renal Agenesis

This section includes text excerpted from "Renal Agenesis,"
Genetic and Rare Diseases Information Center (GARD), National
Center for Advancing Translational Sciences (NCATS), July 1, 2014.
Reviewed December 2017.

Renal agenesis (RA) is a form of renal tract malformation characterized by the complete absence of development of one or both kidneys (unilateral RA or bilateral RA respectively; see these terms), accompanied by absent ureter(s).

Epidemiology

The annual incidence of RA is estimated at around 1/2,000. Fetal prevalence of bilateral renal agenesis in Europe has been estimated at 1/8,500.

Clinical Description

Most patients with unilateral RA are asymptomatic if the other kidney is fully functional and the disease is commonly detected as a chance observation. However, hypertension, proteinuria, and renal failure may develop in the long run (20–50 percent of cases at the age of 30). Unilateral RA is occasionally associated with genital tract anomalies on the same side (e.g., seminal vesicle hypoplasia and absence of the vas deferens), cardiac anomalies (such as atrial or ventricular septal defects) and/or gastrointestinal anomalies (such as anal atresia). Bilateral RA is characterized by complete absence of kidney development, absent ureters and subsequent absence of fetal renal function resulting in Potter sequence with pulmonary hypoplasia related to oligohydramnios, which is fatal shortly after birth.

Etiology

Renal agenesis results from a developmental failure of the ureteric bud and the metanephric mesenchyme (MM). Unilateral renal agenesis can be caused by mutations in many genes, such as *RET* (10q11.2), *BMP4* (14q22-q23), *FRAS1* (4q21.21), *FREM1* (9p22.3), or *UPK3A* (22q13.31). A few cases of bilateral renal agenesis have been found to be caused by mutations in the *RET*, *FGF20* (8p22) or *ITGA8* (10p13) genes. Maternal diabetes mellitus or use of specific drugs during pregnancy can also result in renal agenesis.

Genetic Counseling

In familial cases, unilateral RA is inherited in an autosomal dominant manner with incomplete penetrance. Bilateral RA is inherited autosomal recessively.

Chapter 29

Liver and Pancreatic Defects

Chapter Contents

Section 29.1

Biliary Atresia

This section includes text excerpted from "Biliary Atresia,"
National Institute of Diabetes and Digestive and Kidney
Diseases (NIDDK), September 2017.

What Is Biliary Atresia?

Biliary atresia is a condition in infants in which the bile ducts—
tubes inside and outside the liver—are scarred and blocked. Bile ducts
carry bile from the liver to the gallbladder for storage, and to the first
part of the small intestine, also called the duodenum, for use in digestion. In infants with biliary atresia, bile can't flow into the intestine,
so bile builds up in the liver and damages it. The damage leads to
scarring, loss of liver tissue and function, and cirrhosis.

Biliary atresia is life-threatening, but with treatment, most infants
with biliary atresia survive to adulthood.

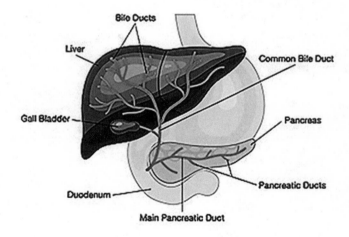

Figure 29.1. *Bile Ducts*

*Bile ducts are tubes that carry bile from the liver to the gallbladder and the duode-
num.*

Are There Different Types of Biliary Atresia?

Doctors have identified different types of biliary atresia.

Biliary Atresia without Birth Defects

In the most common type of biliary atresia, infants have no other major birth defects. Doctors may call this type of biliary atresia perinatal or isolated biliary atresia. A recent North American study found that 84 percent of infants with biliary atresia have this type.

Biliary Atresia with Birth Defects

Some infants have major birth defects—including problems with the heart, spleen, or intestines—along with biliary atresia. Doctors may call this fetal or embryonic biliary atresia. A recent North American study found that 16 percent of infants with biliary atresia have major birth defects.

How Common Is Biliary Atresia?

Biliary atresia is rare and affects about 1 out of every 12,000 infants in the United States.

Who Is More Likely to Have Biliary Atresia?

Biliary atresia only occurs in newborn infants. The disease is slightly more common in female infants and in infants with Asian or African American heritage.

What Are the Complications of Biliary Atresia?

Complications of biliary atresia include failure to thrive and malnutrition, cirrhosis and related complications, and liver failure.

Without treatment, infants with biliary atresia would develop cirrhosis within 6 months and liver failure within 1 year. By age 2, untreated infants would need a liver transplant to survive.

Early treatment with a surgery called the Kasai procedure may slow or, in some cases, prevent the development of cirrhosis and liver failure. Even with treatment, about half of children with biliary atresia will need a liver transplant by age 2. Two-thirds will need a liver transplant sometime during childhood.

Malnutrition

Even after treatment with the Kasai procedure, children with biliary atresia may have reduced bile flow to the small intestine and liver damage, leading to malnutrition and related problems with growth, such as failure to thrive.

Cirrhosis and Related Complications

Cirrhosis is a condition in which the liver breaks down and is unable to work normally. Scar tissue replaces healthy liver tissue, partly blocking the flow of blood through the liver. In the early stages of cirrhosis, the liver continues to work. As cirrhosis gets worse, the liver begins to fail.

In children with biliary atresia, cirrhosis may cause complications, including portal hypertension. Portal hypertension is high blood pressure in the portal vein, a blood vessel that carries blood from the intestines to the liver.

Portal hypertension may lead to specific complications, including:

- a buildup of fluid in the abdomen, called ascites. Infection of this fluid can be very dangerous.

- enlarged blood vessels, called varices, which can develop in the esophagus, stomach, or both. Varices can break open and cause life-threatening bleeding in the digestive tract.

Liver Failure

With liver failure, also called end-stage liver disease, the liver can no longer perform important functions or replace damaged cells. Infants and children with liver failure need a liver transplant to survive.

What Are the Symptoms of Biliary Atresia?

Typically, the first sign of biliary atresia is yellowing of the skin and whites of the eyes, called jaundice, which results from the buildup of bile in the body. Bile contains a reddish-yellow substance called bilirubin.

Infants often have jaundice in the first 2 weeks of life, so it is not easy to identify biliary atresia in newborn infants. Jaundice that lasts beyond 3 weeks of age may be the first sign of biliary atresia. Infants with biliary atresia typically develop jaundice by 3–6 weeks of age.

Infants with biliary atresia may also have pale yellow, gray, or white stools. Stools change color because bilirubin is not reaching the intestines and passing out of the body in the stool.

What Causes Biliary Atresia?

Experts don't know what causes biliary atresia. Research suggests that infants develop biliary atresia in the womb or shortly after birth. Experts are trying to find out if one or more of the following factors could play a role in causing biliary atresia:

- infections with certain viruses
- coming into contact with harmful chemicals
- problems with the immune system
- a problem during liver and bile duct development in the womb
- certain genes or changes in genes—called mutations—that may increase the chances of developing biliary atresia

Biliary atresia is not an inherited disease, meaning it does not pass from parent to child.

How Do Doctors Diagnose Biliary Atresia?

To diagnose biliary atresia, a doctor will ask about your infant's medical and family history, perform a physical exam, and order a series of tests. Experts recommend testing for biliary atresia and other health problems in infants who still have jaundice 3 weeks after birth.

If test results suggest that an infant is likely to have biliary atresia, the next step is surgery to confirm the diagnosis.

Doctors may refer children with suspected biliary atresia to specialists, such as pediatric gastroenterologists, pediatric hepatologists, or pediatric surgeons.

Family and Medical History

The doctor will ask about your infant's family and medical history. The doctor will also ask about symptoms such as jaundice and changes in stool color.

Physical Exam

During a physical exam, the doctor may:

- examine the infant's body for signs of jaundice

- examine the infant's body for other birth defects that sometimes occur along with biliary atresia

- feel the infant's abdomen to check for an enlarged liver or spleen, which may be signs of biliary atresia

- check the color of the infant's stool and urine

What Tests Do Doctors Use to Diagnose Biliary Atresia?

Doctors may order some or all of the following tests to diagnose biliary atresia and rule out other health problems. Doctors may perform several tests because many other diseases can cause signs that are like the signs of biliary atresia.

Blood Tests

A healthcare professional may take a blood sample from the infant and send the sample to a lab. Doctors may use blood tests to measure bilirubin levels and to check for signs of liver disease.

Ultrasound

Ultrasound uses a device called a transducer, which bounces safe, painless sound waves off organs to create images of their structure. Using ultrasound, doctors can rule out other health problems and look for signs that suggest an infant may have biliary atresia. However, an ultrasound cannot confirm a diagnosis of biliary atresia.

Hepatobiliary Scan

A hepatobiliary scan is an imaging test that uses a small amount of safe radioactive material to create an image of the liver and bile ducts. The test can show if and where bile flow is blocked.

Liver Biopsy

During a liver biopsy, a doctor will take pieces of tissue from the liver. A pathologist will examine the tissue under a microscope to look for signs of damage or disease. A liver biopsy can show whether an infant is likely to have biliary atresia. A biopsy can also help rule out or identify other liver problems.

How Do Doctors Perform Surgery to Confirm the Diagnosis of Biliary Atresia?

During diagnostic surgery, a pediatric surgeon makes a cut in the infant's abdomen to directly examine the liver and bile ducts. Alternatively, surgeons may use a device called a laparoscope, which is inserted through a small incision and does not require the abdomen to be opened. If the surgeon confirms that the infant has biliary atresia, the surgeon will usually perform surgery to treat biliary atresia right away.

How Do Doctors Treat Biliary Atresia?

Doctors treat biliary atresia with a surgery called the Kasai procedure and eventually, in most cases, a liver transplant. Thanks to advances in treatment, more than 80–90 percent of infants with biliary atresia survive to adulthood.

The Kasai Procedure

The Kasai procedure is usually the first treatment for biliary atresia. The Kasai procedure does not cure biliary atresia. However, if the procedure is successful, it may slow liver damage and delay or prevent complications and the need for a liver transplant. The earlier the procedure is done, the more effective it may be.

During the procedure, a surgeon removes the damaged bile ducts outside the liver. The surgeon uses a loop of the infant's own small intestine to replace the damaged bile ducts. If the surgery is successful, bile will flow directly from the liver to the small intestine. Within 3 months of the procedure, one has an idea of whether the surgery has worked or not. After a successful surgery, most infants no longer have jaundice and have a reduced risk of developing complications of advancing liver disease.

Complications. After the procedure, a common complication is infection of the liver, called cholangitis. Doctors may prescribe antibiotics after surgery to help prevent this infection. If cholangitis occurs, doctors treat it with antibiotics, usually intravenous (IV) antibiotics given in the hospital.

If the procedure is not successful, the flow of bile will remain blocked. After an unsuccessful procedure, infants will develop complications of biliary atresia and will usually need a liver transplant by age 2. Even after a successful surgery, most children will slowly develop complications of biliary atresia, over years or decades, and will eventually need a liver transplant. In some cases, after a successful procedure, children never need a liver transplant.

Liver Transplant

If biliary atresia leads to serious complications, the infant or child will need a liver transplant. A liver transplant is surgery to remove a diseased or injured liver and replace it with a healthy liver from another person, called a donor.

Most children with biliary atresia eventually need a liver transplant, even after a successful Kasai procedure.

How Does Biliary Atresia Affect Nutrition?

Even after treatment with the Kasai procedure, children with biliary atresia may have reduced bile flow to the small intestine and liver damage, leading to:

• problems digesting fats and absorbing fat-soluble vitamins

• loss of appetite

• a faster metabolism and a need for more calories

• low levels of protein, vitamins, and minerals

These problems may cause children with biliary atresia to become malnourished, and they may not grow normally.

What Should Infants and Children with Biliary Atresia Eat?

To make sure infants and children with biliary atresia get enough nutrients and calories, doctors may recommend:

• a special eating plan

• a special formula for formula-fed infants

• supplements, which may be added to breast milk, formula, or food

Supplements for biliary atresia include vitamins—especially fat-soluble vitamins—and medium-chain triglyceride (MCT) oil. MCT oil adds calories to foods and is easier to digest without bile than other fats. Doctors may recommend other types of supplements as well.

If a child isn't getting enough nutrients from food and supplements taken by mouth, a doctor may recommend using a feeding tube, called a nasogastric feeding tube, to provide high-calorie liquid directly to the stomach. In some cases, children with biliary atresia need to receive nutrition through an intravenous (IV) line. This type of feeding is called total parenteral nutrition (TPN).

Your child's doctor or a dietitian can recommend a specific eating plan and supplements for your child.

What Should Infants and Children Eat after a Liver Transplant?

After a liver transplant, most infants and children can eat a healthy, balanced diet that is normal for their age.

Section 29.2

Cystic Fibrosis (CF)

This section includes text excerpted from "Cystic Fibrosis," National Heart, Lung, and Blood Institute (NHLBI), December 26, 2013. Reviewed December 2017.

What Is Cystic Fibrosis (CF)?

Cystic fibrosis, or CF, is an inherited disease of the secretory glands. Secretory glands include glands that make mucus and sweat.

"Inherited" means the disease is passed from parents to children through genes. People who have CF inherit two faulty genes for the disease—one from each parent. The parents likely don't have the disease themselves.

CF mainly affects the lungs, pancreas, liver, intestines, sinuses, and sex organs.

What Causes CF?

A defect in the cystic fibrosis transmembrane conductance regulator (*CFTR*) gene causes cystic fibrosis (CF). This gene makes a protein that controls the movement of salt and water in and out of your body's cells. In people who have CF, the gene makes a protein that doesn't work well. This causes thick, sticky mucus and very salty sweat.

Research suggests that the CFTR protein also affects the body in other ways. This may help explain other symptoms and complications of CF. More than a thousand known defects can affect the *CFTR* gene. The type of defect you or your child has may affect the severity of CF. Other genes also may play a role in the severity of the disease.

How Is Cystic Fibrosis Inherited?

Every person inherits two *CFTR* genes—one from each parent. Children who inherit a faulty *CFTR* gene from each parent will have CF.

Children who inherit one faulty *CFTR* gene and one normal *CFTR* gene are "CF carriers." CF carriers usually have no symptoms of CF and live normal lives. However, they can pass the faulty *CFTR* gene to their children.

Figure 29.2 shows how two parents who are both CF carriers can pass the faulty *CFTR* gene to their children.

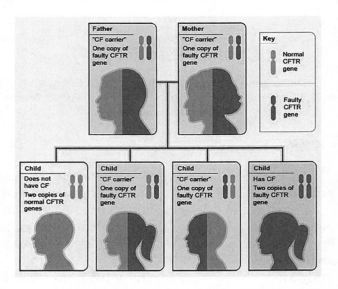

Figure 29.2. *Example of an Inheritance Pattern for Cystic Fibrosis (CF)*

The figure shows how CFTR genes are inherited. A person inherits two copies of the CFTR gene—one from each parent. If each parent has a normal CFTR gene and a faulty CFTR gene, each child has a 25 percent chance of inheriting two normal genes; a 50 percent chance of inheriting one normal gene and one faulty gene; and a 25 percent chance of inheriting two faulty genes.

Who Is at Risk for CF?

CF affects both males and females and people from all racial and ethnic groups. However, the disease is most common among Caucasians of Northern European descent. CF also is common among Latinos and American Indians, especially the Pueblo and Zuni. The disease is less common among African Americans and Asian Americans.

More than 10 million Americans are carriers of a faulty *CF* gene. Many of them don't know that they're CF carriers.

What Are the Signs and Symptoms of CF?

The signs and symptoms of CF vary from person to person and over time. Sometimes you'll have few symptoms. Other times, your symptoms may become more severe. One of the first signs of CF that parents may notice is that their baby's skin tastes salty when kissed, or the baby doesn't pass stool when first born. Most of the other signs and symptoms of CF happen later. They're related to how CF affects the respiratory, digestive, or reproductive systems of the body.

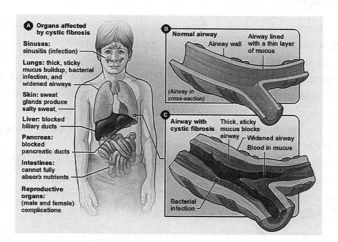

Figure 29.3. *Cystic Fibrosis*

Figure A shows the organs that cystic fibrosis (CF) can affect. Figure B shows a cross-section of a normal airway. Figure C shows an airway with CF. The widened airway is blocked by thick, sticky mucus that contains blood and bacteria.

Respiratory System Signs and Symptoms

People who have CF have thick, sticky mucus that builds up in their airways. This buildup of mucus makes it easier for bacteria to grow and cause infections. Infections can block the airways and cause frequent coughing that brings up thick sputum (spit) or mucus that's sometimes bloody.

People who have CF tend to have lung infections caused by unusual germs that don't respond to standard antibiotics. For example, lung infections caused by bacteria called mucoid *Pseudomonas* are much more common in people who have CF than in those who don't. An infection caused by these bacteria may be a sign of CF.

People who have CF have frequent bouts of sinusitis, an infection of the sinuses. The sinuses are hollow air spaces around the eyes, nose, and forehead. Frequent bouts of bronchitis and pneumonia also can occur. These infections can cause long-term lung damage.

As CF gets worse, you may have more serious problems, such as pneumothorax or bronchiectasis.

Some people who have CF also develop nasal polyps (growths in the nose) that may require surgery.

Digestive System Signs and Symptoms

In CF, mucus can block tubes, or ducts, in your pancreas (an organ in your abdomen). These blockages prevent enzymes from reaching your intestines.

As a result, your intestines can't fully absorb fats and proteins. This can cause ongoing diarrhea or bulky, foul-smelling, greasy stools. Intestinal blockages also may occur, especially in newborns. Too much gas or severe constipation in the intestines may cause stomach pain and discomfort.

A hallmark of CF in children is poor weight gain and growth. These children are unable to get enough nutrients from their food because of the lack of enzymes to help absorb fats and proteins.

As CF gets worse, other problems may occur, such as:

- **Pancreatitis.** This is a condition in which the pancreas become inflamed, which causes pain.

- **Rectal prolapse.** Frequent coughing or problems passing stools may cause rectal tissue from inside you to move out of your rectum.

- **Liver disease** due to inflamed or blocked bile ducts.

- **Diabetes.**

- **Gallstones.**

Reproductive System Signs and Symptoms

Men who have CF are infertile because they're born without a vas deferens. The vas deferens is a tube that delivers sperm from the testes to the penis.

Women who have CF may have a hard time getting pregnant because of mucus blocking the cervix or other CF complications.

Other Signs, Symptoms, and Complications

Other signs and symptoms of CF are related to an upset of the balance of minerals in your blood.

CF causes your sweat to become very salty. As a result, your body loses large amounts of salt when you sweat. This can cause dehydration (a lack of fluid in your body), increased heart rate, fatigue (tiredness), weakness, decreased blood pressure, heat stroke, and, rarely, death.

CF also can cause clubbing and low bone density. Clubbing is the widening and rounding of the tips of your fingers and toes. This sign develops late in CF because your lungs aren't moving enough oxygen into your bloodstream.

Low bone density also tends to occur late in CF. It can lead to bone-thinning disorders called osteoporosis and osteopenia.

How Is CF Diagnosed?

Doctors diagnose CF based on the results from various tests.

Newborn Screening

All States screen newborns for CF using a genetic test or a blood test. The genetic test shows whether a newborn has faulty *CFTR* genes. The blood test shows whether a newborn's pancreas is working properly.

Sweat Test

If a genetic test or blood test suggests CF, a doctor will confirm the diagnosis using a sweat test. This test is the most useful test for diagnosing CF. A sweat test measures the amount of salt in sweat.

For this test, the doctor triggers sweating on a small patch of skin on an arm or leg. He or she rubs the skin with a sweat-producing chemical and then uses an electrode to provide a mild electrical current. This may cause a tingling or warm feeling.

Sweat is collected on a pad or paper and then analyzed. The sweat test usually is done twice. High salt levels confirm a diagnosis of CF.

Other Tests

If you or your child has CF, your doctor may recommend other tests, such as:

- **Genetic tests** to find out what type of CFTR defect is causing your CF.

- **A chest X-ray.** This test creates pictures of the structures in your chest, such as your heart, lungs, and blood vessels. A chest X-ray can show whether your lungs are inflamed or scarred, or whether they trap air.

- **A sinus X-ray.** This test may show signs of sinusitis, a complication of CF.

- **Lung function tests.** These tests measure how much air you can breathe in and out, how fast you can breathe air out, and how well your lungs deliver oxygen to your blood.

- **A sputum culture.** For this test, your doctor will take a sample of your sputum (spit) to see whether bacteria are growing in it. If you have bacteria called mucoid *Pseudomonas*, you may have more advanced CF that needs aggressive treatment.

Prenatal Screening

If you're pregnant, prenatal genetic tests can show whether your fetus has CF. These tests include amniocentesis and chorionic villus sampling (CVS).

In amniocentesis, your doctor inserts a hollow needle through your abdominal wall into your uterus. He or she removes a small amount of fluid from the sac around the baby. The fluid is tested to see whether both of the baby's *CFTR* genes are normal.

In CVS, your doctor threads a thin tube through the vagina and cervix to the placenta. The doctor removes a tissue sample from the placenta using gentle suction. The sample is tested to see whether the baby has CF.

CF Carrier Testing

People who have one normal *CFTR* gene and one faulty *CFTR* gene are CF carriers. CF carriers usually have no symptoms of CF and live normal lives. However, carriers can pass faulty *CFTR* genes on to their children.

If you have a family history of CF or a partner who has CF (or a family history of it) and you're planning a pregnancy, you may want to find out whether you're a CF carrier.

A genetics counselor can test a blood or saliva sample to find out whether you have a faulty *CF* gene. This type of testing can detect faulty *CF* genes in 9 out of 10 cases.

How Is CF Treated?

Cystic fibrosis (CF) has no cure. However, treatments have greatly improved in recent years. The goals of CF treatment include:

- Preventing and controlling lung infections
- Loosening and removing thick, sticky mucus from the lungs
- Preventing or treating blockages in the intestines
- Providing enough nutrition
- Preventing dehydration (a lack of fluid in the body)

Depending on the severity of CF, you or your child may be treated in a hospital.

Specialists Involved

If you or your child has CF, you may be treated by a CF specialist. This is a doctor who is familiar with the complex nature of CF.

Often, a CF specialist works with a medical team of nurses, physical therapists, dietitians, and social workers. CF specialists often are located at major medical centers.

The United States also has more than 100 CF Care Centers. These centers have teams of doctors, nurses, dietitians, respiratory therapists, physical therapists, and social workers who have special training related to CF care. Most CF Care Centers have pediatric and adult programs or clinics.

Treatment for Lung Problems

The main treatments for lung problems in people who have CF are chest physical therapy (CPT), exercise, and medicines. Your doctor also may recommend a pulmonary rehabilitation (PR) program.

Chest Physical Therapy (CPT)

CPT also is called chest clapping or percussion. It involves pounding your chest and back over and over with your hands or a device to loosen the mucus from your lungs so that you can cough it up.

You might sit down or lie on your stomach with your head down while you do CPT. Gravity and force help drain the mucus from your lungs.

Some people find CPT hard or uncomfortable to do. Several devices have been developed that may help with CPT, such as:

- An electric chest clapper, known as a mechanical percussor.

- An inflatable therapy vest that uses high-frequency airwaves to force the mucus that's deep in your lungs toward your upper airways so you can cough it up.

- A small, handheld device that you exhale through. The device causes vibrations that dislodge the mucus.

- A mask that creates vibrations that help break the mucus loose from your airway walls.

Breathing techniques also may help dislodge mucus so you can cough it up. These techniques include forcing out a couple of short breaths or deeper breaths and then doing relaxed breathing. This may help loosen the mucus in your lungs and open your airways.

Exercise

Aerobic exercise that makes you breathe harder can help loosen the mucus in your airways so you can cough it up. Exercise also helps improve your overall physical condition.

However, CF causes your sweat to become very salty. As a result, your body loses large amounts of salt when you sweat. Thus, your doctor may recommend a high-salt diet or salt supplements to maintain the balance of minerals in your blood.

If you exercise regularly, you may be able to cut back on your CPT. However, you should check with your doctor first.

Medicines

If you have CF, your doctor may prescribe antibiotics, anti-inflammatory medicines, bronchodilators, or medicines to help clear the mucus. These medicines help treat or prevent lung infections, reduce swelling and open up the airways, and thin mucus. If you have mutations in a gene called *G551D*, which occurs in about 5 percent of people who have CF, your doctor may prescribe the oral medicine ivacaftor (approved for people with CF who are 6 years of age and older).

Antibiotics are the main treatment to prevent or treat lung infections. Your doctor may prescribe oral, inhaled, or intravenous (IV) antibiotics.

Oral antibiotics often are used to treat mild lung infections. Inhaled antibiotics may be used to prevent or control infections caused by the bacteria mucoid *Pseudomonas*. For severe or hard-to-treat infections, you may be given antibiotics through an IV tube (a tube inserted into a vein). This type of treatment may require you to stay in a hospital.

Anti-inflammatory medicines can help reduce swelling in your airways due to ongoing infections. These medicines may be inhaled or oral.

Bronchodilators help open the airways by relaxing the muscles around them. These medicines are inhaled. They're often taken just before CPT to help clear mucus out of your airways. You also may take bronchodilators before inhaling other medicines into your lungs.

Your doctor may prescribe medicines to reduce the stickiness of your mucus and loosen it up. These medicines can help clear out mucus, improve lung function, and prevent worsening lung symptoms.

Treatments for Advanced Lung Disease

If you have advanced lung disease, you may need oxygen therapy. Oxygen usually is given through nasal prongs or a mask.

If other treatments haven't worked, a lung transplant may be an option if you have severe lung disease. A lung transplant is surgery to remove a person's diseased lung and replace it with a healthy lung from a deceased donor.

Pulmonary Rehabilitation (PR)

Your doctor may recommend PR as part of your treatment plan. PR is a broad program that helps improve the wellbeing of people who have chronic (ongoing) breathing problems.

PR doesn't replace medical therapy. Instead, it's used with medical therapy and may include:

- Exercise training

- Nutritional counseling

- Education on your lung disease or condition and how to manage it

- Energy-conserving techniques

- Breathing strategies

- Psychological counseling and/or group support

PR has many benefits. It can improve your ability to function and your quality of life. The program also may help relieve your breathing problems. Even if you have advanced lung disease, you can still benefit from PR.

Treatment for Digestive Problems

CF can cause many digestive problems, such as bulky stools, intestinal gas, a swollen belly, severe constipation, and pain or discomfort. Digestive problems also can lead to poor growth and development in children.

Nutritional therapy can improve your strength and ability to stay active. It also can improve growth and development in children. Nutritional therapy also may make you strong enough to resist some lung infections. A nutritionist can help you create a nutritional plan that meets your needs.

In addition to having a well-balanced diet that's rich in calories, fat, and protein, your nutritional therapy may include:

- Oral pancreatic enzymes to help you digest fats and proteins and absorb more vitamins.

- Supplements of vitamins A, D, E, and K to replace the fat-soluble vitamins that your intestines can't absorb.

- High-calorie shakes to provide you with extra nutrients.

- A high-salt diet or salt supplements that you take before exercising.

- A feeding tube to give you more calories at night while you're sleeping. The tube may be threaded through your nose and throat and into your stomach. Or, the tube may be placed directly into your stomach through a surgically made hole. Before you go to bed each night, you'll attach a bag with a nutritional solution to the entrance of the tube. It will feed you while you sleep.

Other treatments for digestive problems may include enemas and mucus-thinning medicines to treat intestinal blockages. Sometimes surgery is needed to remove an intestinal blockage.

Your doctor also may prescribe medicines to reduce your stomach acid and help oral pancreatic enzymes work better.

Treatments for CF Complications

A common complication of CF is diabetes. The type of diabetes associated with CF often requires different treatment than other types of diabetes.

Another common CF complication is the bone-thinning disorder osteoporosis. Your doctor may prescribe medicines that prevent your bones from losing their density.

Living with CF

If you or your child has CF, you should learn as much as you can about the disease. Work closely with your doctors to learn how to manage CF.

Ongoing Care

Having ongoing medical care by a team of doctors, nurses, and respiratory therapists who specialize in CF is important. These specialists often are located at major medical centers or CF Care Centers.

The United States has more than 100 CF Care Centers. Most of these centers have pediatric and adult programs or clinics.

It's standard to have CF checkups every three months. Talk with your doctor about whether you should get an annual flu shot and other vaccines. Take all of your medicines as your doctor prescribes. In between checkups, be sure to contact your doctor if you have:

- Blood in your mucus, increased amounts of mucus, or a change in the color or consistency of your mucus.

- Decreased energy or appetite.

- Severe constipation or diarrhea, severe abdominal pain, or vomit that's dark green.

- A fever, which is a sign of infection. (However, you may still have a serious infection that needs treatment even if you don't have a fever.)

Transition of Care

Better treatments for CF allow people who have the disease to live longer now than in the past. Thus, the move from pediatric care to adult care is an important step in treatment.

If your child has CF, encourage him or her to learn about the disease and take an active role in treatment. This will help prepare your child for the transition to adult care.

CF Care Centers can help provide age-appropriate treatment throughout the transition period and into adulthood. They also will support the transition to adult care by balancing medical needs with other developmental factors, such as increased independence, relationships, and employment.

Talk with your child's healthcare team for more information about how to help your child move from pediatric care to adult care.

Lifestyle Changes

In between medical checkups, you can practice good self-care and follow a healthy lifestyle.

For example, follow a healthy diet. A healthy diet includes a variety of fruits, vegetables, and whole grains. Talk with your doctor about what types and amounts of foods you should include in your diet.

Other lifestyle changes include:

• Not smoking and avoiding tobacco smoke

• Washing your hands often to lower your risk of infection

• Exercising regularly and drinking lots of fluids

• Doing chest physical therapy (as your doctor recommends)

Other Concerns

Although CF requires daily care, most people who have the disease are able to attend school and work.

If you have CF, you should talk with your doctor if you're planning a pregnancy. Although CF can cause fertility problems, men and women who have the disease should still have protected sex to avoid sexually transmitted diseases.

Emotional Issues

Living with CF may cause fear, anxiety, depression, and stress. Talk about how you feel with your healthcare team. Talking to a professional counselor also can help. If you're very depressed, your doctor may recommend medicines or other treatments that can improve your quality of life.

Joining a patient support group may help you adjust to living with CF. You can see how other people who have the same symptoms have coped with them. Talk with your doctor about local support groups or check with an area medical center.

Support from family and friends also can help relieve stress and anxiety. Let your loved ones know how you feel and what they can do to help you.

Chapter 30

Musculoskeletal Defects

Chapter Contents

Section 30.1

Arthrogryposis Multiplex Congenita (AMC)

This section includes text excerpted from "Arthrogryposis
Multiplex Congenita," Genetic and Rare Diseases Information
Center (GARD), National Center for Advancing Translational
Sciences (NCATS), January 12, 2015.

Arthrogryposis multiplex congenita (AMC) refers to the development of multiple joint contractures affecting two or more areas of the
body prior to birth. A contracture occurs when a joint becomes permanently fixed in a bent or straightened position, which can impact
the function and range of motion of the joint and may lead to muscle
atrophy. AMC is not a specific diagnosis, but rather a physical symptom that can be associated with many different medical conditions. It
is suspected that AMC is related to decreased fetal movement during
development which can have a variety of different causes, including
environmental factors (i.e., maternal illness, limited space), single
gene changes (autosomal dominant, autosomal recessive, X-linked),
chromosomal abnormalities, and various syndromes. Treatment varies based on the signs and symptoms found in each person, but may
include physical therapy, removable splints, exercise, and/or surgery.

Statistics

AMC affects approximately 1 in 3,000 individuals in the United
States. The condition has been reported in individuals of Asian, African, and European descent. It is more common in isolated populations
such as Finland and the Bedouin community in Israel. The number of
men and women affected is approximately equal.

Symptoms

AMC refers to the development of multiple joint contractures affecting two or more areas of the body prior to birth. A contracture occurs
when a joint becomes permanently fixed in a bent or straightened
position, which can impact the function and range of motion of the

joint. In some cases, only a few joints are affected and the range of motion may be nearly normal. In people who are severely affected, every joint in the body can be involved, including the jaw and back. Muscles of affected limbs may be atrophied or underdeveloped. Soft tissue webbing may develop over the affected joint.

AMC is not a specific diagnosis, but rather a physical symptom that can be found in many different medical conditions. The signs and symptoms associated with AMC can, therefore, vary greatly in range and severity depending on the underlying condition.

Cause

The exact cause of AMC is not fully understood. AMC is thought to be related to decreased fetal movement during development, which can occur for a variety of reasons. When a joint is not moved for a period of time, extra connective tissue may grow around it, fixing it in place. Lack of joint movement also means that tendons connected to the joint are not stretched to their normal length, which can make normal joint movement difficult.

In general, there are four causes for decreased fetal movement before birth:

1. **Abnormal development of muscles.** In most cases, the specific cause for this cannot be identified. Suspected causes include muscle diseases, maternal fever during pregnancy, and viruses which may damage the cells that transmit nerve impulses to the muscles.

2. **Insufficient room in the uterus for normal movement.** For example, multiple fetuses may be present, the mother may lack normal amounts of amniotic fluid or there may be uterine structural abnormalities.

3. **Malformations of the central nervous system (the brain and/or spinal cord).** In these cases, arthrogryposis is usually accompanied by a wide range of other symptoms.

4. **Tendons, bones, joints or joint linings may develop abnormally.** For example, tendons may not be connected to the proper place in a joint.

AMC can be a component of numerous condition caused by environmental factors, single gene changes (autosomal dominant, autosomal recessive, X-linked), chromosomal abnormalities, and various syndromes.

507

Inheritance

AMC is not inherited in most cases; however, a genetic cause can be identified in about 30 percent of affected people. It can be a component of many different genetic conditions, including those caused by a single gene change or a chromosomal abnormality, such as trisomy 18. Genetic conditions sometimes associated with AMC include some connective tissue disorders; muscle disorders such as muscular dystrophies or congenital myopathies; and certain mitochondrial disorders. Depending on the underlying genetic cause, it may be inherited in an autosomal recessive, autosomal dominant or X-linked manner. Some cases are thought to have multifactorial inheritance, which means that both genetic and environmental factors may play a role in causing the condition.

Treatment

The treatment of AMC varies based on the signs and symptoms present in each person and the severity of the condition. Early in life, physical therapy to stretch contractures can improve the range of motion of affected joints and prevent muscle atrophy. Splits can also be used in combination with these stretching exercises. For most types of arthrogryposis, physical and occupational therapy have proven very beneficial in improving muscle strength and increasing the range of motion of affected joints.

Some patients, however, have persistent functional difficulties despite a rigorous physical therapy regimen. In these cases, surgery may be recommended to achieve better positioning and increase the range of motion in certain joints. Tendon transfers have been done to improve muscle function.

Prognosis

The long-term outlook (prognosis) for people with AMC depends on the severity of the condition, the underlying cause, and the affected person's response to therapy. The degree to which muscles and joints are affected varies significantly from person to person. AMC can be associated with a variety of conditions that are each characterized by unique symptoms.

In general, many people affected by AMC have a good prognosis. With physical therapy and other available treatments, substantial improvement in joint function and mobility is normally possible. Most people with AMC are of normal intelligence and are able to lead productive, independent lives as adults.

Section 30.2

Clubfoot

This section contains text excerpted from the following sources: Text beginning with the heading "What Is Clubfoot?" is excerpted from "Descriptive Epidemiology of Idiopathic Clubfoot," U.S. Department of Health and Human Services (HHS), July 1, 2014. Reviewed December 2017; Text under the heading "Treatment" is excerpted from "Clubfoot Disability: Model for Sustainable Health Systems Programs," U.S. Agency for International Development (USAID), February 2015.

What Is Clubfoot?

Talipes equinovarus or clubfoot is a congenital structural defect of several tissues of the foot and ankle, resulting in abnormal positioning of joints. Specifically, the hindfoot is rotated inward, the foot is pointed downward, the midfoot is arched, and the forefoot is turned inward.

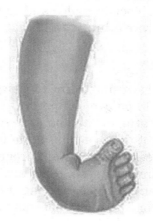

Figure 30.1. *Talipes Equinovarus*

(Source: "Congenital Malformations and Deformations of the Musculoskeletal System," Centers for Disease Control and Prevention (CDC).)

What Causes Clubfoot?

Decades ago, clubfoot was thought to arise from mechanical or constraining forces, such as breech delivery, oligohydramnios, bicornuate uterus, and multiple gestations, which would suggest that pathogenesis occurs later in gestation. Evidences counters this hypothesis on the basis of known embryologic development. Specifically, the foot begins to develop during the 9th week of gestation when the orientation of the limb buds is in a vertical axis.

Early on, the soles of the feet normally face one another, but by the 14th week they should have rotated medially and assumed the position of adult feet. Thus, the pathogenesis of the structural-type of clubfoot is thought to occur during these early weeks of gestational development.

Types of Clubfoot

Structural clubfoot can be confused with positional-type clubfoot which has a generally similar phenotype except that it is possible postnatally to manually move the foot into normal position and is thought to arise from uterine constraint. Structural-type clubfoot is estimated to affect approximately 1 per 1000 births, making it one of the most common congenital malformations. It occurs as part of known syndromes and secondary to bilateral renal agenesis and neural tube defects, but the majority of structural cases are not attributed to another primary anomaly and are labeled 'idiopathic.'

Epidemiologic studies have consistently reported higher prevalences of idiopathic clubfoot in males and in first-born children, but any associations with race/ethnicity and maternal age are not clear.

Treatment

The Ponseti Method is a simple, inexpensive, outpatient treatment that has been proven to be over 95 percent effective when properly administered. This treatment method consists of a series of specific gentle manipulations of the foot and ankle followed by the application of plaster casts weekly to maintain progressively improved joint alignments. Usually from four–six casts are required to correct the deformity. In 85 percent of cases, patients undergo a simple, percutaneous Achilles tenotomy (usually done as an outpatient procedure) as the final stage of the casting treatment. To prevent relapses, a foot abduction brace is usually worn daily for three months and then nightly until the child is from 3–4-years-old or for one year if the patient is older than four when he or she starts treatment. Using the

Ponseti Method, surgery is rarely necessary; the method is now recognized as the preferred treatment worldwide and has been endorsed by orthopedic societies in more than 45 countries.

The Ponseti Method can be used successfully anywhere in the world since diagnosis of clubfoot is primarily based only on physical examination and treatment requires minimal medical supplies (casting material, tenotomy supplies, and braces) along with the skill of the treating healthcare professional and the cooperation of the child's parents or caregivers.

Section 30.3

Fibrous Dysplasia (FD)

This section includes text excerpted from "Fibrous Dysplasia Overview," National Institutes of Health (NIH), June 1, 2015.

What Is Fibrous Dysplasia (FD)?

Fibrous dysplasia (FD) is a skeletal disorder in which bone-forming cells fail to mature and produce too much fibrous, or connective, tissue. Areas of healthy bone are replaced with this fibrous tissue. The replacement of normal bone in FD can lead to pain, misshapen bones, and fracture, especially when it occurs in the long bones (arms and legs). When it occurs in the skull, there can also be a replacement of the normal bone with fibrous tissue, resulting in changes in the shape of the face or skull, pain, and, in rare circumstances, hearing or vision loss.

Some people with FD have only one bone involved (monostotic), whereas other people have more than one bone involved (polyostotic). The disease may occur alone, or as part of a condition known as the McCune-Albright syndrome. McCune-Albright syndrome is characterized by FD and other symptoms such as patches of pigmented skin (light brown or "café-au-lait" spots) and endocrine problems such as early puberty (precocious puberty), hyperthyroidism (excess thyroid hormone), excess growth hormone (gigantism or acromegaly), excess cortisol (Cushing syndrome), and other rare conditions.

FD affect any bone in the body. The most common sites are the bones in the skull and face, femur (thighbone), tibia (shinbone), humerus (upper arm), pelvis, and ribs. Although many bones can be affected at once—and affected bones are often found on one side of the body—the disease does not "spread" from one bone to another; that is, the pattern of which bones are involved is established very early in life and does not change with age.

Who Is Affected?

FD is an uncommon disorder. It is usually diagnosed in children and young adults, and is present throughout life. The likelihood of getting the disease does not appear to be influenced by gender, race, ethnic background, geographic location, or by any environmental exposures.

What Is the Cause?

FD is caused by a defective gene in the cells that form bone and other affected tissues. The defect occurs at some point after conception, most likely early in fetal development. This means that the disorder is not inherited from an affected person's parents, nor can an affected person with the condition pass it on to his or her children.

What Are the Symptoms?

The most common symptoms of the disorder are painful, misshapen, and/or broken bones (fractures). Fractures are more common between the ages of 6 and 10, but often persist into adulthood. The problems a person experiences depend on which bones are affected. For example, the legs can be of different lengths, leading to a limp and the need for a shoe lift. The bones of the sinuses can be affected, leading to chronic sinus congestion. Only very rarely do serious problems such as vision loss or cancer occur.

How Is FD Diagnosed?

The bones in people with FD have a characteristic appearance on X-rays, which is usually sufficient to make the diagnosis. Other imaging tests, such as magnetic resonance imaging (MRI) or computed tomography (CT) may also be indicated. In some cases, a doctor may need to obtain a small bone specimen (a biopsy) to confirm the diagnosis. The usefulness of gene testing is not clear. Since the mutated gene is only present in FD tissues, it is best to test only the deoxyribonucleic acid (DNA) from affected tissue, but even then, doctors do not know with certainty how useful such a test is.

How Is FD Treated?

There is no cure for FD. Like most medical conditions, one treats the symptoms or problems as they arise. Fractures often require surgery, but can sometimes be treated with just a cast. Surgeries are recommended if a fracture is likely to occur, or in an effort to correct the shape of the bone. Surgery may also be indicated to relieve bone pain. Medications known as bisphosphonates—approved by the U.S. Food and Drug Administration (FDA) for the treatment of other bone diseases—have been shown to reduce pain associated with the disease. Bone-healthy strategies such as physical activity (with physician approval), and adequate calcium, phosphorus, and vitamin D intake are also important.

Section 30.4

Other Musculoskeletal Disorders

This section contains text excerpted from the following sources: Text under the heading "Macrodactyly" is excerpted from "Macrodactyly of the Hand," Genetic and Rare Diseases Information Center (GARD), National Center for Advancing Translational Sciences (NCATS), November 30, 2016; Text under the heading "Polydactyly" is excerpted from "Polydactyly," Genetic and Rare Diseases Information Center (GARD), National Center for Advancing Translational Sciences (NCATS), May 8, 2015; Text beginning with the heading "Syndactyly" is excerpted from "Syndactyly Type 3," Genetic and Rare Diseases Information Center (GARD), National Center for Advancing Translational Sciences (NCATS), June 3, 2013. Reviewed December 2017.

Macrodactyly

Macrodactyly of the hand is a rare condition in which a person's fingers are abnormally large due to the overgrowth of the underlying bone and soft tissue. This condition is congenital, meaning that babies are born with it. Although babies are born with the condition, macrodactyly is usually not inherited. Most of the time, only one hand is affected, but usually more than one finger is involved. Macrodactyly may also coexist with syndactyly (a condition in which two fingers are fused together) or clinodactyly (a condition in which a finger or more curves). Macrodactyly is deforming and can cause symptoms in some people. There have been cases of people with macrodactyly also having carpal tunnel syndrome. Surgery, usually involving multiple procedures, can help the condition.

Polydactyly

Polydactyly is a condition in which a person has more than five fingers per hand or five toes per foot. It is the most common birth defect of the hand and foot. Polydactyly can occur as an isolated finding such that the person has no other physical anomalies or intellectual impairment. However, it can occur in association with other birth defects and cognitive abnormalities as part of a genetic syndrome. In some cases, the extra digits may be well-formed and functional. Surgery may be considered especially for poorly formed digits or very large extra digits. Surgical management depends greatly on the complexity of the deformity.

Syndactyly

Syndactyly type 3 (SD3) is a limb abnormality present at birth that is characterized by complete fusion of the 4th and 5th fingers on both hands. In most cases only the soft tissue is fused, but in some cases the bones of the fingers (distal phalanges) are fused. There is evidence that SD3 is caused by mutations in the *GJA1* gene, which has also been implicated in a condition called oculodentodigital dysplasia. SD3 is the characteristic digital abnormality in this condition. SD3 is inherited in an autosomal dominant manner.

Inheritance

Syndactyly type 3 has been shown to be inherited in an autosomal dominant manner. This means that having only one mutated copy of the causative gene is sufficient to cause the condition. When an individual with an autosomal dominant condition has children, each child has a 50 percent (1 in 2) chance of inheriting the mutated gene and a 50 percent chance of inheriting the normal gene and being unaffected.

Section 30.5

Torticollis

Congenital torticollis, also known as wryneck or twisted neck, is a condition in which an infant's neck is twisted as the neck muscle is shortened, making it difficult for the child to turn his or her head. It usually occurs at birth or shortly after birth, and normally it takes 6–8 weeks to discover the condition as the baby begins to gain control over the head and neck; however, it can take up to 3 months to develop. Infants with torticollis do not feel any pain and it happens in both boys and girls. Some babies with congenital torticollis also have hip dysplasia.

Causes of Torticollis

The exact cause of congenital torticollis is unknown; however, a common belief is that the condition can be caused because of the abnormal positioning of the fetus inside the uterus (a breech position, where the buttocks of the baby would face the birth canal). Congenital torticollis can also happen after a difficult birth. If forceps or vacuum devices were used during childbirth, it is more likely that the baby would develop this condition. These devices put pressure on the sternocleidomastoid muscle (SCM), the neck muscle. This muscle extends from the jawbone to the collarbone and breastbone; when the muscle is pulled or stretched it might tear, which causes a bleed or bruise within the muscle. The bruised muscle develops scar tissue (fibrosis) that shortens and tightens the neck muscle, which pulls the child's head to a side. The scar tissue forms a lump that can be felt on the neck side. In few cases, congenital malformation of the cervical spine is another cause of congenital torticollis.

Symptoms of Torticollis

Each child may experience symptoms differently. The torticollis may be seen at birth or several weeks after birth.

Here are the most common symptoms for congenital torticollis:

- The head is titled to one side and the chin faces the opposite shoulder. A majority of infants are affected on the right side of the neck.

- The baby finds it difficult to turn his or her head to the sides and up and down because of a limited range of motion. The baby looks over one shoulder instead of using his or her eyes to follow movements near them.

- If the baby is breastfed, then he or she may prefer breastfeeding only on one breast.

- In the first few weeks after birth, the baby may have a lump in the affected neck muscle—it is not painful but can be felt.

- Some babies develop a flat head on one or both sides due to sleeping on the same side always.

Diagnosis of Torticollis

If an infant has difficulty in turning the head or the head is tilted, a pediatrician needs to be consulted. The healthcare provider would discuss the infant's general health, ask specifically about torticollis symptoms, and do a complete physical examination. Diagnostic procedures for congenital torticollis are as follows:

- **X-ray:** A test using electromagnetic energy beams that captures and produces images of internal tissues, bones, and organs. It helps check abnormality in the neck muscles.

- **Ultrasound examination:** An imaging technique that examines the function of internal organs and assesses blood flow through various vessels. It uses high-frequency sound waves and a computer to produce images of tissues and blood vessels to check the muscle around the mass.

Treatment of Torticollis

If congenital torticollis is not treated, it may result in the child not being able to move the head properly, or it could cause permanent tightening of the muscle with uneven development of the neck and face. The healthcare provider will determine the treatment based on the child's overall health, age, and medical history; and the extent of the condition, child's tolerance toward different treatment methods, and parent's opinion or preference.

The basic treatment for congenital torticollis is a gentle exercise program to stretch the sternocleidomastoid muscle (neck muscle). The healthcare provider will teach exercises that can be performed on the baby. The exercises are as follows:

- **Stretching exercises:** The baby's neck is turned from side to side gently so that the chin touches each shoulder. The head is tilted downward on the unaffected side to help relieve tension and lengthen the neck muscle.

- **Infant stimulation:** This enables the baby to learn to stretch the muscle. The baby is encouraged to turn both ways by placing toys or offering the milk bottle, so that his or her head is turned to see them.

Surgical treatments are also available if the condition cannot be corrected with these exercises. Almost 10 percent of kids with congenital torticollis need surgery. It is a minor procedure and is usually done once the child reaches preschool years.

There is no prevention possible for this condition.

References

1. "Congenital Muscular Torticollis," American Academy of Orthopaedic Surgeons (AAOS), n.d.

2. "Congenital Muscular Torticollis," Children's Hospital of Philadelphia, n.d.

3. "Congenital Torticollis," WebMD, n.d.

4. Solo-Josephson, Patricia. "Infant Torticollis," KidsHealth, July 2017.

Section 30.6

Upper and Lower Limb Reduction Defects

This section includes text excerpted from "Birth Defects—Facts about Upper and Lower Limb Reduction Defects," Centers for Disease Control and Prevention (CDC), November 21, 2017.

Upper and lower limb reduction defects occur when a part of or the entire arm (upper limb) or leg (lower limb) of a fetus fails to form completely during pregnancy. The defect is referred to as a "limb reduction" because a limb is reduced from its normal size or is missing.

How Often Does Limb Reduction Defects Occur?

Centers for Disease Control and Prevention (CDC) estimates that each year about 1,500 babies in the United States are born with upper limb reductions and about 750 are born with lower limb reductions. In other words, each year about 4 out of every 10,000 babies will have upper limb reductions and about 2 out of every 10,000 babies will have lower limb reductions. Some of these babies will have both upper and lower limb reduction defects.

What Problems Do Children with Limb Reduction Defects Have?

Babies and children with limb reduction defects will face various issues and difficulties, but the extent of these will depend on the location and size of the reduction. Some potential difficulties and problems include:

- Difficulties with normal development such as motor skills

- Needing assistance with daily activities such as self-care

- Limitations with certain movements, sports, or activities

- Potential emotional and social issues because of physical appearance

Specific treatment for limb reduction defects will be determined by the child's doctor, based on things like the child's age, the extent and type of defect, and the child's tolerance for certain medications, procedures, and therapies.

The overall goal for treatment of limb reduction defects is to provide the child with a limb that has proper function and appearance. Treatment can vary for each child. Potential treatments include:

- Prosthetics (artificial limbs)

- Orthotics (splints or braces)

- Surgery

- Rehabilitation (physical or occupational therapy)

It is important to remember that some babies and children with limb reductions will have some difficulties and limitations throughout life, but with proper treatment and care they can live long, healthy, and productive lives.

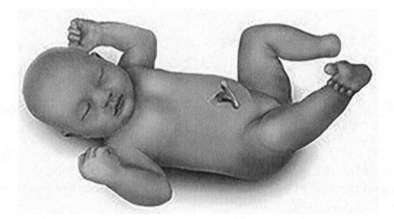

Figure 30.2. *Congenital Absence of Foot and Toes*

What Causes Limb Reduction Defects?

The cause of limb reduction defects is unknown. However, research has shown that certain behaviors or exposures during pregnancy can increase the risk of having a baby with a limb reduction defect. These include:

- Exposure of the mother to certain chemicals or viruses while she is pregnant

- Exposure of the mother to certain medications

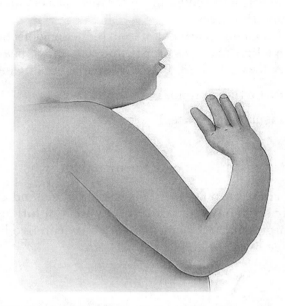

Figure 30.3. *Longitudinal Reduction Defect of Radius*

- Possible exposure of the mother to tobacco smoking (although more research is needed)

CDC works with many researchers to study risk factors that can increase the chance of having a baby with limb reduction defects, as well as outcomes of babies with the defect. Following are examples of what this research has found:

- A woman taking multivitamins before she gets pregnant might decrease her risk for having a baby with limb reduction defects, although more research is needed.

- Certain sets of limb reduction defects might be associated with other birth defects, such as heart defects, omphalocele, and gastroschisis.

Can Limb Reduction Defects Be Prevented?

There is no known way to prevent this type of defect, but some of the problems experienced later in life by a person born with a limb reduction defect can be prevented if the defect is treated early.

Even so, mothers can take steps before and during pregnancy to have a healthy pregnancy. Steps include taking a daily multivitamin with folic acid (400 micrograms), not smoking, and not drinking alcohol during pregnancy.

Chapter 31

Reproductive Organ Defects

Chapter Contents

Section 31.1

Congenital Adrenal Hyperplasia (CAH)

This section includes text excerpted from "Facts about
CAH (Congenital Adrenal Hyperplasia)," National
Institutes of Health (NIH), February 2016.

What Is Congenital Adrenal Hyperplasia (CAH)?

Congenital adrenal hyperplasia (CAH) is a genetic disorder of the
adrenal glands that affects the body's general health, growth, and
development.

What Are the Adrenal Glands?

The adrenal glands are a pair of walnut-sized organs above the
kidneys. They make hormones, which act like chemical messengers
that affect other organs in the body. An organ at the base of the brain,
called the pituitary gland, helps regulate the adrenal glands. Each
adrenal gland has two parts: the medulla (the inner part), and the
cortex (the outer part). The medulla makes the hormone adrenaline.
The cortex makes the hormones cortisol, aldosterone, and androgens.
CAH affects how the adrenal cortex works. In severe cases, the adrenal
medulla also may not function normally.

What Do Adrenal Hormones Do?

Hormones made by the adrenal glands are important for the body's
normal functioning. Cortisol affects energy levels, sugar levels, blood
pressure, and the body's response to illness or injury. Aldosterone
helps maintain the proper salt level and blood pressure. Androgens
are hormones needed for normal growth and development in both boys
and girls. Adrenaline affects blood sugar levels, blood pressure, and
the body's response to physical stress. The adrenal glands help keep
the body in balance by making the right amounts of these hormones.
In patients with CAH, there is an abnormal production of adrenal
hormones.

Symptoms

Too little cortisol may cause tiredness, nausea, and weight loss. During illness or injury, low cortisol levels can lead to low blood pressure and even death. Also, treating a cortisol imbalance with too much cortisol can cause abnormal development in children, obesity, short stature, and decreased bone density (osteoporosis).

Lack of aldosterone, which occurs in three out of four patients with classic (severe) CAH, upsets salt levels. This imbalance may cause dehydration, and possibly death. Chronic salt imbalance may cause abnormal growth.

Too much androgen causes abnormal physical development in children. Boys and girls with CAH may either grow too fast, develop pubic hair and acne early, and/or stop growing too soon, causing short stature. Girls exposed to high levels of androgens before birth may have abnormal external genitalia at birth, and genital surgery is usually performed in infancy. Although their internal female organs are normal, excess androgens may affect puberty and cause irregular menstrual periods.

Classic CAH

The severe form of CAH is called classic CAH, and it occurs in 1 in 16,000 births. The most common is 21- hydroxylase deficiency, which makes up about 95 percent of cases. A child with this type of CAH has adrenal glands that cannot make enough cortisol and may or may not make aldosterone. As a result, the glands overwork trying to make these hormones and end up making too many androgens. The second most common form of classic CAH is 11-hydroxylase deficiency. A child with this type of classic CAH has adrenal glands that make too much androgen and not enough cortisol. Children with this type of CAH may have high blood pressure. These patients do not have aldosterone deficiency. Other rare types of classic CAH include 3-betahydroxy-steroid dehydrogenase deficiency, lipoid CAH, and 17- hydroxylase deficiency.

Nonclassic (Late-Onset) CAH

The mild form of CAH is called nonclassic congenital adrenal hyperplasia (NCAH). This type of CAH is almost always due to 21-hydroxylase deficiency. Only a handful of people have been described as having nonclassic CAH due to other causes. People with nonclassic 21-hydroxylase deficiency (NC21OHD) usually make enough cortisol and aldosterone, but make excess androgens. Symptoms may come and go, beginning at any time, but typically develop in late childhood or early adulthood. Boys often do not need treatment, but girls often need treatment to suppress their excess androgens. Nonclassic CAH is common. One in every 1,000 people has nonclassic 21-hydroxylase deficiency. Incidence is higher in certain ethnic groups including Ashkenazi Jews, Hispanics, Yugoslavs, and Italians.

How Is CAH Inherited?

An inherited disorder is one that can be passed from the parents to their children. CAH is a type of inherited disorder called "autosomal recessive." For a child to have CAH, each parent must either have CAH or carry a abnormal gene. This means that if two parents are CAH carriers (have the gene for CAH but not the disorder), then their children have a 25 percent chance (1 in 4) of being born with CAH. Each sibling without CAH has two chances in three of being a carrier. Tests can be done to find out if someone is a carrier.

How Is CAH Treated?

People with CAH have a normal life expectancy, but CAH cannot be outgrown. Classic CAH requires treatment for life. Some patients with nonclassic CAH may not require treatment as adults. Treatment is tailored for each patient and adjusted during childhood for growth. The standard treatment for children with classic CAH 21-hydroxylase deficiency is hydrocortisone which replaces cortisol and fludrocortisone which replaces aldosterone. For classic CAH 11-hydroxylase deficiency, the treatment is only hydrocortisone. Patients can be started on longer-acting forms of hydrocortisone-like medication (i.e., prednisone or dexamethasone) when they are done growing.

Patients with the nonclassic form of CAH need only hydrocortisone (or a longer-acting form of hydrocortisone-like medication). Some patients with nonclassic CAH are able to come off of medication as adults, but patients with classic CAH need lifelong treatment. Experimental prenatal treatment is available for fetuses at risk for classic CAH. For this treatment, mothers take dexamethasone, a potent form of hydrocortisone-like medication. This medication suppresses androgens in the fetus and allows female genitalia to develop more normally. This treatment lessens or eliminates the need for surgery in girls. It does not, however, treat other aspects of the disorder. Children with CAH still need to take hydrocortisone and fludrocortisone for life.

What If a Child or an Adult with CAH Has an Illness, Surgery, or a Major Injury?

During these times, a patient with CAH needs closer medical attention and should be under a doctor's care. More cortisol is needed to meet the body's increased needs for this hormone. Higher doses of hydrocortisone are given by mouth or sometimes by intramuscular injection (into the muscle). Intravenous medication is needed before surgery.

Medical Alert Identification

In an emergency, it is important to alert medical personnel about the diagnosis of adrenal insufficiency, so wearing a medical alert identification bracelet or necklace is recommended. The information on the medic alert should include, "Adrenal Insufficiency Requires Hydrocortisone." It is important for the adult patient or parent of a child patient to learn how to administer an intramuscular injection of hydrocortisone in the case of an emergency.

Can a Woman with CAH Become Pregnant and Have a Baby?

Increased androgens may cause irregular menstrual periods and make it harder for a woman with CAH to conceive a child. But if she takes her medications as directed, then she can become pregnant and have a baby.

Do Men with CAH Have Fertility Problems?

Men who take medications as directed usually have normal fertility. Rarely, however, they may develop "adrenal rest tissue" in their testes. This is when adrenal tissue grows in other parts of the body, such as the testes. The tissue does not turn into cancer, but it can grow enough to cause discomfort or infertility. Large growths are rare, and surgery is usually not needed.

Can CAH Be Diagnosed Prenatally?

CAH can be diagnosed before birth. Amniocentesis or chorionic villus sampling during pregnancy can check for the disorder. Testing for classic CAH is part of the routine newborn screening done in all states in the United States.

Section 31.2

Hypospadias

This section includes text excerpted from "Facts about Hypospadias," Centers for Disease Control and Prevention (CDC), November 21, 2017.

What Is Hypospadias?

Hypospadias is a birth defect in boys in which the opening of the urethra is not located at the tip of the penis. In boys with hypospadias, the urethra forms abnormally during weeks 8–14 of pregnancy. The abnormal opening can form anywhere from just below the end of the penis to the scrotum. There are different degrees of hypospadias; some can be minor and some more severe.

Types of Hypospadias

The type of hypospadias a boy has depends on the location of the opening of the urethra:

- **Subcoronal.** The opening of the urethra is located somewhere near the head of the penis.

- **Midshaft.** The opening of the urethra is located along the shaft of the penis.

- **Penoscrotal.** The opening of the urethra is located where the penis and scrotum meet.

Other Problems

Boys with hypospadias can sometimes have a curved penis. They could have problems with abnormal spraying of urine and might have to sit to urinate. In some boys with hypospadias, the testicle has not fully descended into the scrotum. If hypospadias is not treated it can lead to problems later in life, such as difficulty performing sexual intercourse or difficulty urinating while standing.

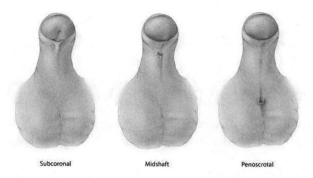

Subcoronal   Midshaft   Penoscrotal

Figure 31.1. *Types of Hypospadias*

Occurrence

It is estimated that each year about 5 boys out of every 1,000 born in the United States have hypospadias, making it one of the most common birth defects.

Causes and Risk Factors

The causes of hypospadias in most infants are unknown. In most cases, hypospadias is thought to be caused by a combination of genes and other factors, such as things the mother comes in contact with in her environment, or what the mother eats or drinks, or certain medications she uses during pregnancy.

In recent years, Centers for Disease Control and Prevention (CDC) researchers have reported important findings about some factors that affect the risk of having a baby boy with hypospadias:

- **Age and weight.** Mothers who were age 35 years or older and who were considered obese had a higher risk of having a baby with hypospadias.

- **Fertility treatments.** Women who used assisted reproductive technology to help with pregnancy had a higher risk of having a baby with hypospadias.

- **Certain hormones.** Women who took certain hormones just before or during pregnancy were shown to have a higher risk of having a baby with hypospadias.

If you are pregnant or thinking about becoming pregnant, talk with your doctor about ways to increase your chance of having a healthy baby.

Diagnosis

Hypospadias is usually diagnosed during a physical examination after the baby is born.

Treatments

Treatment for hypospadias depends on the type of defect the boy has. Most cases of hypospadias will need surgery to correct the defect.

If surgery is needed, it is usually done when the boy is between the ages of 3–18 months old. In some cases the surgery is done in stages. Some of the repairs done during the surgery might include placing the opening of the urethra in the right place, correcting the curve in the penis, and repairing the skin around the opening of the urethra. Because the doctor might need to use the foreskin to make some of the repairs, a baby boy with hypospadias should not be circumcised.

Section 31.3

Inguinal Hernia

This section includes text excerpted from "Inguinal Hernia," National Institute of Diabetes and Digestive and Kidney Diseases (NIDDK), June 2014. Reviewed December 2017.

What Is an Inguinal Hernia?

An inguinal hernia happens when contents of the abdomen—usually fat or part of the small intestine—bulge through a weak area in the lower abdominal wall. The abdomen is the area between the chest and the hips. The area of the lower abdominal wall is also called the inguinal or groin region.

Two types of inguinal hernias are:

- **Indirect inguinal hernias,** which are caused by a defect in the abdominal wall that is congenital, or present at birth

- **Direct inguinal hernias,** which usually occur only in male adults and are caused by a weakness in the muscles of the abdominal wall that develops over time

Inguinal hernias occur at the inguinal canal in the groin region.

What Is the Inguinal Canal?

The inguinal canal is a passage through the lower abdominal wall. People have two inguinal canals—one on each side of the lower abdomen. In males, the spermatic cords pass through the inguinal canals and connect to the testicles in the scrotum—the sac around the testicles. The spermatic cords contain blood vessels, nerves, and a duct, called the spermatic duct, that carries sperm from the testicles to the penis. In females, the round ligaments, which support the uterus, pass through the inguinal canals.

What Causes Inguinal Hernias?

The cause of inguinal hernias depends on the type of inguinal hernia.

Indirect Inguinal Hernias

A defect in the abdominal wall that is present at birth causes an indirect inguinal hernia.

During the development of the fetus in the womb, the lining of the abdominal cavity forms and extends into the inguinal canal. In males, the spermatic cord and testicles descend out from inside the abdomen and through the abdominal lining to the scrotum through the inguinal canal. Next, the abdominal lining usually closes off the entrance to the inguinal canal a few weeks before or after birth. In females, the ovaries do not descend out from inside the abdomen, and the abdominal lining usually closes a couple of months before birth.

Sometimes the lining of the abdomen does not close as it should, leaving an opening in the abdominal wall at the upper part of the inguinal canal. Fat or part of the small intestine may slide into the inguinal canal through this opening, causing a hernia. In females, the ovaries may also slide into the inguinal canal and cause a hernia.

Indirect hernias are the most common type of inguinal hernia. Indirect inguinal hernias may appear in 2–3 percent of male children; however, they are much less common in female children, occurring in less than 1 percent.

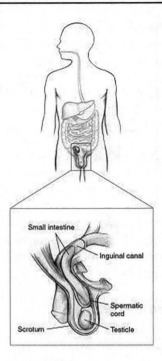

Figure 31.2. *Indirect Inguinal Hernia in a Male*

Direct Inguinal Hernias

Direct inguinal hernias usually occur only in male adults as aging and stress or strain weaken the abdominal muscles around the inguinal canal. Previous surgery in the lower abdomen can also weaken the abdominal muscles.

Females rarely form this type of inguinal hernia. In females, the broad ligament of the uterus acts as an additional barrier behind the muscle layer of the lower abdominal wall. The broad ligament of the uterus is a sheet of tissue that supports the uterus and other reproductive organs.

Who Is More Likely to Develop an Inguinal Hernia?

Males are much more likely to develop inguinal hernias than females. About 25 percent of males and about 2 percent of females will develop an inguinal hernia in their lifetimes. Some people who have an inguinal hernia on one side will have or will develop a hernia on the other side.

People of any age can develop inguinal hernias. Indirect hernias can appear before age 1 and often appear before age 30; however, they may appear later in life. Premature infants have a higher chance of developing an indirect inguinal hernia. Direct hernias, which usually only occur in male adults, are much more common in men older than age 40 because the muscles of the abdominal wall weaken with age.

People with a family history of inguinal hernias are more likely to develop inguinal hernias. Studies also suggest that people who smoke have an increased risk of inguinal hernias.

What Are the Signs and Symptoms of an Inguinal Hernia?

The first sign of an inguinal hernia is a small bulge on one or, rarely, on both sides of the groin—the area just above the groin crease between the lower abdomen and the thigh. The bulge may increase in size over time and usually disappears when lying down.

Other signs and symptoms can include:

- discomfort or pain in the groin—especially when straining, lifting, coughing, or exercising—that improves when resting

- feelings such as weakness, heaviness, burning, or aching in the groin

- a swollen or an enlarged scrotum in men or boys

Indirect and direct inguinal hernias may slide in and out of the abdomen into the inguinal canal. A healthcare provider can often move them back into the abdomen with gentle massage.

What Are the Complications of Inguinal Hernias?

Inguinal hernias can cause the following complications:

- **Incarceration.** An incarcerated hernia happens when part of the fat or small intestine from inside the abdomen becomes stuck in the groin or scrotum and cannot go back into the abdomen. A healthcare provider is unable to massage the hernia back into the abdomen.

- **Strangulation.** When an incarcerated hernia is not treated, the blood supply to the small intestine may become obstructed, causing "strangulation" of the small intestine. This lack of blood supply is an emergency situation and can cause the section of the intestine to die.

How Are Inguinal Hernias Diagnosed?

A healthcare provider diagnoses an inguinal hernia with:

- **Medical and family history.** Taking a medical and family history may help a healthcare provider diagnose an inguinal hernia. Often the symptoms that the patient describes will be signs of an inguinal hernia.

- **Physical exam.** A physical exam may help diagnose an inguinal hernia. During a physical exam, a healthcare provider usually examines the patient's body. The healthcare provider may ask the patient to stand and cough or strain so the healthcare provider can feel for a bulge caused by the hernia as it moves into the groin or scrotum. The healthcare provider may gently try to massage the hernia back into its proper position in the abdomen.

- **Imaging tests.** A healthcare provider does not usually use imaging tests, including X-rays, to diagnose an inguinal hernia unless he or she:

- is trying to diagnose a strangulation or an incarceration

- cannot feel the inguinal hernia during a physical exam, especially in patients who are overweight

- is uncertain if the hernia or another condition is causing the swelling in the groin or other symptoms

Specially trained technicians perform imaging tests at a healthcare provider's office, an outpatient center, or a hospital.

A radiologist—a doctor who specializes in medical imaging—interprets the images. A patient does not usually need anesthesia.

Tests may include the following:

- **Abdominal X-ray.** An X-ray is a picture recorded on film or on a computer using a small amount of radiation. The patient will lie on a table or stand during the X-ray. The technician positions the X-ray machine over the abdominal area. The patient will hold his or her breath as the technician takes the picture so that the picture will not be blurry. The technician may ask the patient to change position for additional pictures.

- **Computerized tomography (CT) scan.** CT scans use a combination of X-rays and computer technology to create images. For a CT scan, the technician may give the patient a solution to drink and an injection of a special dye, called contrast medium. A healthcare provider injects the contrast medium into a vein, and the injection will make the patient feel warm all over for a minute or two. The contrast medium allows the healthcare provider to see the blood vessels and blood flow on the X-rays. CT scans require the patient to lie on a table that slides into a tunnel-shaped device where the technician takes the X-rays. A healthcare provider may give children a sedative to help them fall asleep for the test.

- **Abdominal ultrasound.** Ultrasound uses a device, called a transducer, that bounces safe, painless sound waves off organs to create an image of their structure.

How Are Inguinal Hernias Treated?

Repair of an inguinal hernia via surgery is the only treatment for inguinal hernias and can prevent incarceration and strangulation. Healthcare providers recommend surgery for most people with inguinal hernias and especially for people with hernias that cause symptoms. Research suggests that men with hernias that cause few or no symptoms may be able to safely delay surgery until their symptoms increase. Men who delay surgery should watch for symptoms and see a healthcare provider regularly. Healthcare providers usually recommend surgery for infants and children to prevent incarceration. Emergent, or immediate, surgery is necessary for incarcerated or strangulated hernias.

A general surgeon—a doctor who specializes in abdominal surgery—performs hernia surgery at a hospital or surgery center, usually on an outpatient basis. Recovery time varies depending on the size of the hernia, the technique used, and the age and health of the person.

Hernia surgery is also called herniorrhaphy. The two main types of surgery for hernias are:

- **Open hernia repair.** During an open hernia repair, a healthcare provider usually gives a patient local anesthesia in the abdomen with sedation; however, some patients may have:
  - sedation with a spinal block, in which a healthcare provider injects anesthetics around the nerves in the spine, making the body numb from the waist down
  - general anesthesia

The surgeon makes an incision in the groin, moves the hernia back into the abdomen, and reinforces the abdominal wall with stitches. Usually the surgeon also reinforces the weak area with a synthetic mesh or "screen" to provide additional support.

- **Laparoscopic hernia repair.** A surgeon performs laparoscopic hernia repair with the patient under general anesthesia. The surgeon makes several small, half-inch incisions in the lower abdomen and inserts a laparoscope—a thin tube with a tiny video camera attached. The camera sends a magnified image from inside the body to a video monitor, giving the surgeon a close-up view of the hernia and surrounding tissue. While watching the monitor, the surgeon repairs the hernia using synthetic mesh or "screen."

People who undergo laparoscopic hernia repair generally experience a shorter recovery time than those who have an open hernia repair. However, the surgeon may determine that laparoscopy is not the best option if the hernia is large or if the person has had previous pelvic surgery.

Most adults experience discomfort and require pain medication after either an open hernia repair or a laparoscopic hernia repair. Intense activity and heavy lifting are restricted for several weeks. The surgeon will discuss when a person may safely return to work. Infants and children also experience some discomfort; however, they usually resume normal activities after several days.

Surgery to repair an inguinal hernia is quite safe, and complications are uncommon. People should contact their healthcare provider if any of the following symptoms appear:

- redness around or drainage from the incision

- fever

- bleeding from the incision

- pain that is not relieved by medication or pain that suddenly worsens

Possible long-term complications include:

- long-lasting pain in the groin

- recurrence of the hernia, requiring a second surgery

- damage to nerves near the hernia

How Can Inguinal Hernias Be Prevented?

People cannot prevent the weakness in the abdominal wall that causes indirect inguinal hernias. However, people may be able to prevent direct inguinal hernias by maintaining a healthy weight and not smoking.

People can keep inguinal hernias from getting worse or keep inguinal hernias from recurring after surgery by:

- avoiding heavy lifting

- using the legs, not the back, when lifting objects

- preventing constipation and straining during bowel movements

- maintaining a healthy weight

- not smoking

Eating, Diet, and Nutrition

Researchers have not found that eating, diet, and nutrition play a role in causing inguinal hernias. A person with an inguinal hernia may be able to prevent symptoms by eating high-fiber foods. Fresh fruits, vegetables, and whole grains are high in fiber and may help prevent the constipation and straining that cause some of the painful symptoms of a hernia.

The surgeon will provide instructions on eating, diet, and nutrition after inguinal hernia surgery. Most people drink liquids and eat a light diet the day of the operation and then resume their usual diet the next day.

Section 31.4

Cryptorchidism (Undescended Testicle)

This section includes text excerpted from "Evaluation and
Treatment of Cryptorchidism," Agency for Healthcare Research
and Quality (AHRQ), U.S. Department of Health and Human
Services (HHS), December 2012. Reviewed December 2017.

What Is Cryptorchidism?

Cryptorchidism is a congenital condition in which one or both testicles are not appropriately positioned in the scrotum at birth and cannot
be moved into the proper position manually. The term "cryptorchidism"
literally means "hidden testicle" and is often used interchangeably
with the term "undescended testicle."

How Many People Suffer from Cryptorchidism?

It affects an estimated 3 percent of full-term male neonates and up
to 30 percent of premature infants, making it the most common male
genital anomaly identified at birth.

What Are the Associated Conditions and Consequences of Cryptorchidism?

Associated conditions and consequences of cryptorchidism include
hypospadias, hernia, and testicular torsion. Bilateral, nonpalpable
testicles associated with hypospadias or ambiguous genitalia may
represent severe developmental abnormalities (including intersex-
uality) that can be life threatening, warranting specific testing, and
treatment. Ascertaining the correct treatment plan for cryptorchidism
is therefore important and includes identifying associated conditions.

How Is Cryptorchidism Diagnosed?

Cryptorchidism is often apparent to parents, and examination for
the condition is part of general pediatric care. Therefore, boys with

cryptorchidism are usually identified early in life, often within the first year.

Cryptorchidism is diagnosed on physical examination and is usually fairly obvious to parents and providers when the testicle is not found in the "normal" position in the scrotum. The position of the cryptorchid testicle can vary and may be just above the scrotum, anywhere along the inguinal canal, or in the abdomen. Sometimes the cryptorchid testicle can be palpated and sometimes it cannot. When testicles are located just above the scrotum, it is important to distinguish between truly cryptorchid testicles and retractile testicles. The key difference is that a retractile testicle can be manually milked into a normal position while a cryptorchid testicle cannot. Retractile testicles are usually treated with observation, and they almost always descend into a normal position and remain there as the child grows. Some children with "low-lying" (defined as just above the scrotum) cryptorchid testes will experience spontaneous descent. In general, the further away the testicle is from the scrotum, the less likely it is to descend spontaneously into a normal position.

What Factors Influence Decision Making Regarding Treatment?

Clinical decision making about treatment is influenced by many factors, including whether or not the testicle is palpable, whether or not the condition is present unilaterally or bilaterally, the age at presentation, and coexisting medical conditions. In boys under 1 year of age whose testicle is palpable and is close to, but not quite inside, the scrotum, it may be difficult to distinguish between "true" cryptorchidism and a retractile testicle. In this case, healthcare providers often elect to observe the patient's condition until he is 1 year old.

Although about 70 percent of cryptorchid testicles spontaneously descend within the first year of life (most occurring in the first three months), the number of boys whose condition persists remains constant. Cryptorchidism is both a significant and costly health problem in the United States. Longer-term consequences of cryptorchidism include testicular malignancy and infertility/subfertility, with stronger evidence for the etiologic role of cryptorchidism in malignancy than in disordered fertility. With regard to testicular cancer, it has been clearly established that there is a strong positive correlation between cryptorchidism and testicular cancer. An estimated ten percent of all testicular tumors develop from an undescended testicle.

How Is Cryptorchidism Treated?

Once cryptorchidism is diagnosed, treatment decisions may be guided by results of hormonal stimulation testing and/or imaging. Imaging is used to identify and locate the testicle in order to determine the optimal treatment approach. Imaging approaches include ultrasonography (US), computerized tomography (CT) scanning, routine magnetic resonance imaging (MRI) and MR angiography and venography, some of which require sedation or anesthesia and are thus not without risks. The purpose of hormonal stimulation testing is to determine if viable testicular tissue is present in the setting of bilateral nonpalpable cryptorchidism. Specifically, if a boy has bilateral nonpalpable testicles, hormones such as human chorionic gonadotropin (hCG) are administered to stimulate the testicles. If increased levels of testosterone are noted after administration of human chorionic gonadotropins, it is assumed that there is at least one viable testicle somewhere in the body. If there is no testosterone response in the presence of elevated levels of follicle stimulating hormone (FSH), the boy is usually presumed to be anorchid. Imaging is often used to determine whether there is in fact a testicle and to locate it. In theory, absence of a testosterone increase in response to hormonal stimulation testing or inability to locate a testicle with imaging should preclude the need for surgery as it indicates a lack of a potentially functional testicle. However, the value and predictive power of these approaches for identifying the presence and location of a testicle is currently not well understood, and their ability to prevent unnecessary surgery is an area of clinical uncertainty.

Medical options in the treatment of cryptorchidism consist of hormones intended to increase circulating androgens. This increase in circulating androgens, in turn, is thought to potentially promote testicular descent. The two hormones that are most commonly used for the treatment of cryptorchidism are luteinizing hormone-releasing hormone (abbreviated as LHRH and also sometimes referred to as gonadotropin-releasing hormone [GnRH]) and hCG. Although used much less commonly, human menopausal gonadotropin (hMG) is also occasionally used and is thought to function in a manner similar to hCG. LHRH and its analogs and agonists can be administered intranasally, while hCG and hMG must be injected intramuscularly. This difference in mode of administration makes LHRH more acceptable in pediatric care.

The surgical options for the treatment of cryptorchidism are primarily dictated by the location and appearance of the undescended testicle. Primary orchiopexy (surgical mobilization of the testicle with placement and fixation in the scrotum) is usually performed for palpable cryptorchid testicles that are of relatively normal size and appearance that are located in the inguinal canal. In cases in which the testicle is found to be atrophic with little or no viable germ cell tissue remaining, orchiectomy is often performed. For nonpalpable testicles located just inside the internal inguinal ring or in the abdomen, surgical management is more complicated and is dependent on location in the abdomen and the length of the gonadal vessels. If the testicle is of normal size and appearance and if the vessels are of adequate length, primary orchiopexy is usually performed. If the vessels are so short as to prohibit tension-free placement of the testicle in the scrotum, a Fowler-Stephens orchiopexy (FSO) is performed. This procedure entails ligating the testicular vessels. The testicular blood supply then depends on collateral circulation from the deferential artery and the cremasteric system.

This procedure can be performed one of two ways: either as a single-stage operation, in which the vessels are ligated and the testicle is then placed into the proper position in the scrotum, or as a two-stage procedure. In a two-stage procedure the vessels are ligated in the first operation, the testicle is allowed to develop presumably better collateral circulation in its abdominal position and is then moved to the proper position in the scrotum during a second procedure, usually 3–6 months later. Both primary orchiopexy and the Fowler-Stephens procedure can be performed using laparoscopic or open surgical technique.

There remains clinical uncertainty and lack of guidance on the appropriate clinical pathway for treatment of cryptorchidism. This uncertainty includes selecting the optimal approach to treatment planning (imaging versus no imaging; hormonal stimulation testing or not) and intervention (surgical versus hormonal, one-stage versus two-stage Fowler Stephens, various modifications of each of the surgical techniques, and open versus laparoscopic approach). The immediate goal of most interventions for cryptorchidism is to reposition the undescended gonad in a "normal" position in the scrotum. Intermediate outcomes include psychological benefits in terms of body image, and long-term goals include preservation of fertility and prevention of testicular malignancy. All of these outcomes are important to patients. While there is some preliminary evidence that medical treatment with hormones, such as LHRH or hCG, may result in descent of the cryptorchid testicle into the scrotum, most children with cryptorchidism ultimately undergo surgical treatment for the condition. The standard urology textbook, *Campbell-Walsh Urology*, considers that "early surgical repositioning of the testicle into the scrotum before the onset of histopathological changes can reduce the risk of subfertility," but this statement has not been systematically considered.

Section 31.5

Mayer-Rokitansky-Küster-Hauser (MRKH) Syndrome

This section includes text excerpted from "Mayer-Rokitansky-Küster-Hauser Syndrome," Genetics Home Reference (GHR), National Institutes of Health (NIH), May 2017.

What Is Mayer-Rokitansky-Küster-Hauser (MRKH) Syndrome?

Mayer-Rokitansky-Küster-Hauser (MRKH) syndrome is a disorder that occurs in females and mainly affects the reproductive system. This condition causes the vagina and uterus to be underdeveloped or absent, although external genitalia are normal.

What Are the Signs and Symptoms of MRKH Syndrome?

Affected women usually do not have menstrual periods due to the absent uterus. Often, the first noticeable sign of MRKH syndrome is that menstruation does not begin by age 16 (primary amenorrhea). Women with MRKH syndrome have a female chromosome pattern (46,XX) and normally functioning ovaries. They also have normal breast and pubic hair development. Although women with this condition are usually unable to carry a pregnancy, they may be able to have children through assisted reproduction.

What Are the Types of MRKH Syndrome?

When only reproductive organs are affected, the condition is classified as MRKH syndrome type 1. Some women with MRKH syndrome also have abnormalities in other parts of the body; in these cases, the condition is classified as MRKH syndrome type 2. In this form of the condition, the kidneys may be abnormally formed or positioned, or one kidney may fail to develop (unilateral renal agenesis). Affected individuals commonly develop skeletal abnormalities, particularly of the spinal bones (vertebrae). Females with MRKH syndrome type 2 may also have hearing loss or heart defects.

Frequency

MRKH syndrome affects approximately 1 in 4,500 newborn girls.

Genetic Changes

The cause of MRKH syndrome is unknown. Changes in several genes that are involved in development before birth have been identified in females with MRKH syndrome. However, each has been found in only a few affected individuals, and it is unclear whether these changes cause MRKH syndrome. Researchers are working to determine how genetic changes might lead to problems with reproductive system development in females.

The reproductive abnormalities of MRKH syndrome are due to incomplete development of the Müllerian duct. This structure in the embryo develops into the uterus, fallopian tubes, cervix, and the upper part of the vagina. The cause of the abnormal development of the Müllerian duct in affected individuals is unknown. Originally, researchers suspected that MRKH syndrome was caused by environmental factors during pregnancy, such as medication or maternal illness. However, subsequent studies have not identified an association with any specific maternal drug use, illness, or other factor. Researchers now suggest that in combination, genetic and environmental factors contribute to the development of MRKH syndrome, although the specific factors are often unknown.

It is also unclear why some affected individuals have abnormalities in parts of the body other than the reproductive system. Certain tissues and organs, such as the kidneys, develop from the same embryonic tissue as the Müllerian duct, and researchers suspect that problems during development could affect these organs as well.

Inheritance Pattern

Most cases of MRKH syndrome occur in females with no history of the disorder in their family.

Less often, MRKH syndrome is passed through generations in families. Its inheritance pattern is usually unclear because the signs and symptoms of the condition frequently vary among affected individuals in the same family. However, in some families, the condition appears to have an autosomal dominant pattern of inheritance. Autosomal dominant inheritance means that one copy of the altered gene in each cell is typically sufficient to cause the disorder, although the gene involved is usually unknown.

Section 31.6

Vaginal Agenesis, Obstruction, Fusion, and Duplication

Vaginal Agenesis

Vaginal agenesis is a congenital disorder in which the vagina and the uterus (womb) are not fully developed. It is also known as mullerian aplasia or Mayer-Rokitansky-Kuster-Hauser (MRKH) syndrome. It affects 1 of every 5,000 female infants. The condition can also affect the kidney or heart—30 percent of the girls with vaginal agenesis will have kidney abnormalities. Some girls may have a shorter vagina, a remnant of one, or might not have a vagina at all. However, girls with vaginal agenesis do have functional ovaries, normal breast and pubic hair development, and normal hormones.

Causes and Risk Factors

The exact cause of vaginal agenesis is unknown. Scientists believe the failure of formation of mullerian ducts during fetal development—generally one of the ducts develop into the uterus and the vagina and the other into the fallopian tubes—could be the cause of the condition.

Signs and Symptoms

Mostly vaginal agenesis signs and symptoms go unnoticed until the child reaches puberty. Some of the symptoms include:

- Amenorrhea (lack of menstrual cycle)
- Painful amenorrhea: Girls with a uterus experience this condition
- Painless amenorrhea: Girls without a uterus experience this condition
- Dimple or small pouch where the vaginal opening should be
- Pain in the lower abdomen area if a uterus is present without a connection to a vaginal canal
- Abdominal pain and monthly cramping when there is buildup of menstrual flow from the obstruction due to the missing vagina

Diagnosis

The diagnosis of the condition is generally not done until puberty because the outer sex organs appear normal. However, a vaginal agenesis diagnosis can happen at different stages of life, such as:

- When a baby girl is born, the parents and doctors may discover the condition
- During teen years, while examining for a kidney problem
- During puberty, when the menstrual cycle does not start

The healthcare provider may suggest the following tests to confirm vaginal agenesis. Some of the testing options include external genital exam, ultrasound, modified internal exam, and magnetic resonance imaging (MRI).

Treatment

The treatment for vaginal agenesis is often done during late teens or early 20s. Depending on the individual's condition, the doctor may suggest the following treatments:

Self-dilation: The most common type of treatment or the first step in treating vaginal agenesis is self-dilation. This treatment allows a small, round rod (dilator) to be pressed against the skin or inside the existing vagina in order to create a vagina without surgery. It is usually done for 15–30 minutes a day. The best time to do this treatment is after a warm bath because the skin stretches easily. As time goes by, larger dilators are used and it takes a few months to get the desired result.

Vaginal dilation through intercourse: This option for self-dilation can be done through frequent intercourse. Possible side effects are bleeding and pain in the beginning. The healthcare provider can give proper advice regarding this treatment.

Surgery (Vaginoplasty): Doctors usually keep surgery as an option if self-dilation does not work. Vaginoplasty is a type of surgery used to create a functional vagina. Vaginoplasty options include:

- **McIndoe procedure (skin graft method):** In this method, the surgeon takes skin from the patient's buttocks and uses it to create a vagina. The surgeon makes a small incision in the area where the vagina is supposed to be; he inserts the skin graft to form a structure and places the mold into the newly formed canal. A week after the surgery the mold is removed and a vaginal dilator is placed in that area. This can be removed while having intercourse or using the bathroom. After three months the dilator needs to be used only at night.

- **Bowel vaginoplasty (using a portion of the colon):** In this type of surgery, the surgeon diverts a portion of the patient's colon to an opening in the genital area, creating a new vagina. The remaining colon is reconnected after this procedure. A vaginal dilator is not essential after this surgery.

- **Vecchietti procedure:** In this procedure, an olive-shaped device is placed at the normal vaginal opening. With the help of a laparoscope, the surgeon connects the device to a separate traction device on the lower abdomen. The traction is tightened every day, allowing the olive-shaped device to create a vagina in a week. After removal of the device, manual dilation is necessary.

Vaginal Obstruction

Female infants are born with a thin layer of tissue called the hymen that surrounds the vaginal opening. In rare cases, this space is blocked; this is known as congenital vaginal obstruction. An imperforate hymen is caused when the tissue that develops the hymen fails to split and make a hole; it is one of the major causes of vaginal obstruction. It is rarely caused by a high transverse septum; in this case, the vagina is not fully developed.

The level of obstruction determines the symptoms. Female babies with imperforate hymen will have a visible bulge in the genital area due to retained mucus secretions. If the obstruction is on the higher end, a swelled belly is noted.

Diagnosis

The healthcare provider usually discovers abdominal or genital swelling because the vagina is filled with fluid. The condition is confirmed by doing an ultrasound or MRI. For an X-ray, a needle would also be inserted into the vaginal area to inject dye or to withdraw fluid for examination.

The child may experience pain and swelling. This comes from the buildup of menstrual blood behind the block. During her period, she may not pass blood even with normal ovulation. If no urinary signs or no mass is found, the condition cannot be found until puberty.

Treatment

The treatment for vaginal obstruction is based on the cause. If the patient has:

- **Imperforate hymen:** The doctor makes a simple cut. After drainage, the patient is checked for other problems. Anesthesia is not needed.

- **High transverse septum:** The doctor would cut upward to remove the block and will reconnect the upper and lower vagina' the patient's own skin or a part of their intestine is used to bridge the gap between the upper and lower vagina. The treatment will also depend on the thickness and location of the block. Some methods are also used to prevent vaginal narrowing. After surgery, a mold is placed inside the vagina with a hollow center to help with the menstrual flow.

Vaginal Duplication and Fusion

The female reproductive system consists of ovaries, fallopian tubes, a uterus, cervix, and vagina. The system is formed from two structures called the mullerian ducts. These ducts develop into fallopian tubes, uterus, cervix, and vagina in females during the ninth week of pregnancy. In few cases, the duplication and fusion of the reproductive organs occur, such as:

- **Uterus duplex bicollis**—only one vagina, but two uteruses and cervix

- **Bicornuate uterus**—two uteruses are fused with one cervix and one vagina

- **Uterus didelphys**—two each of a uterus, cervix, and vagina. One vagina is blocked and the other is unblocked.

In vaginal duplication or fusion, there are no signs or symptoms; however, the outer organs may look abnormal. Adult females with this condition may experience infertility. Some symptoms for infants or teen girls could be:

- Puberty discomfort

- A mass or lump found in the lower stomach

- Frequent urination

- Urine leaking from vagina before and after urination

Diagnosis

Diagnosis for vaginal duplication or fusion is done through an ultrasound or magnetic resonance imaging (MRI). In some girls, lumps are formed in the lower belly; a physical examination will help to identify the problem. An ultrasound shows why the lump pushes the vagina back and the bladder forward. MRIs are usually done to get a full analysis of the condition.

Treatment

Treatment is not necessary for everyone. Surgery is necessary when the condition is causing symptoms, a woman is unable to conceive, or when a woman has had a number of miscarriages.

References

1. "Urologic Conditions: Vaginal Abnormalities: Vaginal Agenesis," Urology Care Foundation, n.d.

2. "Diseases and Conditions: Vaginal Agenesis," Mayo Clinic, n.d.

3. Laufer, Marc. "Conditions + Treatments—Vaginal Agenesis," Boston Children's Hospital, 2011.

4. "Urologic Conditions—Vaginal Abnormalities: Congenital Vaginal Obstruction," Urology Care Foundation, n.d.

5. "Urologic Conditions—Vaginal Abnormalities: Fusion and Duplication," Urology Care Foundation, n.d.

Chapter 32

Respiratory System Defects

Chapter Contents

Section 32.1

Pulmonary Sequestration

This section includes text excerpted from "Pulmonary
Sequestration," Genetic and Rare Diseases Information
Center (GARD), National Center for Advancing Translational
Sciences (NCATS), August 14, 2016.

What Is Pulmonary Sequestration?

Pulmonary sequestration is a rare congenital (present from birth)
malformation, where nonfunctioning lung tissue is separated from
the rest of the lung and supplied with blood from an unusual source,
often an artery from systemic circulation. Pulmonary sequestrations
may be defined as intralobular, or extralobular, depending on their
location. Symptoms may include a chronic or recurrent cough, respiratory distress, or lung infection. Treatment depends on the location
and may involve surgery.

What Is Extralobar Pulmonary Sequestration?

Extralobar pulmonary sequestration (EPS) is a mass of pulmonary
tissue without connection to the bronchial tree that has direct blood
supply from a branch of the aorta. EPS is found in the left hemitho-
rax in 90 percent of the cases, but 10 percent can be intra-abdominal.
Intra-abdominal EPS is almost always found on the left side above
the kidney and is often associated with left congenital diaphragmatic
hernia. EPS occurs more often in males and is associated with other
birth defects. It typically is diagnosed in infants prior to 6 months of
age but can be diagnosed at any age.

What Are the Symptoms of Extralobar Pulmonary Sequestration?

Typical symptoms seen in infants with extralobular pulmonary
sequestration include cough, respiratory problems, feeding difficulties,
or congestive heart failure, although many infants have no symptoms.

Chronic infections are not common. Extralobular pulmonary sequestration is commonly associated with other birth defects, including diaphragmatic hernia and other lung malformations such as congenital cystic adenomatoid malformation (CCAM) and bronchogenic cysts, pectus excavatum, pericardial problems, and duplication cysts. This type of sequestration accounts for 25 percent of all sequestrations.

Intralobular pulmonary sequestration is characterized by recurrent infections, hemoptysis, or pleural effusion. A chronic or recurrent cough is common. A chest radiograph may reveal a solid or fluid (cystic) lesion in the lower lobe, more often on the left side. Intralobular pulmonary sequestration (ILS) is often diagnosed later than Extralobular pulmonary sequestration (ELS), in childhood or adulthood. It accounts for 75 percent of all sequestrations and affects males and females in equal numbers. Intralobular pulmonary sequestration is not commonly associated with other congenital anomalies.

What Are the Causes of Pulmonary Sequestration?

Pulmonary sequestration appears to result from abnormal budding of the primitive foregut. The tissue in this accessory lung bud migrates with the developing lung, but does not communicate with it. It receives its blood supply from vessels that connect to the aorta or one of its side branches. The arterial supply is derived in most cases from the thoracic aorta (75%) or the abdominal aorta (20%). In some cases (15%), two different arteries supply the blood.

If the accessory lung bud develops early in embryonic development, the pulmonary sequestration occurs among the normal lung tissue, where it is encased within the pleural sac. This results in intralobular pulmonary sequestration. Venous drainage of intralobular pulmonary sequestration is usually through the pulmonary circulation. If the accessory lung bud develops later, extralobular pulmonary sequestration results. This type of pulmonary sequestration is separated from the normal lung tissue by its own visceral pleura and can occur above, within, or below the diaphragm. Venous drainage is usually through the systemic circulation.

Is Pulmonary Sequestration Inherited?

While the vast majority of pulmonary sequestration cases occur in isolation (without any family history), rare familial cases have been reported. Therefore, a genetic component cannot be ruled out.

What Are the Treatment, Available for Pulmonary Sequestration?

Traditional treatment of extralobular pulmonary sequestration involves surgical removal via mini thoracotomy for patients that are experiencing symptoms. Less invasive surgery techniques may include thorascopic surgery and coil embolization.

Due to the risk for infection and bleeding, intralobar pulmonary sequestrations are usually removed, either by segmentectomy (removal of part of the lung) or lobectomy (removal of the full lobe). Angiography along with computed tomography (CT) scan (with or without contrast) and magnetic resonance imaging (MRI) are generally used to visualize the origins of the blood supply before surgery is performed.

Section 32.2

Tracheobronchomalacia

This section includes text excerpted from "Tracheobronchomalacia,"
Genetic and Rare Diseases Information Center (GARD),
National Center for Advancing Translational
Sciences (NCATS), March 6, 2015.

What Is Tracheobronchomalacia (TBM)?

Tracheobronchomalacia (TBM) is a rare condition that occurs when the walls of the airway (specifically the trachea and bronchi) are weak. This can cause the airway to become narrow or collapse. There are two forms of TBM:

1. A congenital form (called primary TBM) that typically develops during infancy

2. Early childhood and an acquired form (called secondary TBM) that is usually seen in adults

Most cases of primary TBM are caused by genetic conditions that weaken the walls of the airway, while the secondary form often occurs incidentally due to trauma, chronic inflammation and/or prolonged compression of the airways. Treatment is generally only required in those who have signs and symptoms of the condition and may include stenting, surgical correction, continuous positive airway pressure (CPAP), and tracheostomy.

What Are the Signs and Symptoms of TBM?

TBM is a condition that occurs when the walls of the airway (specifically the trachea and bronchi) are weak. This can cause the airway to become narrow or collapse. There are two forms of TBM. Primary TBM (also called congenital TBM) typically develops during infancy or early childhood, while secondary TBM (also called acquired TBM) is usually seen in adults.

Some affected people may initially have no signs or symptoms. However, the condition is typically progressive (becomes worse overtime) and many people will eventually develop characteristic features such as shortness of breath, cough, sputum retention (inability to clear mucus from the respiratory tract), and wheezing or stridor with breathing. Symptoms may become worse during periods of stress (i.e., illness), when reclining, or when forcing a cough. Infants and young children with TBM tend to have more frequent respiratory infections and delayed recovery from these illnesses.

What Are the Causes of TBM?

The underlying cause of tracheobronchomalacia (TBM) varies by subtype. Most cases of primary TBM (also called congenital TBM) are caused by genetic conditions that weaken the walls of the airway (specifically the trachea and bronchi). For example, TBM has been reported in people with mucopolysaccharidoses (such as Hunter syndrome and Hurler syndrome), Ehlers Danlos Syndrome (EDS), and a variety of chromosome abnormalities. Primary TBM can also be idiopathic (unknown cause) or associated with prematurity and certain birth defects (i.e., tracheoesophageal fistula).

The secondary form (also called acquired TBM) is caused by the degeneration (breakdown) of cartilage that typically supports the airways. It is most commonly associated with:

- Certain medical procedures such as endotracheal intubation or tracheostomy

- Conditions that lead to chronic (persisting or progressing for a long period of time) inflammation such as relapsing polychondritis or chronic obstructive pulmonary disease (COPD)

- Cancers, tumors, or cysts that cause prolonged compression of the airway

Is TBM Inherited?

Primary tracheobronchomalacia (TBM) is often associated with certain genetic conditions. In some cases, an affected person inherits the condition from an affected parent. Other cases may result from new (de novo) gene mutations. These cases occur in people with no history of the disorder in their family. When TBM is part of a genetic condition, it can be passed onto future generations.

Secondary TBM (also called acquired TBM) is not inherited. It generally occurs incidentally due to trauma, chronic inflammation and/or prolonged compression of the airways.

How Is TBM Diagnosed?

A diagnosis of TBM may be suspected based on the presence of characteristic signs and symptoms or abnormal pulmonary function tests. Additional testing such as CT scan and bronchoscopy can then be performed to confirm the diagnosis and evaluate the severity of the condition. TBM is considered mild if the trachea narrows to 50 percent of its initial size while the affected person is breathing out, moderate if it narrows to 25 percent, and severe if the walls of the trachea touch.

How Is TBM Treated?

Treatment is only medically necessary in people who have signs and symptoms of tracheobronchomalacia (TBM). Management of symptomatic TBM first involves identifying underlying conditions contributing to symptoms, such as chronic inflammation, compression, or injury. Initial treatment will target these underlying medical concerns.

If symptoms persist, people with TBM may undergo pulmonary function tests (PFT) or other assessments to help guide therapy choice and allow monitoring of the response to treatment.

Treatment options may include:

- Silicone and/or long-term stenting

- Surgical correction

- Continuous positive airway pressure (CPAP)

- Tracheostomy (often used as a last resort as it can sometimes worsen TBM)

Discuss your treatment options with a healthcare provider.

Prognosis

The long-term outlook (prognosis) for people with tracheobron-chomalacia (TBM) varies depending on the underlying cause. In general, the prognosis is good in children with primary TBM (also called congenital TBM) who do not have any associated problems. Most of these cases that develop during infancy resolve on their own when the cartilage of the trachea naturally stiffens (often between ages one and two). However, intervention may be needed in children with episodes of airway obstruction, frequent infections, respiratory failure, and/or failure to thrive. When primary TBM is part of a genetic condition, the prognosis largely depends on the severity of the condition and the other associated signs and symptoms.

Secondary TBM (also called acquired TBM) can remain stable over time, but tends to worsen in the majority of affected people. Without treatment, TBM may cause significant breathing problems, but it is rarely life-threatening. Fortunately, treatment options have progressed significantly in recent decades which have lead to improvements in prognosis and quality of life.

Chapter 33

Spina Bifida

Chapter Contents

Section 33.1

Spina Bifida: Basic Facts

This section includes text excerpted from "Spina
Bifida—Basics," Centers for Disease Control and
Prevention (CDC), September 11, 2017.

Spina bifida is a condition that affects the spine and is usually
apparent at birth. It is a type of neural tube defect (NTD).

Spina bifida can happen anywhere along the spine if the neural
tube does not close all the way. When the neural tube doesn't close
all the way, the backbone that protects the spinal cord doesn't form
and close as it should. This often results in damage to the spinal cord
and nerves.

Spina bifida might cause physical and intellectual disabilities that
range from mild to severe. The severity depends on:

- The size and location of the opening in the spine.

- Whether part of the spinal cord and nerves are affected.

Types of Spina Bifida

- **Myelomeningocele.** When people talk about spina bifida, most
  often they are referring to myelomeningocele. Myelomeningocele
  is the most serious type of spina bifida. With this condition, a
  sac of fluid comes through an opening in the baby's back. Part of
  the spinal cord and nerves are in this sac and are damaged. This
  type of spina bifida causes moderate to severe disabilities, such
  as problems affecting how the person goes to the bathroom, loss
  of feeling in the person's legs or feet, and not being able to move
  the legs.

- **Meningocele.** Another type of spina bifida is meningocele.
  With meningocele a sac of fluid comes through an opening in
  the baby's back. But, the spinal cord is not in this sac. There is
  usually little or no nerve damage. This type of spina bifida can
  cause minor disabilities.

- **Spina Bifida Occulta.** Spina bifida occulta is the mildest type of spina bifida. It is sometimes called "hidden" spina bifida. With it, there is a small gap in the spine, but no opening or sac on the back. The spinal cord and the nerves usually are normal. Many times, spina bifida occulta is not discovered until late childhood or adulthood. This type of spina bifida usually does not cause any disabilities.

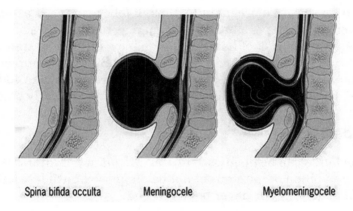

Spina bifida occulta   Meningocele   Myelomeningocele

Figure 33.1. *Three Most Common Types of Spina Bifida*

Causes and Prevention

The causes of spina bifida are unknown. The role that genetics and the environment play in causing spina bifida needs to be studied further.

There are ways for women to reduce the risk of having a baby with spina bifida both before and during her pregnancy.

If you are pregnant or could get pregnant, use the following tips to help prevent your baby from having spina bifida:

- Take 400 micrograms (mcg) of folic acid every day. If you have already had a pregnancy affected by spina bifida, you may need to take a higher dose of folic acid before pregnancy and during early pregnancy. Talk to your doctor to discuss what's best for you.

- Talk to your doctor or pharmacist about any prescription and over the counter drugs, vitamins, and dietary or herbal supplements you are taking.

- If you have a medical condition—such as diabetes or obesity—be sure it is under control before you become pregnant.

- Avoid overheating your body, as might happen if you use a hot tub or sauna.

- Treat any fever you have right away with Tylenol® (or store brand acetaminophen).

Spina bifida happens in the first few weeks of pregnancy, often before a woman knows she's pregnant. Although folic acid is not a guarantee that a woman will have a healthy pregnancy, taking folic acid can help reduce a woman's risk of having a pregnancy affected by spina bifida. Because half of all pregnancies in the United States are unplanned, it is important that all women who can become pregnant take 400 mcg of folic acid daily one month before pregnancy and during early pregnancy.

Diagnosis

Spina bifida can be diagnosed during pregnancy or after the baby is born. Spina bifida occulta might not be diagnosed until late childhood or adulthood, or might never be diagnosed.

During Pregnancy

During pregnancy there are screening tests (prenatal tests) to check for spina bifida and other birth defects. Talk with your doctor about any questions or concerns you have about this prenatal testing.

- **AFP.** AFP stands for alpha-fetoprotein, a protein the unborn baby produces. This is a simple blood test that measures how much AFP has passed into the mother's bloodstream from the baby. A high level of AFP might mean that the baby has spina bifida. An AFP test might be part of a test called the "triple screen" that looks for neural tube defects and other issues.

- **Ultrasound.** An ultrasound is a type of picture of the baby. In some cases, the doctor can see if the baby has spina bifida or find other reasons that there might be a high level of AFP. Frequently, spina bifida can be seen with this test.

- **Amniocentesis.** For this test, the doctor takes a small sample of the amniotic fluid surrounding the baby in the womb. Higher than average levels of AFP in the fluid might mean that the baby has spina bifida.

After the Baby Is Born

In some cases, spina bifida might not be diagnosed until after the baby is born.

Sometimes there is a hairy patch of skin or a dimple on the baby's back that is first seen after the baby is born. A doctor can use an image scan, such as an, X-ray, magnetic resonance imaging (MRI), or computed tomography (CT), to get a clearer view of the baby's spine and the bones in the back.

Sometimes spina bifida is not diagnosed until after the baby is born because the mother did not receive prenatal care or an ultrasound did not show clear pictures of the affected part of the spine.

Treatments

Not all people born with spina bifida have the same needs, so treatment will be different for each person. Some people have problems that are more serious than others. People with myelomeningocele and meningocele will need more treatments than people with spina bifida occulta.

Living with Spina Bifida

Spina bifida can range from mild to severe. Some people may have little to no disability. Other people may be limited in the way they move or function. Some people may even be paralyzed or unable to walk or move parts of their body.

Even so, with the right care, most people affected by spina bifida lead full, productive lives.

Section 33.2

Spina Bifida: Health Issues and Treatments

This section includes text excerpted from "Spina
Bifida—Health Issues and Treatments," Centers for Disease
Control and Prevention (CDC), September 11, 2017.

No two people with spina bifida are exactly alike. Health issues and
treatments for people with spina bifida will be different for each person. Some people have issues that are more severe than other people.
Those born with "open" spina bifida usually have more health issues
and need more types of treatments.

Open Spina Bifida

Sometimes when a baby has open spina bifida, or myelomeningocele, doctors will perform surgery to close the spine before the baby is
born. This surgery is a major procedure for the mother and the baby,
and may not be available where you live.

Hydrocephalus

Many babies born with spina bifida get hydrocephalus (often called
water on the brain). This means that there is extra fluid in and around
the brain. The extra fluid can cause the spaces in the brain, called
ventricles, to become too large and the head can swell. Hydrocephalus needs to be followed closely and treated properly to prevent brain
injury.

If a baby with spina bifida has hydrocephalus, a surgeon can put in
a shunt. A shunt is a small hollow tube that will help drain the fluid
from the baby's brain and protect it from too much pressure. Additional
surgery might be needed to change the shunt as the child grows up or
if it becomes clogged or infected.

Tethered Spinal Cord

Many people with open spina bifida have tethered spinal cords.
Normally, the bottom of the spinal cord floats around freely in the

spinal canal. A tethered spinal cord is attached to the spinal canal. When this happens, the spinal cord stretches as a person grows, which can permanently damage the spinal nerves. The person might have back pain, scoliosis (crooked spine), leg and foot weakness, changes in bladder or bowel control, and other problems. A tethered spinal cord can be treated with surgery.

Mobility and Physical Activity

People affected by spina bifida get around in different ways. These include walking without any aids or assistance; walking with braces, crutches, or walkers; and using wheelchairs.

People with spina bifida higher on the spine (near the head) might have paralyzed legs and use wheelchairs. Those with spina bifida lower on the spine (near the hips) might have more use of their legs and use crutches, braces, or walkers, or they might be able to walk without these devices.

Regular physical activity is important for all people, but especially for those with conditions that affect movement, such as spina bifida. The Centers for Disease Control and Prevention (CDC) recommends 60 minutes of physical activity a day. There are many ways for people with spina bifida to be active. For example, they can:

- Engage in active play with friends.
- Roll or walk in the neighborhood.
- Participate in community programs, such as the Early Intervention Program for Infants and Toddlers with Disabilities and Special Education Services for Preschoolers with Disabilities, which are free programs in many communities.
- Enjoy parks and recreation areas with playgrounds that are accessible to people with disabilities.
- Do exercises recommended by a physical therapist.
- Attend summer camps and recreational facilities that are accessible for those with disabilities.
- Participate in sports activities (for example, swimming) and teams for people with or those without disabilities.

Using the Bathroom

People with spina bifida often cannot control when they go to the bathroom (incontinence). They also can develop urinary tract infections. It is important to develop a plan for going to the bathroom that works and is as simple as possible. This can lead to increased health, participation, and independence, and avoid embarrassment for people with spina bifida. Healthcare providers can help develop a plan for each person. A tube (catheter) inserted in the bladder can help drain urine. In some cases, extra fiber can be added to the diet to keep bowel movements regular. Surgery also might be recommended.

Skin

People with spina bifida can develop sores, calluses, blisters, and burns on their feet, ankles, and hips. However, they might not know when these develop because they might not be able to feel certain parts of their body.

Ways to help protect the skin:

- Check the skin regularly for redness, including under braces.
- Try to avoid hot bath water, hot irons and hot or unpadded seat belt clasps that may cause burns.
- Make sure to wear properly fitting shoes at all times.
- Use sunscreen and don't stay out in the sun too long.
- Do not sit or lie in one position for too long.

Latex (Natural Rubber) Allergy

Many people with spina bifida are allergic to products that contain latex, or natural rubber. This means they should not use items made of natural rubber. For babies, this would include rubber nipples and pacifiers. A person with this type of allergy can wear a bracelet to alert other people of the allergy.

Health Checks

Every person needs a primary care provider, such as a pediatrician, nurse practitioner, general family doctor, or internist. The primary care provider will want to make sure that he or she is healthy; developing normally; and receiving immunization against diseases and infections, including the flu.

In addition to seeing a primary healthcare provider, a person with spina bifida will be checked and treated as needed by doctors who specialize in different parts of the body. These doctors might suggest treatments or surgeries to help the person.

These specialists might include:

- An orthopedist, who will work with muscles and bones.

- A urologist, who will check the kidneys and bladder.

- A neurosurgeon, who will check the brain and spine.

Chapter 34

Urinary Tract Defects

Chapter Contents

Section 34.1

Megaureter

What Is a Megaureter?

The urinary system is made of two kidneys, two ureters, a bladder, and a urethra. Kidneys filter out toxic and extra water from the blood, which then flows out of the kidney through the ureters and into the bladder as urine. Once the bladder is full, urine is passed through the urethra. Most kids are born with a normal urinary tract; however, in some children, a ureter that connects the kidney and bladder gets larger. Ureters are narrow tubes that are normally about ¼-inch wide; the medical condition that enlarges a ureter is known as megaureter— it gets? 3/8-inch wide. This condition can lead to infection due to stagnation of urine and cause serious kidney damage if not treated.

Types of Megaureters

Refluxing megaureter: In this type of a megaureter, vesicoureteral reflux occurs—the ureters are wide and urine flows back up from the bladder. A refluxing megaureter is a sign of vesicoureteral reflux. The backflow expands the ureter. This condition is commonly seen in newborn males. The reflux and the expanded ureter get better over the first year of life. However, if the problem persists, surgery may be recommended. Some health issues are caused due to refluxing megaureters; when the bladder does not drain all the way and sends urine back up the ureters, the bladder swells causing a condition called megacystis megaureter syndrome.

Primary obstructed megaureter: In this type of megaureter, the ureter is too narrow where it enters the bladder. This causes a block of urine flow at that point and makes the ureter wider further up. The thinning can damage the kidney over time. A healthcare provider may recommend surgery to remove the block.

Primary nonobstructed, nonrefluxing megaureter: This type of megaureter results from wide ureters; it is not caused by urine back-flow or blocks. A healthcare provider will monitor to rule out reflux or blocks. The condition improves with time.

Obstructed, refluxing megaureter: This type of megaureter happens when there is both reflux and a block caused by a ureter. This rare condition is dangerous because the ureter gets wider and more blocked over time. Children with this problem are in danger of urinary tract infections.

Secondary megaureter: This type of megaureter occurs due to other health conditions, such as:

- Male urethra getting blocked
- Neurogenic bladder (a bladder that functions poorly due to nerve damage—spina bifida, spinal cord injury, etc.)
- Prune belly syndrome (a partial absence of some abdominal muscles, which gives a prune-like appearance.)

Symptoms of Megaureter

Generally, a megaureter does not have symptoms. Healthcare providers may find them through a prenatal ultrasound. They are discovered as hydronephrosis or a stretched urinary tract in the fetus. A healthcare provider may detect a megaureter when checking a child who has a urinary tract infection; the child's symptoms will normally include fever, vomiting, and back pain. Some other symptoms include:

- Back pain or abdominal pain
- Abdominal mass that can be seen or felt
- Hematuria (blood in the urine)
- Urinary incontinence
- Urolithiasis (stone formation within the urinary tract)

Diagnosis of Megaureter

A healthcare provider conducts certain tests to determine if the child has a megaureter.

The tests are listed below:

- **Ultrasound test:** This test uses sound waves to capture internal tissues and organs inside the body. In order to detect a megaureter, this test is done to see how the kidney, ureters, and bladder function; they are excellent for finding widened ureters. This test is painless.

- **Magnetic resonance imaging (MRI):** This test involves injecting dyes into the urinary tract with the help of magnetic fields. The images are much clearer than an ultrasound, and they are often used for children because the test calls for general anesthesia.

- **Diuretic renal scan:** This test is mainly done to check for blocks. A radioactive liquid is injected into a vein connected to the kidneys. The renal scan helps to track the liquid and see how the kidneys are functioning or if there are any blocks.

- **Voiding cystourethrogram (VCUG):** This X-ray test is done to detect vesicoureteral reflux. A tube is inserted into the ure-thra connecting to the bladder. A special dye is dripped through the tube into the bladder and the dye is traced by an X-ray to see if the liquid remains in the bladder or goes up the ureter. If reflux is present, the dye will flow back into the ureter.

Treatment for Megaureter

Often, a megaureter does not require treatment and is sorted out on its own. However, if treatment is required, it is based on the cause. Here are a few treatments:

- Initial treatment involves antibiotics for treatment to reduce chances of urinary tract infections.

- Surgery is recommended for a megaureter that does not resolve with time. When a test indicates a block or impaired kidney function, a typical surgery would be a ureteral reimplantation (putting a ureter back into the bladder) and ureteral tapering (trimming the widened ureter). If the child does not have a uri-nary tract infection, the surgery can be postponed until the child is 12 months old.

- An open type of surgery is done for obstructed megaureters by removing the block; and, if reflux is present, the backflow of urine is corrected.

- For children over two years, balloon dilation is a treatment option. A long, thin telescope with light at the end is used to examine the urinary tract. A small wire is placed through the bladder up into the ureter. A balloon is inflated and used to stretch the narrow part of the ureter, and a silicon tube is placed in the ureter for 4–6 weeks to allow it to expand. This clears up the block and reflux.

• Laparoscopy is done is certain cases. Thin tubes are placed inside the body through a small cut.

After Treatment

After surgery, several tests may be needed to determine if the surgery was successful. The size of the ureter may not be corrected immediately, and it may need to be checked regularly. Certain issues that can occur from surgery are bleeding, vesicoureteral reflux, and blocked ureter.

Approximately, 5 of 100 cases may experience a block after surgery or after a long period, and require more surgery. Scans and tests need to be followed for a number of years to know if the kidneys and ureters are functioning properly.

References

1.   "Megaureter," University of California, San Francisco (UCSF), n.d.

2.   "Megaureter," Cleveland Clinic, n.d.

3.   "What are the Symptoms of a Megaureter?" Urology Care Foundation, n.d.

4.   "Megaureter Symptoms & Causes," Boston Children's Hospital, n.d.

Section 34.2

Urachal Cyst

This section includes text excerpted from "Urachal Cyst," Genetic
and Rare Diseases Information Center (GARD), National Center for
Advancing Translational Sciences (NCATS), September 29, 2017.

What Is Urachal Cyst?

Urachal cyst is a sac-like pocket of tissue that develops in the urachus, a primitive structure that connects the umbilical cord to the
bladder in the developing baby. Although it normally disappears prior
to birth, part of the urachus may remain in some people. Urachal cysts
can develop at any age, but typically affect older children and adults.
Urachal cysts are often not associated with any signs or symptoms
unless there are complications such as infection. In these cases, symptoms may include abdominal pain, fever, pain with urination, and/or
hematuria. These cysts may be monitored or treated with surgery to
drain the cyst and/or remove the urachus.

What Are the Symptoms of Urachal Cysts?

In most cases, urachal cysts are not associated with any signs or
symptoms unless there are complications such as infection. Possible
symptoms vary, but may include:

- Lower abdominal pain
- Fever
- Abdominal lump or mass
- Pain with urination
- Urinary tract infection
- Hematuria

What Are the Causes of Urachal Cysts?

A urachal cyst occurs when a pocket of air or fluid develops in
the urachus. Before birth, the urachus is a primitive structure that

connects the umbilical cord to the bladder in the developing baby. The urachus normally disappears before birth, but part of the urachus may remain in some people after they are born. This can lead to urachal abnormalities such as urachal cysts.

Can a Urachal Cyst Cause Urachal Cancer?

Yes, a urachal cyst can become urachal cancer, but this is a rare occurrence. One research study showed that urachal cancer was not found in any children with urachal cysts; however, 25 percent of adults with urachal cysts were found to have urachal cancer. The authors of this study suggested that the longer the urachal cyst remained in the body, the greater the chance it could become cancerous.

How Is Urachal Diagnosed?

The diagnosis of a urachal cyst may be suspected based on the presence of characteristic signs and symptoms. The following tests may then be ordered to confirm the diagnosis:

- Ultrasound
- Magnetic resonance imaging (MRI) scan
- Computed tomography (CT) scan

How Is Urachal Cyst Treated?

Treatment of a urachal cyst may depend on whether or not the person is experiencing any symptoms. Sometimes these cysts are not treated but are monitored, particularly if there are no symptoms. In some cases, the urachal abnormalities resolve on their own without treatment. Because there is a small risk that a urachal cyst may become cancerous, surgery may be performed to completely remove the urachus. You can talk to your doctor about the risk of the urachal cyst causing infection or developing into cancer and balancing that with the risks associated with surgical removal.

Prognosis

The long-term outlook (prognosis) for a urachal cyst is generally good. In most cases, urachal cysts are not associated with any signs or symptoms unless there are complications such as infection. There are instances where urachal abnormalities resolve on their own. Because there is a small risk of urachal cancer, the entire urachus may be surgically removed. You can talk with your doctor about the risks associated with surgery. There is usually no need for follow-up or evaluation if the urachus is removed.

Section 34.3

Urine Blockage in Newborns

This section includes text excerpted from "Urine Blockage in Newborns," National Institute of Diabetes and Digestive and Kidney Diseases (NIDDK), September 2013. Reviewed December 2017.

What Is the Urinary Tract?

The urinary tract is the body's drainage system for removing wastes and extra fluid. The urinary tract includes two kidneys, two ureters, a bladder, and a urethra. The kidneys are two bean-shaped organs, each about the size of a fist. They are located just below the rib cage, one on each side of the spine. Every day, the kidneys filter about 120 to 150 quarts of blood to produce about 1 to 2 quarts of urine, composed of wastes and extra fluid. Children produce less urine than adults. The amount produced depends on their age. The urine flows from the kidneys to the bladder through tubes called ureters. The bladder stores urine until releasing it through urination. When the bladder empties, urine flows out of the body through a tube called the urethra at the bottom of the bladder.

The kidneys and urinary system keep fluids and natural chemicals in the body balanced. While a baby is developing in the mother's womb, called prenatal development, the placenta—a temporary organ joining mother and baby—controls much of that balance. The baby's kidneys begin to produce urine at about 10–12 weeks after conception. However, the mother's placenta continues to do most of the work until the last few weeks of the pregnancy. Wastes and extra water are removed from the baby's body through the umbilical cord. The baby's urine is released into the amniotic sac and becomes part of the amniotic fluid. This fluid plays a role in the baby's lung development.

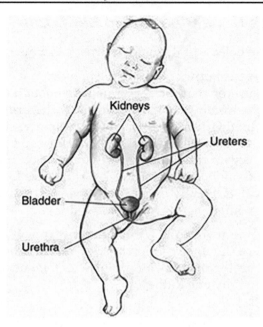

Figure 34.1. *Newborn Urinary tract*

The urinary tract includes two kidneys, two ureters, a bladder, and a urethra.

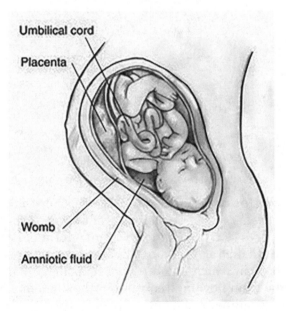

Figure 34.2. *Baby in Mother's Womb*

What Causes Urine Blockage in Newborns?

Many types of defects in the urinary tract can cause urine blockage:

- **Vesicoureteral reflux (VUR).** Most children with VUR are born with a ureter that did not grow long enough during development in the womb. The valve formed by the ureter pressing against the bladder wall does not close properly, so urine backs up—refluxes—from the bladder to the ureter and eventually to the kidney. Severe reflux may prevent a kidney from developing normally and may increase the risk for damage from infections after birth. VUR usually affects only one ureter and kidney, though it can affect both ureters and kidneys.

- **Ureteropelvic junction (UPJ) obstruction.** If urine is blocked where the ureter joins the kidney, only the kidney swells. The ureter remains a normal size. UPJ obstruction usually occurs in only one kidney.

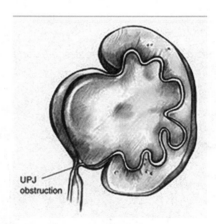

Figure 34.3. *Ureteropelvic Junction (UPJ)*

UPJ obstruction occurs when urine is blocked where the ureter joins the kidney.

- **Bladder outlet obstruction (BOO).** BOO describes any blockage in the urethra or at the opening of the bladder. Posterior urethral valves (PUV), the most common form of BOO seen in newborns and during prenatal ultrasound exams, is a birth defect in boys in which an abnormal fold of tissue in the urethra keeps urine from flowing freely out of the bladder. This defect may cause swelling in the entire urinary tract, including the urethra, bladder, ureters, and kidneys.

- **Ureterocele.** If the end of the ureter does not develop normally, it can bulge, creating a ureterocele. The ureterocele may obstruct part of the ureter or the bladder.

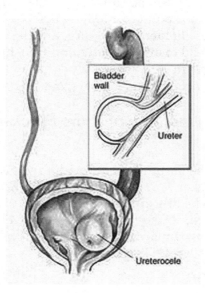

Figure 34.4. *Ureterocele*

Some babies are born with genetic conditions that affect several different systems in the body, including the urinary tract:

- **Prune belly syndrome (PBS).** PBS is a group of birth defects involving poor development of the abdominal muscles, enlargement of the ureters and bladder, and both testicles remaining inside the body instead of descending into the scrotum. The skin over the abdomen is wrinkled, giving the appearance of a prune. PBS usually occurs in boys, and most children with PBS have hydronephrosis—swelling in the kidney—and VUR.

- **Esophageal atresia (EA).** EA is a birth defect in which the esophagus—the muscular tube that carries food and liquids from the mouth to the stomach—lacks the opening for food to pass into the stomach. Babies born with EA may also have problems with their spinal columns, digestive systems, hearts, and urinary tracts.

- **Congenital heart defects.** Heart defects range from mild to life threatening. Children born with heart defects also have a higher rate of problems in the urinary tract than children in the general population, suggesting that some types of heart and urinary defects may have a common genetic cause.

Urine blockage can also be caused by spina bifida and other birth defects that affect the spinal cord. These defects may interrupt nerve signals between the bladder, spinal cord, and brain, which are needed for urination, and lead to urinary retention—the inability to empty the bladder completely—in newborns. Urine that remains in the bladder can reflux into the ureters and kidneys, causing swelling.

What Are the Symptoms of Urine Blockage in Newborns?

Before leaving the hospital, a baby with urine blockage may urinate only small amounts or may not urinate at all. As part of the routine newborn exam, the healthcare provider may feel an enlarged kidney or find a closed urethra, which may indicate urine blockage. Sometimes urine blockage is not apparent until a child develops symptoms of a urinary tract infection (UTI), including:

- fever
- irritability
- not eating
- nausea
- diarrhea
- vomiting
- cloudy, dark, bloody, or foul-smelling urine
- urinating often

If these symptoms persist, the child should see a healthcare provider. A child two months of age or younger with a fever should see a healthcare provider immediately. The healthcare provider will ask for a urine sample to test for bacteria.

What Are the Complications of Urine Blockage before and after Birth?

When a defect in the urinary tract blocks the flow of urine, the urine backs up and causes the ureters to swell, called hydroureter, and hydronephrosis.

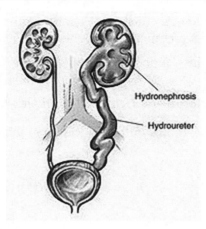

Figure 34.5. *Swelling*

Swelling in the kidney is called hydronephrosis. Swelling in the ureter is called hydroureter.

Hydronephrosis is the most common problem found during prenatal ultrasound of a baby in the womb. The swelling may be easy to see or barely detectable. The results of hydronephrosis may be mild or severe, yet the long-term outcome for the child's health cannot always be predicted by the severity of swelling. Urine blockage may damage the developing kidneys and reduce their ability to filter. In the most severe cases of urine blockage, where little or no urine leaves the baby's bladder, the amount of amniotic fluid is reduced to the point that the baby's lung development is threatened.

After birth, urine blockage may raise a child's risk of developing a UTI. Recurring UTIs can lead to more permanent kidney damage.

How Is Urine Blockage in Newborns Diagnosed?

Defects of the urinary tract may be diagnosed before or after the baby is born.

Diagnosis before Birth

Tests during pregnancy can help determine if the baby is developing normally in the womb.

- **Ultrasound.** Ultrasound uses a device, called a transducer, that bounces safe, painless sound waves off organs to create an image of their structure. A prenatal ultrasound can show internal organs within the baby. The procedure is performed in a healthcare provider's office, outpatient center, or hospital by a specially trained technician, and the images are interpreted by:

- a **radiologist**—a doctor who specializes in medical imaging, or

- an **obstetrician**—a doctor who delivers babies

The below figure shows enlarged kidneys, ureters, or bladders in babies.

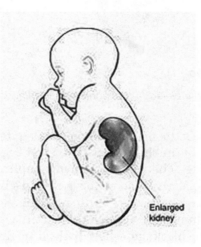

Figure 34.6. *Baby Kidney*

A prenatal ultrasound can show enlarged kidneys, ureters, or bladders in babies.

- **Amniocentesis.** Amniocentesis is a procedure in which amniotic fluid is removed from the mother's womb for testing. The procedure can be performed in the healthcare provider's office, and local anesthetic may be used. The healthcare provider inserts a thin needle through the abdomen into the uterus to obtain a small amount of amniotic fluid. Cells from the fluid are grown in a lab and then analyzed. The healthcare provider usually uses ultrasound to find the exact location of the baby. The test can show whether the baby has certain birth defects and how well the baby's lungs are developing.

- **Chorionic villus sampling (CVS).** CVS is the removal of a small piece of tissue from the placenta for testing. The procedure can be performed in the healthcare provider's office; anesthesia is not needed. The healthcare provider uses ultrasound to guide a thin tube or needle through the vagina or abdomen into the placenta. Cells are removed from the placenta and then analyzed. The test can show whether the baby has certain genetic defects.

Most healthy women do not need all of these tests. Ultrasound exams during pregnancy are routine. Amniocentesis and CVS are recommended only when a risk of genetic problems exists because of family history or a problem is detected during an ultrasound. Amniocentesis and CVS carry a slight risk of harming the baby and mother or ending the pregnancy in miscarriage, so the risks should be carefully considered.

Diagnosis after Birth

Different imaging techniques can be used in infants and children to determine the cause of urine blockage.

- **Ultrasound.** Ultrasound can be used to view the child's urinary tract. For infants, the image is clearer than could be achieved while the baby was in the womb.

- **Voiding cystourethrogram (VCUG).** VCUG is an X-ray image of the bladder and urethra taken while the bladder is full and during urination, also called voiding. The procedure is performed in an outpatient center or hospital by an X-ray technician supervised by a radiologist, who then interprets the images. While anesthesia is not needed, sedation may be used for some children. The bladder and urethra are filled with a special dye, called contrast medium, to make the structures clearly visible on the X-ray images. The X-ray machine captures images of the contrast medium while the bladder is full and when the child urinates. The test can show reflux or blockage of the bladder due to an obstruction, such as PUV.

- **Radionuclide scan.** A radionuclide scan is an imaging technique that detects small amounts of radiation after a person is injected with radioactive chemicals. The dose of the radioactive chemicals is small; therefore, the risk of causing damage to cells is low. Radionuclide scans are performed in an outpatient center or hospital by a specially trained technician, and the images are interpreted by a radiologist. Anesthesia is not needed. Special cameras and computers are used to create images of the radioactive chemicals as they pass through the kidneys. Radioactive chemicals injected into the blood can provide information about kidney function.

How Is Urine Blockage in Newborns Treated?

Treatment for urine blockage depends on the cause and severity of the blockage. Hydronephrosis discovered before the baby is born rarely requires immediate action, especially if it is only on one side. The condition often goes away without any treatment before or after birth. The health-care provider should keep track of the condition with frequent ultrasounds.

Surgery

If the urine blockage threatens the life of the unborn baby, a fetal surgeon may recommend surgery to insert a shunt or correct the problem causing the blockage. A shunt is a small tube that can be inserted into the baby's bladder to release urine into the amniotic sac. The procedure is similar to amniocentesis, in that a needle is inserted through the mother's abdomen. Ultrasound guides in placement of the shunt, which is attached to the end of the needle. Alternatively, an endoscope—a small, flexible tube with a light—can be used to place a shunt or to repair the problem causing the blockage. Fetal surgery carries many risks, so it is performed only in special circumstances, such as when the amniotic fluid is absent and the baby's lungs are not developing or when the kidneys are severely damaged.

If the urinary defect does not correct itself after the child is born, and the child continues to have urine blockage, surgery may be needed to remove the obstruction and restore urine flow. The decision to operate depends on the degree of blockage. After surgery, a small tube, called a stent, may be placed in the ureter or urethra to keep it open temporarily while healing occurs.

Antibiotics

Antibiotics are bacteria-fighting medications. A child with possible urine blockage or VUR may be given antibiotics to prevent UTIs from developing until the urinary defect corrects itself or is corrected with surgery.

Intermittent Catheterization

Intermittent catheterization may be used for a child with urinary retention due to a nerve disease. The parent or guardian, and later the child, is taught to drain the bladder by inserting a thin tube, called a catheter, through the urethra to the bladder. Emptying the bladder in this way helps to decrease kidney damage, urine leakage, and UTIs.

Section 34.4

Vesicoureteral Reflux

This section includes text excerpted from "Vesicoureteral Reflux," National Institute of Diabetes and Digestive and Kidney Diseases (NIDDK), June 2012. Reviewed December 2017.

What Is Vesicoureteral Reflux (VUR)?

Vesicoureteral reflux is the abnormal flow of urine from the bladder to the upper urinary tract. The urinary tract is the body's drainage

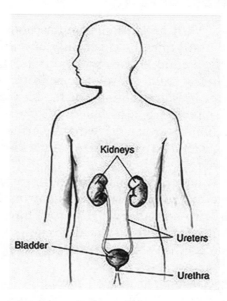

Figure 34.7. *Urinary Tract*

system for removing wastes and extra water. The urinary tract includes two kidneys, two ureters, a bladder, and a urethra. Blood flows through the kidneys, and the kidneys filter out wastes and extra water, making urine. The urine travels down two narrow tubes called the ureters. The urine is then stored in a balloonlike organ called the bladder. When the bladder empties, urine flows out of the body through a tube called the urethra at the bottom of the bladder.

In VUR, urine may flow back—reflux—into one or both ureters and, in some cases, to one or both kidneys. VUR that affects only one ureter and kidney is called unilateral reflux, and VUR that affects both ureters and kidneys is called bilateral reflux.

Who Gets VUR?

Vesicoureteral reflux is more common in infants and young children, but older children and even adults can be affected. About 10 percent of children have VUR. Studies estimate that VUR occurs in about 32 percent of siblings of an affected child. This rate may be as low as 7 percent in older siblings and as high as 100 percent in identical twins. These findings indicate that VUR is an inherited condition.

What Are the Types of VUR?

The two types of VUR are primary and secondary. Most cases of VUR are primary and typically affect only one ureter and kidney. With primary VUR, a child is born with a ureter that did not grow long enough during the child's development in the womb. The valve formed by the ureter pressing against the bladder wall does not close properly, so urine refluxes from the bladder to the ureter and eventually to the kidney. This type of VUR can get better or disappear as a child gets older. As a child grows, the ureter gets longer and function of the valve improves.

Secondary VUR occurs when a blockage in the urinary tract causes an increase in pressure and pushes urine back up into the ureters. Children with secondary VUR often have bilateral reflux. VUR caused by a physical defect typically results from an abnormal fold of tissue in the urethra that keeps urine from flowing freely out of the bladder.

VUR is usually classified as grade I through V, with grade I being the least severe and grade V being the most severe.

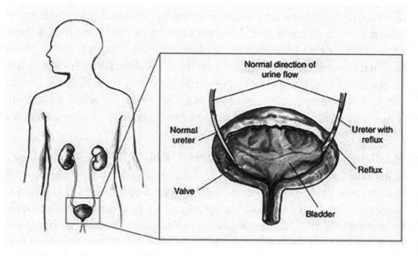

Figure 34.8. *Primary Vesicoureteral Reflux*

What Are the Symptoms of VUR?

In many cases, a child with VUR has no symptoms. When symptoms are present, the most common is a urinary tract infection (UTI). VUR can lead to infection because urine that remains in the child's urinary tract provides a place for bacteria to grow. Studies estimate that 30 percent of children and up to 70 percent of infants with a UTI have VUR.

What Are the Complications of VUR?

When a child with VUR gets a UTI, bacteria can move into the kidney and lead to scarring. Scarring of the kidney can be associated with high blood pressure and kidney failure. However, most children with VUR who get a UTI recover without long-term complications.

How Is VUR Diagnosed?

The most common tests used to diagnose VUR include:

• **Voiding cystourethrogram (VCUG).** VCUG is an X-ray image of the bladder and urethra taken during urination, also called voiding. The bladder and urethra are filled with a special dye, called contrast medium, to make the urethra clearly visible.

The X-ray machine captures a video of the contrast medium when the child urinates. The procedure is performed in a healthcare provider's office, outpatient center, or hospital by an X-ray technician supervised by a radiologist—a doctor who specializes in medical imaging—who then interprets the images. Anesthesia is not needed, but sedation may be used for some children. This test can show abnormalities of the inside of the urethra and bladder.

- **Radionuclide cystogram (RNC).** RNC is a type of nuclear scan that involves placing radioactive material into the bladder. A scanner then detects the radioactive material as the child urinates or after the bladder is empty. The procedure is performed in a healthcare provider's office, outpatient center, or hospital by a specially trained technician, and the images are interpreted by a radiologist. Anesthesia is not needed, but sedation may be used for some children. RNC is more sensitive than VCUG but does not provide as much detail of the bladder anatomy.

- **Abdominal ultrasound.** Ultrasound uses a device, called a transducer, that bounces safe, painless sound waves off organs to create an image of their structure. An abdominal ultrasound can create images of the entire urinary tract, including the kidneys and bladder. The procedure is performed in a healthcare provider's office, outpatient center, or hospital by a specially trained technician, and the images are interpreted by a radiologist; anesthesia is not needed. Ultrasound may be used before VCUG or RNC if the child's family or healthcare provider wants to avoid exposure to X-ray radiation or radioactive material.

Testing is usually done on:

- infants diagnosed during pregnancy with urine blockage affecting the kidneys

- children younger than five years of age with a UTI

- children with a UTI and fever, called febrile UTI, regardless of age

- children with a family history of VUR, including an affected sibling

- males with a UTI who are not sexually active, regardless of age or fever

VUR is an unlikely cause of UTI in some children, so these tests are not done until other causes of UTI are ruled out for:

- children five years of age and older with a UTI
- children with a UTI but no fever
- sexually active males with a UTI

What Other Tests Do Children with VUR Need?

Following diagnosis, children with VUR should have a general medical evaluation that includes blood pressure measurement, as high blood pressure is an indicator of kidney damage. If both kidneys are affected, a child's blood should be tested for creatinine—a waste product of normal muscle breakdown. Healthy kidneys remove creatinine from the blood; when the kidneys are damaged, creatinine builds up in the blood. The urine may be tested for the presence of protein and bacteria. Protein in the urine is another indication of damaged kidneys.

Children with VUR should also be assessed for bladder/bowel dysfunction (BBD). BBD symptoms include:

- having to urinate often or suddenly
- long periods of time between bathroom visits
- daytime wetting
- pain in the penis or perineum—the area between the anus and genitals
- posturing to prevent wetting
- constipation—a condition in which a child has fewer than two bowel movements in a week; the bowel movements may be painful
- fecal incontinence—inability to hold stool in the colon and rectum, which are parts of the large intestine

Children who have VUR along with any BBD symptoms are at greater risk of kidney damage due to infection.

How Is Primary VUR Treated?

The standard treatment for primary VUR has included prompt treatment of UTIs and long-term use of antibiotics to prevent UTIs, also called antimicrobial prophylaxis, until VUR goes away on its own.

Antibiotics are bacteria-fighting medications. Surgery has also been used in certain cases.

Several studies have raised questions about long-term use of antibiotics for prevention of UTIs. The studies found little or no effect on prevention of kidney damage. Long-term use may also make the child resistant to the antibiotic, meaning the medication does not work as well, and the child may be sicker longer and may need to take medications that are even stronger.

Current recommendations from the American Urological Association (AUA) include the following:

- **Children younger than 1 year of age**—continuous antibiotics should be used if a child has a history of febrile UTI or VUR grade III through V that was identified through screening

- **Children older than 1 year of age with BBD**—continuous antibiotics should be used while BBD is being treated

- **Children older than 1 year of age without BBD**—continuous antibiotics can be used at the discretion of the healthcare provider but is not automatically recommended; however, UTIs should be promptly treated

Surgery has traditionally been considered for a child with kidney infection, fever, and severe reflux that has not improved within a year. However, some healthcare providers recommend surgery when a scan of the kidneys shows evidence of inflammation. Several surgical approaches can be used to alter the ureter and prevent urine from refluxing.

Deflux, a gel like liquid containing complex sugars, is an alternative to surgery for treatment of VUR. A small amount of Deflux is injected into the bladder wall near the opening of the ureter. This injection creates a bulge in the tissue that makes it harder for urine to flow back up the ureter. The healthcare provider uses a special tube to see inside the bladder during the procedure. Deflux injection is an outpatient procedure done under general anesthesia, so the child can go home the same day.

How Is Secondary VUR Treated?

Secondary VUR is treated by removing the blockage causing the reflux. Treatment may involve:

- surgery
- antibiotics
- intermittent catheterization—draining the bladder by inserting a thin tube, called a catheter, through the urethra to the bladder

Part Four

Additional Help and Information

Chapter 35

Glossary of Terms Related to Congenital Disorders

agenesis, aplasia: Congenital absence of a body part or organ, implying that the structure never formed. Result of an error in development, as opposed to an external process.

abdominal wall defects: Incomplete development of the skin and muscles of the belly, allowing internal organs to protrude into the umbilical cord (omphalocele) or outside the body (gastroschisis). Also called ventral wall defects.

alcohol-related birth defects (ARBD): Children who had prenatal alcohol exposure, but do not manifest the full symptoms of fetal alcohol syndrome (FAS) may exhibit alcohol-related birth defects. Caused by prenatal alcohol exposure and refers to alcohol induced physical anomalies.

alcohol-related neurodevelopmental disorder (ARND): Children who had prenatal alcohol exposure but do not manifest the full symptoms of fetal alcohol syndrome (FAS) may exhibit alcohol-related neurodevelopmental disorder. Caused by prenatal alcohol exposure and refers to alcohol-induced cognitive and behavioral problems without the characteristic facial or growth abnormalities seen among children with FAS.

This glossary contains terms excerpted from documents produced by several sources deemed reliable.

alpha-fetoprotein (AFP): A plasma protein normally produced by the fetus that can be found in the mother's blood (the maternal serum AFP). It provides a screening test for neural tube defects. Prenatal maternal lab tests are done at fifteen to twenty weeks' gestation.

amniocentesis: A prenatal test where amniotic fluid is withdrawn using a needle inserted into the uterus. The fluid and the cells it contains can be used to perform tests on the fetus, including chromosome testing. Usually performed in the second trimester.

amniotic bands: Strands of tissue that float in the amniotic fluid as a consequence of tears or ruptures in the amniotic membrane which surrounds the fetus during development.

anal atresia: Incomplete development of the lowest part of the large intestine, preventing passage of stool (feces).

anencephaly: Neural tube defect where the brain and skull do not form completely. Affected babies die, either before birth (stillbirth) or shortly thereafter. Because the brain is only partly formed, affected newborns cannot control basic life functions like breathing.

anotia: A congenital absence of one or both ears.

aortic artery/valve (stenosis) (AVS) defect: Heart defect involving the aorta (the main blood vessel leading from the heart). Defects include narrowing or complete closure of the vessel (artery) or valve (connection between the heart and the aorta).

arthrogryposis: Multiple congenital contractures of various joints.

atresia: Absence or blockage of an opening such as the intestinal tract.

atrial septal defect (ASD): An atrial septal defect is a hole (defect) in the wall (septum) that separates the two upper chambers of the heart, called atria. This hole between the heart chambers disrupts the flow of blood and oxygen to the body.

bilateral: Occurring on both sides. For example, bilateral limb defects affect both arms or both legs.

biliary atresia: Congenital absence or closure of the major bile ducts, the ducts that drain bile from the liver.

birth defect: Congenital abnormalities of structure, function, or metabolism present before birth.

bladder exstrophy: A defect in the lower abdominal wall and anterior (front) wall of the bladder through which the lining of the bladder is exposed to the outside.

branchial cleft, fistula, tag, cyst: Congenital abnormality of the neck or area just below the collarbone (clavicle). Includes skin pits (cleft), tissue tags, or cysts.

cataract: An opacity (clouding) of the lens of the eye.

cerebral palsy: Condition where the brain does not properly control muscles and movement. Some people with cerebral palsy have additional disabilities, such as mental retardation or seizures. Although not a structural birth defect, cerebral palsy may have its origins in prenatal development and is sometimes accompanied by structural birth defects.

chorionic villus sampling (CVS): A prenatal test usually done in the first trimester to detect fetal abnormalities. A small piece of the developing placenta is withdrawn; because this has the same genetic make-up as the developing fetus, it can be used for genetic or chromosome tests.

cleft lip: Congenital defect of the upper lip in which there is incomplete closure.

cleft palate: Incomplete development of the roof of the mouth. It can occur alone or accompanied by a cleft lip.

cluster: An apparently unusual concentration of a health condition in a particular area and time period.

coarctation of the aorta: Occurs when the aorta is pinched or constricted. This obstructs blood flow to the lower body and increases blood pressure above the constriction.

congenital: Abnormality or problem present at birth. Includes defects detected prenatally and those not recognized until after the newborn period.

congenital abnormality: A problem present at birth (see birth defects).

congenital heart defect (CHD): Abnormal heart structure present at birth. Includes defects detected prenatally, and those recognized after the newborn period.

corpus callosum: The area of the brain which connects the two cerebral hemispheres.

craniofacial: Involving the face and skull.

craniosynostosis: Too early closure of the skull bones, causing unusual head shape.

Dandy-Walker malformation: Congenital defect of the cerebellum involving a small cerebellar vermis and cystic dilation of the fourth ventricle.

diaphragmatic hernia: A failure of the diaphragm to form completely, leaving a hole. Abdominal organs can protrude through the hole into the chest cavity and interfere with development of the heart and lungs. Usually life-threatening and requires emergent surgery.

Down syndrome (Trisomy 21): The chromosomal abnormality characterized by an extra copy of chromosome 21. In rare cases this syndrome is caused by translocation. The extra copy can be free-lying, or can be attached to some other chromosome, most frequently number 14. Down syndrome can occur in mosaic. So that there is a population of normal cells and a population of trisomy 21 cells. Down syndrome is characterized by moderate to severe mental retardation, sloping forehead, small ear canals, flat bridged nose and short fingers and toes. One third of infants have congenital heart disease, and one third have duodenal atresia. (Both can be present in the same infant.) Affected people can survive to middle or old age. There is an increased incidence of Alzheimer disease in adults with Down syndrome.

dysgenesis: Abnormal formation of an organ or body structure.

dysplasia: Abnormal cell organization of an organ. Usually congenital, may be acquired.

Edwards syndrome (Trisomy 18): The chromosomal abnormality characterized by an extra copy of chromosome 18. The extra chromosome can be free lying or attached to another chromosome. Trisomy 18 can occur in mosaic. Edwards syndrome is characterized by mental retardation, neonatal hepatitis, low-set ears, skull malformation and short digits. Cardiac and renal anomalies are also common. Survival for more than a few months is rare.

encephalocele: The protrusion of the brain substance through a defect in the skull.

esophageal atresia: Congenital discontinuity of the lumen of the esophagus. Usually associated with a tracheoesophageal fistula (TEF) which is an abnormal connection between the esophagus and trachea.

fetal alcohol spectrum disorder (FASD): Physical findings and development disabilities caused by drinking alcohol during pregnancy. Characteristics include: low birth weight, poor growth after birth, small head, small eyelid openings, smooth philtrum (the area between the nose and lip) and thin upper lip. Alcohol-exposed children with developmental delays and behavior problems, but few of the physical features of FAS, may be designated as having "fetal alcohol effects."

fetal alcohol syndrome (FAS): A constellation of physical abnormalities (including characteristic abnormal facial features and growth retardation), and problems of behavior and cognition in children born to mothers who drank alcohol during pregnancy.

fetal death (stillbirth): Spontaneous delivery of an infant or fetus at twenty weeks or greater gestation that does not exhibit signs of life. Transient cardiac contractions and fleeting respiratory efforts or gasps are not necessarily considered signs of life by all programs. A late fetal death is a fetal death that occurs at twenty-eight weeks or greater gestation.

fistula: An abnormal passage from an internal organ to the body surface or between two internal organs or structures.

folate: B vitamin necessary for red blood cell production; folate deficiency can lead to anemia and, during embryogenesis, can affect the normal development of the fetus' neural tube; found in liver, green leafy vegetables, beans, beets, broccoli, cauliflower, citrus fruits, and sweet potatoes.

folic acid: B vitamin found in green leafy vegetables and dried beans as well as in fortified cereal and flour. When taken around the time of conception and in early pregnancy, folic acid is associated with lower risk for neural tube defects, oral clefts, limb and heart defects.

gastroschisis: Condition where the intestines protrude through a hole in the abdomen to the side of the umbilical cord; part of the category abdominal wall defects.

gestation/gestational age: Pregnancy time span. For example, "twenty weeks' gestation" refers to the twentieth week of pregnancy. The normal human gestation is thirty-seven to forty-two weeks.

heart defects: Abnormal structures of the heart and/or large vessels leading from the heart; impairing distribution of oxygen and nutrients throughout the body. Also called cardiac defects.

hernia: A protrusion of an organ or part through connective tissue or through a wall of the cavity in which it is normally enclosed.

Hirschsprung disease (HD): A condition where sections of the intestine lack nerve stimulation; food is not moved through the gut, which becomes distended. Requires surgery to remove the faulty sections.

holoprosencephaly: Serious brain abnormality where the developing forebrain fails to undergo normal division into two lobes. Facial development is often altered—there may be a single eye, closely spaced eyes with a single nostril, a midline cleft lip or a single central front incisor tooth. Holoprosencephaly often causes severe mental retardation and/or death.

hydrocephalus: The abnormal accumulation of fluid within the spaces of the brain.

hydronephrosis: Enlargement of the urine-filled chambers (pelves, calyces) of the kidney.

hyperplasia: Overgrowth due to an increase in the number of cells of tissue.

hypertrophy: Overgrowth due to enlargement of existing cells.

hypoplasia: A condition of arrested development in which an organ or part remains below the normal size or in an immature state.

hypoplastic left heart syndrome (HLHS): The structures of the left side of the heart (the left ventricle, the mitral valve, and the aortic valve) are underdeveloped and unable to pump blood adequately to the entire body.

hypospadias: Birth defect of the penis where the urinary opening is misplaced (on the shaft or in the scrotum in the more serious forms).

imperforate anus: Absence of an external opening from the rectum/intestinal tract. Surgery is needed to allow the infant to pass feces.

intestinal atresia: Condition where abnormally formed segments in the intestine obstruct food movement during digestion. Often classified according to the part of the gut affected: from the stomach to the colon (small intestine), the colon and rectum (large intestine) or anus. See colorectal atresia and anal atresia.

intrauterine growth restriction: Refers to the poor growth of a baby while in the womb. Specifically, it refers to a fetus whose weight is below the tenth percentile for its gestational age.

kidney defects: Absence, underdevelopment or other structural abnormality of the kidneys. Also called renal defects.

limb reduction defects: Missing or malformed arms, legs, hands, fingers, feet, or toes.

malformation: A major anomaly that arises during the initial formation of a structure, i.e., during organogenesis. For most organs, this occurs during the first eight weeks after fertilization. The resulting structure may be abnormally formed, incompletely formed, or may fail to form altogether. Examples of malformations include spina bifida and hypoplastic left heart.

malrotation of the intestines: Unusual configuration of intestinal (bowel) loops.

meninges: Membranes that cover the brain and spinal cord.

microcephaly: The congenital smallness of the head, with corresponding smallness of the brain.

microphthalmia: The congenital abnormal smallness of one or both eyes. Can occur in the presence of other ocular defects.

microtia: A small or maldeveloped external ear and atretic or stenotic external auditory canal.

miscarriage: Pregnancy loss occurring before twenty weeks gestation (the first half of pregnancy). Also called spontaneous abortion.

neonatal death: Death of a live-born infant within the first twenty-eight days after birth. Early neonatal death refers to death during the first seven days. Late neonatal death refers to death after seven days but before twenty-nine days.

neural tube defects (NTD): Abnormalities arising during early fetal development when the neural tube—the precursor of the spinal cord and brain—does not form correctly. Can cause absence of the brain (anencephaly) or spina bifida (open spine defect).

newborn screening: The examination of blood samples from a newborn infant to detect disease-related abnormalities or deficiencies in gene products. Newborn screening (NBS) programs collect dried blood spots (DBS) in every state.

oligohydramnios: A condition in pregnancy where there is a lack of, or decrease in, amniotic fluid surrounding the fetus.

omphalocele: Condition where the abdominal wall is incompletely formed, allowing internal organs to protrude into the umbilical cord. Surgery to replace the organs can crowd the lungs, causing breathing problems. Omphalocele is part of the category abdominal wall defects.

patent ductus arteriosus (PDA): A blood vessel between the pulmonary artery and the aorta. This is normal in fetal life, but can cause problems after birth, particularly in premature infants. This condition causes abnormal cardiac circulation and pressure in the heart during contractions. The vast majority close spontaneously and cause no problems. Medical or surgical correction may be done. This is only an abnormality if it causes significant medical problems.

phenylketonuria (PKU): An inherited disorder of metabolism that can cause mental retardation if not treated. In PKU, the body cannot process a portion of the protein called phenylalanine (Phe), which is in almost all foods. If the Phe level gets too high, the brain can become damaged. All babies born in U.S. hospitals are now routinely tested for PKU soon after birth.

polydactyly: Extra fingers or toes which may be medial (preaxial) or lateral (postaxial).

polyhydramnios: The presence of excessive amniotic fluid surrounding the unborn infant.

postnatal: After delivery.

pregnancy termination: Abortion; often done when birth defects are detected with prenatal diagnosis.

premature birth: Birth of a baby before the standard period of pregnancy is completed. Prematurity is considered to occur when the baby is born sooner than thirty-seven weeks after the beginning of the last menstrual period (LMP). Also known as preterm birth.

prenatal diagnosis: Tests done during pregnancy to detect abnormalities. Some tests are for screening, determining whether a pregnancy is at higher or lower risk, such as the expanded AFP blood test. Other tests—like amniocentesis—are diagnostic, telling for certain whether the fetus is affected.

prenatal: Before delivery.

preterm infant: An infant born before thirty-seven completed weeks of gestation.

pulmonary atresia: Congenital heart defect characterized by absence of the pulmonary valve or pulmonary artery itself. May occur with an intact ventricular septum (PA/IVS) or with a ventricular septal defect, in which it is more properly called Tetralogy of Fallot with pulmonary atresia (TOF/PA).

pulmonary hypoplasia: Incomplete or defective development of the lungs.

pulmonary stenosis (PS): Congenital heart defect characterized by narrowing of the pulmonary valve.

renal agenesis or dysgenesis: The failure, or deviation, of embryonic development of the kidney.

spina bifida: Structural birth defect where the spine and spinal cord don't develop correctly. Depending on the size and location of the defect, it may cause paralysis or inability to control muscles in the legs or arms—affected children often use wheelchairs, walkers, or braces.

stenosis: A narrowing or constriction of the diameter of a bodily passage or orifice.

stillbirth (fetal death): Infant or fetus at twenty weeks or greater gestation that does not exhibit signs of life. Transient cardiac contractions and fleeting respiratory efforts or gasps are not necessarily considered signs of life by all programs.

structural birth defects: Problems in prenatal development affecting the body structure, whether external (for example, cleft lip or missing limbs) or internal (such as heart defects, kidney defects). Also called malformations.

teratogen: An exposure that interferes with normal fetal development, causing a birth defect. Known teratogens include certain illnesses in the mother (German measles, diabetes), medications (thalidomide, Dilantin) and other exposures (excessive alcohol).

term infant: An infant born after thirty-seven completed weeks and before forty-two completed weeks of gestation.

tetralogy of fallot (TOF): A congenital cardiac anomaly consisting of four defects: ventricular septal defect, pulmonary valve stenosis or atresia, displacement of the aorta to the right, and hypertrophy of right ventricle. The condition is corrected surgically.

tracheoesophageal fistula: An abnormal passage between the esophagus and trachea. Leads to pneumonia. Corrected surgically. It is frequently associated with esophageal atresia.

transposition of the great vessels/arteries (dTGA): Major heart defect where the main blood vessels leading from heart are reversed, resulting in improper circulation of oxygenated and oxygen depleted blood.

tricuspid atresia (TA): Congenital heart defect characterized by the absence of the tricuspid valve.

trisomy: A chromosomal abnormality characterized by one more than the normal number of chromosomes. Normally, cells contain two of each chromosome. In trisomy, cells contain three copies of a specific chromosome.

trisomy 13: Chromosome abnormality caused by an extra chromosome 13.

trisomy 18: Chromosomal abnormality caused by an extra chromosome 18.

truncus arteriosus: A conotruncal heart defect where a single blood vessel replaces the pulmonary artery (leading to the lungs) and the aorta (leading to the rest of the body); this results in mixing of oxygenated and oxygen-depleted blood.

ultrasound: Prenatal test using sound waves to create a picture of the developing fetus. Ultrasound can measure growth and examine body structures such as the heart and spine.

urethra: The tube leading from the bladder to outside the body.

urinary defects: Defects of the structures for collecting and excreting urine. This includes the bladder, the tubes connecting the kidneys to the bladder (ureters), and the tube leading from the bladder to outside the body (the urethra).

urinary tract obstruction: Defect in the tubes leading to and from the bladder, preventing normal urination. Backed-up urine damages the kidneys—children often need corrective surgery and possible dialysis (mechanized help with filtering waste from the blood). In severe cases, the absence of amniotic fluid (which comes from fetal urine) prevents the fetal lungs from growing and expanding; once born, these babies cannot breathe and soon die.

ventricle: One of the two lower chambers of the heart (plural ventricles). The right ventricle sends blood to the lungs, and the left ventricle passes oxygen-rich blood to the rest of the body.

ventricular septal defect (VSD): Heart defect where a hole between the two bottom pumping heart chambers (ventricles) allows oxygenated and oxygen-depleted blood to mix.

very low birth weight: Birth weight less than 1,500 grams, regardless of gestational age.

Chapter 36

Congenital Disorders: Resources for Information and Support

General

American Pregnancy Association
3007 Skyway Cir. N.
Ste. 800
Irving, TX 75038
Toll-Free: 800-672-2296
Phone: 972-550-0140
Website: www.americanpregnancy.org
E-mail: info@americanpregnancy.org

Boston Children's Hospital
300 Longwood Ave.
Boston, MA 02115
Toll-Free: 844-BCH-PEDS (844-224-7337)
Phone: 617-355-6000
TTY: 617-730-0152
Website: www.childrenshospital.org

Resources in this chapter were compiled from several sources deemed reliable; all contact information was verified and updated in December 2017.

Centers for Disease Control and Prevention (CDC)
1600 Clifton Rd.
Atlanta, GA 30329-4027
Toll-Free: 800-CDC-INFO (800-232-4636)
Toll-Free TTY: 888-232-6348
Website: www.cdc.gov

Children's Hospital Colorado
Anschutz Medical Campus
13123 E. 16th Ave.
Aurora, CO 80045
Toll Free: 800-624-6553
Phone: 720-777-0123
Website: www.childrenscolorado.org

Children's Hospital of Philadelphia
3401 Civic Center Blvd.
Philadelphia, PA 19104
Toll Free: 800-879-2467
Phone: 215-590-3800
Fax: 215-590-1415
Website: www.chop.edu

Children's Memorial Hermann Hospital
Texas Medical Center
6411 Fannin St.
Houston, TX 77030
Toll-Free: 713-222-CARE (713-222-2273)
Phone: 713-704-KIDS (713-704-5437)
Website: www.childrens.memorialhermann.org

Cincinnati Children's Hospital Medical Center
3333 Burnet Ave.
Cincinnati, OH 45229-3026
Toll-Free: 800-344-2462; Toll-Free: 877-881-8479 (outside of tri-state area)
Phone: 513-636-4200
TTY: 513-636-4900
Website: www.cincinnati childrens.org

Fetal Hope Foundation
9786 S. Holland St.
Littleton, CO 80127
Toll-Free: 877-789-HOPE (877-789-4673)
Phone: 303-932-0553
Website: www.fetalhealthfoundation.org
E-mail: info@fetalhope.org

Johns Hopkins Children's Center
The Charlotte R. Bloomberg Children's Center
1800 Orleans St.
Baltimore, MD 21287
Phone: 410-955-5000
Website: www.hopkinsmedicine.org

Lifespan
167 Pt. St.
Providence, RI 02903
Phone: 401-444-3500
Website: www.lifespan.org

March of Dimes
1275 Mamaroneck Ave.
White Plains, NY 10605
Website: www.marchofdimes.org

MotherToBaby
Organization of Teratology Information Specialists (OTIS)
5034A Thoroughbred Ln.
Brentwood, TN 37027
Phone: 615- 649-3082
Website: www.mothertobaby.org
E-mail: contactus@otispregnancy.org

SSM Health
1465 S. Grand Blvd.
St. Louis, MO 63104
Toll-Free: 877-SSM-FETL (877-776-3385)
Phone: 314-994-7800
Website: www.ssmhealth.com

University of California San Francisco (UCSF) Benioff Children's Hospital
505 Parnassus Ave.
San Francisco, CA 94143
Phone: 415-476-1000
Website: www.ucsfbenioffchildrens.org

University of California San Francisco (UCSF) Fetal Treatment Center
1855 Fourth St.
Second Fl. Rm. A-2432
San Francisco, CA 94158-2549
Toll-Free: 800-RX-FETUS (800-793-3887)
Fax: 415-502-0660
Website: www.fetus.ucsf.edu
E-mail: fetaltreatmentcenter@ucsf.edu

University of Michigan C.S. Mott Children's Hospital
1540 E. Hospital Dr.
Ann Arbor, MI 48109
Toll-Free: 877-285-7788
Phone: 734-936-4000
Website: www.mottchildren.org
E-mail: mottchildren@umich.edu

The University of Texas Health Science Center at Houston (UTHealth)
7000 Fannin St.
Ste. 1800
Houston, TX 77030
Phone: 713-500-4472
Website: www.uth.edu

Birthmarks

Vascular Birthmarks Foundation
P.O. Box 106
Latham, NY 12110
Toll-Free: 877-VBF-4646 (877-823-4646)
Website: www.birthmark.org

Brain and Spinal Cord Defects

Dandy-Walker Alliance, Inc.
10325 Kensington Pkwy
Ste. 384
Kensington, MD 20895
Toll-Free: 877-Dandy-Walker (877-326-3992)
Website: www.dandy-walker.org
E-mail: comments@dandy-walker.org

Hydrocephalus Association
4340 East West Hwy
Ste. 905
Bethesda, MD 20814-4447
Toll-Free: 888-598-3789
Phone: 301-202-3811
Fax: 301-202-3813
Website: www.hydroassoc.org
E-mail: info@hydroassoc.org

National Hydrocephalus Foundation (NHF)
12413 Centralia Rd.
Lakewood, CA 90715-1653
Toll-Free: 888-857-3434
Phone: 562-924-6666
Website: www.nhfonline.org
E-mail: info@nhfonline.org

National Institute of Neurological Disorders and Stroke (NINDS)
NIH Neurological Institute
P.O. Box 5801
Bethesda, MD 20824
Toll-Free: 800-352-9424
Phone: 301-496-5751
Website: www.ninds.nih.gov
E-mail: me20t@nih.gov

National Organization for Disorders of the Corpus Callosum (NODCC)
18032-C Lemon Dr.
PMB 363
Yorba Linda, CA 92886
Phone: 714-747-0063
Fax: 714-693-0808
Website: www.nodcc.org
E-mail: info@nodcc.org

Pediatric Hydrocephalus Foundation
10 Main St.
Ste. 335
Woodbridge, NJ 07095
Phone: 732-634-1283
Fax: 847-589-1250
Website: www.hydrocephaluskids.org
E-mail: info@hydrocephaluskids.org

Spina Bifida Association
1600 Wilson Blvd.
Ste. 800
Arlington, VA 22209
Toll Free: 800-621-3141
Phone: 202-944-3285
Fax: 202-944-3295
Website: www.spinabifidaassociation.org
E-mail: sbaa@sbaa.org

United Cerebral Palsy
1825 K St. N.W.
Ste. 600
Washington, DC 20006
Toll-Free: 800-872-5827
Phone: 202-776-0406
Fax: 202-776-0414
Website: www.ucp.org
E-mail: info@ucp.org

Cardiovascular Defects

Adult Congenital Heart Association (ACHA)
3300 Henry Ave.
Ste. 112
Philadelphia, PA 19119
Toll Free: 888-921-ACHA (888-921-2242)
Phone: 215-849-1260
Fax: 215-849-1261
Website: www.achaheart.org
E-mail: info@achaheart.org

American Heart Association (AHA)
7272 Greenville Ave.
Dallas, TX 75231
Toll-Free: 800-AHA-USA-1 (800-242-8721)
Phone: 214-570-5978
Website: www.heart.org
E-mail: inquiries@heart.org

National Heart, Lung, and Blood Institute (NHLBI)
NHLBI Health Information Center
P.O. Box 30105
Bethesda, MD 20824-0105
Phone: 301-592-8573
TTY: 240-629-3255
Website: www.nhlbi.nih.gov
E-mail: nhlbiinfo@nhlbi.nih.gov

Craniofacial Defects

American Cleft Palate-Craniofacial Association (ACPA)
1504 E. Franklin St.
Ste. 102
Chapel Hill, NC 27514-2820
Phone: 919-933-9044
Fax: 919-933-9604
Website: www.acpa-cpf.org
E-mail: info@acpa-cpf.org

Ameriface
P.O. Box 751112
Las Vegas, NV 89136-1112
Toll-Free: 888-486-1209
Phone: 702-769-9264
Fax: 702-341-5351
Website: www.ameriface.org
E-mail: info@ameriface.org

Children's Craniofacial Association (CCA)
13140 Coit Rd., Ste. 517
Dallas, TX 75240
Toll-Free: 800-535-3643
Phone: 214-570-9099
Fax: 214-570-8811
Website: www.ccakids.org
E-mail: contactCCA@ccakids.com

Cleft Palate Foundation
1504 E. Franklin St.
Ste. 102
Chapel Hill, NC 27514-2820
Toll-Free: 800-242-5338
Phone: 919-933-9044
Fax: 919-933-9604
Website: www.cleftline.org

FACES: The National Craniofacial Association
P.O. Box 11082
Chattanooga, TN 37401
Toll Free: 800-332-2373
Phone: 423-266-1632
Website: www.faces-cranio.org
E-mail: faces@faces-cranio.org

myFace
333 E. 30th St. Lobby Office
New York, NY 10016
Phone: 212-263-6656
Fax: 212-263-7534
Website: www.myface.org
E-mail: info@myface.org

National Institute of Dental and Craniofacial Research (NIDCR)

National Institutes of Health (NIH)
31 Center Dr. MSC 2190
Bldg. 31 Rm. 5B55
Bethesda, MD 20892-2190
Toll-Free: 866-232-4528
Phone: 301-496-4261
Fax: 301-480-4098
Website: www.nidcr.nih.gov
E-mail: nidcrinfo@mail.nih.gov

World Craniofacial Foundation

7777 Forest Ln.
Ste. C-616
Dallas, TX 75230
Toll-Free: 800-533-3315
Phone: 972-566-6669
Website: www.worldcf.org
E-mail: info@worldcf.org

Digestive Tract Defects

American Liver Foundation (ALF)

39 Bdwy.
Ste. 2700
New York, NY 10006
Toll-Free: 800-GO-LIVER (800-465-4837)
Phone: 212-668-1000
Fax: 212-483-8179
Website: www.liverfoundation.org

Association of Congenital Diaphragmatic Hernia Research Awareness and Support (CHERUBS)

152 S. White St.
Upstairs Ste.
Wake Forest, NC 27587
Phone: 919-610-0129
Fax: 815-425-9155
Website: www.cherubs-cdh.org
E-mail: cpab@cherubs-cdh.org

Children's Liver Association for Support Services (C.L.A.S.S.)
P.O. Box 15061
Monaca, PA 15061
Phone: 724-888-2568
Website: www.classkids.org
E-mail: info@classkids.org

Children's Organ Transplant Association (COTA)
2501 W. COTA Dr.
Bloomington, IN 47403
Toll-Free: 800-366-2682
Fax: 812-336-8885
Website: www.cota.org
E-mail: cota@cota.org

North American Society for Pediatric Gastroenterology, Hepatology and Nutrition (NASPGHAN)
714 N. Bethlehem Pike, Ste. 300
Ambler, PA 19002
Phone: 215-641-9800
Fax: 215-641-1995
Website: www.naspghan.org
E-mail: naspghan@naspghan.org

National Institute of Diabetes and Digestive and Kidney Diseases (NIDDK)
Office of Communications & Public Liaison
31 Center Dr. MSC 2560
Bethesda, MD 20892-2560
Toll-Free: 800-860-8747
Phone: 301-435-8116
Toll-Free TTY: 866-569-1162
Website: www.niddk.nih.gov
E-mail: healthinfo@niddk.nih.gov

Pull-Thru Network
c/o Lori Parker
1705 Wintergreen Pkwy
Normal, IL 61761
Phone: 309-262-0786
Website: www.pullthrunetwork.org

Kidney and Urinary Tract Defects

American Association of Kidney Patients (AAKP)
14440 Bruce B. Downs Blvd.
Tampa, Fl 33613
Toll-Free:800-749-AAKP (800-749-2257)
Phone: 813-636-8100
Fax: 813-636-8122
Website: www.aakp.org
E-mail: info@aakp.org

American Kidney Fund (AKF)
11921 Rockville Pike
Ste. 300
Rockville, MD 20852
Toll-Free: 800-638-8299
Phone: 301-881-3052
Website: www.kidneyfund.org
E-mail: info@kidneyfund.org

American Society of Pediatric Nephrology (ASPN)
6728 Old McLean Village Dr.
McLean, VA 22101
Phone: 703-556-9222
Website: www.aspneph.org
E-mail: info@aspneph.org

American Urological Association (AUA)
1000 Corporate Blvd.
Linthicum, MD 21090
Toll-Free: 800-828-7866
Phone: 410-689-3700
Fax: 410-689-3800
Website: www.auanet.org
E-mail: aua@AUAnet.org

Association for the Bladder Exstrophy Community (A-BE-C)
204 37th Ave. N.
Ste. 157
Saint Petersburg, FL 33704
Website: www.bladderexstrophy.com

Bladder Exstrophy Research Foundation
P.O. Box 13083
Newport Beach, CA 92658
Phone: 949-922-9865
Website: www.exstrophyresearch.org
E-mail: info@exstrophyresearch.org

Georgia Urology
1930 Brannan Rd.
McDonough, GA 30253
Toll-Free: 855-STONE11 (855-786-6311)
Phone: 678-284-4053
Website: www.gaurology.com

Hypospadias and Epispadias Association, Inc.
P.O. Box 607
Amserdam, NY 12010
Website: www.heainfo.org

Kidney & Urology Foundation of America (KUFA)
63 W. Main St.
Ste. G
Freehold, NJ 07728
Toll-Free: 800-633-6628
Phone: 732-866-4444
Website: www.kidneyurology.org

National Kidney Foundation (NKF)
30 E. 33rd St.
New York, NY 10016
Toll-Free: 855-NKF-CARES (855-653-2273)
Phone: 800-622-9010
Fax: 212-689-9261
Website: www.kidney.org
E-mail: info@kidney.org

Limb and Joint Defects

American Academy of Orthopaedic Surgeons (AAOS)
9400 W. Higgins Rd.
Rosemont, IL 60018
Phone: 847-823-7186
Fax: 847-823-8125
Website: www.aaos.org

American Society for Surgery of the Hand (ASSH)
822 W. Washington Blvd.
Chicago, IL, 60607
Phone: 312-880-1900
Fax: 847-384-1435
Website: www.assh.org
E-mail: info@assh.org

Fibrous Dysplasia Foundation
2885 Sanford Ave. S.W. 40754
Grandville, MI 49418
Website: www.fibrousdysplasia.org
E-mail: info@fibrousdysplasia.org

Maternal Alcohol Abuse

National Institute on Alcohol Abuse and Alcoholism (NIAAA)
5635 Fishers Ln.
Bethesda, MD 20892-9304
Phone: 301-443-3860
Website: www.niaaa.nih.gov
E-mail: niaaaweb-r@exchange.nih.gov

National Organization on Fetal Alcohol Syndrome (NOFAS)
1200 Eton Ct. N.W.
Third Fl.
Washington, DC 20007
Phone: 202-785-4585
Fax: 202-466-6456
Website: www.nofas.org
E-mail: information@nofas.org

Index

Index

Page numbers followed by 'n' indicate a footnote. Page numbers in *italics* indicate a table or illustration.